WITHDRAWN
UTSA LIBRARIES

Wretched Rebels

Rural
Disturbances
on the Eve of
the Chinese
Revolution

Harvard East Asian Monographs 323

Wretched Rebels

Rural Disturbances on the Eve of the Chinese Revolution

Lucien Bianco

with the assistance of Hua Chang-ming

Translated by Philip Liddell

Published by the Harvard University Asia Center
and distributed by Harvard University Press
Cambridge (Massachusetts) and London, 2009

Original French edition © 2005, Éditions de La Martinière, Paris, France

English translation © 2009 by the President and Fellows of Harvard College

Printed in the United States of America

The Harvard University Asia Center publishes a monograph series and, in coordination with the Fairbank Center for Chinese Studies, the Korea Institute, the Reischauer Institute of Japanese Studies, and other faculties and institutes, administers research projects designed to further scholarly understanding of China, Japan, Vietnam, Korea, and other Asian countries. The Center also sponsors projects addressing multidisciplinary and regional issues in Asia.

Library of Congress Cataloging-in-Publication Data

Bianco, Lucien.
   [Jacqueries et révolution dans la Chine du XXe siècle. English]
   Wretched rebels : rural disturbances on the eve of the Chinese Revolution / Lucien Bianco ; with the assistance of Hua Chang-ming ; translated by Philip Liddell.
      p. cm. -- (Harvard East Asian monographs ; 323)
   Revised and shortened translation of: Jacqueries et révolution dans la Chine du XXe siècle. Paris : Martinière, c2005.
   Sequel to: Peasants without the party / Lucien Bianco. Armonk, N.Y. : M.E. Sharpe, c2001.
   Includes bibliographical references and index.
   ISBN 978-0-674-03542-3 (cloth : alk. paper)
   1. China--History--20th century. 2. China--Social conditions--20th century. 3. Revolutions--China--History--20th century. 4. China--Rural conditions. 5. Peasants--China--History--20th century. 6. Peasant uprisings--China--History--20th century. I. Hua, Chang-Ming. II. Bianco, Lucien. Peasants without the party. III. Title.

DS774.B4413 2009
951'.036--dc22

2009047453

Index by the author

∞ Printed on acid-free paper

Last figure below indicates year of this printing

19 18 17 16 15 14 13 12 11 10 09

Contents

Boxes, Maps, and Tables	vii
Conventions	ix
Preface	xi

1 Typology I: Movements Opposed to the Administration 1
    Resistance to Tax Collection 1
    Special Levies and Mixed Incidents 14
    Non-Tax Movements Directed Against the Administration 23
    Movements Directed Against the Army and Military Service 30

2 Typology II: Movements Within Society 36
    Social Movements 36
    Horizontal Conflicts 43
    Sects and Secret Societies 44

3 Repertoire of Action 52
    Nonviolent Action 52
    Handing over Farm Tools 56
    Violent Actions 57
    Peasant "Excesses" 63

4 Exploitation or Oppression? 69
    Social Questions Without Social Movements 69
    From Exploitation to Oppression 78

5 Taxation — 90

Against the Increase in the Tax Burden 91
Abuses, Frauds, Smuggling, and Repression 99
Updating the Cadastre 110
The Social Component of Antifiscal Resistance 117

6 Reforms — 130

Resistance to the New Policies 130
Under the Republic 143

7 Conscription — 159

Military Service 160
Mixed Cases: Conscription and Something Else 171
Not So Much Conscription, Just the Army 174
Major Revolts 176

8 Permanencies — 190

In France Long Ago, but Yesterday in China 190
Today in China 200

Appendix

The Various Categories of Rural Disturbances — 211

Reference Matter

Notes — 217
Works Cited — 241
Index — 263

Boxes, Maps, and Tables

Boxes

1.1	Resistance to Land Surtaxes: Yangzhong, Jiangsu, 4–5 October 1932	3
1.2	Revolt Against the Salt Tax: Western Shaanxi, 1903	5
1.3	Revolt by Drafted Laborers: Southeast Sichuan, March 1936	18
1.4	Resistance to *Bingchai*: North China, 1929–30	20
1.5	Resistance to Military Service: Xindu, Sichuan, November 1938	34
2.1	Advance Warning of Looting: Xingwen, Sichuan, 1934	38
2.2	Murder of a Local Tyrant: Baoji, Shaanxi, 1933	43
2.3	The Sect of the Heavenly Gate (Tianmenhui)	49
3.1	From Petition to Riot: Yongji, Shanxi, 1903	55
3.2	Handover of Farm Tools: Weinan, Shaanxi, 1923	58
4.1	Mechanical Irrigation in the Village: Lücheng, Jiangsu, 1926	81
4.2	Local Despots: Maozhai, Jiangsu, 1935	84
5.1	Resisting a New Tax: Siyugang, Jiangsu, 2–4 August 1912	93
5.2	Salt Workers and Fishermen Take on the Fiscal Inquisition: Daishan, Zhejiang, July 1936	103
5.3	Commonplace Encounter between Salt Workers and the Salt Police: Rudong, Jiangsu, 1932	108
5.4	Resistance to the Cadastral Review: Jiangdu, Jiangsu, 1932	114
5.5	Targeting the Powerful, More Than the Rich: Hengxiang, Jiangsu, Winter 1924–25	120

5.6	Peasants Manipulated in Other People's Interests: Liuqiao, Jiangsu, 1928	125
6.1	Opposition to the Census and House Number Plates: Lian Xian, Guangdong, 1910	138
6.2	Maneuvers by Priests and Monks: 1928–29	146
6.3	Resistance to the Cutting of Queues: Ankang, Shaanxi, 1913	149
6.4	Fighting the Ban on Praying for Rain: Shehong, Sichuan, 1928, 1936, and 1941	150
6.5	Spring Silkworms: Zhejiang, 1933	151
7.1	Opposition to the Draft Lottery: Guanghan, Sichuan, 31 May–4 June 1940	164
7.2	Resistance to Tax and Conscription: Zhongjiang, Sichuan, December 1938	172
7.3	Resistance to the Army, Not Conscription: Tianhekou, Hubei, June 1944	175

Maps

6.1	Northern Zhejiang	155
7.1	Eastern Guizhou	178
7.2	Southern Gansu	184

Tables

5.1	Price (in *yuan*) of a Picul of Salt in Pinghu and Haiyan, Zhejiang	106
A.1	The Various Categories of Rural Disturbances	213

Conventions

Weights and Measures

WEIGHT
dan (picul): about 133 pounds (59.6 kilograms)
jin: 1/100 of the *dan*, about 1.3 pounds (or 596 grams)
liang: 1/16 of the *jin*, about 1.3 ounces (37 grams)

VOLUME (FOR GRAIN)
dan: about 27 gallons (102 liters)
dou: 1/10 of a *dan*, about 2.7 gallons (10.2 liters)
sheng: 1/10 of a *dou*, about 0.27 gallons (1.02 liters)

DISTANCE
li: 1/3 of a mile (0.576 kilometer)

AREA
mu: about 1/6 of an acre (6.14 ares, 1/15 of a hectare)

Abbreviations

CQ	*China Quarterly*
CYB	*China Yearbook*
DFZZ	*Dongfang zazhi*
JAS	*Journal of Asian Studies*

NCH	*North China Herald*
QMN	"Qingmo minbian nianbiao" (Zhang and Ding 1982–83)
SB	*Shenbao*
USDS	United States, Department of State Archives
WSZL	*Wenshi ziliao*
WSZLXJ	*Wenshi ziliao xuanji*
XGQSJMDS	*Xinhai geming qian shinian jian minbian dang'an shiliao* (Zhongguo diyi lishi dang'an guan 1985)
XZ	*Xianzhi*
ZD2LDG	Zhongguo di'er lishi dang'an guan (archival file)
ZGNC	*Zhongguo nongcun*
ZJNSZ	*Zhongguo jindai nongye shi ziliao* (Zhang Youyi 1957)
ZLN	*Zhongguo laodong nianjian*
ZMDZH	*Zhonghua minguoshi dang'an ziliao huibian* (Zhongguo di'er lishi dang'an guan 1988)
ZYRB	*Zhongyang ribao*

Preface

This book is a revised and shortened account of *Jacqueries et révolution dans la Chine du XXe siècle* (Paris, 2005). It may also be read as a sequel to *Peasants Without the Party* (M. E. Sharpe, 2001; hereinafter *PWP*) and is based upon the same range of material that was introduced and evaluated there (*PWP*, xviii–xxi). The book excludes from consideration the same kind of big events, those that "made history" either before 1911 (such as the Boxer and Tongmenghui uprisings), or, under the Republic, the GMD-led Peasant Unions, the CCP-led peasant movements, the anti-Japanese guerrilla campaigns, and so on.

In the first three chapters, I introduce the subject of peasant resistance, leaving detailed description for later in the book. Chapters 1 and 2 set out the various categories of resistance, separately identified according to their targets and their motivations. Chapter 3 describes the range or repertoire of its forms of protest, in the terms defined by Charles Tilly (1986).

Chapters 4 to 7 are more thematic, systematizing the questions raised in *PWP*. These were inspired by the preoccupations of Chinese revolutionaries themselves: preoccupations before they won power (the class consciousness of the peasants) and their concerns of today over how to modernize their country.

The low level of class consciousness among the peasant masses is illustrated by a striking contrast. On the one hand, antitax resistance was ubiquitous; on the other, tenant farmers' riots were infrequent and confined within narrow geographical limits. Riots against taxation outnumbered by seven times those against rents, whereas land rent charges averaged seven times more than land tax—which, admittedly, represented only a portion of the tax burden. Examined as a category, only the poorest (apart from farm laborers) were involved in resistance to land rent, while antitax resistance brought together a broad front of taxpayers including the landlords themselves. Pillaging and food riots made up the other great movement of the poor (apart from that of the tenants), but the rebels attacked not so much the persons of the rich as their grain reserves, or in other words, their means to live through hard times. Chapter 4 lists the other categories of social movements that, in one way or another, set the poor against the rich. Twin lessons may be drawn from them. In the first place, resistance to rich people's exploitation of the poor was less significant than resistance to the oppression of the weak by the powerful—even though, naturally enough, those in power were also rich or became so thanks to the legal or illegal authority they exercised at the local level. Secondly, social questions as desperate as the poverty of farm laborers or as weighty as the torments suffered by insolvent debtors practically never gave rise (unless exploited by the CCP) to collective or violent resistance. At the same time, the frequency of *xiedou* (armed conflicts) comes into stronger relief, since they involved two camps mixed in social composition but alike in that very heterogeneousness, each acquiring the unanimity of "our side" against the outsiders (a clan or neighboring village).

Chapter 5 merges two chapters of *Jacqueries*. Antitax resistance was touched on in my earlier book in relation to a particular revolt (*PWP*, Chapter 5), but is here the focus of the central chapter: it is the book's longest, yet still hardly long enough to do justice to the subject. More than looting, which was merely a short-term means of survival, antitax resistance is the fullest expression of peasant protest. And it is present as well in a significant proportion of the various categories of unrest explored in the book's remaining chapters.

This is particularly true of resistance to the late Qing New Policies (*xinzheng*) recalled at the start of Chapter 6. Did peasant resistance hamper, time and time again, the efforts undertaken to modernize and strengthen the country? I venture this sacrilegious hypothesis in Chapters 6 and 7. Chapter 6 first examines the forms of and motivations behind rural opposition to the New Policies, an audacious but belated project that precipitated the fall of the Dynasty. A quarter of a century later, the resistance of silkworm cultivators to the modernization of their trade left it still less fit to survive the Great Depression or to overcome the competition from Japanese silk (though I make absolutely no claim that these "technocratic" reforms would have been on either count successful had there been no peasant resistance at all). Five years later, the Japanese invasion was of a wholly different order: it proved a challenge utterly beyond China's capacity to defend herself. So there is no question that peasants were responsible for the inadequacies of the Chinese defense, still less for masking the ill-treatment of conscripts, who were nearly all of peasant origin, or the tragic suffering (economic and human) inflicted on farming families by the unequal imposition of military service. The fact remains that draft-dodging and desertion did seriously handicap the nation's resistance (Chapter 7).

I should indicate briefly those chapters of *Jacqueries* that have been omitted from this abridged edition. Firstly, Chapter 5, devoted to the leaders (the initiators and organizers) of collective actions. A fair number of them were not peasants; among those who were, the "poor peasants" celebrated in communist historiography were far fewer than either the so-called middle or rich peasants. Yet, I concede that my count cannot possibly represent a true quantitative analysis; quite soon, that will become a feasible project, thanks to the ever-growing abundance of evidence and biographical details available from a multiplicity of studies and compilations—and also from the less grudging opening of archives (police archives, among others). Similarly, I have left out the bulk of Chapter 6, a rather restrictive estimate of the strength of the insurgent peasants and the danger they represented for those in power. The response by authorities at various levels to rural unrest, their vertical or horizontal divisions (internal conflicts within the elite), their handling of disturbances, and the combination of concessions with pitiless repression (inherited from imperial prescriptions) were the subject of *Jacqueries* Chapter 7.

The content of the other *Jacqueries* chapters not retained for the English-language edition has been more or less treated in *PWP*. In one case, however, the earlier treatment of "Peasant Responses to CCP Mobilization Policies" has been appreciably changed. Chapter 11 of *PWP*—the reprinted text of a paper presented in Leiden in 1990 and revised in 1993 for publication in Saich and Van de Ven eds. 1995—did not take into account the monumental study by Odoric Wou that came out immediately afterwards (1994) or (for obvious reasons) later studies, such as Benton (1999), DeVido (1995 and 2000), Esherick (1994, 1995, 2000), Feng Chongyi and Goodman eds. (2000), Goodman (1994 and 2000), Keating (1994 and 1997), Ngo (2003), Saich (1996), Selden (1995), and Wou (2004). The development of the sub-discipline "rural communist bases" was not interrupted in 2004, the year when the manuscript of *Jacqueries* was passed to the publishers. The studies published between 1994 and 2004 have nevertheless enabled me to flesh out, and on one point (*PWP*, 233, item 2), to correct my initial treatment of "peasant responses."

All in all, the chapters that I have left out of the present edition are those that seemed to me the least important. I trust that I have retained the essentials. In addition, I have added a final chapter, written specially for this new edition: Chapter 8 outlines a number of permanent features of collective actions by the peasantry. These features are common to French peasants in the seventeenth century and Chinese peasants in the twentieth century, revealing as well many continuities between the actions of the latter and those that make today's headlines.

Let me finally express my thanks to at least a handful of people and institutions. My research has benefited greatly as a result of the decision by the École des Hautes Études en Sciences Sociales to grant me in 1992 the half-time collaboration of a research assistant. The zeal and competence of this assistant, Madame Hua Chang-ming, have fulfilled all my expectations. In particular, she helped me to draw upon the wealth contained in *Wenshi ziliao*, now rendered easily accessible thanks to the precious five-volume index published by Yantai shifan xueyuan 1992, as presented by Sherman Cochran (1996, 92) and extolled in *PWP* (xx and xxvi). I should add that after she retired in 1997, Madame Hua continued for several years her collaboration with me on a purely generous basis.

Dr. Fu Hung-chung, who is the author of an excellent doctoral thesis entitled "Le service militaire en Chine à la veille de la Révolution chinoise" (Military Service in China on the Eve of the Chinese Revolution, Paris, 2007), located and made available to me a variety of material from the Taiwan archives referred to in Chapter 7 of the present work. Further discoveries presented in his thesis encouraged me to redraft and flesh out this chapter.

I wish also to thank Mark Selden and Elizabeth Perry for having taken the initiative in submitting *Jacqueries* to the Harvard University Asia Center, as well as the anonymous reader for the publications program, whose pertinent suggestions greatly improved the manuscript. Lastly, working with Philip Liddell has been a constant pleasure—and not only because of the excellence of his translation.

Wretched Rebels

Rural
Disturbances
on the Eve of
the Chinese
Revolution

ONE

Typology I: Movements Opposed to the Administration

Movements directed against the administration, the police, and the army are far more numerous than struggles between social classes or local communities (examined in Chapter 2). In each case, my approach will be more detailed when I deal with categories or sub-categories of incidents that are not central to the subject matter of this book, and less so dealing with others, that is, with subjects taken up in a subsequent chapter or already dealt with in *Peasants Without the Party* (PWP). In both cases, as in the rest of the book, I shall illustrate within boxes certain themes presented more abstractly in the course of the text.

We shall begin with resistance to taxation, which far outweighs all other forms of rural agitation, with the possible exception of banditry (Billingsley 1988).

Resistance to Tax Collection

When a source tells us, without elaboration, that the peasants "resisted taxes and levies" (*kangjuan, kangshui*), we can identify the fiscal charge referred to only when the context is explained—which, fortunately, it usually is. In most cases what is meant is simply the land tax, which is calculated on the area of land owned and not agricultural output, unlike most of the taxes we shall examine later. Other taxes were imposed not on what peasants might produce but on what they consumed or transported (transit tax): on their holidays, their homes, their persons (head tax), their work implements, and so on.

LAND TAX

At first sight, it is surprising that the land tax provoked so many revolts (see Appendix) because it was very light and not at all proportionate to the continuing predominance of agriculture in the Chinese economy. What is more, from 1912 to 1941, the state exacted almost no income from it. For the first three decades of the Republic, the bulk of its tax revenues were shared between provinces and counties: de facto during Yuan Shikai's presidency (1915–16) and in the decade of the warlords (1916–26), de jure from 1928 to 1941 (since the new Nationalist government preferred to sanction existing practices rather than push the regional powers into combining against it). By that time, inflation and the need to finance wartime military expenditure and supply grain for the troops obliged the government to reimpose the land tax and to exact payments in kind.

What made these modest levies so unpopular were the forms they took and their irregular increases. The burden of the land tax grew throughout the half-century, not continuously but in fits and starts (see Chapter 5). Each time the authorities encountered a new requirement, it tended to impose a new land tax (*mujuan*, payment of so much per *mu*), sometimes referred to not by its source but its purpose: *xuejuan* (tax for schools), *jingjuan* (tax for the police), and so on. Even more often the local authorities imposed a new surcharge (*fujiashui*), indexed to the original land tax (*zhengshui*, the regular land tax), which rose very little or not at all. It was these new taxes and surtaxes that provoked most uprisings (Box 1.1). The taxpayers' indignation and, less often, their uprisings were directed less at the growing burden of tax than at each particular new imposition—at the small change, in sum, of this general tendency. The peasants would hit out at the new surtax, or at the authorities' refusal to allow the usual tax remission following a bad harvest, at the anticipated collection of taxes (and sometimes the umpteenth collection during a single countryside campaign), at an illegal exaction, a fraud or a blatant abuse. Or conversely they might resent reforms of the land registry, which inhibited tax evasion. In short, most

Typology I: Movements Opposed to the Administration

Box 1.1   Resistance to Land Surtaxes: Yangzhong, Jiangsu, 4–5 October 1932

At the start of the Republic, the fluvial island of Yangzhong ("in the middle of the Yangzi") was established as a county. About twenty years later, two members of the local gentry, delegates to the fourth and fifth *qu* (wards) of the county, campaigned unsuccessfully for Yangzhong, the smallest of the 63 counties in Jiangsu, to be merged with a neighboring county. Their initiative had a fiscal motive: administrative spending would be reduced by the merger. Though outgoings would admittedly be higher for a larger county, they would be funded by surcharges indexed to land taxes levied on more than a million *mu* of cultivated land, instead of on Yangzhong's 200,000.

Throughout the summer of 1932, these two notables, Dai Shifu and Huang Zhisan, maintained their opposition to the increase of one of these surtaxes. The county magistrate sent out Secretary Lin Murong to persuade the village heads of the two wards, as well as the members of the local gentry, of the necessity to increase the taxes. Confronted by a crowd of people refusing to disperse, Lin fled disguised as a woman (August 1932). The magistrate resigned, and a new magistrate, a tough character, decided to raise three new taxes and six surtaxes. Local taxpayers contrasted the failure of the petitions for merging the two counties with the success of the demonstration that had frightened off Lin and forced the magistrate to resign: they decided to resist. Dai Shifu and Huang Zhisan, naturally enough, assumed leadership of the movement. On October 2, Dai Shifu proposed that each family should send one representative to an antitax demonstration in front of the county yamen. Each demonstrator was to bring a bale of straw, so that he could sleep on the spot until the county government granted the right of exemption from the new surtaxes, as demanded by the demonstrators.

The straw served a quite different purpose. Since the officials would not relent, the crowd's mood hardened. Two ringleaders, Dai Zhongxuan and Liu Shifu, quickly supplanted the two notables who led the movement during its first peaceful phase. On 4 October, on Dai's call, peasants gathered—30 to 40 at first, and eventually thousands—in front of the offices of Ward 4, where Liu trussed up the official in charge. Thence they moved on to the offices of Ward 5, but because they could not find its chief, who had fled, they set fire to his house, the first of seven such blazes. The peasants burned the homes, one by one, of a member of the Guomindang county committee, the commander of the militia, the head of Ward 3, the chief tax collector, a middle-ranking official, and, lastly, the island's biggest landowner. Along the way, the crowd had swollen to around ten thousand people, whom Dai led into an attack on the county government building. The police opened fire, killing one peasant, and arrested Dai.

The next day, the peasants turned out again intending to set fire to the county yamen, but military reinforcements arrived by river from Zhenjiang (upstream) and Nantong (downstream). Four peasants were killed, and the others dispersed. The seven families whose homes were burned down demanded the arrest of 42 "criminals," most of whom had run away. During his trial, Dai Zhongxuan struck the public prosecutor and was condemned to three-and-a-half years in prison; he appealed, as did twelve fellow combatants. The Suzhou court overturned the sentence of the Zhenjiang court and acquitted all the accused, for lack of proof—while the Yangzhong magistrate committed suicide for not having prevented or contained the revolt.

SOURCES: Dai Wen 1957; *ZLN*, vol. 3, 1933, section 2, 67; Bianco and Chevrier 1985, 157–59.

revolts were limited reactions to such-and-such an innovation perceived as unbearable. They were not part of any concerted resistance to ever more repressive taxes, and even less of a challenge to the principle of taxation.

This applies to anti-tax agitation as a whole, which would extend to disturbances directed against not land taxes but levies imposed on a wide variety of products.

RESISTANCE TO TAXATION ON AGRICULTURAL PRODUCTS

Many taxed products, such as clothes made by peasants, are not mentioned in the following list for a good reason: the tax on them did not provoke any uprisings that we know of. Apart from (slight) exceptions, the following list ranks these products by the number of revolts to which their taxation led, in descending order.

Salt

Resistance to the taxing of salt (*yanshui*) is in second place, far behind resistance to the land tax, and far in front of all other forms of antitax resistance (Box 1.2). The two products heading this list (salt and opium) were both subject to significant illegal trafficking. Repression of salt smuggling provoked the most numerous and bloodiest confrontations. Unlike opium, salt is a basic necessity, used for preserving meat and fish as once it was in Europe. It is, even more than in Europe, an essential

Box 1.2	Revolt Against the Salt Tax: Western Shaanxi, 1903

After the Boxer Uprising, which had degenerated into a war between the Imperial Court and the foreign powers, the treaty of 7 September 1901 had imposed on China the payment of an enormous sum in war reparations to the eleven countries whose Peking legations had been besieged, or whose missionaries (and one diplomat: the German Ambassador) had been murdered. The treaty stipulated that these reparations would be funded out of China's customs duties (maritime customs in particular) and the salt tax. So it is not surprising that the Shaanxi provincial government should have practically doubled the price of its salt, so as to amass its share of the first installments, payable as early as 1902. To forestall the smuggling that this brutal price hike would inevitably cause, the government set up many inspection offices in charge of salt sales: the main offices in prefectures and some counties and their sub-offices in the other counties and main townships.

In the west of the province, the Fengxiang main office closed all shops specializing in selling salt and entrusted the salt trade to a corporation of big licensed merchants, each of which held a sales monopoly in one or two counties. Anything up to 200 *yanyong* (salt guards) patrolled these offices to stop looting and prevent smuggling, with one to several dozen guards posted at each outlet. The main source for this information (who, it is true, is not wholly impartial) accuses these guards of all the misdeeds traditionally ascribed to the *yanjing* and the *yanbing* (salt soldiers): violence, extortion, imposing heavy fines or confiscating salt found in people's homes, pursuing searches right into women's bedrooms (and frequently raping them). The Fengxiang office also acquired a hundred camels to transport the salt in escorted caravans from the neighboring province of Gansu, which provided a good proportion of the salt consumed in western Shaanxi. As that was not enough, the Fengxiang office also hired mule drivers, not escorted but supervised, and ordered them to pay toll charges on leaving and arriving, check in at a whole series of points along the route, and deliver to Fengxiang the exact quantity of salt that they loaded in Gansu. The smallest deficit meant a fine, and if repeated, carried penalties up to the confiscation of the entire load and the mules as well.

This is what happened in early December 1903 to a certain Wang Laiwa, who found himself fined the amount of three mules at the toll office in Tiandang, Fengxiang county. He asked Wang Yaoyao, an associate from a nearby village, to plead his case for restitution. The latter failed in the enterprise, which prompted him to organize with Li and Chao (like him, peasants and occasional mule drivers as well as martial arts experts) a raid on the salt offices. They had no trouble enlisting about a thousand more peasants. On 13 December they attacked five sub-offices across the region. Meeting no resistance from managers or guards—who ran away—they destroyed the premises and carried the salt into storage. The next day, they marched on the main office in Fengxiang, their ranks swollen en route by peasants from three counties: Fengxiang, Qishan, and Baoji. The *yanyong* opened fire, killing one peasant and wounding many others. So the rioters set fire to the camel shed adjoining the office and attacked the main building. Guards and staff fled—except for one unfortunate who was beaten to death on the spot. After that, the rioters set fire to the office itself.

Since these events took place outside the walls of Fengxiang, the prefect and the general commanding the garrison simply shut the gates to keep the unrest out of the city. A few days later, two columns of soldiers, each 800 to 900 strong, arrived on the scene and arrested over 70 villagers, releasing them soon afterwards. But when the soldiers started looting, burning, and raping (at least according to our source), the three ringleaders mustered a thousand men on a nearby hilltop to fight them off. The prefect of Fengxiang and a judge eventually persuaded them to disband and go home—upon which the prefect gave orders for the ringleaders to be seized. Chao was arrested a month later in a county nearby, and Wang Yaoyao was reported to the authorities by the man sheltering him (and was himself killed in revenge by Wang's son the following year). The remaining leader, Li, managed to take refuge further away in Gansu, where the authorities picked him up during the winter of 1904–1905. With his two comrades already executed, Li was secretly dispatched one day in February 1905, when the inhabitants of Fenxiang had gone to watch a drama production, with fireworks, at the Temple of the God of Fire, five *li* from the city. As for Wang Laiwa, whose three mules were confiscated at the start of the affair, he was put in irons (specifically, chained to an enormous rock) and sentenced to life in prison (where, in fact, he died).

After that initial blunder—the 70 temporary arrests—the penalties were, as usual, selective and merciless at the same time (see Chapter 3), but counterbalanced by major concessions: the authorities provisionally gave up their monopoly of salt deliveries, closed the salt sub-offices and toll offices, and most importantly, lowered the price of salt. Indeed, their clash with the mule drivers was just the incident that sparked off the uprising. Added to the violence and searches of the *yanyong*, the rise in salt prices, which had put this essential commodity beyond the means of many villagers, explains why a thousand peasants rushed to support the three ringleaders.

SOURCES: The main source is the substantial but not always reliable *Qishan WSZL* (vol. 3, 1988, 6–32), which was completed and corrected on minor points of detail in Xibei daxue lishixi 1984.

component of human nutrition, the Chinese diet being low in meat, and rice being low in salt. Again, unlike opium, salt is heavy and cumbersome. Overland transport was prohibitively costly except over short distances; accordingly, it was transported mainly by water—not by sea, like the salt for medieval Venice, the Ottoman Empire, and British India, but by river, as in France during the Ancien Régime (Adshead 1983, 226). River transport is easier to control than maritime transport: leaving aside the large lakes such as Lake Tai, used by fleets of smugglers, this common feature may be added to other resemblances between taxation, trade, and salt trafficking in China and France (see Chapter 8).

At the start of the Republic, vigorous reforms were applied to salt administration making it more efficient (Adshead 1970) and, at the same time, better adapted to the fight against smuggling. Trafficking in salt had become almost inevitable, given the wide variations in price between various (geographic) Salt Divisions and given the very high price of *guanyan* ("official salt") compared with *siyan* ("private," or black market salt). Our research includes resistance to the repression of smuggling, but not smuggling as such. Some gangs of smugglers comprising hundreds of men and junks under the leadership of secret societies turned to banditry rather than resistance.

From now on I shall restrict myself to a brief description of each category and sub-category of antitax resistance and to one or two examples of related incidents without further details. Those seeking further information will find it in *Jacqueries* (67–78).

Opium

Opium was taxed even more heavily than salt and likewise encouraged smuggling. Yet the two commodities were subject to sharply different forms of taxation. For the greater part of the half-century, poppy growing was officially forbidden, which obliged the authorities—particularly during the "warlords" decade—to impose on the growers heavy fines that disguised taxes. What provoked most revolts against the poppy tax (for example, those in Su Xian and Lingbi in 1932, see *PWP*, Chapter 5) were the abuses and corruption of the tax authorities and collectors, whereas the resistance to the salt tax was often linked to the prevention and repression of fraud and smuggling.

Cattle

By itself, the slaughter tax provoked more than one-third of the 45 instances of resistance to taxes on cattle in my sample. In Guangdong province alone during the single year of 1904, it caused three incidents each involving over a thousand people (*QMN*, no. 49, 1982, 123 and 127). Further taxes were aimed at livestock, including animals sold. Sometimes they applied without distinction to head of cattle (*shengkou juan*), but in general the species of livestock was named. In these cases, two named animals at once might be taxed, such as oxen and pigs (*niuzhu juan*) or steers and horses (*niuma juan* or *niuma shui*); or it might be a single species, usually pigs (*zhu juan*), but also steers or buffaloes (*niutou shui*), and so on. Among the rare cases of resistance to the trade in cattle is a late example from 1932: in Sanguanmiao, Henan, where the peasants refused to pay a tax of 0.5 *yuan* for each head of cattle sold (*Gong Xian WSZL*, vol. 7, 1990, 137–38). Unlike this latter case, most instances of resistance to cattle taxes date from the Empire or the early days of the Republic.

Wines and spirits

More so here than under the previous heading, uprisings occurred in the early part of the half-century: 16 of the 23 recorded cases date from the closing stage of the Empire and none is later than 1935. The New Policies (see Chapter 6) introduced in the last years of the Empire led to the raising of existing taxes plus new taxes (on spirits, tobacco, meat, and other products) that few counties maintained under the Republic.

In principle, the production of wine (or tobacco) for home consumption was not taxed. In this case, it was the sudden imposition of a tax (thus, its newness) that provoked a peaceful petition and (when the petition was rejected or repressed) a riot. So it was in Yongji, in the autumn of 1903 (see Chapter 3). In the absence of any new tax, revolts were commonly sparked off either by the sudden increase of an existing tax, as in Liangnong in March 1933 (see Chapter 5), or, as with salt, by fiscal controls aimed at preventing or unmasking frauds. Whether or not they were concealing extra wine production intending to sell it, the producers were unified in reproaching the tax controllers for their nit-picking searches, their brutality, or their corruption: the example of Liuqiao in April 1928 (see Chapter 5) illustrates this latter scenario.

Fishing and fish

It is not always easy to say whether such incidents concerned peasants who fish or full-time fishermen. Being unable in some cases to tell, I have taken the risk of listing a couple of incidents not involving peasants. Some of these revolts led to fatalities: seven ringleaders killed in Shidao, Shandong, on 14 June 1917 (*Yantai WSZL*, vol. 3, 1984, 167–69); 60 peasants killed and over a hundred arrested in Muping, in the same province, during the summer of 1928 (*Muping WSZL*, vol. 3, 1990, 124–36); eight killed in the autumn of 1935 in the south of Hainan Island (*Guizhou WSZL*, vol. 15, 1984, 40–43). In the last case, the fishermen were going in for salt smuggling; and the arrest of one of them triggered the revolt. Then we have a mixed case, arising also from salt taxation, which united fishermen and salt-workers in a memorable and bloody uprising in Daishan in July 1936 (see Box 5.2).

Agricultural food products

More than half the incidents and revolts under this heading arose from taxes either on sugar (*tangjuan*) or fruit/fruit trees (*guomu juan*). Nearly all those linked to sugar broke out in the two Guangs (Guangdong and Guangxi), southern provinces where sugar plantations abound. The most significant (the Sanna uprising in April 1907) was launched by the Wanrenhui (Society of the Ten Thousand), numbering, in fact, from 2,000 to 3,000 men (*QMN*, no. 49, 1982, 166; *XGQSJMDS*, 456–57). The following year, at the other end of the country, resistance to a fruit tax mobilized over 3,000 peasants from 28 villages in Zunhua county, Hebei (Prazniak 1999, 97–100; *Zunhua XZ*, 1990, 10).

Among other products, we should mention oil, tea, and vegetables. The oil tax triggered a revolt affecting 121 villages in early summer 1910 in Huaiyuan county, Guangxi (*DFZZ* 7:7, 1910, 17875–76). A year later on 28 July 1911, peasants in Xinhui county, Guangdong, destroyed the offices responsible for collecting the taxes on tea, spirits, and pigs and set fire to the home of the clerk who collected the tax on polders, or reclaimed land (*QMN*, no. 50, 1983, 117). Three years later, in May 1914, following a tax strike by tea vendors in Liuxia, Zhejiang, about a thousand tea growers unable to sell their crop destroyed the dwelling of a member of the tax-collecting committee (Zhejiang sheng zhengxie wenshi ziliao weiyuanhui 1990, 135). To campaign against a new tax on vegetables introduced in September 1929, thousands of street vendors from the suburbs of Peking refused to do business and abandoned their empty carts in the streets; they soon formed a Peasant Union. The struggle lasted several months (*ZLN*, vol. 2, 1932, section 2, 185–86).

Non-food agricultural products

Bamboo, which is not only eaten but also serves ten other purposes,[1] provides a transition between food products and non-food products. Resistance to taxation affecting bamboo shoots and roots provoked two riots each rallying several thousand peasants in Wukang, Zhejiang, in April 1908 (*QMN*, no. 50, 1983, 92), and then in the northwest of the neighboring province of Fujian in 1923. In the second case, peasants from Wufu and Baishui forced the authorities to put up a stela confirming their resolve never again to raise this kind of tax (*Wuyishan shizhi*, 1994, 28).

Taxes on tobacco were often combined with those on wines and spirits, as well as other taxes. The tax that rallied over a thousand peasants in Shilong Zhen, in Dongguan county, Guangdong, in September 1911, set some kind of record. The rioters were objecting to a whole range of taxes: on tobacco, silk, spirits, steers and the slaughter of cattle (two separate taxes), poultry, fish, and a medicinal plant (*QMN*, no. 50, 1983, 119).

Like the revolts against the land tax, some of the incidents in this category were provoked by increases, as when the tax on silk rose from 7 to 12 copper coins per ounce in Xiaoshan, Zhejiang, in August 1907 (Shen 1981, 43). And as with antitax resistance in general, many other groups, too numerous to be cited here, fought the imposition of new taxes. Some incidents remained minimal, even peaceful, while others led to fatalities: five men were killed in November 1924 in Gushi (in Weinan county, Shaanxi), when troops fired on tens of thousands of farmworkers who had come with their tools to demonstrate against the tax on cotton (*Weinan XZ*, 1987, 14). Twenty years earlier, the increase of a tax on indigo had provoked a still more bloody and well-documented revolt in Leping, Jiangxi (*Leping XZ*, 1987, 161–64 and 411–12; Li Wenzhi 1957, 963–64; Sheel 1989, 51–52 and 122–25; Zhang Zhenhe 1954, 188–97; *QMN*, no. 49, 1982, 125–26; *Jacqueries*, 72–73).

Typology I: Movements Opposed to the Administration

Handcrafted products

The Gushi uprising, which mobilized so many peasants against the cotton tax (see above), was a separate matter from cases of resistance to the tax on dyed cotton fabrics, such as those in Guanlitu, Henan, during the autumn of 1906 (*QMN*, no. 49, 1982, 153). Among the products handmade by peasants as a secondary—but occasionally their main—occupation were mats, woven sometimes from reeds, as in Fengtai, Hebei, in 1909 (*QMN*, no. 50, 1983, 85), and sometimes from straw, as in Laixi, in neighboring Shandong, the scene of the victorious resistance of the *ximin* (the peasants who made these mats) in January 1922 (*Laixi XZ*, 1990, 665–66).

We should also mention the tax on straw hats, the object of successful resistance in 1906 in Longyang and Dongguo, in the southwest of Shandong (*Teng XZ*, 1989, 14); on saucepans; and on china. In 1920, the villagers of Houfotang, Gansu, opposed a tax on saucepans (*Wudu WSZLXJ*, vol. 1, 1986, 24–25). A thousand kilometers east of there, the peasants of Ci Xian, Hebei, resisted in 1927 an additional tax on china imposed by the warlord Feng Yuxiang (Thaxton 1989, 256–57).

Raw materials

Wood was hewn sometimes from trees planted by farmers. More usually it was cut down or gathered in the forests by peasants. The other products under this heading were similarly excavated by peasants from the soil or sub-soil. On 21 April 1910, taxes on firewood, coal, and boats provoked a riot in Zhangxing, Zhejiang (*QMN*, no. 50, 1983, 94). More revolts were related to coal than to wood. A bodyguard to the Emperor returned to his native village in the county of Shahe, Zhili, where, in June 1903, he led the villagers' resistance to the tax on a coal mine (*XGQSJMDS* 1985, 49). In the neighboring province of Shanxi, where more coal is produced, two incidents occurred fifteen years apart. The first was peaceful: in February 1911, over a thousand peasants in the Dongye region went to Wutai county town to present a petition for the coal tax to be repealed (*Wutai XZ*, 1988, 696). The second turned into a riot: peasants from villages southwest of Linfen county refused to pay the coal tax (*meishui*)—and they ultimately won their case (*ZLN*, vol. 1, 1928, section 2, 470).

The only instance I have found relating to the tax on lime was a mere request for the tax to be repealed, which was rejected by the county government of Yangchun, Guangdong, in December 1933 (*Nanhua ribao*, 8 December 1933, cited in *ZLN*, vol. 4, 1934, section 2, 69). By contrast, several riots, some both significant and bloody, arose after officials refused to repeal a tax on saltpeter, but I have chosen to list these under the important first heading of salt tax revolts.

RESISTANCE TO OTHER TAXES

We have been dealing so far with peasant resistance to taxes on products supposed to have provided them with incomes. There were other taxes, not on what peasants grew or made but on transport, trade, the consumption of these same products (or others), or again on tools for work or measurement, even on the clearance of new farmland. We must also take account of the head tax, registration fees, residential taxes, taxes on village festivals—though there were some known taxes (for example, on matches, cooking-stoves, straw sandals, cement, or guarding fields by night) that are not mentioned because they did not lead to revolts or riots known to me.

Trade, transit, and consumption

The notorious *lijin* taxed goods in transit, whether farm products or not. Since it was repealed in 1931, only before that date—and, in the main, before 1911—did it provoke peasant resistance. The most serious outbreak was in May 1909 in Zhenyuan, Guizhou (*Zhenyuan WSZL*, vol. 3, 1989, 37–38).

The *lijin* was repealed by a consolidated tax, the *tongshui* (Tien 1972, 78–79). This term also designated a local tax paid by peasants taking their products into town. In March 1922, 30,000 peasants from twenty villages around Shanhaiguan, at the eastern end of the Great Wall, rose up against this tax (*Qinghuangdao WSZL*, vol. 1, 1987, 109–11).

The same term, *tongshui*, also included indirect taxes on various products. In November 1932, a tax on sweet potatoes mobilized the peasants of Chaoyang, Guangdong, to ask for an exemption on the grounds that the potatoes were a significant staple food for poor people (*ZLN*, vol. 3, 1933, section 2, 103).

Means of production

We should include among the taxes on work and measurement tools those other levies on farm instruments, manure, boats, and bushels (*dou*).[2] The word *dou* refers to a grain receptacle in the form of a truncated pyramid as well as the volume it holds (one *dou* equal to ten *sheng*, which is more or less ten liters). Each time peasants used a *dou* they had to pay the tax on bushels (*doujuan*). In February 1910 this sparked resistance by the peasants of Yongning, Henan (*QMN*, no. 50, 1983, 90–91).

The only affair linked to the clearance tax (*kenwu juan*) could have been added to the very first categories of antitax resistance, since it involved clandestine salt workers and is calculated on *mu*, just like the land tax. It was introduced in spring 1919 and applied in coastal, marshy, or salty areas in Dongtai county, Jiangsu. Resistance by 30,000 taxpayers peaked in two bloody confrontations in 1922 and especially in 1923 and ended only with the eventual repeal of the tax in 1927 (*Jiangsu WSZL*, vol. 18, 1986, 167–73).

Head tax and residential taxes

By definition, the head tax (*diding*) hit everyone. In July 1910, thousands of peasants in Guni, Ghizhou, rose up against a specific variety of head tax named *rentou shui* or "tax per head" (*QMN*, no. 50, 1983, 101; *SB*, 29 September 1910). More often, peasants rebelled, not at the tax, but at increases to it, as in Jingchuan, Gansu, in July 1915 (*Jingchuan XZ*, 1996). Some locally based taxes were proportionate to the total number of humans and animals registered in each household; one such tax provoked a riot in Qian'an, Zhili, in September 1909 (*QMN*, no. 50, 1983, 83).

After people and animals, there was their accommodation. On 11 May 1904 in Zhenjiang, Jiangsu, over 10,000 men (not all of them peasants) demonstrated in front of the county government offices against the residential tax (*fang juan*) and other taxes raised to fund the requirements of the police—who killed four demonstrators (*QMN*, no. 49, 1982, 123). The tax on doors and dwellings echoes the French Ancien Régime tax on doors and windows. Residents of Longchang, Sichuan, resisted the tax from November 1924 to March 1925 (*Longchang WSZL*, vol. 4, 1984, 25–28). The tax on door name-plates (*menbian juan*) also hit every family. During the 1920s, several thousand peasants in Jiangsu protested it (*ZJNSZ*, vol. 2, 701).

From November 1908 to June 1909, a monthly tax on chimneys drove 200 peasants (according to one source) or 1,000 (according to the other) from Mizhi, Shaanxi, to resist (Xibei daxue lishixi 1984, 163–65; *Mizhi WSZL*, vol. 1, 1964, 57–67).

Various other taxes

To finish, we should mention resistance to various taxes ranging from payments on property transfers to taxes on public entertainments.

In May 1914, peasants in Xingtang, Hebei, demanded the abolition of taxes on registering deeds on land sales (*qishui*), which had risen tremendously during the nineteenth century (*Xingtang WSZL*, vol. 1, 1989, 98–102; Reed 2000, 176). In 1922, several thousand peasants in Chifeng, Inner Mongolia, refused to pay these registration taxes, or more precisely, the payments on property transfers (*Chifeng shijiaoqu WSZL*, vol. 2, 1990, 34–36). The requirement to purchase tax stamps (*yinhua*) also provoked resistance and riots. A stationer's shop in Tianle, Xiaoshan county, Zhejiang, that collected registration charges was targeted by rioting peasants in August 1921 (*Xiaoshan XZ*, 1987, 23).

As for entertainments, the magistrate of Zhushan county, Hubei imposed a tax on opera productions in January 1910. This aroused opposition from hundreds of villagers (*QMN*, no. 50, 1983, 89). Other taxes, sometimes resisted, applied to theater productions and processions.

Special Levies and Mixed Incidents

It is not enough to say that the revolts and riots against taxation were by far the most numerous. We should not forget that further unrest arose from different exactions—government demands for labor and military demands for both labor and goods—and that most other mixed sources of unrest added taxation to some further grievance.

NON-TAX EXACTIONS: CORVÉE

Statute labor, also known as corvée, demanded no money from taxpayers and no material contributions (not even the grain required when taxes were collected in kind): it demanded their labor. At the outset we should state that cases of resistance to statute labor were rare—barely 1.3 percent of all the incidents examined in this book (48 out of 3,648).

Yet the statute labor requirements were unpopular and did weigh heavily, especially between 1935 and 1949; admittedly, though, they weighed less heavily than under the Qing, when they could represent, together with the land tax, the main peasant contribution.[3] Statute labor was demanded with increasing frequency after Chiang Kai-shek's directive was published in December 1934 authorizing provincial governments to use peasant labor to push through all sorts of public works projects: digging irrigation canals, dredging rivers, shoring up dikes, clearing and reforesting land, and particularly building roads and railways. The directive assured officials that this work would benefit directly the laborers who were recruited from villages in the region. In fact, the rich landowners, who had more fields to be irrigated and protected from flooding and who were more likely to use modern roads, escaped the labor draft. Either they paid to be exempted—legally or by bribing the head of the *baojia* in charge of recruiting the laborers— or else the recruiters did not even dare to call on them.[4] The exemption of notables and rich people increased the load on the poor, who had no need for modern roads alongside paths and waterways and, often enough, were forbidden to pull their wooden carts on them anyway. What is more, the Nationalist government built most of its modern roads for military purposes (Eastman 1974, 210–12; Cochran et al. 1983, 98). During the war, the authorities mobilized armies of drafted laborers to extend airstrips or build new ones, especially in southwest China where the central government had sought refuge.[5]

The draftees were often required to turn up bringing their own pickaxes or shovels and sometimes their own lunchboxes. Others were fed, meagerly, and some even received modest pay, but this was unusual.[6] Sometimes the foremen would refuse to feed them on rainy days (since they did not work) even though they had no possibility of returning home, or a corrupt *baojia* head might extort from each of them a handful of copper coins to cover the "charges for calling out the draft." And the call for labor, far from being restricted exclusively to the farmers' quiet periods, might come at the worst moment of their year. For example, near Wuxi in Jiangsu, it came during the second fortnight of May, the moment when the silkworm breeders had to hurry to settle the spring silkworms onto the planks where they would spin their silken cocoons. Most silkworm breeders could not afford to pay someone to stand in for them while they worked on building a road: a road that sometimes ran across their own land, for the loss of which any compensation would be very little, very late (Cochran et al. 1983, 102–4; Eastman 1974, 210). If the draftees arrived late for work or did not work at the required rhythm, the foremen—or in more cases the guards (army or militia) supervising them—were liable to beat them and wound them, sometimes to kill them.

More often than not, it was ill-treatment, abuse, or more simply hunger that drove people into "resistance to the corvée" (*kang liyi*). Sometimes the practice of selecting by lot who had to work was enough to set off a riot: in 1935 in Biyang, Henan, a thousand old women destroyed the *baojia* registers containing the names of able-bodied adults (their husbands and sons) and wounded an officer in the process (*ZJNSZ*, vol. 3, 1025). As a general rule, however, it was the workers themselves who protested against the poor quality, insufficiency, or lack of food; the worsening of their living and working conditions; and the corruption and brutality of the officials and guards. Being unable to satisfy their hunger with the daily rations served them, 20,000 draftees in Jintan, Jiangsu, fought in 1935 against the troops sent to "protect the road"— which, in fact, meant supervising the corvée (*ZJNSZ*, vol. 3, 1025). The same year in the same province, the draftees in the second ward of Lianshui county asked the bureau regulating maintenance works on the Huai River to issue them with wheat flour. When the authorities refused, they went and helped themselves, looting the office storehouse. The police killed two draftees and wounded a third, upon which a thousand draftees went and burned down a thousand sheds along a large section of building sites (*Huaiyin WSZL*, vol. 2, 1984, 228). In Gaoyou (same year, same province), draftees heard that the authorities would distribute food to those sent to reinforce the dikes to prevent flooding and that each worker, once he had moved a certain volume of earth, would be issued four *fen* for his water and tea expenses. After a while, those supervising the laborers no longer fed them or paid them anything; they even charged them small sums in call-out charges. Six thousand peasants, draftees, and "civilians," both men and women, went and destroyed the county government buildings, thrashing those officials they came across, ward heads, village heads, and even court officials (*ZJNSZ*, vol. 3, 1025). Badly fed, badly clothed—and with the ward heads taking a cut from the pay they had been promised—more than 30,000 draftees in Guanyun, Jiangsu, rebelled in May 1936. They put to flight most of the ward heads and village heads and won their case (*Guanyun WSZL*, vol. 2, 1985, 138–40; also *ZJNSZ*, vol. 3, 1027). Further south in the same province, the foremen speeded up the work rate of laborers sent to dredge two riverbeds in Haimen and Wuxi counties. When they started locking up some draftees and shooting others, the laborers went on strike (*ZJNSZ*, vol. 3, 1025).

Striking, which was very rare among agricultural workers (see Chapter 4), was a favored form of action among corvée laborers. These were peasants, temporarily drafted into labor: they experimented with an unfamiliar form of struggle, especially in regions such as Jiangsu, far away from Shaanxi and its *jiaonong* tradition (see Chapter 3). The draftees' strength lay certainly in their numbers, enabling them on occasion to take more violent action, as when ten or twenty thousand of them attacked with their pickaxes the escort force (*ludui*) responsible for preventing their escape. When they rose up in smaller numbers—numbers more than ample for other forms of peasant resistance—they were exposed to the greatest danger. The authorities were only too aware of the risks posed by the huge mobilizations that they themselves had ordered; they lost no time when reinforcements were needed. Thus, when a thousand draftees rose against them in Jinshan, near Shanghai, at the end of March 1935, the militia promptly put them down, and the leaders of the revolt hanged themselves without waiting to be captured (*Jinshan XZ*, 1990, 26). In Suining, Sichuan, in December 1935, in reprisal for three policemen killed, draftees and demonstrators suffered ten times as many losses: more than 30 killed and over 100 wounded. (*Sichuan WSZL*, vol. 13, 1964, 173–76).

Readers will have noted not just the often considerable numbers involved in resisting the corvée but also the historical concentration of such incidents: most of the affairs mentioned date from 1935 or 1936. Our sample is hardly representative, since our main source in this field covers precisely those two years (*ZJNSZ*, vol. 3, 1025–28). Nevertheless, even cases reported by other sources were concentrated in the years 1935 and 1936, which allows me to assert another factor, observed also in relation to other forms of peasant resistance: what infuriated and

Box 1.3   Revolt by Drafted Laborers: Southeast Sichuan, March 1936

Everyone knows that the Long March of the Chinese communists lasted a full year (from October 1934 to October 1935). It is less known that they spent more than two-thirds of that year (from the end of January to 10 September 1935) crossing, from south to north, a single province: Sichuan, the largest in the country. To fight them, Nationalist leaders undertook to link Sichuan with four adjoining provinces: Shaanxi, Hubei, Hunan, and Guizhou. From the outskirts of Chongqing to the Hunan border, the third of these "roads to crush the bandits" (*gonglu jiaofei*) crossed seven counties—Qijiang, Fuling, Nanchuan, Pengshui, Qianjiang, Youyang, and Xiushan—and took fourteen months (from November 1935 to January 1937) to build. By the time the road was finished, it was too late to fight the communists, who had withdrawn into the northwest of the country, but its completion gave an advantage to the central government, in that the pursuit of the communists enabled it to strengthen its hold over the province at the expense of the local warlords.

Despite wastage and corruption, the building of the road was not expensive, because the bulk of the work was done by laborers locally drafted to lay the roadway crossing their region. All along the way, road construction committees ordered township and village heads to mobilize the able-bodied men. Landlords and rich peasants would pay to be exempted from corvée, placing the entire burden on the poor peasants. Their wives and mothers feared for their lives, all of them having heard and chanted the song lamenting the fate of the husband of Meng Jiangnü, who was killed while working on the Great Wall. The draftees of the 1930s survived, but had the right only to one meal a day; none were paid except for those cutting stones. In Fuling, where even stonecutters received no pay, many draftees ran off and those recaptured were jailed.

Indeed, it was in Fuling county, at a place called the White Horse, that the first riot broke out: the draftees beat a guard to death. The guards and foremen (most of them members of the Gelaohui from Chongqing) treated the laborers badly, beating them when they stopped to rest after particularly hard work, such as transporting over dozens of kilometers the tree trunks needed for building wooden bridges. There was no one to care for the injured or the sick.

The second riot, breaking out on the Qianjiang section, was a real revolt. It was supported by a sect originally from a band of *shenbing* ("divine soldiers") in Hubei: the Lianyingjiao or Lianyinghui (Sect or Association of United Heroes). Starting in 1930, these "divine soldiers" adopted the title of *lianying* and their organization quickly swelled with numerous recruits among peasants in the Qianjiang and Pengshui areas who were exposed to natural disasters and military exactions. At dawn on 16 March 1936, at a place known as Bailayuan, between kilometer markers 363 and 364 of the road under construction, a hundred or so *lianying* arrived to lend a hand to the laborers. Repeating slogans devised by the sect leader ("hit the road"; "hit the county offices"; "no tax payments"), the draftees with their tools and the *lianying* with their daggers or guns attacked and killed the guards and foremen and wrecked and burned the local road-building offices. It took until 20 March for the uprising to be put down by the militia and a company of soldiers, who suffered serious losses.

SOURCES: *Qianjiang WSZL*, vol. 1, 1986, 42–52; *ZGNC*, vol. 3, no. 7, July 1937, 72–74. On the legend of Meng Jiangnü, see Waldron 1990, 197–201.

mobilized the peasants was the newness of the recourse to corvée, which became general in response to Chiang Kai-shek's directive in December 1934. It was invariably the scourge of the present moment that aroused the peasants' most violent reactions, such as the late Qing campaigns to eradicate poppy cultivation (*PWP*, Chapter 6) and the military conscription imposed during the Sino-Japanese War (see below, Chapter 7). And when the scourge lasted, it was likely to be more passionately fought at its outset (for example, the proliferation of surtaxes on the land tax between 1926 and 1928) than at its peak (between 1931 and 1934, when the burden of taxation became intolerable).

NON-TAX EXACTIONS: *BINGCHAI* AND DRAFTING OF COOLIES

We may also include under non-tax exactions the occasional military requisitions (*bingchai*), imposed in a similar way to ordinary taxes. The army had merely to indicate to the administration the sum of money, the quantity of cereals, or the number of mules, donkeys, or carts that it needed to be commandeered. The administration then passed the order on down to village level and supervised the collection process. These requisitions were carried out in response not so much to people's ability to pay as to the needs of various armies. So it is not surprising that their golden age—so to speak!—should have coincided with the end of the warlords' hegemony and the beginnings of the Nationalist regime in the regions that experienced "residual militarism."[7] That was the situation in the Yellow River basin provinces (Shaanxi, Shanxi, Henan, Hebei, and Shandong), where these requisitions became very heavy between 1929 and 1931. At that time, the first three of these five provinces were stricken by famine, which increased the burden of military requisitions.

Box 1.4 Resistance to *Bingchai*: North China, 1929–30

An estimated 20,000 peasants in Zhouzhi county, Shaanxi, had to flee the region during a famine in which 40,000 died. In 1929, the tension between Feng Yuxiang (who controlled Shaanxi) and Chiang Kai-shek led to increased exactions. On 16 December, the army demanded payments of 90,000 *yuan* by the people of two counties, Zhouzhi and Hu (a little further east). This demand was reinforced by a threat: 100 strokes of the cane for *lijia* heads and other notables if payment was not made within a week.

Responding to the call of a martial arts master, the self-defense militias banded together as an "Army of Peasants" (*nongmin jun*) also called, in reference to its origins, the Army of the People's Militias (*mintuan jun*). This army could muster only 300 men, but it was enough to frighten the police, who fled. What is more, after their early successes, the 300 had become 800 by the time they reached the county headquarters (Zhouzhi) where, in December 1929, they massacred the magistrate and numerous officials. Then they released prisoners and confiscated five to six guns, some money, and some opium. After a few days, they moved off to seize Hu county town, where they killed an even larger number of policemen. That was the end of their epic adventure: army reinforcements sent to Hu defeated them. The survivors fell back in a disorderly retreat to Zhouzhi.

The following year, on 4 November 1930, the south of Hebei was the scene of an equally serious riot, sparked off by the retreat of Yan Xishan's Shanxi army, which before leaving demanded mules and carts in numbers proportionate to the land area of the supplying villages. Once the mules had been handed over, the army demanded food. There were numerous well-established sects and secret societies in the region (southwestern Hebei): Hongqianghui (Red Spears), Baiqianghui (White Spears), Lanqianghui (Blue Spears), Huangshahui (Yellow Sand Society), Zhenwuhui (Real Fighters Society), Tianmenhui (Heavenly Gate Society) and many others. So the police, fearing that they would face resistance, refused to approach the villages. The exception was one officer, called Wu, who escorted some collectors to Lulu township in Shunde county. The Red Spears asked for extra time; Wu started making threats; a member of the Red Spears replied in the same tone; Wu killed him. At once, the bystanders threw themselves on Wu and the collectors and stabbed them to death. Various secret societies were summoned by the ringing of bells, and after consultations, it was agreed to parade Wu's body, with hands severed, from village to village. Along the way, Wu's ears were cut off, and after three days' walking, his head as well. The Shanxi army made no request for his remains, and in its precipitous retreat westward it abandoned much of its food—the demands for which sparked off the riot.

SOURCES: These two episodes, together with a third that occurred in Yizheng, Shanxi, are reported in Wang, Shi, and Xue 1931. This text, 73 pages long, is reprinted in Feng 1936, 355–97. The report by Wang, Shi, and Xue has been summarized in Institute of Pacific Relations 1939, 101-09. On the first episode, additional details, not always corroborating Wang, Shi, and Xue, are given in *Zhouzhi WSZL*, vol. 4, 1989, 79–83.

The military's needs, as we have seen, were often mixed: contributions in money and in kind, including animals, to which was added as needed the draft of men, not to fight, but to carry food and equipment. The conscription of coolies for the army is a separate issue from the corvée, the drafting of laborers as described above. In any case, we have not included among the 48 instances of resistance to corvée the revolts provoked by the army's coolie roundups. Of course, these roundups, like those for conscripts, became particularly massive and frequent during the Sino-Japanese War; and most of the incidents linked to such raids date from that period. We shall mention just one, providing a transition to the following paragraph. During the autumn of 1941, the villagers of Xiaocun Xizhai, in Yanshi county, Henan, fought against the recruitment of coolies and servants for officers, as well as the pressure for paying taxes after harvests had been ruined by a severe drought. As soon as the police had received reinforcements, the rebels were crushed: thirteen peasants killed, houses burned down, and possessions looted (*Yanshi WSZL*, vol. 1, 1987, 89–93).

MIXED EPISODES

Jean Nicolas distinguishes two types of motivation behind some incidents: the "basic type" or primary motivation and the "secondary type or by-product."[8] Among other examples, he cites that of a subsistence riot that turned into an antitax dispute (Nicolas 2002, 28). In China, it was taxation in most cases that supplied the incidental target of a revolt initially motivated by another grievance. Often, it was far more than just an incidental target added along the way: it was present from the start, jointly with the other cause, and it is difficult to tell which target was the more important. We describe as "mixed" these complex affairs, which straddle the categories established in our typology and in which were pursued two or several objectives, of comparable if not always equal significance (it might happen that one objective remained the priority or that another might supplant the first).

When the rioters' various grievances converge on one target (very often taxation), I shall simply indicate it within the relevant category. A revolt may, for instance, be motivated at once by a surtax on the land tax, an increase in the tax on spirits, and the establishment of a new tax on the slaughter of pigs. Real mixed incidents are aimed at various targets, such as the tax officials and the army (the most common case). Had I followed my first impulse, I should have doubled, even tripled, their number, but I later reduced it by systematically favoring the "basic type," which enables me to ascribe incidents to such-and-such a category.

It was above all during the Sino-Japanese War that, in many incidents, resistance to conscription and to taxation were mingled, the blend being symbolized by two pairs of characters: *bu na liang, bu dang bing* ("no taxation, no military service"). One example will suffice, that of a revolt involving over 10,000 participants (eventually defeated) in Duyun, in southern Guizhou, between February and March 1943 (Zhou, He, and Zhang 1987, 40). One less common variation is *bu chu bing, bu jiao liang* ("not to leave as a soldier, not to pay tax in kind"): the example is from the village of Daping, Jiangxi, in December 1940 (*Lichuan WSZL*, vol. 2, 1991, 64–67). Still fighting those twin antagonists, the army and the taxman, peasants sometimes combined not just two but four grievances: *bing fu liang kuan* ("military service, corvée demanded by the army, tax payments in kind, and in money"). It was against these four scourges that around one thousand peasants rebelled in Gucheng, Hubei, between June and July 1945. Nine of them were shot and fifteen others sentenced to long prison terms (*Gucheng WSZL*, vol. 1, 1987, 77–81).

Outside the years 1937 to 1945, the resistance to taxation was always dominant, but was often associated with other targets. One such target was the army, but not because of conscription: in Ning Xian, Gansu, in 1926, peasants resisted the raising of a "contribution to purchasing guns" decided upon by "Zhang the Wolf," the nickname of commander Zhang Zhaojia. Rioters killed two policemen. Twenty of the rebels were executed, and the heads of the two ringleaders were hung from the wall of the county capital (*Ning XZ*, 1988, 404–5). Another target was the civilian administration, particularly at the time of the New Poli-

Typology I: Movements Opposed to the Administration

cies (1901–11): in November 1910, 10,000 to 20,000 peasants in Ye Xian, Henan, fought against a new tax on wine, and at the same time, battled the local administration (new as well) controlled by local notables (*DFZZ*, vol. 7, no. 12, January 1911, 18, 903–4). Yet another example would be looting or subsistence riots: in September 1910, starving people in Yancheng, Jiangsu, looted not just any building but the local tax office (*QMN*, no. 50, 1983, 94).

Lastly, there are instances (though rare) of movements directed against two or more targets without taxation being involved. This was the case in Qinglongjiao, Zhejiang, in October 1928: farmers on land owned by a landlord attacked the surveyors' office, which at first sight suggests a movement directed against the local authorities. However, it was at the landlord's request that a corrupt surveyor had increased by one-twentieth the area of each of the fields rented to the farmers, which proportionately increased their rents. As such, we could say that this incident arose equally from resistance to land rent (*Cixi XZ*, 1992, 16).

In still more exceptional ways, some originally mixed episodes developed to the point of acquiring one or more new targets and taking on a new character. A case in point is the revolt that shook the Changle region in Fujian during the winter of 1931–32 (Bianco 1986, 297–99).[9] This complex affair was at once an antitax movement and a struggle against the military (the navy, as it happened) that degenerated into a war between villages. This third phase, *xiedou*, was the last, because it was easier to put down. By contrast, the great uprisings narrated at the end of Chapter 7 could not be so easily repressed, which was why there was time for them to become still more complex.

Non-Tax Movements Directed Against the Administration

These movements arise out of the injustices and corruption of officials; out of administrative decisions that are unfavorable or not in the peasants' interests (or decisions not made owing to administrators' incompetence and failure to take necessary measures); and lastly, out of decisions aimed at benefiting the people, even attempts at reform.

CORRUPTION AND EXACTIONS

Some revolts were targeted at the corruption of officials in general, such as that calling "for corrupt officials to be beaten, pursued and killed in order to save the people" in Xingjie, Xichou county, Yunnan, from May to July 1937 (*Wenshan Zhou WSZL*, vol. 3, 1985, 91–98). More usually, the peasants attacked one or more named, corrupt officials, starting with the magistrate himself: a corrupt magistrate who had misappropriated emergency funds (in Duchang, Jiangxi, in 1926; *ZLN*, vol. 1, 1928, 468), another who had put into his own pocket the money extorted by his predecessor (in Hancheng, Shaanxi, in 1918; *Hancheng WSZL huibian*, vol. 2, 1983, 99–101), a third who had shared with local leaders the credits intended for building an airport (in Zhijiang, Hunan, in 1938; *Xiangxi WSZL*, vol. 5, 1985). In January 1943, 300 "Heavenly Soldiers" (*shenbing*) attacked Daozhen county town in Guizhou. They suffered heavy losses during the following days and months (their leader was killed on 13 May). In November 1943, a delegation of nine natives of Daozhen county declared in front of the provincial assembly that the revolt (by that date already crushed) had been provoked by magistrate Han Xuchu, a "cruel and corrupt man, who breaks the law and kills people" (*Daozhen Xilaozu Miaozu zizhi XZ*, 1992, 15–16).[10]

Just as frequently, villagers raged against local leaders who were not all officials, strictly speaking, but nevertheless wielded power and influence. The villagers of Baishuishi, Guangxi, fought a stubborn battle for three years against a village head (*xiangzhang*) and other corrupt members of the administration (*Pubei Xian WSZL*, vol. 2, 1988, 63–72). In 1934, the villagers of Xiyan, Shanxi, succeeded in ridding themselves of a tyrannical village head (*cunzhang*) who used his official connections to exploit the people mercilessly (*Yu Xian WSZL*, vol. 1, 1985, 168–69). Elsewhere, a mere *xiangtong* (local administration agent) incurred the villagers' wrath, as in Fenjing in October 1911. Nine villagers were killed in punitive action after they destroyed the corrupt agent's house, several schools, and the local self-government office (*Jintian WSZL*, vol. 4, undated, 12–13). Sometimes the target was a lowly rural guard (*dibao*), such as the one accused of harboring bandits in Matang, Jiangsu, in May 1913 (*Rudong XZ*, 1983, 504 and 513).

Kangbao douzheng ("struggle against oppression"): that is how our sources often express the resistance to exactions, especially when they are accompanied by violence. Another expression, *fan ba* ("opposing despots"), draws attention to the *eba* ("local despots"), who embodied a widespread scourge in the ill-regulated countryside of the Republican interregnum. These local barons (also known sometimes as *du huangdi*, "the village emperor") ruled with a rod of iron the petty fiefdoms they carved out using connections within the administration (some of them being nominally part of it) or quite simply by force (often they had private militias) and intimidation. During the Sino-Japanese War, an *eba* who had a score of young people abducted for army service demanded opium in exchange for releasing them. More than a hundred villagers surrounded the headquarters of the ward administration (*qu gongsuo*) in Shuanlongjing, Qiubei county, Yunnan, in February 1942 and freed the draftees detained there (*Wenshan Zhou WSZL*, vol. 3, 1985, 104–6).

In the latter case, resistance to exactions accompanied the resistance to conscription. In other cases, it was related to antitax resistance: when taxes were paid in kind, peasants were quick to blame the collectors, accusing them of fiddling the weighing of grain and embezzling some of it (see a case in east Shanxi at the end of the Empire in *Yu Xian WSZL*, vol. 1, 1985, 205–9). Still more incidents turned into mini-*xiedou* (Chapter 2): in 1941, a peasant in Luoping village, Gansu, killed a corrupt and tyrannical head of *bao*. This murder sparked off numerous killings, arson attacks, and hostage takings—revenge upon revenge, *xiedou* in its purest form (*Kang XZ*, 1989, 577–79). More usually, the struggle against the corruption and greed of those in power was a portent of social conflict to come (Chapters 2 and 4), because of collusion between the authorities and the rich. In Huangdian, Anhui, where fir trees were the main produce, a landlord called Zhu Qingchuan appropriated a wooded hill belonging to the peasant Cheng Shenzhong and installed a tenant farmer there. In July 1932, Zhu and the commander of the local militia arrested Cheng and made him sign, under torture, an ownership acknowledgement: "This hill belongs to Zhu Qingchuan." Enraged, 40 villagers from Huangdian invaded the militia headquarters, seized seven guns, set Cheng free, and recovered the paper he had signed. The affair might have stopped there if Zhu, with the complicity of two senior officials, had not persuaded the Xiuning magistrate, responsible for Huangdian, to grant him justice against the "bandits"— the Huangdian villagers who had forcibly occupied "his" hill. The magistrate stuck by this version. On 7 November he marched on Huangdian at the head of a hundred men including the local militia. The villagers, still celebrating, were setting off firecrackers: the magistrate, thinking they were a call to battle, ordered an attack. Four villagers were killed, but the others fought back, killing the magistrate and beating a dozen soldiers to death. Zhu and his two accomplices fled and the police, finally seeing the light, gave orders for their arrest. All the same, the authorities considered the magistrate as having died doing his duty (in fact, it seems Zhu had bought him off): they awarded his wife 1,000 *yuan* in funeral expenses and a civil pension (*Xiuning XZ*, 1990, 22 and 421).

OTHER ADMINISTRATIVE MEASURES

All kinds of other administrative measures excited the villagers' resistance. Most of these harmed or threatened their interests, beginning with expropriations, especially when the owners got very little in the way of compensation, which was often the case. About ten of the riots in our sample broke out in response to expropriations, most under the Nationalist government (*ZJNSZ*, vol. 3, 1026–28 cites several cases). We should recall the most recent example—before, of course, the many such incidents occurring since the 1990s. To make room for building an airport in Songming, Yunnan, in spring 1945, more than 380 hectares of land, including fourteen villages, had to be expropriated and thousands of homes cleared. On 18 April, delegates from the fourteen villages petitioned the provincial government to abandon the project; nevertheless, work began on 1 May. Next, the peasants asked that the airport be built on uncultivated land. The next day, since the work went ahead, nearly 1,000 peasants took direct action. They wounded the magistrate, who died of his injuries, and killed one of his guards. The authorities responded with a hundred or so arrests, and the following year, executed a prisoner who had admitted killing the magistrate (*Songming WSZL*, vol. 1, 1989, 66–70).

After expropriations there follows a whole series of concrete grievances arising from government regulations, interventions, or projects damaging to peasants' interests. Recurring problems arose from water. The following list, leaving out dates and locations, gives a quick idea. Peasants protested the digging of a canal and the building of a pumping station that caused damage to neighboring fields (*Jianwei XZ*, 1991, 15). More than 300 peasants asked the authorities to stop building locks along another canal (*Dagong Bao*, 28 November 1933, cited in *ZLN*, vol.

4, 1934, 64). They were objecting to irrigation projects that had been badly carried out, flooding some fields during storms, so they organized a mock demonstration of welcome for the site foreman hoping to force him out (*Feng Xian WSZL*, vol. 4, 1986, 33–35). Peasants who had suffered losses from flooding launched a petition to be allowed to cultivate fields covered with reeds alongside the river, which until then the authorities had wisely forbidden (*ZYRB*, 14 January 1934, cited in *ZLN*, vol. 4, 1934, 65).

It was not only the authorities' actions that excited resentment and revolts: it was sometimes also their inaction. During the great floods of 1931, the Yangzi caused widespread damage to Yangzhong Island: dikes were breached in 32 places, 100 square kilometers were flooded, and 119 people were drowned. The peasants, judging that the dikes had been badly maintained, demonstrated and demolished the county Office of Public Works (*Yangzhong XZ*, 1991, 8 and 435). Another flood, less serious, occurred three years later, in a region dotted with lakes, tributaries of the Yangzi, and canals; this time, it was the flood report by the magistrate of Mianyang county, Hubei, that angered the peasants. In their view, he had underestimated the damage, which spurred the peasants of Datonghu into setting fire to the administrative buildings of one ward and one large village. More than 150 peasants were killed in terrible repressions (*Honghu XZ*, 1992, 13).

Other riots targeted the police, because of their actions or misdeeds. When a policeman injured a peasant, the crowd attacked a police station (*Yong'an shizhi*, 1994, 21). Patrolmen ordered to break a butchers' strike looted the meat, including some that villagers had already paid for, and kicked outside anyone who objected. The peasants demonstrated in the streets against this injustice (*Rudong XZ*, 1983, 504). Other clashes with the police or soldiers were aimed at preventing arrests. In December 1943, in the village of Bending, Guizhou, the mere attempt to arrest a single man, Pan Fusheng, aroused violent resistance in which two policemen were killed. The village head was furious, ordered the village burned, and profaned the tomb of Pan's father. Pan gathered 300 villagers in protest, occupied several villages, and brought in 1,000 militiamen. In January 1944, reinforcements finally overcame the rebels. Pan fled, and escaped death only by making lavish payments to corrupt officials (*Sandu XZ*, 1992, 20).

History does not relate the exact motivation behind Pan's arrest nor why the villagers so wholeheartedly backed him. Were they, as in other cases, expressing solidarity with one of their own, without troubling to question the rightness of the cause they were espousing? Many affairs quite simply resembled private vendettas that became public because local people supported one of the parties engaged in a dispute, not necessarily with the administration, but with an administrator. Other incidents betrayed hostility toward innovations and changes. When a magistrate altered the site and the dates of a market, traditionally set for the third, sixth, and ninth days of each ten-day period of the Chinese calendar, unhappy villagers demolished the county yamen and injured a ward head (in May 1938, in Mingshan, Sichuan; *Mingshan XZ*, 1992, 13). Lastly, in many another case, what motivated the rioters was parochialism, even if they harbored many legitimate grievances on which our sources remain dumb. Affairs like this occupy a gray or uncertain area between the majority of revolts, provoked by known injustices, and those which, as we shall see, broke out in reaction to sometimes clumsy but often necessary measures.

REFORMS OR ATTEMPTS AT REFORM

A third series of riots and revolts, sparked off again by the administration's initiatives, was targeted at measures that might cause suffering to the peasants, or from which they might expect little or no benefit, or lastly, others that might have benefited them if better managed and more generally accepted. However diverse they were, such measures had something in common: they were, on balance, desirable or necessary. We may reproach the administration for having introduced them with excessive brutality, but not for undertaking them.

The most spectacular measure from which the peasants suffered was undoubtedly the eradication of the poppy, which was resolutely pursued during the last years of the Qing (*PWP*, Chapter 6). Poppies were a more risky crop than some others for climatic terms (rain or a humid atmosphere at the moment of harvesting could be ruinous) but they were also far more profitable. They even represented the main source of income in many regions in the west of the country: from Shaanxi and Gansu in the northwest to Sichuan, Yunnan, and Guizhou in the southwest. In these regions, the ban on producing and selling opium was regarded as a catastrophe, one that deprived the poppy growers of their livelihood. A good many of the growers found ways around the ban or defied it, concealing their poppies among other crops or physically resisting soldiers sent to enforce the ban.

A few years before its first campaign against opium was launched, the imperial court introduced the New Policies. They were ambitious but belated, having mainly the effect of accelerating the fall of the dynasty they were intended to save.[11] The policies included the creation of a "new army" (*xin jun*) capable of facing up to the imperialists and repressing domestic unrest, a dose of constitutional monarchy and local administrative autonomy, and above all, the creation of modern schools (*xin xue*), like the army designated "new," where the teaching of mathematics and science would supplant that of the classics. The peasants—or at least a minority of villagers—fought against those reforms affecting rural society (the new schools and local autonomy) but did not resist the institutional changes at the central level; for instance, they opposed the strengthening of the police rather than the creation of the new army. Admittedly, there was an antitax element to the arson attacks on schools, police stations, and the offices of the "autonomous" local authorities, attacks that became endemic during the last years of the Qing. All of these fine projects were financed by taxes and surtaxes, but the villagers' hostility was fueled by many motives beyond hatred of taxation.

One of the last projects launched under the New Policies was the census of 1910. The peasants hunted down, wounded, and sometimes killed the census takers, mostly recruited among teachers, again because villagers attributed taxation plans to the official wish to count the population. Also, villagers gave credence to wild rumors (as detailed in Chapter 6). Born of the same fears, opposition to censuses continued under the Republic, combined into a movement of pervasive hostility to the sacrilegious innovations perpetrated by iconoclastic modernizers, who were fiercely overturning statues in village temples and banning processions to bring rain, along with other ceremonies they regarded as superstitions.

There was one last category of administrative measures and reforms that might have benefited the peasants (in the same way as reforming the land registry mentioned earlier in the context of antitax resistance). In the 1930s, the Nationalist government undertook reforms, in truth more economic than social in their impact. Some were aimed at improving farmers' productivity, some at enabling Chinese silk producers to resist competition from Japan. The peasants' hostility impeded or slowed the implementation of these reforms, which admittedly would not have solved their problems but might have relieved their poverty and furnished a partial answer to the crisis of Chinese agriculture.

Movements Directed Against the Army and Military Service

All of the incidents listed so far were targeted at the civilian administration—or, in some cases, the police. There remain, on one hand, the actions directed against the army, not many, as it was dangerous to take them on. These were mainly defensive reactions, sometimes the last resort, provoked by the troops' exactions or violence. On the other hand, and most importantly, there were incidents arising from compulsory military service, especially between 1937 and 1949, when foreign or civil wars were continuous but for one year (August 1945 to June 1946). Such incidents, by contrast, were very frequent, particularly in the southwest of the country where the government took refuge during the war, but peasants attacked local administrators as well as recruiting officers.

THE ARMY

It is not always easy to distinguish the requisitions known to be legal, and supported by the civilian administration from the extortions practiced directly by the army. The distinction even loses all meaning during the warlords' era: within the boundaries of their fiefdoms, local authorities—often appointed by the warlords—would obey their slightest wishes. To provide for his immediate expenses, the least of the warlords would please himself in raising special contributions at irregular intervals. In protest at one of these, the inhabitants of three villages in Liping county, Guizhou, rebelled in October 1924. A day's fighting ended with several hundred villagers killed (*Liping XZ*, 1989, 16).

Eight years later, a comparable incident had a quite different outcome, simply because in the meantime the Nationalist government had imposed its rule on the "residual" warlords, particularly the minor ones. Warlord Ma Hongxun was no sooner installed in Mingxi, Fujian, in March 1932, than he emptied the public stores of grain to pay his soldiers, forcibly bought grain cheap and sold it dear, and imposed ten tax collections and various charges in the space of two months. His exactions had the immediate effect of strengthening the Red Turbans and the Big Knives. In May, a battle between these two secret societies and Ma's 1,000 men caused many deaths. On 28 June, thousands of peasants (mostly from the secret societies) surrounded the county capital where Ma had dug in. On 1 July, a Nationalist force arrived in support of the besiegers. Exhausted by four weeks of siege, Ma Hongxun nevertheless succeeded in breaking out and fleeing on 26 July (*Mingxi XZ*, 1997, 18–19). The Mingxi rebels suffered many losses, like those in Liping, but eventually the central army had taken their side and rescued them.

The distinction between legal contributions and illegal exactions became much clearer when the soldiery went in for looting pure and simple. They did so frequently, especially in the years between 1910 and 1920. Resisting these depredations was dangerous, but once the peasants had made up their minds, they gave no quarter. In September 1913, 400 soldiers under a certain commander Ni raided the eastern suburbs of Shou Xian, Anhui, and abducted some locals, intending to ransom them. Within a few hours, the villagers mobilized. Armed with guns, pikes, knives, and sticks, they surrounded the soldiers, killed several dozen of them on the spot, and captured some others, whom they shot immediately. The affair did not end there: under the command of a former militia leader, 20,000 men crossed the Huai river, occupied Fengtai county town, and appointed one of their men as magistrate. They did not stay long. Pursued by Ni's army, many of them met their deaths as they returned over the river (Weng et al. 1990, 449–51).

Robberies and looting were sometimes accompanied by brutality, woundings, or killings. Some movements were not directed, or not exclusively, against the army's extortions and exactions, but at its violence. This ranged from mere "bad behavior" by the soldiers—forcing shopkeepers to sell at low prices or molesting women—to rape and murder. Once again, it was during the time of the warlords that excesses of this kind were most widespread, but they continued into the Nanjing decade in provinces or parts of provinces less controlled by the national government. These regions were not being fought over by the "residual" warlords; but they were still being stalked by groups of "soldier-bandits" (*bingfei*) whom the government imagined they could domesticate by enrolling them in regular forces, but who were all the more tempted—because they were seldom paid on time—to resume their former practices. In this case, again, the peasants who dared to resist them showed no mercy, as is attested by the bloody Longtian incident (Bianco 1986, 291–92).

CONSCRIPTION

All of the affairs linked to the army that we have just reviewed add up to less than half the cases of resistance to military service. We should remember, however, that the latter were often targeted at the civil authorities and that a good half of them were mixed affairs: resistance to military service and to something else, usually taxation. Nearly 90 percent of the numerous riots provoked by conscription date from the years 1937 to 1949, which is hardly surprising. Most broke out during the Sino-Japanese War and quite a few during the Civil War.

China enjoys a superabundance of manpower. But from the very beginning of the war, Japan occupied the most populous provinces—in truth, quite loosely, having too few troops to manage its vast acquisitions. China's recruitment pool ought to have been enough, even when restricted to "Free" China: the province of Sichuan alone was more populous than France. Yet the paradox is that China was short of soldiers throughout the war, while still meeting resistance from those forced into military service. Conscription by lottery persisted, confirming the surfeit of potential recruits: the country did not need to enroll everyone within the relevant age groups. Further confirmation was the application of physical standards to eliminate the unfit (though by the war's latter stages the services became much less choosy) and the exemption of students, government officials, and state enterprise employees, who were judged more useful in their education or jobs than at the front. It was the same with taxes, before and during the war. Tax revenue was insufficient to finance development, but in view of its inequality, of the irregularities, frauds, and abuses to which tax collection gave rise, it was more than enough to fuel discontent and resistance. During the war, the military deficit was quantitative—due to a defective census, to poor coordination between civilian and military administrators, and (last but not least) to the corruption of local officials—and qualitative—conscripts were illiterate or sick and unable to master sophisticated equipment such as American tanks. This dual deficit was never really absorbed; but conscription was resented as an unbearable scourge by households subjected to it.

Nine out of ten of these families were peasants and overwhelmingly poor. Looking beyond the sociological composition of the Chinese people and the exemption of various categories of citizens, this skew is explained by the practice of buying exemption, legally or fraudulently. Rich people could thus sidestep the lottery, or if they drew the wrong number, could pay for a stand-in. In the provinces supplying the most conscripts (Sichuan, to begin with, as it was the seat of the central government and therefore better controlled), manpower, abundant before the war, came to be insufficient for farming needs. This development was good for farm laborers, whose wages soared; but it frequently turned out catastrophically for soldiers' parents. The economic distress suffered by families deprived of one or several workers in their prime of life would be enough by itself to explain how unpopular military service was among the farming community. Still worse, as most conscripts could not write, enjoyed no leave, and would not be demobilized until the war's end (if they survived that long), their families considered them as lost children.

It was the selection of draftees by lottery that provoked the greatest number of riots. Frauds and injustices were so frequent that the local authorities were regularly suspected of embezzlement. In addition to selection by lottery, many other abuses aroused conscripts and their parents to resistance. Variations in the number of yearly recruitment drives were a further source of discontent, flight, and agitation. In a famous memorandum addressed to Chiang Kai-shek, the American General Wedemeyer wrote, "For a Chinese peasant, conscription is a scourge comparable to famine or floods, except that it strikes them more regularly (twice a year) and leaves more victims" (Romanus and Sunderland 1959, 66). If recruitment had only been limited to twice a year! There were frequently four recruiting drives and sometimes twelve. From 1941 onward, the administration redoubled its emergency recruiting campaigns (*jinji zhengbing*). Just like taxes collected in advance, there were recruitments in advance (*yuzheng*) on future quotas. When these means were not enough, army units made up their numbers by sending squads into the villages and townships to "welcome" (in fact, to press-gang)

Box 1.5   Resistance to Military Service: Xindu, Sichuan, November 1938

A simple misunderstanding or rumor about cheating during the drawing of lots could trigger a riot when discontent was already smoldering. This was the case in Xindu, where local leaders had lost their influence to the benefit of "foreign" officials in Sichuan; people grumbled at the haughty attitudes of these same officials, judging their lifestyle too free; and, of course, they resented the unequal allotment of conscription. When the police called in the young men on 8 November for the preliminary inquiry that was to exempt only sons and select the able-bodied for the lottery, their families believed the lots were already being drawn. The young men wrecked the conscription office and the staff fled. The authorities opened fire and found themselves, after a few hours, facing a huge gathering of youths who had come running in from surrounding townships. In Taixing town, the rioters killed four policemen and an employee of a model farm (managed by the state); in Xindu, the dead were being carried out from both camps. Soon, their numbers boosted by militiamen from neighboring counties, 20,000 peasants jammed the county government building for six days until negotiations mediated by local notables, backed by reinforcements from the provincial government, restored calm. The Xindu magistrate was dismissed.

SOURCES: Dai Gaoxiang 1983, 161; "Sichuan Xindu shibian jingguo wenjian" (Documents relating to the unfolding of the incident in Xindu, Sichuan province), Archives of the Dangshihui (Committee of the History of the Party [Guomindang]), Taipei, file 502/209. Both sources were kindly passed on by Fu Hung-chung. Our account is a compromise between the two sources, which differ as to dates and other points. The second includes a fairly long report by the magistrate Luo, who succeeded the sacked magistrate. It is more detailed, but partisan toward the police.

soldiers (*jiebingdui*). This practice, often referred to in the crudest way as "picking up soldiers" (*labing*), consisted of seizing peasants working in their fields, tying their hands quickly behind their backs, and dragging them off, or with the same dexterity, in grabbing onlookers standing around a juggler or acrobat: "Any man with time to watch a street show had better be in the Army!" (Eastman 1984, 149). Lastly, even those whom the recruiting sergeant enlisted legally were often captured, rather than recruited, for fear they would run away.

Sometimes, conscripts would use force in resisting the recruitment squads, as in Xiapu, Jinxian county, Jiangxi, 19 April 1945 (*Jinxian XZ*, 1989, 19). At other times, they would deliberately kill the person in charge of enlisting conscripts. This happened at the same time a little further south, in Meifang, Yihuang county, Jiangxi (*Yihuang WSZL*, vol. 3, 1991, 46).

In all, the riots and revolts provoked by the recruitment of soldiers were so numerous (nearly 60 recorded between 1937 and 1945 in the provinces of Sichuan and Guizhou alone) that, for a time, they supplanted antitax riots at the head of the resistance list. Or, more exactly, they would have supplanted them had not most of the riots against conscription been mixed affairs, targeted also at taxation.

TWO

Typology II:

Movements Within Society

Movements setting classes or social groupings against each other, being less frequent than riots directed against the civil or military administration, are subdivided into two mutually incompatible types. We may designate the first as social movements (or vertical social movements), pitting poor against rich, and the second as horizontal conflicts, ones that set neighbors (clans or villages) against one another, the social composition of each camp being similar but otherwise rarely of much significance.

As this chapter is very short, I shall add to it a sort of appendix to the typology, devoted to movements of various kinds sparked off by religious sects or secret societies.

Social Movements

The best known of such movements are food disturbances and resistance to land rents.

LOOTING AND FOOD DISTURBANCES

The movements described in Chapter 1 were targeted at the authorities, tax or otherwise. Here, the targets were different. Admittedly, while sometimes looters helped themselves from public granaries, they would usually go for the storehouse of a better-off neighbor, a rice shop, a barge—in short, their targets were private citizens, or more precisely, their possessions. In most cases looters did no harm to the other person: it was a share of his reserves that they wanted, just to survive.

A second difference with the previous chapter: most of the incidents there were on a small scale, while these were tiny. Limited to one village or a handful of villages, the incidents in Chapter 1 lasted in general for a day or two, involving small numbers (a few hundred or perhaps a thousand men), and they left a number of buildings demolished or burned down and few people killed—in most cases none at all. Most cases of looting, however, were even smaller affairs, the most basic of all those examined in this book. But these minor incidents were more frequent than the others, apart from antitax disturbances. They were so common, even innocuous, that reporters and other observers were usually content to mention them without further comment: "There have been cases of looting in such-and-such a locality or county." Innocuous because they did not represent a serious threat to public order—though they certainly did in the despair they reveal (see Box 2.1).

A real subsistence riot is not at all the same thing, of course. They did occur and could be very serious, but such riots—though no less significant than other forms of social unrest—make up only a small minority of food disturbances. The rest, more than nine out of ten, were merely cases of looting: people were hungry and helped themselves to any available food. The trouble is that there is no clear division between looting and rioting: looting may degenerate and it is not always easy to determine the point where the imperceptible buildup of violence alters the nature of the incident.[1]

Outbreaks of looting are far and away the most numerous social movements. In my sample, which admittedly only estimates their numbers (see the Appendix), they are five times more numerous than the most representative and often mentioned social movements: those that set farmers against landlords.

RENT RESISTANCE

From the outset, we should stress the paradox: tenant farmers rarely rebelled (*PWP*, Chapter 7), whereas their circumstances represented the most conspicuous social problem in the Chinese countryside. Debtors,

> **Box 2.1**   Advance Warning of Looting: Xingwen, Sichuan, 1934
>
> Written in a notice (*gaobai*) posted in Xingwen "so that everyone will be informed": "For years we have been suffering from drought and have been able to harvest practically nothing. Sell our children? No one wants them. Our wives? All our families are poor and no one would take them on. . . . If only Heaven would bless us with a shower of grain, perhaps we could survive. But as money does not grow out of the ground, we have no means of satisfying our hunger. . . . So we have gathered our poor people together, those left with nothing at all, to form an organization whose members will go and eat at rich people's houses. We shall ask them for anything that can fill our bellies. But clothes and other objects, those we must not take, to distinguish us from bandits and to prolong our pitiful lives."
>
> SOURCE: *Sichuan WSZLXJ*, vol 3, 1962, 140–41.

admittedly, were almost as numerous as tenant farmers and their fate sometimes more tragic, but the two categories overlap: many tenants were indebted and, moreover, some became tenants because they had been insolvent debtors, forced to cede ownership of their plots of land to their creditors. Demographic pressure, though not the only cause, is sufficient to explain why rents and interest rates were high—so high, indeed, that very few tenants or debtors succeeded in escaping the vicious circle: chronic debt leading to farming someone else's land.

In truth, some tenant farmers (known as "semi-tenants") owned fields too small to feed their families: they made up the difference by renting a field. The "semi-tenants" were even more numerous than the mere tenants. Between them these two categories amounted to just under half of all farmers. It is helpful to recall the same proportion (a little less than half, about 44 percent, of the harvest from the rented field) to give us an idea of the average level of rent. But these rates varied enormously from one region to the next or according to the legal status of the landowner, individual or collective.[2] Taking all categories together, we may estimate that, of every four tenants, two handed over to the landlord between a third and a half of their crops, the third gave more than half, and the fourth less than a third of the field's output.

I use the generic term "tenant or tenant farmer" to translate the Chinese *diannong*, although some *diannong* were in fact sharecroppers. As with sharecropping, sharing the crop (*fenzu*) accounted for more than a quarter of all arrangements between landowners and tenants. As it enabled both to share the risks, it was common where the output from the land was unstable. One drawback: it deterred the sharecropper from investing since he could keep only part of any additional harvest this expense might yield.

Renting in kind (*guzu*) could be found in a good half of cases. For each *mu* under cultivation, the tenant paid his landlord a given quantity, fixed in advance, of rice or wheat, or both at the same time, or of different cereals. This system encouraged the tenant to improve the rented field and to produce more, and it rarely pushed him into excessive risks, since both custom and sometimes also the law required that the amount of rent be reduced in the event of poor harvests.

In one case out of five, or a little more, the rent was paid in cash (*qianzu*). As with the previous system, the amount was fixed in advance and independent of the success of the harvest, but it forced the tenant to sell his grain immediately after harvesting, when prices were at their lowest. The system operated mostly on the outskirts of great cities, such as Shanghai, areas where commercial farming was fairly well developed, and also on land rented by collectivities (including clans, schools, and temples).

The duration of the lease varied as widely as forms of payment. In nearly 30 percent of cases it was not specified: tenure could then tacitly be carried over. Most leases varied between one and ten years, but some were longer. What the tenant preferred was indefinitely renewed tenure that, ideally, could be inherited. Tenure of that kind did exist, de facto, in many a region (the landowner could not, without very good reason, evict his tenant) and even in law: this was permanent tenancy (*yongdian*), in decline by the twentieth century. As an additional advantage, permanent tenancy was often combined with fairly low rents. The tenant could acquire it in different ways: he could buy permanency when signing the lease by paying the equivalent of three years' rent; he could enrich a mediocre piece of ground; or he might acquire it if, as the landowner, he had to cede his title of ownership to an influential notable for purposes of tax avoidance or to sell his field while retaining rights to the "land surface" (*dianmian*). This distinction between owning the "surface" and owning the "subsoil" (*diandi*) often went hand in hand with permanent tenancy: the landowner could not drive the tenant off a field if they shared its ownership. The right to the land surface was inherited and could be traded like any other ownership title; in general, it was more valuable than the title to ownership of the subsoil. It is tricky to discuss in the abstract the tenants' condition without distinguishing, for example, between the permanent tenure of the owner of the land surface and the precarious situation of the tenant who could be evicted at the end of the year.

Inequalities did not stop there. A small minority of tenant farmers had to pay rent in advance, another minority had to pay in installments all through the year, while most had nothing to pay before the harvest. More importantly, one tenant out of every three or four (less than 1 percent of those in Shandong and more than 96 percent of those in Sichuan) had to pay, on signing the contract, a deposit that on average was the equivalent of a year's rent—sometimes much less (a tenth, for example), sometimes more. The anticipated payment of the rent, as well as the deposit, amounted to a significant advance of money that the tenant did not always have available. So the landowner would sometimes lend him this sum, charging interest—all of it staying in his pocket. Some landowners provided farm implements and draft animals, even seeds and fertilizer; others nothing at all. As a general rule, the rent was lower when such investments were left to the tenant. These few examples give only a glimpse of the manifold variables affecting average levels of rent and making our appreciation of the tenants' condition so complex a task. Some of the land controlled by clans in Yunnan were rented by rich peasants who preferred to increase their output by renting fields—rather than buying them—and paying farm laborers to work them. Like their counterparts in a Guangdong county where one rich peasant in every six had not even the smallest field, renting land proved very profitable (Fei and Chang 1948, 77; Bergère, Bianco, and Domes 1989, 272–73). Had they judged it more profitable to buy land, they would have done so.

The circumstances of tenant farmers were not uniform across China, but this fact should obscure neither the extreme poverty of most of them nor the brutality with which they were sometimes treated by rent collectors, the landowners themselves, or their henchmen. Around 1930, a short distance (30 miles) from Shanghai, fifteen people were imprisoned in the Kunshan detention center for tenant farmers, on the strength of a simple arrest order (*qiejiao*) signed by the landowner. Their crime: non-payment of rent—or being in arrears. Of the fifteen prisoners, none owed more than about 30 *yuan*, and five were women arrested in lieu of their runaway husbands. Defaulting tenants had to pay for their own food, at twice the market price (their families were not allowed to bring them anything), and also contribute to the guards' expenses (*yafei*) while in detention (Feng 1933, 109). In addition to detention centers for defaulting tenants, there were, in less developed regions, private landlords' courts. The landlord sat like a judge, the tenant crouched in front of him, on his knees; all around, displayed in the "court," were implements of torture and weapons (planks, ropes, knives, and guns). In Guanyun in 1932, in the northern and more traditional part of the same province (Jiangsu), the verdict of the landlord/judge/prosecutor was final. The tenant had insulted him for having slept with the tenant's wife (which explains the insult): he ordered the man's tongue to be cut out, and had another tenant drowned by his servants (Feng 1933, 536). While such excesses were unusual, ill-treatment, killings, and rapes were more common, perpetrated either by the landlords, their sons, or their managers, or by village heads who were often beholden to them (Institute of Pacific Relations 1939, 16; Ash 1976, 43–44; and especially *DFZZ*, vol. 27, no. 6, 1930, 72).

The subordination of tenants to their "masters" and their precarious economic condition made it less surprising how rarely they revolted, but the very fact that tenant riots were rare nonetheless requires attention. If we are careful to exclude revolts incited by third parties (communists or other radical intellectuals, or Peasant Unions during the 1920s), as well as legal actions and individual quarrels between tenants and landowners (or managers), in other words, if we apply to the resistance by tenant farmers the same rule as to all categories of rural disturbances in our sample, the modest total of tenants' revolts is remarkable. There were fewer of them, in half a century, than the riots provoked by the New Policies in six years (from 1905 to 1911); half as many as those provoked by conscription between 1937 and 1949; much fewer than disturbances linked to the single salt tax—not to mention the land tax—or than episodes linked to opium (the tax and the eradication of the poppy); and finally, two-and-a-half times fewer than *xiedou* (feuds). They became a little less rare during the second quarter of the century, and simple refusals to pay the rent became more frequent, partly because non-spontaneous resistance (incited by communists or others) may have influenced the spontaneous, preexisting, category. Lastly, they were, on the model of other categories of resistance, reactive and defensive: to rebel required at least that the landowner was refusing to allow the usual reduction in rent after a bad harvest. Even then the links between the three phenomena were far from automatic: bad harvests were recurrent, refusal to lower the rents not so unusual, and resistance exceptional.

OTHER SOCIAL MOVEMENTS

Other social movements, being still rarer than tenant riots, did not break out where expected. The most underprivileged and most exploited social categories (farm laborers and debtors) hardly ever rebelled—except, of course, when their unrest was incited by communists (*Jacqueries*, 248–60).

One can certainly find social movements other than those. There were those peasants who paraded with banners displaying the four characters *dafu jipin* ("hit the rich and help the poor"). Other peasants, suffering the first and worst effects of modernization, rose up against the formation of, for example, a syndicate to control the market of such-and-such a product, or the promoters of mechanical irrigation, or competition from a big forest-clearing firm. In all these cases, the peasants were victims only of the weapons available to those in possession of capital. But the law of the strongest was not always applied legally, far from it. The rich and powerful would seize land not yet cleared, or sometimes even arable land that villagers considered commonly owned by all the residents. To convert it into private property, all the notables had to do was give a good thrashing to the poor wretches trying to cultivate it, and then to pay something resembling a tax to some complicit or intimidated officials.

The unfair acquisition of land lies somewhere between competition "within the rules" and the numerous perks and privileges available to the rich and powerful and, still worse, the exactions practiced by many in positions of authority in villages or wards. Were the peasant victims of these hated petty tyrants suffering social exploitation or oppression

Box 2.2   Murder of a Local Tyrant: Baoji, Shaanxi, 1933

Sun Chao, who had completed only a few years in school, carefully cultivated his *guanxi* (relations) in order to become rich and powerful. He succeeded, and was appointed head of the fifth ward of Baoji county in Shaanxi, and then commander of the local militia. From then on, he came on strong, in every possible way. He imposed taxes whenever he pleased (and pocketed them), bought for almost nothing the land owned by starving victims of the 1929 famine, charged high rents to the former owners, lent them food in the spring, and charged 50 percent interest in the autumn.

Eighteen young people, who had become sworn brothers, became informed that Sun's guards were armed only with daggers and old, locally made guns. On the morning of 21 November 1933, they attacked his house, found him crouching in his kitchen, and decapitated him.

The police arrested four of the eighteen, while the others succeeded in escaping. One of the four was executed, and two others were tortured to death in prison.

SOURCE: *Baoji Xian WSZL*, vol. 6, 1988, 43–49.

of a political kind? Both, no doubt; but it was the second that gave rise to the first. It was the tyrants' access to a particle of power that enabled them to extort money or goods and, by the same token, to inflict on peasants both humiliations and ill-treatment (cf. Box 2.2). We may conclude then that, in this chapter devoted to peasant movements "in society," we have found some movements directed against local representatives of the administration, just as in Chapter 1.

While still looking within society, the following paragraphs introduce movements of quite a different kind.

Horizontal Conflicts

In contrast with social movements setting the poor against the rich or powerful, other conflicts could involve a local collectivity (a clan or village) fighting another. As each of these comprised a minority of rich people and a majority of poor or destitute people, the two opposing groups were of heterogeneous (and similar) social structure. We shall describe as "horizontal conflicts" these struggles between groups (or forces) of equivalent wealth, which the Chinese call quite simply "armed conflicts" (*xiedou*). This definition, deliberately vague, does not specify how deep, long, or serious the struggle might be, or its place on the scale between simple clash and real local war.

Readers would be justified in asking why I include conflicts of this kind in a book about peasant struggles (*PWP*, Chapters 9 and 10). How better may I reassure them than by confessing my initial surprise at discovering movements quite different from those I was looking for, but far more common, significant, and bloody than revolts by tenants or many others? Most villagers, however poor, felt more involved in the smallest *xiedou* than in rent protests or farm laborers' strikes.

Sects and Secret Societies

In the first half of the twentieth century, a villager living in Shandong, Henan, Sichuan, or some other province was very likely—at one time or another—to have sought protection from a sect or secret society or suffered from their actions. They were ever-present, like the Mafia in Sicily, but differed from it, however, despite obvious points in common. We may regard them, roughly speaking, as fraternities offering mutual aid and protection to their members. The distinction between religious sects and secret societies largely became blurred in the twentieth century, many of them changing names, even categories (a dissolved sect reappearing as a secret society or vice versa), to escape repression. Under the Republic their numbers redoubled, any distinctions quite often lost in confusion. Repression forced them to go underground for a while, even to disappear, until a new wave of insecurity helped them to revive, and thanks to their success against troublemakers, to prosper.

Here, I am not concerned with popular religion or with the numerous aspects of a phenomenon increasingly being studied in China and elsewhere.[3] I consider sects and secret societies only as they relate to peasant resistance. Most of them, other things being equal, did not rebel (Overmeyer 1976; Naquin 1981, xiii), which has not deterred many contemporary observers of the Republican period from associating peasant movements with secret societies. The association is mistaken, largely arising from the fact that sects and secret societies, being capable of undertaking more far-reaching actions and sustaining them for longer, were often the only movements known in the cities.

The link between "spontaneous" peasant movements and sects or secret societies is close—and not only because the latter recruited mainly from among peasants—but ambivalent. Local self-defense was a shared priority. Sects and secret societies protected villagers against bandits and also against other attacks from outside: soldiers, tax collectors, or any others acting for political authorities whose intrusion exceeded the limits tolerated by the rural community. Thus, crime caused the reemergence of sects and secret societies in Shandong and Henan in 1920–21. They grew and multiplied in resistance to the warlords' armies in 1925–26, they were repressed by Wu Peifu in 1927 and then by the Nationalist government over the following decade, they reappeared to confront the insecurity caused by the Japanese invasion, they resisted conscription during the foreign and civil wars, and they were finally liquidated by the new communist government in the early 1950s. In addition to providing local self-defense and preserving the status quo, the sects and secret societies and the peasant movements described in this book had other defining features in common: hostility to outsiders and innovations, reactive activity without specific political goals, and fighting alternately for or against law and order (against bandits, then against taxation).

Sects and secret societies, though very active in antitax resistance, were less so against ordinary looting—which does not mean they refrained from it! By contrast, they took for themselves a leading role in resisting the army and military service; indeed, at some moments (1925–27, the 1940s) they occupied the front line. These variations can be easily explained: basic actions such as looting did not require the help and support of an organization, whereas it is difficult and dangerous for unorganized peasants to take on the army. Unable to confront troops by themselves, peasants flocked to join any society that resisted them, especially if it demonstrated its effectiveness. It was in the wake of decisive victories against troops (or bandits) that sects and societies saw peasant membership soar.

This brings us to the most original aspect of the secret societies, the most important of all, in the peasants' eyes: neither their superstitions, which made the first impression on city observers, nor their deficient sense of organization—so deplored by the revolutionaries—but on the contrary their organizations in themselves, their discipline, their effectiveness, and in a word, their strength. The secret societies could sustain more important and durable revolts than most of those studied in this book, and their participation could often transform a mere riot into a large-scale uprising. While rioters were usually counted in their hundreds, or occasionally in their thousands, the forces lined up by the secret societies numbered quite often in tens of thousands.[4] The peasants enrolled in the societies were less well armed than their enemies (though better than ordinary rioters) and were massacred in great numbers,[5] but they inflicted considerable losses on the opposing forces.[6] To sum up, they were more dangerous to the bandits, the warlords, or the tax officials than the anonymous heroes of the numerous incidents recalled in this volume, and therefore more effective and tougher in terms of peasant self-defense: their opponents could never be quite sure of finally being rid of a secret society. When beaten, its members melted back into the civil population, conspicuously available for action when the situation allowed or demanded it. The Red Spears, for example, crushed in 1927, reappeared a decade later when the Japanese invasion destabilized the countryside.

The secret societies came back to life, but they did not modernize. The militant communists who lost contact with the Party during the White Terror of 1927–28 and rejoined years later came back matured and battle-hardened. They learned lessons from failure, and if they did not, the Party did it for them. From the "revolution" of 1925–27 to the Eyuwan Soviet and the resistance to Japan, the Chinese Communist Party (CCP) was constantly adapting, refining, and polishing its strategies according to earlier experience and new circumstances. (Wou 1994, Chapters 2, 3, and 5). The Red Spears (or any other societies, names being unimportant), their inevitable partners—now allied, competing, or opposed—had hardly developed.

While the communists remained very aware of the limits of the sects (particularism and superstitions that exceeded even those of the secret societies), what they blamed them for above all was being the instrument of the traditional rural elite. This was frequently borne out, especially in regions of strong vertical cohesion in village society, where sects and secret societies became quite naturally the landowners' agents, though mainly recruiting among the poor peasants. Their leaders, on the other hand, often came from more favored rural classes (Wou 1994, 67–69; Tai 1985, 32 and ix, x, and xv from Elizabeth Perry's preface; Chinese edition Dai 1973, 191, 230–31; Park 2002, 198, 213,

236, 241, and 267). The case of the landowner Deng Wenming, who is best remembered today by his eldest son, renamed Deng Xiaoping, was not unusual (Yang 1997, 12). In the early years of the twentieth century, Deng was leader of the Gelaohui (Elders and Ancients Society, often referred to as the Elder Brothers Society) in Paifang, Sichuan. At the end of the Empire and under the Republic, the influence of the Gelaohui or the Paoge (Gowned Brothers), both headed by the most powerful families, was predominant in many Sichuan counties (Ruf 1988, 60–61; *Guan XZ*, 1991, 715). Just as any magistrate newly appointed in Yingshan (in the northeast of the province) under the Qing had to pay an immediate courtesy visit to leading gentry, now he checked in with the *daye*, the county Paoge leader. When a conflict broke out, it was not the magistrate but the Paoge who awarded arbitration (*Yingshan XZ*, 1989, 741). In Shehong, in the same province, it was the Paoge who collected the slaughter tax and many other taxes. In other words, the society, whose leading figures were regularly consulted by the legal authorities, had nothing clandestine or "secret" about it (*Shehong XZ*, 1990, 647–48 and 959–60).

While we cannot share the communists' point of view, since "autonomous or spontaneous" rural unrest was certainly not aimed exclusively at defending the poorest peasants, not even as a priority, the fact remains that many sects or secret societies slipped—or never even needed to slip—from defending village autonomy to maintaining village power in the gentry's hands. However, it is not always easy to determine the exact political orientation of these societies. They might defend the established privileges of the rich, and then ally themselves with the communists against the Guomindang when it repressed them, even if it meant, once the communists had won power, fighting against them alongside the Guomindang, deeming it the lesser of two evils. Later, sects and secret societies would fight, now against the Japanese occupiers, now with them against the resistance, because they too were "outsiders," intruders in the region. In this latter case, the deal might simply be concluded by an ambitious leader, whom the successes of the secret society or sect he commanded had pushed up to the rank of local potentate.

The peasants did not particularly object to the changing loyalties of sects and societies, often dictated by the primary defense of local autonomy, a sacred cause for them as well; but they dreaded the growing and uncontrollable ambition of leaders transformed by the interplay of power into little warlords, like those they were supposed to be fighting. Just like the internal struggles between warlords, those between sects and/or secret societies, and indeed between factions of the same society (or sect) were not uncommon. Many important *xiedou* (PWP, Chapter 9) pitted one sect or secret society against another. In April 1927, the *xiedou* that broke out in Ci Xian, Henan (today in Hebei), between the Red Spears and the Heavenly Gate Sect mobilized thousands of combatants on either side. It lasted for nine months of operations extending across a dozen villages; and each of the two secret societies suffered very heavy losses, to the great benefit of their common enemy, the Fengtian Army (Qiao 1993, 91).

Sometimes the Hongqianghui joined forces with bandits in looting and killing. As a result, village opinion, initially favorable toward the secret societies, turned against them. In November 1927, the villagers of Xishuibo, Shandong, had to defend themselves against a sect whose protection they had been counting on. It murdered about 30 people, which brought villagers running in from many neighboring villages to attack the sect members and set fire to their headquarters (*Qihe XZ*, 1990, 21).

Be it gangsterism, racketeering, or smuggling (opium trafficking in Sichuan was often the business of the Gelaohui and the Paoge), leaders in the service of the rural elite or of their own ambitions made secret societies, as David Ownby emphasizes (2001, 153), "undependable as representatives of popular struggle." Nevertheless, this instrument, though it could sometimes turn against them, when measured against the peasants' usual means of action was exceptionally effective.[7] This sad paradox illustrates an insecurity that was tragically confirmed by their followers' faith in their own invulnerability: (*dao qiang bu ru*, "daggers and bullets will not penetrate").Whether they worked for or against the spontaneous peasants' movement, secret societies and religious sects were representative of village culture or sub-culture (the "little tradition" described in Redfield 1956). They were the authentic children of the countryside, unlike the officials fearfully glimpsed on their infrequent rural tours or the intellectuals who came to preach revolution to the villages. As an example, Box 2.3 describes a religious sect in Henan that has been the subject of a detailed study.

Box 2.3   The Sect of the Heavenly Gate (Tianmenhui)

The sect was founded in 1923 in Lin Xian, on the borders of three provinces, Henan, Shanxi, and Hebei. It drew its inspiration from the teachings and rites of the ancient sect of the White Lotus, though it had no direct link with it. It claimed to open the gate of heaven but reflected a more immediate concern, shared by most villagers: to be protected from bandits, soldiers, and warlords.

The Tianmenhui's early successes over the bandits helped it to consolidate itself rapidly. Soon it had more than 100,000 members in Lin Xian. As the society deepened its roots in Lin Xian, it expanded—or, more precisely, extended—its grasp to other counties: 26 in all, with a membership totaling some 400,000 by 1927.

While the rural elite controlled most sects and secret societies, it was not so here. Han Genzi, one of the two founders of the sect, was very poor and illiterate. Because his family owned only two *mu* of land, Han earned his living carving wood or cutting stone. Having changed his given name to Yuming ("he who would desire to be enlightened"), Han Yuming established himself as the all-powerful head of an authentically peasant movement. He put to flight or shot his particular enemies: big landlords, "bad scholar gentry" (*lieshen*), and "local despots" (*tuhao*).

It was an authentic peasant movement, though not exclusively, because its success attracted members of the elite confronted, like the rest of the villagers, by crime. Contemptuous at first, then mistrustful, landowners incapable of resisting bandits by themselves were eager to learn from the Tianmenhui its tried and tested recipes. In 1926, bandits took hostage and killed several members of a rich landowner's family in Xun Xian, a neighboring county. Afterwards, the landowner sent twenty young people, among them his son Yang Guanyi, to follow the martial arts courses run by the sect. On their return, these new followers were quick to set up branches in 110 villages in Xun county. Yang Guanyi would later become one of the leading figures in the Tianmenhui.

His promotion does not imply that control over the society escaped from the peasants who founded it. The society did evolve in the end: indeed, it was restructured and unified. In 1931, the official militia responsible for keeping order in Lin county was entirely composed of Tianmenhui followers who had not broken with the mother society. But this evolution was the creation of the peasant leaders and, at the start, of the first of them, men who learned their lesson from defeat and from a sociopolitical environment that was unfavorable to maintaining the methods, rituals, and beliefs that supported their early successes.

Han Yuming's transformation, eloquently described by Qiao Peihua, is instructive. Having been defeated in March 1928 and crushed in January 1929, he found refuge with the warlord Zhang Xueliang. While his forces, dispersed and hiding in the villages of several counties, maintained some proportion of their strength, Han stayed for a year in Mukden (Shenyang). Under Zhang's tutelage, he came to appreciate modernity and knowledge. Although he had occasionally employed old-style scholars, he had hitherto been inclined to arrest and kill anyone who had received a modern education. Up until 1928, he had invariably worn a pigtail and scorned people wearing Western clothes as "foreign devils." In Mukden in 1929, he convinced himself of the need for an open mind, if only to create a modern army, one fundamentally different from his own force of ill-equipped peasants. From then on, he dropped all superstitions, dismissing them as ridiculous.

Zhang Xueliang's power impressed Han: he concluded that, to play the role to which he still aspired, he would need an official title for his army. Back on home territory during the winter of 1929–30, Han appointed himself commander. The Lin Xian county magistrate, obliged to maintain good relations with the Tianmenhui, threw a party for Han, who paraded in Western costume, with leather hat and shoes, white gloves, and cane. Now Han abandoned the old forms of organization, to which the peasants were very attached, but failed to win over the scholar gentry, who had not forgiven him for having massacred many of them a few years before. We should be careful not to attribute to these spectacular changes the difficulties of a movement that seems never to have recovered from its defeat in January 1929—nor even the arrest and death of Han Yuming himself, killed with 200 of his soldiers in December 1931 or January 1932. The Tianmenhui, commanded thereafter by one of Han's nephews, based itself in the mountains.

But it was the Japanese invasion that stimulated the true revival of the society, under the leadership this time not of an illiterate peasant but of an intellectual, born of a rich and powerful family: none other than Yang Guanyi, who twelve years before had come to learn the rudiments of the martial arts from the Tianmenhui. We should not conclude that a society founded by a poor illiterate peasant was taken over by a member of the elite, who molded it for purposes foreign to the preoccupations of the peasant masses: the fight against the national enemy. Yang was personally a patriot, but he was responding all the same to the peasants' wishes, after they begged him to reorganize the Tianmenhui. Why? For one thing, just that, to fight the occupiers, that is to say, to prevent new atrocities: the Japanese had just massacred 4,500 inhabitants of Xun Xian county while indulging in looting and arson attacks. For another, to protect themselves from bandits, whose numbers had been boosted by wartime disorders. And lastly, to resist the exactions, mainly taxes, of the county magistrate. So the revival of the Tianmenhui did arise from the peasants' unvarying objective of protecting and defending the group against anyone that attacked it. This continuity is more fundamental than the innovation identified by Chalmers Johnson (1962): the emergence of mass nationalism during the Second World War. We may add that, despite Yang Guanyi's initial successes, the society's greatest days were back in 1926–27, when it was under the firm leadership of Han Yuming.

SOURCE: Qiao 1993.

THREE

Repertoire of Action

This chapter is devoted to the repertoire, or range of actions, available to popular movements, as defined by Charles Tilly (1986, 15, 57–58, 541–42). It classifies the various forms of peasant action, from the least to the most violent.

Nonviolent Action

Everyday forms of resistance, as defined by James Scott (1985), are often the only ones possible under a communist dictatorship. So they are to be encountered in China mainly after 1949 (see *PWP*, Chapter 13). All the same, the weakest were not averse to trying it even before 1949.

Around 1930, peasants in North China subjected to military requisitions (*bingchai*) mutilated or blinded their cattle. They made them useless for farming but also for requisitions: they could be used for grinding flour or sold to the butcher (Feng 1936, 387). The peasants were anticipating the attitude of the next generation, who would cripple or kill their draft animals rather than hand them over to the production cooperative. Also confined within the limits of everyday resistance were the tenant farmers who added water and sand to payments of grain in rent, the taxpayers who tried just about anything to achieve tax evasion, or the conscription draftees who skedaddled rather than present themselves for the lottery.

Unlike the everyday forms of resistance, which were preferably concealed, petitions (*qingyuan*) were by definition public. They were nonetheless peaceful, at least to begin with, and indeed couched in respectful terms. That was true of the petition by taxpayers in Sanshui, Guangdong, published in July 1933 in a Cantonese daily. Pointing to several consecutive years of flooding and drought, which had lowered the yield of low-lying land to 30 or 40 percent of the average, it asked that those farming these low-lying areas should be exempted from paying a police surtax (ZLN, vol. 4, 1934, 68–69).

The same year, about ten similar petitions launched all over China requested reductions of, or exemption from, particular taxes, or more rarely, the land tax itself. As in Sanshui, some justified the request citing repeated natural disasters (floods and drought) since 1930—particularly serious in that year of 1933, as claimed by the Xuancheng Farming Association (*nonghui*) in Anhui. For good measure, it added other frequently adduced arguments: the general economic crisis, competition from foreign fabrics, poor sales of silk, tea, and hemp, and coal mines threatened with closure (ZLN, vol. 4, 1934, 65).

The authors of petitions were rarely identified, and we may exclude only the illiterate. It is likely that members of the local elite inspired, wrote, or signed many of them. The farming associations, like that in Xuancheng, were official organizations usually controlled by landlords or rich peasants. After all, did not the same association go so far as to mention colliery closures that, though scarcely affecting the average farmer's income, would be of greater concern for higher taxpayers with investments in industry?

The 70 to 80 petitions counted represent only a small minority of the incidents examined in this book. In Huailu county, Hebei, subjected to a meticulous study, petitions (sometimes backed by pressure or negotiations) eclipsed all other forms of antitax resistance (Li 2005, Chapter 3). They were all launched by the local elite and many were successful, so much so that tax increases remained fairly modest during the first two decades of the Republic—or less onerous at least than if the elite had given the authorities free rein. Only after 1930, when the Nationalist government set out to impose its authority locally, at the expense of the elite, did they fail to defend their interests and those of other county taxpayers (Li 2005, 75–76 and 246). Before that date, in terms of effectiveness, this peaceful resistance could be favorably compared with violent resistance in the rest of the country.

The petitioners of Huailu and other counties, just like those pursuing legal and procedural resistance in the PRC today, followed the same tactics, consisting of setting one level of the administrative hierarchy against another (Li 2005, Chapter 9 and O'Brien and Li 1995). In January 1922, more than 200 petitioners asked the Zhejiang provincial government to dismiss the Deqing magistrate, who had forged false land tax registers (*Deqing XZ*, 1992, 9). In July 1936, by contrast, over 300 petitioners appealed to the magistrate of Yixing, Jiangsu, asking his support in their grievances against the Dapu village head who had imposed a "tax for the public welfare" (*gongyi juan*) on his own authority (*ZJNSZ*, vol. 3, 1023).

In these last two cases, the petitioners went in person to Hangzhou (the capital of Zhejiang) and Yixing. Petitions of this kind, transmitted not by letter or telegram but by hand and with a mass attendance, are not far removed from demonstrations (*shiwei*). Far more numerous than petitions, demonstrations were, in principle, nonviolent. The demonstrators sometimes specified that they were marching without weapons (*tushou*: "their hands empty"); whether they said so or not, it was almost always the case. Sometimes, though infrequently, the demonstrators won satisfaction, as in Fengxi, Fujian, in January 1946, where they demanded exemption from the land tax (*Mingxi WSZL*, vol. 5, 1988, 93–94). It was their numbers that impressed or intimidated, especially when the demonstration of strength was made in front of the magistrate's office. Violent demonstrations (*relie zhi shiwei*) were exceptions—a few examples were recorded in Jiangxi in 1926 and 1927 (*ZLN*, vol. 1, 1928, 468). It was more common, however, for a demonstration to start by being peaceful and then to degenerate, usually following a violent reaction on the part of the police. In Daishan, Zhejiang, in July 1936, the police, frightened by the very large number of demonstrators, opened fire and killed a fisherman, which triggered a serious riot (see Box 5.2,). Even less frequently, however, a demonstration would degenerate by itself, without the slightest provocation by the police. In Zhenyuan, Guizhou, in May 1909, 10,000 peasants (men and women) and lumberjacks, who were being required to pay the *lijin* office a percentage of the price of vegetables, shoes, straw, and logs that they were coming to sell in the market, ended by burning down the office and killing its director along with four other people (*Zhenyuan WSZL*, vol. 3, 1989, 37–38).

Box 3.1   From Petition to Riot: Yongji, Shanxi, 1903

In 1903, the Yongji magistrate imposed a new tax on persimmon brandy, a product representing a fairly widespread secondary activity in eighteen of the county's villages. Persimmon growers elected three delegates to carry their petition to the county government. It read: "The low yield of the land makes this secondary production indispensable—though, as it happens, not very profitable; since the brandy is distilled from the fruit of a tree rooted in a field already subject to the land tax, there is no reason for paying another tax on the alcohol."

Faced with these arguments, the magistrate remained adamant. He ordered that the tax should be collected immediately. When the tax officials started destroying stills and vats, the distillers' responded by planning a new petition, coupled with a mass demonstration: if their claims were still not considered, they would go into town on 29 September and turn over their farm tools as a sign of protest.

On the appointed day, thousands of villagers—men, women, children, and old people—marched on the town and demanded to see the magistrate. He merely sent out a score of mounted police to disperse the procession. As soon as the demonstrators arrived in town, the horsemen opened fire, killing two peasants and wounding many others. The peasants fought back and in their turn wounded several policemen. The other horsemen galloped off, the magistrate fled, and the demonstrators attacked the county government building. The prefect of Puzhou, responsible for Yongji, then promised to abolish the tax, and the villagers returned home. With peace restored, the magistrate arrested the three delegates, intending to have them condemned to death—which sparked off new petitions. The provincial government was forced to get a grip on things. It sent out two investigators, who demanded the dismissal of the magistrate, but they also concluded nevertheless that the delegates must be convicted to save the government's face. One was sentenced to ten years in prison (after eight, come the 1911 revolution, he was released) and the other two men to six months.

SOURCE: *Jindaishi ziliao*, no. 6, 1957, 61–66.

Escalation, spontaneous or provoked by the authorities' clumsiness, violence, or merely their refusal to listen, could transform petitions and demonstrations into riots. In May 1930, during the hungry season between harvests, rice was beginning to run short in Jiangshan, Zhejiang. A petition addressed to the magistrate asked him to forbid tradesmen and well-off individuals from speculating by stockpiling rice. As the magistrate refused to intervene, angry citizens looted several shops and private stores (*Jiangshan XZ*, 1990, 11–12). This was still nothing more than looting. In Yongji, Shanxi, in September 1903, the situation escalated into something far more serious (see Box 3.1).

In all, petitions (like those in Jiangshan and Yongji) and demonstrations (like those in Daishan and Zhenyuan) that led to full-blown riots are, according to my figures, about as numerous as those that stayed peaceful. Many other incidents classified under the two following headings also began with a nonviolent phase. This was particularly true of the handover of farm implements (*jiaonong*), which formed a halfway stage between nonviolent and violent actions. In its initial phase, it was a mass demonstration that was peaceful in principle, but it often ended in a riot.

Handing over Farm Tools

Jiaonong is an abbreviation of *jiaona nongju* ("the handing over of farm tools"), a practice in which hard-pressed taxpayers would down their tools in front of the county or ward office building to show they were abandoning an occupation that had ceased to be profitable. Natural disasters often contributed to their ruin, but what they fought above all were tax increases that, even in good years, cut their incomes to little or nothing—or, conversely, taxes that the authorities persisted in collecting despite the disasters.[1] *Jiaonong*, then, was a way of exerting pressure to win a reduction in taxation or the abolition of a particular tax, often a new one. Considered as an inoffensive form of action, sometimes similar to a mere demonstration (Li 1959, 56), *jiaonong* could nevertheless win the day by its impact as a spectacle: thousands, sometimes tens of thousands, of peasants massed with their tools in front of the county government buildings, which at any moment they might attack.[2] Not only could the tools serve as weapons if the demonstration became violent, but sometimes also the demonstrators would conceal their tools and brandish them in front of the magistrate's yamen, surrounding it, and on occasion, wrecking it. To escape exposure to this kind of incident, magistrates who saw a troop of farmers approaching, carrying spades and pickaxes, would often order the gates in the city walls to be shut. If the peasants retaliated by throwing stones and bricks at the gates or at the soldiers on guard, if the soldiers fired on the demonstrators, if the peasants battered down the gates or set fire to them,[3] then the movement took on the appearance of a classic antitax riot, except that the slogan *jiaonong* was explicitly proclaimed, even written on banners.[4] If we disregard the insistence with which the peasants were repeating, "Hand over our tools! Give up our jobs!" there is no difference between the riot of December 1923, Weinan, Shaanxi (Box 3.2), and those described in Chapter 5.

In Shaanxi, *jiaonong* is a deep-rooted tradition, so much so that sources are usually content to indicate them without resorting to superfluous explanations: *you jiaonong* ("there was a handover of tools") or *jiaonong yundong* ("handover of tools movement"), as would be said of some forms of looting (*chi dahu yundong*; see *PWP*, 146).[5] Leaving aside the episodes mentioned generally in these sources,[6] I have identified 59 instances of *jiaonong*, 48 of them in Shaanxi, concentrated particularly on a level with Xi'an, between Tongguan (to the east) and Baoji (to the west).[7] Occurring at intervals throughout the first half of the twentieth century (the earliest case in 1900, the latest in 1947), the 59 *jiaonong* of the sample were especially frequent during the last decade of the Empire (14 cases) and still more so during the warlord era and the first half of the Nanjing decade: 34 cases between 1922 and 1932. To supply their armies' needs, the warlords set new records for fiscal extortion and "military requisitions" (*bingchai*), not excluding the years of bad harvests and even during the famine of 1928–31. From 1927 onward, the fresh upsurge of *jiaonong* incidents arose also from the fact that the communists were striving to appropriate for their own purposes this weapon from the traditional armory.[8]

Violent Actions

If we combine in an artificial way the components usually shared between various riots or revolts, we shall see how a "complete" revolt would look. Firstly, anonymous letters or notices would call for action against such-and-such a target.[9] Then those involved would meet, preferably late at night, in or in front of a temple. They would sacrifice a cock or another animal, cutting its throat, drinking its blood, and swearing an oath that all those present would pledge themselves to

Box 3.2   Handover of Farm Tools: Weinan, Shaanxi, 1923

The riot of 25 and 26 December in Weinan, in the Wei valley to the east of Xi'an, confirms that the causes of *jiaonong* were no different from those of a very great number of "classic" antitax riots: the accumulation of surtaxes and special contributions, the increase in the overall burden of them, and the brutality in collecting them—any or all combined with a poor harvest. Among all the special contributions, the most burdensome was the monthly tax on wheat, which had to be paid a month in advance. The *jiaonong* movement was pledged to get it abolished. But what lit the fuse was the special contribution of 2,000 *yuan* for a local warlord's army, demanded on 22 December by magistrate Sun Pingwen. The drought that struck Weinan county in 1923 particularly affected Dongyuan and Xiyuan, where the movement was launched. Harvests there fell to 30 or 40 percent of normal, and many peasants were obliged to mortgage their houses or sell their land, while many others fled the region. And the ward head and his officials did the same, when they received orders to impose this new contribution that they knew they could never collect.

On 25 December, Magistrate Sun sent about 30 soldiers and policemen to Dongyuan to collect the special contribution in their place, an act they performed with extreme brutality, up until the moment when the peasants sounded the gong calling on villagers to defend themselves. The crowd gathered in Dongyuan township, putting the security forces to flight; they addressed to all the villages dependent on Dongyuan and Xiyuan an "urgent message" (*jimao xin*) inviting farmers to turn over their tools the next day at the county yamen, with each family required to delegate one member to the demonstration. All around, and all through the night of 25–26 December, the gongs were sounded. Before dawn, the peasants were on their way. By the time they arrived at the edge of the county town, their numbers had swollen to tens of thousands.

Magistrate Sun turned up on horseback, and the crowd surged around him demanding exemption from the taxes and special contributions. Sun made verbal promises, but the peasants called on him to write them down, which he did: "Exemption from the special contributions, and free elections for heads of *lijia*" (groups of about a hundred families or more). The peasants were suspicious: they asked again for the contributions suppressed to be listed precisely and authenticated with the magistrate's seal. Coming to the magistrate's rescue, a scholar gave his opinion that it would be quite enough for the magistrate to reduce contributions to one-half, "without which we should not be able to feed our soldiers." The peasants bashed his head in with their farm tools and wounded two other scholars—but they left the magistrate unharmed. He threw himself onto his knees and signed and sealed just about anything they want, in particular their exemption to the monthly wheat tax.

The peasants dispersed and the magistrate was free to leave. No sooner was he back in Weinan than he learned that another crowd of peasants, much the same size, was approaching the town. At once, he ordered the gates closed. The peasants wrecked a salt shop and the collection offices of the *lijin*, shouting, "Let's give up our jobs, let's hand in our tools!" (*bu zuo zhuangjia le, jiaonong! jiaonong!*). The soldiers started firing from the top of the city walls, killing a peasant and wounding a dozen more. A call for revenge burst from 10,000 throats. The magistrate agreed to sack the brigade commander and to have the soldier shot—the one who fired the fatal bullet—and to take care of the victim's funeral expenses. The peasants' exemption to the monthly wheat tax and the other special contributions was not challenged thereafter.

SOURCES: The most important is *Shaanxi WSZL*, vol. 9, 1981, 223–31. See also *Weinan XZ*, 1987, 13; *ZJNSZ*, vol. 2, 701; *Xiangdao*, 20 February 1924, 405–6 (article signed Chen Duxiu).

---

stay united until victory.[10] Sometimes a leader would be designated or elected on the spot.[11] If the revolt was not to be immediate, participants would inform other villages, inviting them to join the movement and giving details of place and time, grievances, and objectives. If it was imminent, the other villagers would be summoned by sounding gongs or by means of "chicken-feather letters" (*jimaoxin*) or "messages sent with a chicken feather attached" (*jimao chuantie*) sent hastily around to each village.[12] In general, the cause was popular or enjoyed near-unanimous support within the village, and volunteers were never wanting. Even so, it could happen that the organizers gave precise instructions, such as "one participant per family" or "those with money should donate it" (or its variant "those with food should bring it"), while "those without should lend their strength" and join the fight.[13] Nor was it unusual for people to be obliged to join and warned of serious penalties to be suffered by anyone tempted to abstain.[14]

On occasion, the peasants would employ a diversion so as not to alert the authorities. In Lantian, Shaanxi, in 1915, they sounded the gong and gathered at the temple with the ostensible purpose of organizing a ceremony of prayers for rain (*Shaanxi WSZLXJ*, vol. 2, 1962, 113). Ten years later, peasants in Hengxiang, Jiangsu, turned out for a show in Yucaizhuang, a poor village nearby, merely in order to make contact with the locals and to win their support in resisting the tax on pigs (see Box 5.5). In other cases, the show was in the street: with consummate theatrical skill, peasants displayed their determination by tying themselves together with ropes to demand a tax reduction,[15] or they invaded the county town carrying coffins to show they were ready to die for their cause.[16] More often, they would carry the corpse of a villager killed during an earlier demonstration, mutely appealing for justice.[17] The peasants were well aware that they were risking their lives by rebelling. Sometimes they said so in a tone, not of bravado, but of resignation: we have reached the point where we have no choice.

Just occasionally, a banner spelled out the reasons behind the dispute, purely defensive reasons, along these lines: "The mandarins do harm to the people: the people put an end to the harm."[18] The names that bands of rebels adopted might express the reasons for their determination, or their plans.[19] Names with a legal or social flavor were not unusual either.[20] The most common names referred quite simply to the color of the turbans worn or flags carried by the activists, especially when the latter were members of sects or secret societies.[21] Lastly, some names, openly moral or emotional, would have been incomprehensible to anyone unfamiliar with the cause or the grievance that had sparked off the rising.[22]

The demonstrators would generally march toward the county capital, or much less often, toward the ward administration offices (*qu gongsuo*), or more rarely still, toward the prefecture or the provincial capital.[23] The marchers might also limit themselves to attacking specific targets including tax collectors, the tax office, a salt warehouse, or a rice shop. It could happen that several columns marching in from all parts of the county would converge on the capital. The magistrate would sometimes go to meet them, attempting to soften them up and talk them out of going any further; scholars sometimes came to help, explaining to the peasants that the magistrate was not responsible for their troubles, that anyway he would work to find a remedy, and intervene with higher authorities, and that the tax might be reduced, though not abolished. As a rule, the peasants were not convinced and would respond by expressing their grievances and their demands. After which, they might surround the magistrate and his escorts, or let them leave, then continue marching toward their objective. In the first case, as happened during the

Weinan *jiaonong* (Box 3.2), they were less ready to attack the magistrate himself than the scholars and other notables who spoke up for him. Some of these rash individuals were beaten to death, others merely injured or taken hostage.

In cases when the magistrate was set free, once back in town he would hurry to close the town gates. This would usher in the next act, which could often be bloody. The peasants would attempt to break down one of the gates with a tree trunk, or to set fire to it. From the top of the walls, soldiers would fire into the air or else directly upon the crowd massed below. If they caused casualties, this would rarely provoke a rout; more often, it would further inflame people's anger. The demonstrators would usually force their way in, invading the narrow streets. Apart from looting rice and salt, the peasants ignored the now closed shops, making their way toward the magistrate's yamen, the headquarters of a notables' association, the salt toll office or any other tax office, a school or a police station (which could be ransacked for arms and ammunition), or even the prison, where they would free the inmates. Their adversaries were incomparably better armed, but were nevertheless overwhelmed by the encircling crowd. It was not unusual for them to go to ground or flee, the magistrate making off by the back door of his residence disguised as a poor servant or an old woman. The rioters were at last in a position to avenge deaths or injuries: they smashed doors and windows, wrecked offices, burned or carried off files from the register office or the land registry, beating, sometimes killing or taking prisoner the few occupants unable to get away in time.

The foregoing scenario, the most common sequence of events, illustrates a riot, rather than a revolt. In the event of a real uprising, rampaging and looting gave way to setting up a short-lived rebel administration. In general this development followed one or several battles, waged in the open countryside rather than in town or city. Equally, it was the countryside that suffered the greatest damage: electricity poles felled, railway tracks torn up, and above all else, tax offices, schools, and the homes of rich landlords demolished or burned down. Before saying anything more on battles as such, let us stay with fires for a moment: if I had to propose one symbol for the peasant movements, I would pick this "poor man's weapon" (Ploux 2002, 74).[24]

This symbol so dominated all protagonists' minds that the mere threat to set the county town alight could be enough to have the city gates opened, after the magistrate had ordered them shut, or to persuade the magistrate instantly to grant a suspension of the land tax as the demonstrators were demanding.[25] Accounts of antitax revolts were even entitled "Zhendong in flames" (Jiang 1988b) and "Fire in Yangzhou" (Dai 1957). In the latter case, the revolt consisted mainly of the burning of seven houses. The targets were not chosen at random, they had been selected. In other riots one target was sometimes spared for fear that the two next-door houses, belonging to peasants, might also be set alight (*Shaanxi WSZLXJ*, vol. 2, 1962, 117). It could also happen that a target might be changed along the way: in Qin county, Shanxi, in February 1912, peasants were protesting against the seizure of their temple for other purposes by the leaders (and profiteers) of the New Policies. They had planned to burn down the school, but in the end, they set fire to 48 houses belonging to "local despots" (*Qin Xian WSZL*, vol. 2, 1986, 44–60). Needless to point out that peasants' houses too were frequently set afire when the revolts were put down, especially when the owners had fled their villages to escape impending massacres.[26] In addition, there were the arson attacks launched by bandits.[27]

Burnings of buildings were much more common than pitched battles. Almost all riots and a considerable number of revolts ended without a single battle between peasants and the police. At the most, the peasants might venture a surprise attack or an ambush.[28] Frontal assaults were a more useful tactic for soldiers and policemen attempting to block the progress of a peasant column in open country, along a road, or approaching a bridge. They rarely turned out well for the rebels, whose only advantage lay in numbers. Certainly, they fought bravely, including hand-to-hand combat, but firepower, discipline, and training were on the side of their opponents (*Jacqueries*, 163–67). The peasants came out better when they were led by a professional, either by hiring his services or persuading him to lead them.[29] And a revolt could have better chances of success when it was launched or taken in hand by a sect or secret society, one led by semi-professionals and armed with acquired or captured weapons. To that could often be added further advantages: the fanatical faith of the more seasoned members and the sense of invulnerability instilled in sect believers as a whole. But when someone invulnerable collapsed in front of you, mortally wounded by a bullet that was supposed to be unable to penetrate his "hard belly,"[30] your ardor was likely to be dulled, unless you still had faith in the leaders' explanation: this fighter had become vulnerable following sexual relations or having taken alcohol when he ought to have abstained or because he had not observed the secrecy to which members were bound.

Although the revelation of the sectarians' vulnerability or quite simply the terrifying firepower of their adversaries provoked on occasion a sudden rout in mid-battle, a sudden stampede was less of a threat to rebel fighters in the midst of a battle than to rioters and mere demonstrators. The latter were more likely to behave like a crowd, duped by the authorities' promises and honeyed words or recalled by some sudden event to their own private interests.[31]

Peasant "Excesses"

The founder and first Secretary General of the CCP, Chen Duxiu, expressed strong disapproval of the "excesses" committed by the peasants during the 1926–27 "revolution," thereby opening himself to sarcastic comments from Mao Zedong (1955, 29–31). One can identify similar excesses not only in the fury of the peasant unions that were then proliferating, but even in the tumult of the riots and spontaneous revolts that this book examines.

What, or rather who, were the rioters' favorite targets? First of all, tax collectors and policemen. After that, the officials sent by the administration to speed up tax payments or apply other unpopular measures, village and ward heads and the staff of the *qu gongsuo* (ward offices), "bad scholar gentry" (*lieshen*) and other "local despots" (*eba*), teachers during the time of the New Policies and the 1910 census, the officials and employees of the county government, and lastly the magistrate himself. How they were treated varied considerably according to circumstances and to the attitudes of the authorities, whether conciliatory or repressive. At the end of April 1932, the head of the Finance Bureau of Hu county, Shaanxi, was marched through the town wearing a paper hat on which were inscribed eight characters: "I am the running dog of Qian Yuncheng." When he reached the temple, he made public confession of his misdeeds and was showered with excrement before being released.[32]

In June 1915, Yuan'an, Hebei, suffered a lengthy drought, which did not prevent the magistrate from raising transfer taxes. About 100 peasants stripped off his clothes and made him walk barefoot in the sun, just to teach him the meaning of drought (*Yuan'an XZ*, 1990, 10). Still under the heading of harmless misadventures (compared with what follows), an official was shut into a pigsty (in Quanzhou, Guangxi, in August 1910: *DFZZ*, vol. 7, no. 8, 18121), a tax collector was thrown into the latrines (in Henglou Cun, Jiangsu, in June 1946: *Qingpu XZ*, 1991, 24), and some policemen were forced to eat excrement (in Rudong, Jiangsu, in October 1913: *Rudong XZ*, 1983, 504). More often, policemen or tax collectors were tied up and taken hostage, or beaten up, even beaten to death.[33] Of course, two of these options might be applied at once: tax collectors were dubbed "running dogs of the tax authorities" and then beaten up, as in Jietouji, Shandong, in September 1930 (*Wulian XZ*, 1992, 10) or marched about naked, then killed, as in the southeastern ward of Ning county, Gansu, in June 1926 (*Ning XZ*, 1988, 404).

It was common for policemen to be killed, and tax collectors even more so.[34] Less usual was paying a fee for each killing,[35] killing the members of a target's family,[36] or committing acts of terrible brutality. For example, rioters used scissors to put out the eyes of a village head and his deputy (the former did not survive) in Qinshui county, Shanxi, in 1922 (*Qinshui XZ*, 1987, 598–99); and protesters put out the eyes and cut out the tongues of six minor officials in Shiquan county, Shaanxi, in June 1926 (*Shiquan XZ*, 1991, 701).[37] Exceptionally, some sources, even studies published in the PRC, mention cannibalism: in October 1942, in Qingxi ward, Guizhou, the rebels executed an officer, after which "the masses" carved off his flesh with a knife, ate it, and drank his blood (Zhou, He, and Zhang, 1987, 368). As a general rule, the worst cruelties came about not during revolts directed against the authorities but during *xiedou* setting clan against neighboring clan: in Laifeng, Hubei, under the Republic, factions and clans buried alive members of opposing communities (women and children included), drowned them, or cut off their arms and legs (*Laifeng XZ*, 1990, 311).

Such cruelties appear to have been more frequent in the west of the country, particularly among some national minorities: for example, in 1906, in Duyun, Guizhou, where the Miao and the Shui joined forces in rebellion (*Duyun WSZLXJ*, vol. 5, 1986, 66). This was also true when secret societies were involved: in Ziyang, Shaanxi, where tax officials were killed "all over the county," the unrest, which was endemic up until 1937, was mainly whipped up by sects and secret societies.[38] In many cases, cruel acts by peasants were reprisals born of anger, acts of revenge for the death of a comrade or a leader, or punishments for those responsible for abuses or atrocities in the course of tax collection.[39] Generally speaking, the victims of particularly savage treatment were not chosen at random. As for Tong Qing, the officer whose flesh the crowd ate and whose blood they drank, we are assured that there was "no misdeed that he was not guilty of" (*wu e bu zuo*), though the expression is a cliche, advanced perhaps to excuse the "popular masses" (Zhou, He, and Zhang, 1987, 368). The family members of the local despot, who were all massacred along with him in Caoguan (see note 36), were universally hated by the village residents for having grabbed three-quarters of their land and lent them money at ruinous rates (*Baiyun WSZL*, vol. 5, 1988, 111).

We should add that, under the cloak of repression, individuals could seek revenge, pure and simple—to which peasants responded by taking revenge in their turn, in payback cycles like those associated with *xiedou* (*PWP*, Chapter 9). In Luokong, Honghe county, Yunnan, a revolt broke out during summer 1937 against the head of a tribe (*tusi*) belonging to a national minority. This man, Chen Zemin, had imposed a special contribution and stockpiled grain as a speculation. On 12 August, the peasants killed Chen and three of his brothers. The mother of the four victims organized a meeting at which she had eight leaders of the revolt murdered, then confiscated their land and goods. To cover her children's funeral expenses she imposed a new special contribution, and to round things off, ordered the arrest of many participants in the revolt. There followed a new revolt or a further episode of the same revolt on 22 September, when the peasants surrounded the administration offices and the house of Chen Yongwen, the uncle of the tribal chief killed six weeks earlier. In their turn, they slaughtered eight people, uncles, nephews, and brothers of the tribal chief (*Honghe XZ*, 1991, 494).

Lastly, as with arson attacks, the acts of cruelty committed by peasant rebels did not exceed—and were often eclipsed by—the suffering inflicted upon them by authorities, soldiers, bandits, or hunger. For example, in a case where twelve members of a family in Yong'an Cun, in Wushan county, Sichuan, took cover in a cave to escape conscription, neither the militia nor the local police were able to dislodge them. In September 1942, the authorities resorted to overwhelming force (rifles and artillery), and then smoked out the cave. All thirteen occupants died: the entire family and a person whom they had invited in (*Wushan XZ*, 1991, 15–16).

Soldiers might belong to the regular army, as did those the authorities called upon in the preceding case, or to the warlords' private armies. The latter were the champions when it came to exactions and ill-treatment, but the regular army were not far behind them.[40]

As for bandits, we shall limit ourselves to adding three cases to Philip Billingsley's list of their exploits (1988). In Yichang county, Hubei, in 1926, if one ventured from one to three miles outside the towns, one found oneself in bandit country, a territory given over to looting, burning, killings, and kidnappings. The villagers did not complain to the administration, for it would have achieved nothing beyond drawing the bandits' revenge upon themselves. Once all those who owned anything had taken refuge in the towns, the bandits essayed a new way of squeezing the poor: after sending a warning—a family had to pay a given sum by a given date—if by the deadline they had received nothing, the bandits wrecked the family's ancestral tombs, throwing the bones into the latrines. Out of filial piety and for fear of the misfortunes that this desecration could not fail to bring upon their descendents, the villagers paid up (*DFZZ*, vol. 23, no. 6, 25 October 1926, 66.686). Two years later, around Jiuxianshan, Shandong, the thousand or so bandits commanded by Liu Guitang, not content with burning, killing, and looting, forcibly requisitioned porters to carry off their booty and killed several hundred of them for not walking fast enough (*Wulian XZ*, 1992, 9). A little later still, to the north of Baishui county, Shaanxi, Yang Mouzi led no more than 300 outlaws, not including those on horseback, but the diversity of their crimes defies the imagination (*Baishui XZ*, 1989, 497–98).[41]

If we add natural disasters and famine, we must recognize that the peasants existed in an environment where human life was cheap. It would have been surprising had this environment not influenced their behavior.[42] Perhaps we might overlook the theories of Gustave Le Bon on the psychology of crowds (Le Bon 1895) but certainly not the modern history of China, as revisited by David Der-wei Wang: "an endless brutality," suffered and committed by a multitude of victims and executioners (Wang 2004).

I have described the repertoire of peasant actions in a static way. It did evolve in the course of the half-century, but not much. The temple ceremonies, in which participants drank blood and swore oaths, were more frequent and more elaborate under the Qing Dynasty. The defeat of the Thousand People (in November 1911) was no surprise to most of the fighters: the pig whose throat was slit by their leader, Zhou Tianbao, had survived its wounds (*PWP*, 210–11 and 17). For contrast, let us consider two other rent resistance movements a generation later. They were launched against two big capitalist companies with thousands of tenants cultivating vast stretches of reclaimed land along the Subei coast (*PWP*, 222–23). Whereas the Thousand People revolt had been crushed in two days, these resistance movements lasted for over a year. No blood was shed (not one animal's throat was slit), but the Shanghai press was mobilized into a public opinion campaign backing the tenants' rights: this was lobbying (which, as it happened, succeeded) rather than an all-out revolt. However, we should resist the idea that this contrast illustrates a trend. The defeat of the two big Subei companies remained absolutely atypical under the Nationalist regime, which saw its share of oaths, animal sacrifices, uprisings to enthrone new emperors (or child emperors designated thanks to a congenital deformity), and of secret society members exposing their naked chests, reputedly bulletproof, to hostile gunfire. All we can suggest is that such rituals were less often observed than in the early years of the century, and that alongside the persistent fancy for numerous superstitions, we can identify others that were clearly in decline, and still more that had all but disappeared. The belief that the imperialists were sacrificing Chinese people under the wheels of trains or against bridge supports was rarely vouched for after 1911, and the attribution of harmful properties to civil status registration continued until about 1925, but did not provoke any revolts during the remaining years of the Republic.

While the modernization of the repertoire was uncertain, its relative flexibility was more striking. Certain forms of action common in other latitudes, strikes for instance, remained extremely rare.[43] Strikes by farmworkers were unusual and continued to be submerged by the taxpayers' *jiaonong*, though even the latter became less frequent in subsequent years. On the other hand, demonstrations became more common in the 1930s. Some additions to the repertoire attest villagers' willingness to adapt. During the Second World War, some peasants adapted for use against police and soldiers the mines they had seen used by anti-Japanese guerrillas. We should not now exaggerate how significant or widespread were such innovations. The repertoire was not fixed; it evolved and adapted, but not to the point of dissolving its specificity and richness while being converted to less traditional or more functional practices.

FOUR

Exploitation or Oppression?

Besides resistance to land rent and food disturbances (*PWP*, Chapters 7 and 8), there were other social conflicts, but these were rare and did not break out where one might expect. The most disadvantaged social categories (farm laborers) and the most exploited (debtors) hardly ever rebelled—except, of course, when their unrest was incited by communists. On the other hand, whole villages, or at least most villagers, took action occasionally against rich people for other reasons than their holding onto grain stores in times of shortage or refusing to reduce land rent after a bad harvest. In some cases, this was still economic exploitation; in others, more usually, this exploitation was scarcely distinguishable from the political oppression that made it possible. In extreme cases, uprisings of this kind, targeted at representatives of the administration, accredited or not (the *eba,* for instance, "local tyrants"), assumed a more political than social character.

Social Questions Without Social Movements

Firstly, we must deal briefly with two serious social questions—farm wages and moneylending—that hardly ever gave rise to social movements.

AGRICULTURAL PROLETARIAT

Admittedly, farm laborers made up only a tenth of all villagers, but they were even poorer and more exploited than the tenant farmers or sharecroppers. Their destitution was linked to their limited numbers: so long as a peasant could make do on his plot of land—whether rented or his own—he took care not to work for anyone else (in China, working as a family was the rule, working for wages the exception). Pure proletarians, who had not the smallest patch of ground and no other income, were still less numerous: perhaps one villager out of 25.[1] For the most part they were farmhands (*changgong*, "long-term laborers") who lived with landowners (in general, big landowners) and were fed by them.

Better paid than farmhands, short-term laborers had, however, no job security. They could be seen gathering in the pre-dawn twilight, by tens or hundreds, at the labor markets; only a minority could hope to be taken on. According to a survey carried out on the eve of the Japanese invasion, provision of the midday meal accounted on average for one-third of a day worker's wages.[2] That result is fairly close to other research (for example, Huang 1985, 193) that estimated the daily wages of a male farm laborer at the equivalent of two days' worth of foodgrains. These pay levels were slightly lower than the average for unskilled urban workers, but may have increased over the long term (Rawski 1989, 346 and 348). During the war, they rose spectacularly as manpower became scarce, large numbers being needed as conscripts, coolies for the military, and laborers on construction projects, such as airports or strategic roads.

These wages, while suggesting that contemporary descriptions and analyses may have exaggerated levels of destitution, were extremely low. The plentiful supply of manpower kept pay at levels more compatible with survival than population growth. In Xingguo, Jiangxi, in 1933, 99 percent of farm laborers were single men (Mao 1933, translated in Schram 1995, 629). Elsewhere, too, the majority of farm laborers (and most farmhands) stayed single, their incomes being insufficient to start families. And people were quick to tease them, warning them to beware of extravagant women: "Once in her clutches, you'll be ruined!" Or, "Anyway, old Wang, what you'll be earning in ten years' time is hardly enough to start dreaming about taking a wife!" (Fei and Chang 1948, 60). Their employers did not always treat them any better and sometimes more roughly: one account describes a farmer beating a kneeling laborer for having stolen a squash.

And yet, while competition in the labor market drove farm laborers to be very tough on each other,[3] relations between farm owners and laborers were rarely strained (Institute of Pacific Relations 1939, 70)—or rarely openly so—because such relations were usually tinged with paternalism in the Confucian tradition: both parties to a bilateral relationship had a duty to observe *ganqing* (good feelings). More importantly, workers who grumbled risked dismissal and unemployment.

So we should not be too surprised by the obvious disproportion between an almost nonexistent social movement and a social problem (the condition of farm laborers): the preceding page gives us only a glimpse of it.[4] The only three strikes by farm laborers that we know of—apart from the large number of those launched by the communists in the teeth of repression and, obviously, those organized by different categories of rural workers—all took place in the same county (Haicheng, Liaoning) and were reported by a single source! (*Haicheng XZ*, 1987, 200 and 12 of the chronology, paginated separately).[5] The first two broke out four months apart, in April and August 1926. As with numerous tenant revolts, one might consider the drought responsible for the first of these strikes, the most interesting, except that the drought provoked an initiative . . . by the landowners themselves! On seeing withered cereals presaging a bad harvest, the landowners of Dajia Cun acted jointly in putting up grain prices. Their laborers, finding themselves able to afford only one *dan* of grain instead of four at the old price, went on strike for a better price. On 18 April, a religious holiday, 30 of them swore an oath before the Temple of the God of Wealth: "If the grain price does not fall, we shall never work again." Six days went by and the landowners had not given in; so on 24 April, the laborers left Dajia Cun to seek work elsewhere. The landowners were obliged to bring in farm laborers from other villages by offering them much higher wages.

These farm laborers had gone on strike in their capacity as consumers. The other two strikes were more classic: during each of them, the laborers demanded and won higher pay. On 25 August 1926, 23 farm laborers in Xi'ai Cun refused to bring in the crops: they went on strike over the autumn harvest (*ba qiu*), and were victorious despite the intervention of the police. In June 1941, in two villages in the same county, 30 laborers began a work slowdown and then refused to hoe, in order to win a pay raise. In all three cases, numbers were modest: from 23 to 30 strikers.

These three strikes broke out in Manchuria, a recently colonized region where, during the busy periods of summer and the autumn harvest, land was more plentiful than labor. The situation was very different south of the Great Wall where, with very few exceptions, landowners had no difficulty recruiting unemployed laborers ready to work at existing wage levels.

Less unusual than strikes in the strict sense, everyday forms of resistance (as defined by Scott 1985) were nonetheless rare—little mentioned at any rate by our sources. We must be content with two examples, drawn from a much reduced sample. Zhang Suicheng, who was orphaned at eight years old, worked from childhood onwards for the three Huang brothers, big landowners who hired farm laborers to work their entire estate. Zhang was hired initially to feed the oxen and pigs. As a child, and later as an adolescent, he hated his employers, sneered at them, botched his work, and eventually ran off. His employers' family searched for him in vain, then he reappeared almost on their doorstep, and the whole village shook with laughter. The game went on for ten years, from 1903 to 1913, after which Zhang joined the White Wolf band (led by the famous bandit Bai Lang) in Henan, where he was killed in March 1914 before reaching his twentieth year (*Long Xian WSZLXJ*, vol. 2, 1982, 152–57). The adolescent's lone rebellion was played out on the desolate borderland between Shaanxi and Gansu. Much further east (in northeastern Liaoning) and three decades later, half a dozen farm laborers deliberately mixed rye grass into the landowner's seed and threw excrement into a jar before setting fire to a building (*Kaiyuan WSZL*, vol. 3, 1988, 88–91). This latter action, we must acknowledge, was outside the limits of everyday resistance.

Riddled with cliches, these two texts leave the reader unsatisfied. For lack of anything better I have recorded what they relate—which confirms the utmost rarity of sources relating to "spontaneous" actions, individual or collective, violent or nonviolent, by the agricultural proletariat.

MONEYLENDING

Moneylending caused greater misfortune than the poverty wages of farm laborers, quite simply because debtors outnumbered farm laborers by four to one. Admittedly, not all debtors were equally pitiable: rich peasants took out interest-bearing loans to buy equipment, and landowners borrowed money that they lent out at a higher interest rate. Moreover, rich people borrowed far larger sums because they had collateral and were trusted. When poor people owed as much as they, it was either an accumulation of small debts that they could not manage to repay or else because they were faced with an exceptional expense (a funeral or a marriage), something that might have equaled their entire yearly income.

Once we classify debtors according to their numbers rather than the total of their borrowings, their distribution changes completely: the poor were in the overwhelming majority—but not the very poor, to whom no one wanted to lend, apart from a parent or close friend who could not deny them a small advance. While loans often ended in tragedy, they were at first considered as an opportunity, one that farm laborers found hard to acquire, and farm laborers were far less often in debt than tenants or sharecroppers. The latter were themselves less often indebted than the semi-tenants (*ban diannong*) because they had not the smallest patch of land to mortgage.

Where the loan's term was specified, it rarely exceeded one year. People took out loans mainly in the winter (to balance their end-of-year accounts, pay the land rent, celebrate the New Year holiday, and pay off old loans now due) and in spring (to tide them over the off season or for the resumption of farming activities). The term set was in principle until the following New Year (according to the lunar calendar), or sometimes until the end of the autumn harvest.

As a general rule, such short-term loans were modest and "unproductive" in the sense that debtors made no profitable reinvestment. Modest firstly and above all else: borrowers could rarely find a local lender capable of furnishing more than 50 *yuan*. Even in nearby townships, the negligible value of objects pawned is evidence of the small sums borrowed. In 1930, out of 167 pledges accepted by various Zhejiang pawnbrokers, 158 were collateral for loans of less than 3 *yuan*, and 54 borrowers, less than a third, walked away with under 0.5 *yuan* (Institute of Pacific Relations 1939, 189–90)! Secondly, unproductive: among the six winter and spring loans mentioned above, only the last could be described as reinvested. The annual re-launch of farming activities demanded seed and sometimes other things, such as fertilizers, tools, or mulberry leaves for feeding silkworms. All of these purchases were likely to impose the need for loans. In all, only about a quarter of the money borrowed was reinvested, not so much the small loans as the much larger borrowings by rich peasants planning to buy cattle and equipment.

The poor, that is, the great majority, made a distinction, not between productive and unproductive, but between urgent loans (for sowing as well as for eating) and loans that could be deferred. Most of the needed investments belonged in the second category, and there was no guarantee that the expected returns would compensate for the interest charges.

Apart from the small free loans agreed to by family or close friends and the loans from credit unions, which at their peak (just before and at the start of the Sino-Japanese War) furnished hardly more than 1 percent of all the money borrowed by villagers, the credit available to them was very expensive. Even so, it was less expensive than is claimed by numerous sources, who were inclined to embroider a reality that hardly needed exaggerating. Let us say that the interest on many loans was between 2 percent and 3 percent per month, generally nearer the former than the latter. Admittedly, we come across many loans that were more expensive, indeed much more expensive, starting with borrowings in kind: here, the interest was higher by a quarter or a third than that charged for cash loans. Cases where lenders charged 100 percent over the year, recovering twice what they had given, were not unusual.

Interest rates varied greatly from one region to another. They were higher in the interior and even more so in the west of the country than in the coastal provinces, where money circulated more freely and risks were smaller. They were higher also in northern Jiangsu (less developed) than in the south. Conversely, in the two neighboring provinces of Henan and Shandong, the highest rates were found in counties where the commercialization of agriculture had progressed furthest. By borrowing in order to pay for the large quantities of fertilizer required for tobacco, the farmers increased the local demand for credit. The absence of regulation at the national or even regional level lent disproportionate weight to local variations in supply and demand.

The rates varied sometimes just as much within a single locality: a debtor might borrow from half a dozen lenders, each time at a different rate (Fei and Chang 1948, 122). Rates depended not only, as we have seen, on the type of loan (repayable in cash or in kind, in cereals, tools, buffaloes, opium, etc.), as well as duration (short-term loans were more expensive), amount (the more borrowed, the lower the interest rate), season (winter more expensive than summer), circumstances, and relations between lenders and borrowers.[6] There were lower rates for well-off borrowers and for borrowers offering securities.

The combination of lenders' risks with the ceaseless and ever more pressing demand from legions of borrowers is enough to explain the high cost of credit. Additionally we must take into account the shortage of supply consequent upon the absence of a national credit market and the scarcity of available capital in the countryside. Neither the modern banks, which found more secure business in the cities, nor the traditional banks (*qianzhuang*), less reluctant but in decline, nor the tontines accessible only to villagers with collateral, nor the few and unevenly distributed credit unions lent as much to peasants as the pawnshops. And, as a rule, these were more expensive. In all, these various bodies and institutions, pawnshops included, provided less than a fifth of the credit obtained by the peasants. There remained the apparently long list—though a petitioner might quickly do the rounds without striking lucky—of individual lenders: professional moneylenders, shopkeepers, grain stores, landowners, rich peasants, or even a parent or neighbor less unfortunate than oneself.

For these village lenders, it was much more profitable to lend money than to lease one's land; but, as it was more risky, they were careful not to lend too much. So the lenders' prudence imposed a limit on poor people's indebtedness. Yet, this voluntary restriction of supply seems not to have had the effect of ratcheting up credit. In the course of a century or more, different forms of credit did eventually spread and compete to some small extent. Making allowance for seasonal and historical fluctuations, average interest rates did not change much between the nineteenth (even the end of the eighteenth) century and 1930 (as confirmed in northern China (Hebei and Shandong) by Ramon Myers (1970, 243). Over the shorter term, the real cost of money climbed steadily from 1931 onward as prices began to fall, but the almost continuous rise in prices during the first two decades of the Republic favored the debtors, as their principal sums depreciated from year to year.

This applied—all the more so—during the Sino-Japanese War when inflation offered some peasants the opportunity to write off debts accumulated over one or several generations, though the circumstances were too exceptional for lessons to be drawn.

In ordinary times, the vicious circle of borrowing and debt changed many small farmers into tenants working their fields for the benefit of former creditors. There was sometimes a halfway stage, a temporary transfer of ownership: the lender would take over the debtor's field, drawing the profit from it in lieu of interest. The switch became permanent when the debtor found himself unable to repay the principal. Even so, the proletarianization of the peasants did not progress at the pace suggested in many studies, and this was partly because the families of those condemned to single status were extinguished with them. Perhaps it did not progress at all. Over the long term (from the end of the nineteenth century until 1949) we cannot detect any significant or rapid land concentration. Quite the opposite: such concentration seems to have been very slow (landowners sold because taxation was heavy and rents unprofitable, or in order to invest in business and industrial affairs in the cities, or to send their sons off to study abroad) and, in particular, intermittent. It progressed only sporadically, during food crises.

Even though we have to dispel the myths, one thing remains inescapably true. In the early part of the twentieth century, in China as in most rural societies where small producers were in the majority, much hardship, perhaps most, was caused by credit. The hardship was chronic, firstly before people could find any credit, later and most of all after they had. Although the two categories partly overlapped, debtors were almost as numerous as tenants and semi-tenants combined. In cases where the moneylender was not the same person as the landlord, it was the former who bore down hardest on the peasants. When payback time came, if a creditor proved intractable, a peasant might commit suicide on his doorstep, hoping that someday his ghost would avenge him and, more immediately, that the creditor might have to write off the debt (Fei 1939, 279). Shylock would lose face, but those exposing him lost their lives.

I do not know of a single case where peasants rose up against hardhearted creditors. I can report one case of collective violence in response, not to lenders refusing to defer payment, but to ill-treatment inflicted on insolvent debtors. Furthermore, to unearth this example I had to look outside the time frame of my present research: in 1892, the villagers of Chenjiaba, north Sichuan, wounded a dozen agents of the "eight big firms" (*ba da hao*), commercial companies that loaned money and were in the habit of tying up and brutalizing borrowers unable to repay their debts. One of them, who owed twenty silver taels, had even been beaten to death (*Mianyang Shi WSZL*, vol. 5, 1990, 171–84).

To sum up everything that is, in our sample, more or less linked to credit (to be repaid or unsuccessfully sought), we should add the following instances: rioting (in Shanxi in the 1930s) against bank staff and other creditors coming to claim what was owed (Gillin 1967, 158); the murder of a peasant in Jing'an, Jiangxi, who had refused to lend to members of his lineage (*Shenbao*, 26 May 1930, cited in *ZJNSZ*, vol. 3, 1029); and lastly, peasants using force against rich people to make them advance two or three piculs of rice until harvest time (Feng 1935, 427). The first case strongly resembles the riots stirred up by collection of land rent and, in particular, of taxes. The last case, even though it presages the *yingjie* (forcible borrowing) applied later on a quite different scale by the communists, is merely a lesser form of another use of force: when starving peasants obliged rich people to share their food (*PWP*, Chapter 8). As to the second case, more serious but of the same kind, the man murdered was not a moneylender but someone unwilling to become a creditor. The case also illustrates the obligations undertaken by members of the same lineage.

Put simply, revolts and collective attacks on moneylenders occurred even less frequently than strikes by farm laborers. The relationship between debtor and creditor worked two ways, more so than that between a tenant and a possibly absentee landlord. The creditor was supposed to provide a service to the debtor, a service the latter would be obliged to call for again: the need to borrow overrode all other considerations. This need impelled debtors to pay their debts even ahead of the rent. Similarly, the fear of not being able to repay drove many a peasant to sell his wife or his children before mortgaging his land.

Moneylending embodies, even more than farm wages, the contrast between an almost nonexistent social movement and a social issue conspicuously present in every village. That is, unless we include under the heading of resistance to moneylending the many revolts where the moneylender's greed was an additional grievance. Let us take the example of an uprising with various causes, first among them the exactions of a local despot. Even so, we should not forget that this despot was also a landlord who charged rent on his eight hectares of land—and practiced moneylending (see below p. 85).

From Exploitation to Oppression

Having considered social questions too important to be left out of this book even though they provoked scarcely any popular resistance, let us look now at real social conflicts and their significance. Outside the two main categories of food disturbances and resistance to land rent, our sample brings together a miscellany of social conflicts. They gave rise to fewer incidents (fewer even than cases of resistance to land rent), but were still ten times more numerous than farm laborers' strikes and debtors' revolts put together. To try and make sense of them, we should start by dealing quickly with the dozen incidents and revolts that, while setting rich against poor, can hardly enlighten us, the sources being too cursory or too vague and too inclined to trot out the same old cliches. Another series of documents do illustrate more usefully the kind of conflicts that pitted peasants (as producers or consumers) against more comfortably off citizens. There is a disparity between the small number of cases arising from "fair" competition (including the advantages available to the person with capital) between social classes of divergent interests and the significantly more numerous cases of fraud, manipulation, monopoly, misappropriation of public property, and extortion pure and simple. This disproportion reveals the often decisive role of oppression at the root of social exploitation.

"HIT THE RICH AND HELP THE POOR!"

In the countryside everyone knew the slogan, "Hit the rich and help the poor!" (*dafu jipin*). Many different groups would use it: brigands even printed these four characters on their banners, intending to pass as Robin Hood and his Merry Men—while robbing the poor as well as the rich. The three Ding brothers, euphemistically nicknamed "the three Ding flowers" (Ding sanhua), did the same, but using the variant "Rob the rich and help the poor!" (*jiefu jipin*). In alliance with the secret society of the Sanyuanhui (Three Lords of Heaven), they unleashed in August 1914 a significant uprising in northern Jiangsu. Although they claimed to have a political program (restore the Ming Dynasty, fight Yuan Shikai, and start a third revolution to succeed the second, crushed the year before), it seems they had no greater ambition than to live off the land and win power locally (*ZD2LDG*, Archives of the Infantry Ministry of the Beiyang Government, widely cited in Jiang 1988c, 2–7).

Our sources, when they had little data (not just the communists but also the Nationalists before they won power) were content to quote this watchword, at the risk or with the purpose of integrating the brigands into the popular movement. Sometimes, however, peasants (without bandits) did come to play a role. In 1913, more than 5,000 poor peasants from the borderlands between Jiangsu and Shandong created a Qingshajun (Army of Green Gauze), whose banners proclaimed, "Kill the rich and help the poor!" (*shafu jipin*). With the support of local peasants, they did indeed become a formidable army, maintaining their campaign until eventual defeat with the death of their leader in October 1917 (*Pei Xian WSZL*, vol. 3, 1985, 106–12). Fifteen years later, in February 1928 in northwestern Hubei, a Huangjinjun (Yellow Towel Army) grew from 300 to 4,000 men and attacked, not just the rich, but also the tax authorities. It killed 110 militiamen, after which the troops were reinforced and, in their turn, killed or wounded a good half of the 4,000 fighters (*Fang XZ*, 1991, 11 and 172). In the northeast of the neighboring province of Henan, rebel peasants besieging the Qingfeng county town in February 1925 assaulted without distinction "rich shopkeepers and big families" (*fushang dahu*; *Qingfeng XZ*, 1990, 33). And occasionally rebels would invoke divine justice, as did the 180 armed men who, in May 1920, killed 30 soldiers in Wuchang county, Heilongjiang, under a banner proclaiming, "As the Way of Heaven requires, kill the rich and help the poor!" (*Wuchang XZ*, 1989, 8).

In southern Guizhou, in 1928, the struggle against the rich took a particularist tone: "Attack the rich, not the poor, those who are far, not those who are close!" (*dafu bu dapin, dayuan bu dajin*), but as the rebels were Miao, "those who are far" probably meant Han people (*Huishui XZ*, 1989, 426).

FAIR AND LESS FAIR COMPETITION

Leaving slogans behind us, we are faced with an infinite variety of concrete grievances, accompanied almost always by a feeling of injustice. Sometimes the injustice and dishonesty of the exploiters was more alleged than established, but that was not usually the case.[7]

We shall begin with a social conflict that may seem familiar, in that it was a classic struggle between producers and buyers: 4,000 to 5,000 tea farmers demanded a higher purchase price by demonstrating in April 1939 outside the magistrate's office in Yuyao, Zhejiang. But there was nothing spontaneous about the demonstration: the Communist Party had organized it. (*Yuyao WSZL*, vol. 2, 1986, 20).

In a small minority of cases, peasants and villagers were merely the losers in the battle against stronger competitors—those who had money and invested it without worrying too much about the poor people they were throwing onto the street. In 1926, some lumberjacks attempted to save their livelihoods, threatened by a capitalist enterprise that had acquired tens of thousands of *mu* in the forest of Yuntaishan, in northeastern Jiangsu. They founded the Biandanhui (Society of Yokes), and in March 1927, 300 of its members, backed by another thousand lumberjacks, destroyed some 20 hectares of young saplings planted by the company. The police arrested one of the leaders, 200 of his comrades tried to free him, two of them were injured, and the lumberjacks lost the argument (*Lianyungang WSZL*, vol. 4, 1986, 31–40). Further south in the same province, the famous industrialist, reformer, and educator Zhang Jian grew cotton on large stretches of land hitherto used for saltworks. The former salt workers, now jobless, invaded the cotton works (in Sanyu on 15 August 1912), beat two employees to death, seized money, grain, and equipment, which they shared out among peasants and the company's workforce, then set fire to the buildings (*Nantong WSZL*, vol. 3, undated, 80–81). In further incidents, fishermen destroyed the fisheries office in protest against the takeover of the fish market by a minority of their competitors (in spring 1911 in two coastal localities near Shanghai; *Chuansha XZ*, 1990, 20), peasants fought (in Jintan, Jiangsu in 1922) to prevent the opening of a fish syndicate controlled by notables (Jiangsu sheng nongmin yundong dashi nianbiao 1981, 429), and salt workers clashed with a shop-

Box 4.1 Mechanical Irrigation in the Village: Lücheng, Jiangsu, 1926

During the drought of summer 1926, some businessmen in Lücheng formed a company that acquired a mechanical pump and charged the peasants a high price for using it—just under three *yuan* per *mu*. What particularly angers the peasants is the ban (publicised on posters) on drawing water from the nearby river, applying to any farmers not paying "rent" to the company, and warning that any of them caught secretly taking water would be fined.

A peasant society "for promoting progress" suggested forming a cooperative that would buy, in everyone's name, a mechanical pump. The investment (1,400 *yuan*) was just about the sum that the entire village would have to pay in a year to rent the rich people's pump. In no time at all, everyone was using the cooperative's pump, and no one used the one belonging to the company. The "bad scholar gentry" (*lieshen*, whom the Guomindang were quick to identify as the company shareholders) then persuaded the warlord Sun Chuanfang that the Society for Promoting Progress is "red"—in other words, communist. Sun sent soldiers, arrested four peasant activists, and dissolved the peasant Society. One of our sources is none other than Mao Zedong: he records that the troops found no adult men in the village (they had all gone to hide in the fields), but that the villagers were obliged to make a "gift" of 1,000 *yuan* to the commanding officer, to prevent any further arrests.

SOURCES: *ZLN*, vol. 1, 1928, 466–67; *Danyang XZ*, 1992, 20; Geisert 2001, 59; *Xiangdao zhoubao*, no. 79, 25 March 1926. Mao's article is translated in Schram 1994, 416–17.

keeper (they called him a "traitor," probably because he had been in contact with a Japanese man) who had acquired for 3,000,000 *yuan* exploitation rights over large areas of salt marshes in the Qingdao region, Shandong, in 1923 (*Xiangdao Zhoubao*, 17 October 1926, cited in *ZJNSZ*, vol. 2, 703). Box 4.1 illustrates this kind of movement rather well: villagers harmed by rich people's investments and fighting back.

This is an interesting affair in more than one respect. Firstly, it was not violent. Secondly and more importantly, it ran counter to the argument put forward in the third chapter of this book. These were not angry peasants obstructing modernization; rather, they were adapting it to their needs. On the other hand, it is not certain that their action was entirely spontaneous: one of our sources ascribes the initiative to the local section of the Guomindang. For our immediate purposes this affair provides us with an apt transition between the collateral damage (the externalities) of modernization and the abuses of power: the ban on continuing to draw water from the river and the appeal to military forces.

Struggles against monopolies were not very different from the cases mentioned above.[8] Let us briefly consider the defense of the village's collective resources when threatened or destroyed by rich people's initiatives (this may still be classed as resistance to investments threatening the peasants' chances of survival). In 1926, Rong Desheng, the "Chinese Rockefeller," wanted to build a road across Xuxiang township, near Wuxi, Jiangsu. To this end, he set out to acquire all the surrounding land and to flatten the houses in Xuxiang. The peasants organized a "peasant club" to resist Rong. In the end, they forced him to pay 200 *yuan* per *mu* of expropriated land, plus 0.10 *yuan* per mulberry tree growing on the land, and made him promise not to demolish any houses in the township (*ZJNSZ*, vol. 2, 706–7; Bergère 1986, 9 and 160–61 on Rong Desheng and the Rong family). In western Fujian in 1928, a natural spring was threatened by the projects of two investors from the provincial capital, Fuzhou. The spring dried up as the villagers had feared, but they did not win any compensation (*Sha Xian WSZL*, vol. 2, 1983, 28–29).

The worst of it, what outraged the peasants and mobilized them to action, was the favors, the cheating, the conspicuous injustices—all benefiting privileged people with direct access to the authorities—and the expropriation of land by the rich and powerful.[9] We should pause a moment on this last point: a recurrent theme was complaints about the forcible occupation of farmland (*qiangzhan nongtian*) to the benefit of the local swells, or rich landowners and/or those with government connections. The peasants of Yuanjiahu, Hubei, resisted for three years (from 1914 to 1917) the seizure of land by private individuals who fenced off the areas they planned to expropriate (*Daye WSZL*, vol. 2, 1987, 116). In a region inhabited by national minorities (northwest of Kunming, in Yunnan) the seizure of land by a *tusi* (a native official in the service of the Chinese authorities) stirred up a far longer conflict. At the outset, it was not violent: in 1912, two army veterans returning to their homeland formed a federation of fifteen villages and sued the *tusi* demanding that he return the land to the community. The authorities were fearful of the *tusi*'s power: they dithered and reached no decision. By 1914, the villagers were sufficiently incensed to widen their federation, which soon numbered 51 villages. At last, Peking reached a judgment, against the *tusi*, but he appealed and would not comply. As he was no longer entitled to collect taxes, all 51 villages refused to pay them. In 1919, the *tusi* formed an alliance with a bandit chief from neighboring Sichuan. Each of the federated villages mustered up to several hundred armed men, and inconclusive skirmishes and looting ensued throughout the 1920s. Only in 1937 did 38 of the federated villages manage finally to recover their land (*Wuding XZ*, 1990, 387–88).

It was not only the expropriation of unused land that peasants were resisting. They also fought the speculation that enriched at their expense a minority of rich and powerful people. Thus, in 1923, the Liqing enterprise, which allied landowners with notables under the aegis of the Qingpu magistrate in Jiangsu, sold land for 12 *yuan* per *mu*, land that it had bought for a quarter of that price and then cleared. To fight its stranglehold, peasants in western Qingpu villages formed their own clearance association (*kenwu lianhehui*) and more than 600 of them demonstrated outside the magistrate's office. They even mustered a regiment of 10,000 men, according to a probably exaggerated report. The opposition to the Liqing enterprise was sustained for several years. In spring 1927, in the climate created by the arrival of the Northern Expedition more than 200 members of peasant unions seized some "bad scholar gentry" charged with having cornered some of this disputed land and delivered them by force to the stadium where they were to be judged.[10]

ILL-TREATMENT AND OPPRESSION: THE "LOCAL TYRANTS"

Let us come to the last point, which sums up the essence of my argument: resistance to oppression (*kang bao*). Admittedly, it could happen that a conflict rooted in oppression might also have an undeniable social aspect. That was the case in Sishang, Shaanxi, in November 1930, when a "holy brigade" (*shen tuan*) of 600 peasants was decimated in a battle with landlords. Their fight was above all against the landlords' authority, as was illustrated by their declared intention to "resist tyranny" (*fankang baozheng; Xixiang XZ*, 1991, 18 and 245). And the same is true of the events described in Box 4.2, which constitute a Subei replica of cases described in other provinces by the scholarly literature.[11]

Box 4.2   Local Despots: Maozhai, Jiangsu, 1935

The big landowner Liu Dashen, who owned 170 acres of land in the Xuzhou region, in northwest Jiangsu, was in his family context a tyrant who forced his daughter-in-law into an abortion and raped his granddaughter. He was also, in his Maozhai fiefdom, a local despot; and hardly anyone dared to confront his six bodyguards.

This episode begins with an instance of personal, or rather family, revenge. Liu Guangqing's father (we will henceforth call the Lius by their given names), having been despoiled of three *mu* of land by Dashen, fell out with him. Dashen killed him. Later, when a murder was committed, Dashen accused Guangqing of having allowed a criminal to escape and had him arrested. Guangqing, once released after the murderer is caught, prepared his revenge with the help of all the men in the family, cousins included. In 1935 he thrashed the tyrant right in the center of Maozhai market. Dashen left the village and killed himself soon afterward. This was the end of the first act of this family drama.

Dashen's brother and two sons disputed his inheritance and came to blows. The brother came off best and succeeded him as local administrator (*yutong*) of Maozhai. The family, bitterly divided, still ruled its fiefdom. Zixiu, a nephew, became village head. In his turn he aroused the people's anger for allegedly embezzling common property (wood, in particular) and pressuring the victims of a flood (in August 1935) instead of rescuing them. It was natural that people should turn to Guangqing, "the avenger," asking him to organize resistance. It was peaceful resistance at first: Guangqing sent several spokesmen for talks with Zixiu, who arrested one of them (Li Chengdong, the only one who is not called Liu). The crowd stormed Zixiu's house and he fled, dragging his prisoner along with him.

To rescue Li, 3,000 to 4,000 peasants made their way to the ward headquarters, about seven miles away. The ward head refused to see them and threatened to call in the troops. The crowd invaded the administrative building, tied up an employee, destroyed furniture and registers, as well as some maps pinned up on the walls, and a portrait of Chiang Kai-shek. After much bargaining and various demonstrations (during which a Guomindang dignitary ran off with 3,000 men at his heels), the peasants finally secured Li's release. He was given responsibility for administering half the village, while the other half was still subject to Zixiu's exactions.

The villagers celebrated this modest success as a great victory, and while they were in the mood for it, they formed the Qiongrenhui (Association of the Poor), which committed itself to provide help to any tenant whose lease is cancelled by their landlord. The Association represented fifteen villages and was presided over by Guangqing. The latter is, in our day, famous as a martyr for having been buried alive in 1944 by the Nationalists.

Despite this epilogue, the communists seem to have played no part in the foregoing affair (like many villagers, Guangqing was content to act as informant to the Red Army). On the other hand, the Association of the Poor and its help to evicted tenants underline the social implications of this mini-revolt, which pitted a family of big landlords against the little people whom Guangqing embodied perfectly: he farmed the land with the youngest of his four sons, the eldest being a tenant himself, and the other two lumberjacks. Even so, the big landlords were fought as local tyrants, as it was their official functions that enabled them to oppress and then to exploit the villagers. The latter reacted, in their usual way, to the concrete misdeeds: it all began with a vengeful family. Just as much as its beginning, the outcome of the conflict was significant in how the authorities dithered and then split the difference. In such regions (the far north of Jiangsu), the Nationalist government from its base in the south was rarely in a position to impose its will on the local potentates governing in its name.

SOURCE: *Tongshan WSZL*, vol. 2, 1983, 75–82.

More usually, the rebels expressed different grievances, but the context clearly showed what counted most in their eyes: it was almost always *bao*, oppression, cruelty, or the authorities' exactions. In Baoji county, Shaanxi, a man was killed one morning in November 1933 by eighteen "sworn brothers." He was a moneylender, who charged rent on his 20 acres of land, but it was in his capacity as local despot, militia chief, and head of the fifth ward that he imposed endless exactions and made himself hated (*Baoji Xian WSZL*, vol. 6, 1988, 43–49). Here, and this was not unusual, the local despot combined administrative duties with maintaining law and order.

Militia commanders are, in fact, along with small local heads, the most common targets of this kind of movement. By contrast, the county magistrate rarely incurred the masses' resentment or hatred, far less often anyway than did the petty tyrants. Not all such figures occupied formal posts in the civil or military administration, but that did not prevent them terrorizing the community with their personal militias, their wealth, or their membership in the local gentry.

The hatred aroused by local despots was in proportion to their misdeeds, and it bears repeating that such misdeeds coupled social exploitation and extortion with exactions enforced by their authority or by brute force. The following incident, which occurred in the final period of the Qing Dynasty, gives us a sense of that hatred. One night during the commemoration of the dead (*qingmingjie*), the inhabitants of Caoguan village, in Guizhou, massacred the family of a local despot called Yu, who had seized three-quarters of the locals' land and was oppressing them in a thousand different ways, exploiting the posts that he and various members of his lineage held in and outside the village. Later that night, the villagers demolished the Yu ancestral tomb and emptied the family pond, "shaped like the mouth of a living dragon" (*huo long kou*), with the purpose of ruining the family's fengshui (*Baiyun WSZL*, vol. 5, 1988, 111–13).

Among some ethnic minorities, the predominance of the political over the social in any conflict combining the two types of grievances has a near-institutional basis. So it was with the Uyghur shepherds' revolt, in Xinjiang, against the head of their tribe: he was forcing them to work for him or his flocks (an unpaid corvée) before they could work with their own animals or on their own farms. In 1907, 1,000 shepherds demanded the right to serve their master only three days a month, and to devote the remainder of their time to their own concerns. Waving banners proclaiming "We are not the slaves of the *qinwang* ["prince of royal blood," in other words the chief or one of the chiefs of their tribe]!" or even "Down with royalty!" they resisted for three months, before being defeated for lack of firearms and because the imperial army supported the *qinwang*. Eight rebels were condemned to death and more than 160 to prison terms (*Xinjiang WSZLXJ*, vol. 13, 1985, 47–51).[12] But it was a different matter with the Yi revolt in western Yunnan in February 1935. There was no institutional basis behind the exploitation—as much social as political—to which peasants were subjected by landlords and despots backed by about 100 outlaws. True, in its moment of victory, the 1,000 rebels won concessions of a social nature (exemption from rent for the rebel tenants), but these were eclipsed by the decidedly political profile that the "incident" took on: the son of one of the instigators of the revolt "mounted the throne" and shared out the official posts among his companions. He was eventually executed but government forces had to intervene on three occasions before bringing down his new "dynasty." Some 80 of his followers were killed with him or during the fighting (*Yongsheng XZ*, 1989, 506–7).

By contrast, areas more or less controlled by the administrative hierarchy occupied only a small part of the territory, though it was much more densely populated than the ethnic minority regions. Most of the country was made up of all sorts of intermediate areas, populated mainly by Han but more or less autonomous. If we made our way northward from the capital Nanjing, we would quickly enter "gray" areas (ill controlled) even without leaving the province (Jiangsu). Judging from a description that we must acknowledge is more famous than representative, we could find in 1930, in the Xuzhou region, semi-feudal "lords," absolute masters of their fortified villages (*zhai*) guarded by militias. The most powerful of them, owning three times as many guns as did, for instance, the magistrate of Pei county, were hardly minded to obey him. They refused to pay the smallest sums in tax on estates ten to twenty times more extensive than those owned by the local tyrant described in Box 4.2. All the same, the holdings of these secular "lords" were surpassed by those controlled by some Buddhist monasteries, such as Jile'an in Suqian county. According to the author Wu Shoupeng, the monks' main occupation was land rent collection and moneylending. One of them was appointed to each village to serve as its head. The peasants in the area were mostly tenants of the monastery, and worked for the monks. A "tenants' revolt" that occurred in Suqian county just before 1930 was launched by the monks themselves, who wanted to protest against the confiscation of religious buildings to convert them into schools (*DFZZ*, vol. 27, no. 6 and 7, 1930; also dealt with in Feng 1935, 330–61; partly translated in Institute of Pacific Relations 1939, 11–13; commented on in Nedostup 2001, 351–55; also *DFZZ*, vol. 27, no. 27, 1930; cited in Park 2002, 206).

We cannot leave it there. We are at the point where social analysis inevitably encroaches upon political territory. Not only are social exploitation and political oppression often indistinguishable, the general rule is that political, administrative, or military oppression engendered the other monster. In the interregnum between the two "empires" (between 1911 and 1949), order was reestablished in a lasting form only in a small part of the Chinese countryside. Insecurity, endemic banditry and the brutalities and looting of the military were widespread, and where law and order did prevail, the arbitrary powers and greed of the local administrators caused as much or more suffering as did the daily exploitation of the poor by the rich.

We should not, for all that, exonerate the rich. They were fairly often also the ones in power, and the landlords too played their part in the local administration and its abuses. More exactly, the rural elite in modern times (the first part of the twentieth century) was composite, as indicated by the time-honored expression *tuhao lieshen* (local tyrants and bad scholar gentry). Nevertheless, the expression was as vague as it was widespread: alongside corrupt members of the administration and sub-administration, it covered all those village swells and local tyrants whose reign of terror was enforced by gangs of heavies or private militias. As their name suggests, the *lieshen* belonged to scholar gentry families and the *tuhao* were more nouveau riche; but the catchphrase, picked up by Nationalist, then communist, propaganda, made so little distinction between the two categories that it was sometimes condensed into a generic term: the *tulie*.[13] The abolition of public exams in 1905, the fall of the Empire in 1912, the violent attacks against Confucianism in 1919: all these developments undermined the scholar gentry's "normal" expectations of upward social mobility and challenged their legitimacy. Some of the gentry became less fastidious about the means, not just of "advancing themselves," but also of holding on to their family patrimony which, under the Republic, became difficult to maintain intact if none of the family members occupied any post of authority in the local administration.

Criticizing the local administration (its shortcomings as well as its misdeeds) boils down to criticizing the political system, including the Nationalist government. The latter was a failure in the countryside, where inherited influence was strong: that of the warlords; the 1911 Revolution, which had dealt a heavy blow to Chinese unity; and last but not least, the Empire, not only the crisis-ridden Empire of the past half-century, but also the secular Empire and its administration "on the cheap" that had scarcely penetrated the villages.

The Republic did attempt to remedy the inadequacies of the local administration in the countryside. From 1914 onwards, the creation of *qu* (wards) provided an intermediate stage between counties and villages (*xiang*). On average there were between five and ten wards per county and the ward head (*quzhang*) was supposed to represent the county magistrate in a ward comprising 50,000 to 100,000 inhabitants. The trouble was that the majority of the *quzhang*, along with the lower-ranking administrators (from the *xiangzhang* to the *baozhang*), were these self-same evil and despised people, the *tuhao*.

We should not forget that they were joined by many commanders of local militias and, as we have pointed out, local tyrants who thrived without needing to rely on posts within either the administration or the police. Chiang Kai-shek who, in his way, was both centralizing and bureaucratic, did attempt to control more closely the ward heads and junior ranks that he could not modify or change—although he did dismiss or punish some of them (Kuhn 1975, 294–98; Zhang Xin 2000, 234–37). But during the short decade preceding the Japanese invasion, he failed to create a more efficient, less predatory, rural administration.

The Nationalist officials did not even succeed in bringing "up" to their level the bulk of the tax revenues collected locally, in other words the supplementary taxes and land tax surcharges raised at will by the "sub-administration." The proliferation of different taxes and the increase in existing taxes caused far more discontent and unrest than social exploitation as such. Antitax disturbances, which we shall now go on to address, did not have the same social implications as resistance to land rent or the looting of granaries. It was brought about by taxpayers possessing taxable funds, first among them the big payers such as landowners who found it difficult to maintain their patrimony without having connections within—or better still a direct hand in—the local administration.

FIVE

Taxation

Among the forms of spontaneous rural unrest in China during the first half of the twentieth century, antitax riots were by far the most numerous (see Appendix). Even that fact does not adequately convey the predominance of antitax resistance, which played a part in many incidents classified under other headings, such as resistance to the New Policies (Chapter 6), or to wartime conscription (Chapter 7). The antitax revolts were the best and most consistent expressions of the discontent of the great majority of Chinese villagers.

Rebellion by taxpayers has not taken on the social significance accorded to that by tenant farmers, which has been studied (for example, in *PWP*, Chapter 7) on the basis of documentation ten times less abundant than that drawn upon in the present chapter. And yet, tenants' uprisings themselves did not always express any obvious class consciousness. While not excluding a sometimes sharp resentment toward landlords, tenants' revolts were more often provoked by bad harvests than by intensified social exploitation. Antitax riots and revolts, being reactive like the tenants' revolts, did sometimes also follow one or several bad harvests, but in general it was the growing burden of taxation that gave rise to them, a burden that by definition affected only landowners.[1] Of course, we should not deny any social component in antitax resistance, the less so in that most taxes were regressive in practice, if not in theory. The fact remains that those leading the resistance—peaceful (petitions) or violent—originated often among landlords or better-off farmers. Most antitax revolts brought together a broad united front of taxpayers, but a fairly good number were led by the biggest taxpayers, harnessing to the purpose the small payers' discontent.

At first sight it is paradoxical that taxation should have been resented to the point of stirring up large numbers of revolts or riots (on average over 20 per year in our sample, or about 30 counting those where its impact was combined with other causes), because it was very light. Although it is easy to list local (and temporary) examples of very high levels of taxation, the average tax burden was restricted to within 5 percent and 10 percent of farm produce, sometimes a little more under the Nationalist government, but less up until 1905, and still worlds away from the 44 percent of the harvest that tenants had to hand over to their landlords. The overwhelming contribution of agriculture to the Chinese economy (still 65 percent of GDP in 1933) is quite out of proportion to the small share of national income that the state drew from the agricultural sector.

Against the Increase in the Tax Burden

Though modest, the tax burden did nevertheless grow over this period, and this increase was the primary source of discontent. If we focus primarily on the land tax, which continued to represent the main part of peasant contributions, it had never been so low as at the very beginning of the period. With the exception of the rich eastern part of Jiangnan, where fiscal levels were traditionally higher, the tax varied almost everywhere else between 2 percent and 4 percent (Wang 1973, 127–28). From the second half of the first decade onward, it rose sharply because of the heavy reparations inflicted on China by the Eight-Nation Alliance following the Boxer Uprising and, still more so, to fund the New Policies. At the start of the Republic, taxes rose under Yuan Shikai, particularly in North China, after which they stabilized for a decade (1916–25). In all, the first fifteen years of the Republic saw a moderate (though unevenly distributed) rise, but on a national scale it did not lead to a notable increase in the effective burden, since prices and especially farm prices tended to go up by at least as much as taxation. It was only during and after the 1926–28 period, marked by the Northern Expedition (Beifa), and then the establishment of the victorious revolutionary government, that taxes increased noticeably faster than farm prices. At the start of the 1930s, when the global economic crisis suddenly drove down farm prices, the persistent increases in taxation assumed disastrous proportions for many small taxpayers, who were sometimes forced into debt to pay what they owed. Farm prices stopped falling in 1934, the Nationalist government finally heeded the peasants' abject poverty and discontent, and their tax burden diminished somewhat in 1935 and 1936. It diminished further at the beginning of the Sino-Japanese War (inflation provisionally easing the load), but then quickly turned upward. The government had to confront growing military spending while no longer accessing revenue from the Maritime Customs or any contributions from the rich coastal provinces occupied by the Japanese. Despite the effects of growing inflation, in 1941 the relief to taxpayers ran out, and they had to pay the land rent in kind. Still worse, the army subjected them to endless requisitions (see Chapter 7). In the immediate aftermath of the war, the government was imprudent enough to grant a one-off remission of land tax. With this single exception, the last decade (the 1940s) had represented, alongside the periods 1906–11 and 1931–34, a high point in the tax demands inflicted on the farming population.

Not counting the 1940s, our sample of antitax revolts reflects quite clearly the growth in the tax burden, with 62.6 percent (725 incidents out of 1,158) of the recorded riots or uprisings occurring during two main periods: from 1906 to October 1911 and from 1926 to 1936. Admittedly, these two periods were less exceptional in reality than in our sample, firstly because the sources favored these two periods (*PWP*, 55–56), and secondly because I have myself diminished the share of the war years by classifying as resistance to military service numerous incidents that also had an antitax character. But in the same way that I have classified as resistance to the New Policies many revolts during the years 1906 to 1911 that were also motivated by taxation. Even if the sources had not favored certain periods and if I myself had counted, not the incidents, but the possibly multiple causes of each incident, more than half (rather than the recorded 62.6 percent) of the antitax revolts would still have been concentrated within the last six years of the Empire (1906 to October 1911) and the Nanking decade, including the Beifa and the final intensification of the struggles between northern warlords (1926 to 1936).

A second source of discontent was the form taken by tax increases, which were slapped on piecemeal. The authorities, local or national, whenever funding problems arose, rarely hesitated to raise new taxes (see Box 5.1) or add surcharges to existing ones.

Box 5.1   Resisting a New Tax: Siyugang, Jiangsu, 2–4 August 1912

The short but bloody revolt that erupted during summer 1912 in Siyugang, near Pingchao on the northwestern tip of Nantong county (Jiangsu), occurred in resistance to the imposition of a new land tax (*mujuan*). This *mujuan* (just like others, in theory) was proportionate to the field areas owned by the taxpayers. And, like the majority of new taxes and surtaxes, it was dedicated to a specific project, in this case the strengthening of the Yangzi's banks. Nevertheless, it had several original features. Firstly, being even more localized than the multiplicity of other taxes and surtaxes imposed by the counties and their subdivisions, the new tax affected only those living along the river banks, the presumed beneficiaries of the work it was supposed to finance—so only the land on the left bank of the Yangzi, a strip about four miles long and two wide, was subject to the tax. Secondly, it took the form of a payment varying according to the land's proximity to the river. The closer, the greater the amount: four *yuan* per *mu* for fields less than three *li* (one mile) from the Yangzi, falling to two *yuan* for fields lying beyond. Lastly, it hit tenants as well as landlords: they were to share the burden (two *yuan* each for land lying less than three *li* from the river, and one *yuan* each beyond). There was a further clause, but not really an original one: the tax imposed in June 1912 in and around Siyugang and Lujinggang (upstream from Siyugang) was in principle temporary. That was the case with many land tax surtaxes, which nevertheless continued to be collected after the bridge, school, or road they were intended to fund had been built and paid for. This one was set for a term of twenty years, the time needed to repay both interest and principal (a sum estimated at 500,000 taels).

This costly work would have to wait. The revolt threw everything into doubt. No one denied that it was necessary for the Yangzi to be held in check at the point where the estuary widened into a sound. After a long period during which the cultivated land had been extended at the expense of the riverbed, from the sixteenth century to the end of the eighteenth century, the last century of the Qing Dynasty and the start of the Republic coincided with the shrinkage of the recovered land. In the Lujinggang-Siyugang section the cultivable area now submerged was estimated at some 100,000 *mu* (16,000 acres). The only question was whether the local taxpayers could by themselves bear the cost of the project. It had been developed, in consultation with foreign engineers, by the celebrated industrialist and reformer Zhang Jian, brought in as early as 1907 by local leaders anxious about the crumbling banks. The decision to go ahead had been taken in 1910 by the Local Autonomy Bureau of Nantong prefecture, but originally, according to one of our sources, the amount of the payment demanded was no more than 1.6 *yuan* per *mu* for fields verging the river and 1.2 *yuan* for land further away, and the expectation was still of a one-off contribution to be paid over two years.

When the duration and final amount of the new tax were officially announced on 25 June 1912, the response was general outrage and immediate preparation for resistance. In this region, the average rent for land was not quite two *yuan* per *mu*. Along the strip of land lying less than a mile from the riverside, the landlords would be out of pocket, since the incomes they raised on their fields was slightly less than the amount of the new tax demands. As for the tenants, their burden would be more than doubled.

During the month of July, notices appeared calling for resistance, a self-defense militia was formed, and on 20 July, about 1,000 peasants filed in procession into a neighboring temple where they burned incense and pledged their "unanimous hearts" to resistance. In every village thereabouts, blacksmiths forged daggers, javelins, and spears. A few old "indigenous" (*tu pao*) cannons were brought out of storage and a fortress was built out of earth to surround the house of Lin Men, one of the leaders behind the revolt. In the event, the uprising was short-lived (it broke out on 2 August and was crushed within two days) but violent—and the repression still more so. In this watery landscape, where a dense grid of canals divided up the low-lying land into a checkerboard, the main battles were fought on or at the approaches to bridges, on or in sight of the water controlling access to nearby hamlets, and the battles pitted thousands of peasants against squads of river police ferried up the Yangzi. The police, with far more modern weapons than their village opponents, had no great difficulty in defeating them, especially after the arrival of reinforcements dispatched by the authorities in light of the unexpected determination of the "bandits."

History or legend records that, at the decisive moment, on 3 August during the attack on the Lin Men fortress, the cannons did not work, the powder having been dampened by a traitor. But there is no need to blame treachery, ill luck, or strategic misjudgments (these being notorious as usual) for an outcome determined by the disparity of force. Once the rebel leaders were convinced that prolonging their resistance would be suicidal, they swam to safety. None would ever reappear in his native village. Just one, Lin Men, was later tracked down, arrested, and executed. The possessions of the fugitive "bandits" were auctioned off to compensate those families whose houses had been burned or destroyed by the rebels. The authorities decided to "suspend" (a euphemism, since the suspension was indefinite) collection of the tax that had triggered the revolt.

In fact, the project to shore up the river banks was not revived until much later. In 1923, a bad poem by Zhang Jian would celebrate its completion, glossing over the fact that the achievement was much less ambitious than had been planned. Since the banks were still crumbling, Nantong county government imposed a new tax in 1928, with the agreement of the Provincial Construction Management, in order to strengthen them. The payment demanded was half as much as in 1912 (two *yuan* per *mu*), but still it provoked a new riot, limited to Lujinggang and quickly put down—but as in 1912, the collection of the tax was "suspended" after the riot.

The 1912 Siyugang revolt, more disciplined (no looting is recorded) and more violent (more than twenty people killed between the two camps) than the average, has further claims upon our interest. Firstly, as we have noted, because the tax hit landlords and tenants at the same time, it promoted even more than usual the local solidarity characteristic of antitax resistance. Secondly, it bore the marks of its time: the transition between the Empire and the Republic. The project to repair and strengthen the Yangzi's banks was a product of the New Policies, in the last days of the Qing Dynasty. All the same, I have refrained from adding the Siyugang revolt to those to be examined in the next chapter (which will be about resistance to modernization, whereas Siyugang was an uprising against a tax). Had they not been threatened with losing money, the riverside dwellers would not have opposed work that would have protected their fields. The new climate created with the change of government perhaps encouraged the rebels, but such an assumption would be based mainly on suspect testimony by members of the local elite, who went to great lengths to induce the authorities to send in reinforcements. The notables who signed a letter to the Jiangsu governor on 10 July identified one of the rebel leaders (Zheng Jianrong, alias Zhu Tianrong) as a former member of the Red Band (Hongbang) who had been a full-time salt smuggler. On the basis of this one fact, they claimed that since the Republic was repressing smuggling more vigorously than the previous administration, the smugglers, who had been accustomed to trafficking undisturbed in this isolated village at the edge of Nantong county, had used the "tax to defend the banks" as a pretext for deceiving and stirring up the peasants.

Although this might seem a little hasty, we have no excuse for failing to mention smuggling, which was left out of two accounts written long after the fact, in the PRC. One of them (Jiang 1988a) has Zheng Jianrong as a salt trader and the other (Fei 1986) says nothing about him. And this is another interesting point that the Siyugang revolt shares with other episodes: the contradictory accounts of the same revolt by partisan sources. Unlike the smuggling explanation, the accusation of corruption, never mentioned in the elites' version, is central to the accounts reaching us from the PRC: they say a clique of notables cornered the management of the Yangzi project and profited nicely from it. The way in which the Siyugang revolt unfolded seems to confirm that accusation, and by the same token, to lend political and social coloring to the antitax resistance movement. Apart from the school and the Local Autonomy Bureau, all the buildings destroyed by the rebels were the private homes of about ten powerful families who controlled the "four ports" (Siyugang, Lujinggang, and two neighboring ports). Similarly, apart from the soldiers and policemen killed in the battle, members of these same families were the only ones (a good half-dozen in all) to have been deliberately slaughtered by the insurgents.

A final point: it is extremely rare for sources to provide us with so many pointers toward understanding—though incompletely and hypothetically—the social allegiances of the leaders and instigators of a revolt.

SOURCES: On the 1912 riot: Yangzhou shifan xueyuan lishixi 1961, 223–29; Fei 1986, 5–9; Qian 1986, 10–25; Jiang 1988a, 1–5. On the 1928 riot: *Tongtong ribao*, Nantong, 9–10 August 1928, 14 June 1929, and 19 October 1929; Jiang 1988a, 5–7; an untitled three-page manuscript with not a single reference, snatched in a keen contest in Nantong on 15 October 1987.

MULTIPLE TAXES

The Siyugang peasants rebelled against one particular tax (*mujuan*) and they were far from being the only ones.[2] There remain those cases, more or less the same number, where their fellows rose up against a multiplicity of taxes and surtaxes. In Yangzhong (discussed in Box 1.1), the taxpayers were apparently paying 9 taxes (Dai 1957, 8) and that was not a record. At the same time (in 1930), the authorities were collecting 10 in Kaiping county (Guangdong), 13 in Yiwu (Zhejiang), 18 in Yuanmou (Yunnan), 20 in Sui Xian (Hubei), 21 in Xushui (Hebei), and 26 in Jiangpu (Jiangsu) (Sun Zuoqi 1935, 157; Duan 1935, 53–54). The figures tell only half the story. Here, for example, is a rundown of taxes and surtaxes in Laiyang in 1910 at the time, it is true, when the New Policies were causing a tax explosion. There was a tax for schools; a tax to renovate the Confucius temple; a police tax; a tax for the blind; a tax on theater performances; two taxes on accommodation; excise duties on linen, peanuts, oil, potatoes, tobacco, and rope; a registration tax on land transfers; a head tax; and a tax called, simply, *mujuan* (tax per *mu*), without any specific application (Wang 1954, 210–11; Prazniak 1980, 52–53 and 1999, 68). At the provincial level in the early 1930s, 105 different surtaxes were in force in Jiangsu and 739 in neighboring Zhejiang (Chen

1966, 239). In each sector, the surtaxes accumulated little by little as spending requirements grew.³ When a "surtax for construction" proved insufficient, authorities added a "special contribution to construction"; then came dedicated surtaxes "for bridge construction," "for road construction," the latter being supplemented in its turn by a "special contribution for road construction." Successive add-ons were rarely balanced by abolishing old taxes no longer applicable. In some provinces people were still paying by the early 1930s the surtax imposed twenty years earlier to cover installation expenditure on the first Parliament created by the new Republican government. Other stopgap surtaxes were labelled more crudely (recalling the twentieths raised in France under Louis XIV and Louis XV): for example, "surtax of a tenth," "surtax of two-tenths," "surtax of three *yuan*," or "surtax to cover the budget deficit." Ordinarily, however, there was no shortage of imagination among financial administrators, as was confirmed by a popular saying, "Since Ancient Times we'd never heard of a tax on shit—but today only farts are free" (Dai 1957, 3; saying also recalled in many other sources). Listing and counting the surtaxes is easy; it is another thing to measure their accumulation or to estimate their overall amount at any given moment, if only because both varied enormously from one province to another, and even between two neighboring counties. We must be content to note that, in 1912, Guangdong was the only province where the overall burden of surtaxes slightly exceeded the basic land tax, whereas by 1933 there remained only three provinces (Anhui, Jiangxi, and Fujian) where it was lower. That same year, 1933, in all Jiangsu counties, surtaxes were more costly than the basic tax; in over half of them, they were more than three times the basic tax; in two-fifths, six times; and the record, for this one province, reached 26 times the amount of the basic tax (Sun Xiaocun 1935, 25).⁴ This situation breached the provisions of a 1928 law prohibiting tax authorities from imposing surtaxes beyond the amount of the basic tax. The same law had another article capping the overall burden of tax—basic tax and surtaxes together—at 1 percent of the land's value. The authorities found a way around this as well.⁵

In some counties, by the end of the Empire, the amount of the surtaxes was very low; in others, it had risen almost to the level of the basic tax. In China overall, in 1908, all surtaxes taken together made up 47 percent of overall land tax revenue, the remaining 53 percent provided by the basic tax. This proportion had already grown considerably since the heyday of the Qing. In 1753 it had amounted to about one-fifth of national tax income, the remaining four-fifths being supplied from the basic tax (Wang 1973, 80). So the increase in surtaxes began well before the Republic. The rigidity of the fiscal system in operation since the start of the Ming Dynasty had already favored their proliferation (Wang 1973 and Huang 1974). The land tax took account only of the surface areas of land, ignoring their value or farm incomes. The area of a field (estimates were rarely updated) was multiplied by a rate (so much per *mu*), itself variable according to the supposed fertility of the field. Sometimes, tax inspectors were content to adjust the land area by means of a fiscal *mu*, which was smaller in irrigated paddy fields than on dry slopes. This rate itself remained fixed for a long time. When adaptations were made, they came a long way behind the rate of change in every department (including demographic progress, agricultural advances, and price rises) and were largely inadequate. The county magistrates could not possibly finance their growing expenditure—not even to pay their administrative staff who could not keep pace as the population tripled—out of a "regular" income that was too inflexible. They had no recourse other than to impose surcharges indexed to the land tax, which again did not provide enough. They had to find other sources of funding, to create or increase other taxes, as is demonstrated by the century-long fall in the share of public revenues derived from land tax, including the surtaxes (Wang 1973, 49–66, also 10, 19, 33, 83; Huang 1974, 184–86).

The growth in the number of surcharges on the land tax under the Republic, as well as taxes and various surtaxes, continued—but the amounts grew as well, as had been common under the Empire. Another inheritance from the Empire was the role assigned to legions of clerks, messengers, tax collectors, and other agents, paid little or nothing, who were the administration's drudges rather than its junior officials: a sub-administration, as it were, or a para-administration. A magistrate, whose time in the post was usually quite short and who could rely only on a handful of qualified officials, was reduced to handing out numerous jobs (usually the unpopular ones) to this string of agents, his control over whom, being proportionate to their pay, was negligible. They tended to take their money where they could find it, in this case from the taxpayer, rather like pre-revolutionary France's Farmers-General handing over to the Treasury what was due—and skimming something off the top.

As we have seen, the Republic, especially under the Guomindang, attempted to take things in hand and to extend the administration's hold over the countryside by dividing each county into wards (*qu*), from five to ten, and each *qu* into *xiang* (large villages). The posts created in each ward were financed by the county, which then had to shoulder extra administrative spending, to which was soon added, thanks to modernization, the growing costs of security, education, and infrastructure. Since the counties enjoyed wide financial autonomy, they multiplied the surcharges on the land tax (their main source of revenue) and various surtaxes, without informing the central government of the tax increases they were introducing (Duara 1988, Chapter 3).

Abuses, Frauds, Smuggling, and Repression

Up until now, I have hardly mentioned corruption.[6] I did just suggest it in relation to the para-administration, most of whose members are likened by Prasenjit Duara to "courtier-entrepreneurs" always tempted to become "courtier-predators," in contrast to the "courtier-protectors" of the traditional gentry, who were less present in the countryside in Republican times because of the insecurity prevailing there and the attractions of urban civilization (Duara 1988, Chapters 2, 3, and 6).[7] Contrary to what we might infer from a considerable amount of testimony, corruption was not the primary cause of the growth in the tax burden. The most honest magistrate could scarcely avoid multiplying and raising surtaxes simply to fulfill his obligations.

That being said, not only was corruption widespread but the authoritarian, if not brutal, approach of the most junior of administrators to the mass of village taxpayers threatened constantly to make their tax obligations more distressing or more burdensome. Sometimes the administration would install public strongboxes in the villages during the period of tax collection. Taxpayers would come to deposit what they owed, which for them represented the least expensive solution: they had simply to pay a modest surcharge to cover the expense of installing and guarding the strongboxes. In other cases, especially when the tax was paid in kind, taxpayers were required to transport it into town and to wait in line at the public granary, where often they were forced to sleep on the spot to keep an eye on their load. By the time the staff did grudgingly consent to inspect their grain, taxpayers might have lost one or several work days in delivering it and spent as much as—or even more than—the value of the grain itself. Even when payment was in money, it took time to travel to the yamen, and illiterate taxpayers were likely to be bullied or cheated by the staff. Some other counties collected taxes directly from the taxpayers' homes. This spared them those expenses and unpleasantness but exposed them to others. For lack of staff, the administration entrusted this task to agents of the para-administration, who often extorted from taxpayers their transportation expenses (adding, for example, a land tax surcharge for "wear on shoe leather"), sometimes demanded overnight accommodation and food, and in the worst cases, forced ignorant or timid people to pay more than they owed, pocketing the difference.[8]

Although the latter case, strictly speaking, falls into the category of corruption, we should linger a moment over mixed situations that might combine legal and illegal profits. In Wujin county, Jiangsu, the subject of a meticulous study (Wan, Zhuang, and Wu 1934), neither the Finance Bureau responsible for administering the land tax nor the Second Division of the county government, which took over its functions in September 1932, was in a position effectively to supervise the setting of tax rolls, which remained in the hands of the traditional collectors. The latter set the tax rolls on the basis of the "authentic registers" drawn up by the *liangfang* (custodians of the land register). The registers were actually owned by the *liangfang*, who passed them from father to son, or in default of a son, sold them to a colleague. The administration, being obliged to employ those who had acquired the register or who controlled its tax base, was supposed to remunerate them. But the commitment of officials to their work and *liangfang* to their registers was not prompted by their pay, which was extremely low: ten *yuan* per month (the wages of an unskilled worker in the textile industry) for the staff and even less for the *liangfang*. Raising these wages would have been a step—but not the only one—toward winning the loyalty of tax employees. If the authorities did not do this, it was undoubtedly because of their financial difficulties but mostly because they knew that these employees derived far more substantial incomes from their responsibilities than their measly pay.

Some of this income was legal. The authorities passed on to the staff part of the collection expenses that every taxpayer had to pay on top of the land tax. Another category of registry agent, separate from the *liangfang*, did not receive any fixed wages at all, but he was authorized to take a commission on the property transfer fees paid by purchasers. This was not enough to live on, but a clever agent could make it pay more by adapting a fixed transfer fee of 0.1 *yuan* into a fee of 0.1 *yuan* per *mu* (Sun Zuoqi 1935, 365). Here we have moved on to illegal pickings, of which I shall give just a few examples. When the peasants in Tongcheng, in the northwest of Anhui, came to make a "disaster declaration" in order to win a tax remission, the staff who registered their declarations extorted from them a "tax" payment, quite illegally, of 120–130 copper coins per *mu*. Still in northern Anhui, collectors made peasants pay for their tax statements (Sun Zuoqi 1935, 367). Profits of this kind were small, but they mounted with repetition, as did tax collectors' fiddles when converting one coinage into another.[9] Other practices, far more profitable, were widespread enough to win places in the swindlers' jargon. For example, "putting on a hat" (*daimao*) or "wearing boots" (*chuanxie*) meant leaving a space before or after the tax amount and adding above (the hat) or below (the boots) an extra figure that was rubbed out once the taxpayer had paid (Sun Zuoqi 1935, 365). Similarly, when it was time for the autumn disaster assessment, a clerk (*lishu*) could "sell a disaster" (*maizai*), a nonexistent one, to the taxpayer, thus swapping a tax reduction for a sweetener. Conversely, he could "hide a disaster" (*nizai*), a real one, unless his victim came across with a bribe (Zhang 1935, 968).[10] Selling disasters was more common than hiding them. The usual victim of frauds was the administration, rather than the taxpayer. Either the tax agent pocketed money due to the Treasury or more often he would share the profit with a complicit taxpayer. For example, he might register a slightly less fruitful than normal harvest as a serious disaster or pass off a long-cultivated field as one recently cleared (and thus less highly taxed), or even as uncultivated land and not subject to tax (Zhang 1935, 362).

And there were deliberate errors that did not involve connivance between taxpayer and tax employee. The agent could pretend to confuse two homonyms: a Wang Xiao'er (Little Wang 2) who had paid his tax and a Wang Xiaosan (Little Wang 3) who had not. By classing Xiao'er among the *minqian* (debtors), the agent put his payment to one side, then pocketed it when the inevitable write-off of arrears occurred. Instead of cancelling the arrears, sometimes the administration awarded bonuses to agents who succeeded in forcing defaulters to pay their debts. In such cases, collectors were content to pick up the payment as usual, writing up the returns as "payment of arrears" and classing an equal sum as "unpaid" (and thus future "arrears") for the current tax year.

Sometimes collectors would write off (as dead, fled, or simply defaulting) taxpayers who had paid their taxes as usual, then lend back to the administration the money they had stolen from it. Similarly, magistrates and their assistants would use the Treasury's money to invest on their own account. Instead of paying money owed to the provincial authorities straightaway, they would lend it out at interest or invest it in business ventures. Or a magistrate might declare that only seven-tenths of the sums due had been paid and share with his accomplices the remaining three-tenths. Or he might overstate staff numbers in the tax offices by declaring twenty employees where there were only ten, paying to himself the extra ten salaries, just as army officers did (on a greater scale) with the pay and food of phantom soldiers (Sun Zuoqi 1935, 359–66 for all the cases cited in the last two paragraphs).

Although corruption was markedly more widespread within the para-administration, it was present at all levels, from county government to village heads, by way of the local tax collectors and the police charged with picking up late payments (cf. the case of the magistrate who orchestrated the embezzling himself, in *PWP*, Chapter 5). A survey by Nankai University based on eleven Hebei counties uncovered cases of corruption in every one of them (Sun Xiaocun 1935, 21). I have relied mainly on the most detailed of available sources (Sun Zuoqi 1935), but there are hardly any contemporary accounts that do not mention flagrant examples of corruption. Year in and year out, the sums milked by officials and corrupt agents added up to a significant proportion of the tax owing.

The administration, faced with the corruption of its regular staff and, even more, of its agents (para-administration), combined with the inexhaustible ingenuity of the taxpayers, was driven to impose countless controls and nitpicking regulations in order to fight tax evasion. Some revolts arose from these controls or from new regulations perceived as unbearable or iniquitous. This was the case on Daishan Island, off Ningbo, during summer 1936 (see Box 5.2).

Taxation

Box 5.2   Salt Workers and Fishermen Take on the Fiscal Inquisition: Daishan, Zhejiang, July 1936

The multiplicity of taxes relating to salt and the nitpicking regulations and partial withdrawal of some privileges were at the root of a bloody revolt by the salt workers and fishermen of Daishan Island, in the Zhoushan Archipelago. The island was the primary center for salt production and the principal maritime fishing port of Zhejiang. Its population, estimated between 50,000 and 70,000, swelled in late spring to double that number with the arrival of fishermen from the mainland. From early May to late August, between 2,000 and 3,000 fishing boats were permanently crammed into its ports taking on supplies of salt for preserving fish while at sea. For the island's salt workers, sales to the fishermen represented the better part of their meager incomes. Their sales to the *aoshang* (salt traders approved by the administration) and the *aozhu* (public salt storehouses) amounted only to a third or a quarter of their annual production of 45,000 tons. The rest, apart from what the islanders consumed (no more than 500 tons) and what the smugglers took (which is hard to estimate) went to the fishermen subject to a tax far lower than that imposed on the "official salt" sold to the *aoshang*.

The basic tax on the official salt amounted to more than half of the price of the salt (two *yuan* per picul, sold for between three and four *yuan*); on top of this, salt workers had to pay a series of extra taxes that they viewed as illegal and blamed on the greed of the administration and the local police: a tax on each salt pan, a "tax on "horses and carriages" (intended to cover the transportation costs of salt administration officials), as well as taxes on drying, stockpiling, and weighing the salt. The huge price difference between salt for nutrition and for salting fish induced the Weights and Measures Bureau, where the salt was weighed before being taxed, to have it colored red or black when destined for the fishermen, to stop them from reselling any of it. So the fishermen complained that they could not find anyone to buy fish stained red or black from the salt. Then a new measure fanned the flames: until then, the fishermen had been able to buy all the salt they needed from the Daishan saltworks, once they paid a fixed tax of four *yuan* and received a certificate valid for the whole season. But with the new regulations, this certificate restricted them to buying only 100 piculs of salt, scarcely one-seventh or one-eighth of a fishing boat's average yearly consumption. The salt workers, for their part, grumbled about the new obligation to pile the salt into heaps, in order to facilitate tax controls. They complained that it is difficult to dry salt when it is piled into small mountains.

The 1936 revolt was not the first. In 1919, the change in the color of salt destined for the fishermen had already provoked a riot, during which fishermen from Fenghua killed the manager of the Daishan saltworks administration. In 1935, a demonstration supported by a petition signed by 34 notables rallied 1,000 salt workers. In 1936, a good fishing season had forced salt prices up and fish prices down: the fish market was glutted, or else the fish rotted for lack of salt. So it was fishermen who launched the movement, but they were supported from the outset by the salt workers, who were infuriated by over-regulation and tax controls. On 8 July, more than 2,000 fishermen and salt workers gathered at the Temple of Wealth and Happiness and agreed to present a joint petition to the Weights and Measures Bureau, expressing their respective grievances: the salt workers seeking an end to stockpiling their salt and the fishermen an end to coloring theirs. Over the next few days, the movement was reinforced by two bands of mainland fishermen: the Hongqibang (Red Flag Band, fishermen from Fenghua county) and the Lanqibang (Blue Flag Band, from Taizhou prefecture). The last meeting took place in another temple on 12 July. Then, the following afternoon, more than 3,000 fishermen and salt workers launched a demonstration. They surrounded the headquarters of the salt police (*jisidui*), charged with combating smuggling.

The demonstration was peaceful in principle, but it degenerated when the police fired on a crowd they considered threatening and killed a fisherman, or according to another source, a salt worker. The demonstrators became enraged and seized the policemen's guns, then invaded their headquarters looking for more weapons and ammunition. The clashes redoubled, the shops closed, the number of rioters swelled to between 5,000 and 6,000 salt workers and fishermen. Piling up wood and coal along two sides of the building, the rioters set fire to the Weights and Measures Bureau, then killed the Bureau head and three employees. The police, now under siege, fired from inside their police stations and from the headquarters of the *jisidui*. At about ten in the evening, the police came running out of a burning building and some rioters stoned them, hurling enormous rocks at their heads, cutting their throats, and stabbing them in their bellies. Others grabbed their guns and turned them against the fleeing policemen. At around four in the morning, after laborious preparations, the insurgents set a second building on fire. Inside, they seized 40 to 50 guns. By dawn on 14 July, 20 or so policemen were dead (more than one-tenth of the force deployed), while among the rioters there were over 30 dead and 100 wounded. In the evening, the fishermen fled the island, and the police, reinforced by sailors from Haizhou and Qingdao (two ports quite a distance from Daishan), machine-gunned them while still at sea. They killed a score of them over the coming days, pursuing other fishermen as far as Ningbo and Fenghua on the mainland. Still more rioters, again about 20 or so, were arrested and transferred to Hangzhou for trial, while voices were being raised in sympathy for the poverty-stricken salt workers of Daishan, calling for action on their behalf.

While it is likely that it was the large number of the demonstrators that frightened the police into firing and that, in turn, it was the killing of the petitioner that sparked off the disturbance, that riot owed much to the strengthening of fiscal controls and the challenge to a traditional privilege: the unlimited purchase of lightly taxed salt for fishermen's professional needs. The administration resorted to these unpopular measures, not so much to boost its income from the salt tax as to combat smuggling. It suspected, often rightly, the salt workers and fishermen of being inveterate smugglers themselves—while they considered themselves persecuted by it. If a little *siyan* (contraband salt) was discovered on a boat, the whole cargo was taxed. Moreover, so the fishermen said, sometimes the rain altered or washed out the salt's color. And, if salt workers and traders were to be believed, the character *guan* ("official") printed with a seal on a salt load was sometimes rubbed off by the effect of jolting when the already taxed salt was being transported. In such cases, the police confiscated the salt and fined heavily those considering or claiming themselves innocent, and sometimes they ended up in prison. In Daishan and elsewhere, the salt police considered that, for many salt workers, smuggling on a day-to-day basis was really a "second job" (*fuye*). Alongside well-armed and organized "salt bandits," how many peddlers were going round the villages with salt hidden under rice or wood at the bottom of their jute sacks, and how many salt workers' wives feigned pregnancy to carry around their bellies the tiny quantities of salt they delivered to the tradesmen!

SOURCES: Beyond a brief mention in *ZJNSZ*, vol. 3, 1024–25, see Meng Yu (pseudonym) 1936, 69–73; Sheng 1936, 54–57; and especially *Ningbo ribao*, 16, 22, 23, 24, 25, 26, 27, and 28 July 1936, of which the very long article of 16 July is the most substantial). These three sources do not agree on all points; and I have not been exclusively faithful to any of them. For the economic, fiscal, and social background, see Li Guoqi 1982, 28–31 and 408–10; *Zhoushan shizhi*, 1992, 237, 239, 243, 246, 250; and Muscolino 2005.

SALT SMUGGLING AND THE BATTLE TO STOP IT

The state's crackdown on traffickers and the sometimes bloody clashes it led to was reflected in the numerous taxes on goods, starting with opium; but, as in Daishan, it was the salt tax that aroused by far the most confrontations. The "private salt" might be either the contraband salt as I briefly described it, or the lower quality "earth salt" extracted from the soil by the inhabitants of some regions for their personal

Table 5.1
Price (in *yuan*) of a Picul of Salt in Pinghu and Haiyan, Zhejiang

Purchase price from producer	Tax	Expenses + profit	Sale price to consumer
Official salt 1.2	6.9	3.29 (for *yan ao*)	11.39
Private salt 1.66 to 2	n/a	about 5 (for smuggler)	up to 7

NOTE: The *yan ao* were the traders licensed to sell the official salt.
SOURCE: Wu Xiaochen 1935, 85–90.

consumption and to eke out the meager incomes they could wrest from their near-barren land. To give an idea how dear was the official salt and how rich the profits from smuggling, we shall cite the example of two coastal counties, Pinghu and Haiyan, in northern Zhejiang.

The huge profit to the smuggler did not prevent everyone else from benefiting as well, from the producer who was better paid to the consumer who paid much less for his picul of salt.

At the official price, the salt worker could get by if he owned a furnace and a salt marsh from which he could extract the brine.[11] If he was a tenant, he could feed his family only by keeping part of his production hidden from the rigorous controls to which he was subjected. In the case of salt obtained by pan and furnace, he was required to declare every day the time at which he lit his furnace and to deliver every evening the whole of his production to the *yan ao*. The authorities would estimate the quantity produced by the length of the boiling time. The salt worker tried to have his pan of salt on the furnace by dawn before going to ask authorization to proceed, so by the time it came through, the first panful was ready. In the evening, he did the same: before delivering his day's production, he took care to put an extra panful on the fire.

The salt workers who concealed a little bit of their output were the small fry of the smuggling business. We can say this much for the peddlers who marketed this "private salt" across the region and for their customers who bought it for their own consumption: smuggling was ubiquitous and every one tried to profit from it. On a wholly different scale, the professional traffickers—the equivalent, you might say, of the "faux-sauniers" (salt smugglers) of pre-revolutionary France—were capable of financing fleets of 100 to 200 junks, flanked by armed escort vessels and preceded by spies whose job was to look out for the salt squads and policemen. The latter were not always eager for battle. Often, they were content to stop three or four junks (this being enough to guarantee them a bonus from the administration) and to let the rest of the convoy pass unchallenged. In some regions, bribing the police became routine. The traffickers paid for their right of way, just as merchants paid fees to the brigands to smooth their cargos' passage along unsafe roads (Wu Xiaochen 1935, 89). Nevertheless, not all the police were for sale; sometimes they confronted the smugglers in murderous battles. And the "salt bandits" (their official title, justified for once), far from confining themselves to smuggling and fighting only when attacked, caused all sorts of trouble. Some of it was in connection with their business: they robbed the "official salt" warehouses and attacked the salt administration offices. Some was not: they looted rice shops, pawnshops, the homes of rich scholar gentry (*shenfu*), besieged police stations, and stole guns and ammunition.[12]

Although the police did take action against these assaults and looting, they were accused of showing less zeal against big organized trafficking than against small smugglers and of cracking down on the petty criminals—and indeed on some who were not. Some people claimed that police officers had planted salt in their homes in order to demand bribes. Such stereotyped accusations were freely plugged in compilations published in the PRC and had already been current during the 1930s, even in specialized official publications (*yanwu tekan*; magazines devoted to "salt affairs") and from the mouths of Nationalist leaders. The latter cited the hatred and fear excited by the "salt police," in terms recalling the repeated warnings by licensed representatives of French kings between the sixteenth and eighteenth centuries: "Ask the man in the street: 'What causes the greatest suffering to the people?' He will unfailingly reply, 'The salt police'" (Report by the Jiangsu Provincial Governor to the Finance Ministry, 31 December, 1934, cited in Ding, ed. 1990, 290).

Here are three examples from the litany of incidents involving the foot soldiers of the trafficking business (taken from Ding, ed. 1990, 289–91). In August 1935, a peasant whose wife was sick had no money to pay the doctor. So he set off to give him five pounds of "private" salt.

Box 5.3   Commonplace Encounter Between Salt Workers and the Salt Police: Rudong, Jiangsu, 1932

On 15 July 1932, in Dingjiabuzi (Rudong county, Jiangsu), a salt worker called Ding Weiyong took home a picul of brine, saying it was for salting his cucumbers. On the dike, he was accosted by two salt policemen, who accused him of smuggling. After being slapped, punched, and threatened, Ding seized one officer's pistol and fired it at him, injuring the man's shoulder blade. Ding's neighbors, hearing the shot, came running up with pitchforks and, in their turn, wounded the other policeman. Salt police reinforcements arrived and arrested Ding and several other workers, taking them to the neighboring township and torturing them. The gong was sounded and 400 to 500 salt workers and peasants armed with pitchforks turned out in response, chasing after the salt police, who opened fire, killing one of their pursuers and wounding two others. The authorities, to calm the villagers, released the men arrested.

SOURCE: Zhonggong Rudong xianwei dangshi bangongshe ed. 1986, 40–41 and 180.

Along the way he met a salt policeman, who confiscated the basket, beat up the peasant, and pushed him into the water, where he drowned. On an unknown date but still during the 1930s, a man named Qiu went to the pawnshop in Yincheng, Hubei, to redeem a pledge, taking with him six pounds of "private" salt. He came across some members of the salt police who arrested him and shot him. In December 1936, in Nanxiyang, Dongyang county, Zhejiang, several salt policemen intercepted a peddler on his way to market with two pounds of smuggled salt in a bamboo basket. They ordered him to reveal the identity of the person who sold him the salt. His reply being less than clear, they started hitting him. A crowd gathered, the salt police opened fire, and two people were killed. Sometimes, however, the petty criminals stood up for themselves, provoking clashes between salt police and villagers (Box 5.3).

Far more serious affairs fairly often set salt workers and villagers against the salt police, especially in the north of the country, on the borders of Hebei, Henan, and Shandong. In a dozen counties close to the Yellow River and its former tributaries, the soil was more propitious for salt extraction than for agriculture (Thaxton 1997). The upper basin of the Yellow River crosses vast stretches of salty ground. As the rate of drop declines in the middle and lower reaches, the slower water flow allows the infiltration of part of the salt content in the water. During the summer when evaporation increases, salt tends to accumulate near the surface of the exposed ground, and villagers scrape the earth to extract it.

Because it was not costly other than in labor, this form of production apparently began under the Ming Dynasty. For a long time, the imperial administration closed its eyes to an activity which, it presumed, provided people too poor to afford the official salt with enough for their own needs. This was never truly the case. And, by the twentieth century, the extension of a traffic that provided a living, not just to producers, but also to a dense network of peddlers was competing—because it escaped the tax—with the official salt or "sea salt" produced along the shores of the Bohai Sea and transported from the coast in convoys by the company holding the legal monopoly of salt trading in the region. Successive governments during the Republican period were increasingly intolerant of this shortfall in revenue. With the coming to power of the Nationalists, repression intensified. Offices for controlling salt sales were opened in each of the three provinces, and salt police squads were attached to them. (The monopoly company had its own police, as feared as the state police.) Security squads patrolled the producing regions in all directions, upturning the pans where the villagers dried the salt, smashing the salt furnaces (where, as in southwestern Shandong, this method coexisted with the drying method), destroying the tools that could be used to extract or produce salt, confiscating salt stocks found in salt workers' homes, arresting many of these salt workers and peddlers, and sometimes killing any who looked likely to resist (Ding ed. 1990, 277–78 and particularly Thaxton 1997).

Between 1930 and 1935, the upsurge of unrest among the northern *xiao min*—"nitrate people," or as they were more usually called on official charge sheets, *xiao fan* ("nitrate criminals"), or indeed *xiao fei* ("nitrate brigands")—was a classic defense reaction (Thaxton 1997 and Ding ed. 1990; see also *DFZZ*, vol. 32, no. 10, 1935, 128–29). The *xiao min* felt they were resisting a government attack on their livelihoods and protecting themselves against the violence of the security forces. As always, this resistance developed only as a last resort, when it proved too dangerous simply to disobey the law by producing and clandestinely selling salt. After all, until recently, they had been producing and selling it with little need for concealment.

Updating the Cadastre

At first sight, it was surprising that taxpayers should have opposed the surveying of their properties and the updating of the land register, which might have distributed the tax burden more fairly. That was not the administration's main purpose: it wanted to increase its revenue by identifying what were called "black fields" (*heidi* or *heitian*; properties not registered and not taxed), but those few cases where it did succeed in updating the register resulted in fairer distribution of the tax burden.

The administration's initiative was not merely justified but indispensable and urgent, so flagrant was the disparity between the tax rolls and the real ownership of land. In innumerable localities across the length and breadth of China, the cadastre had not been reviewed for decades, sometimes not for centuries. In central and southern China, many rolls had never been restored since the Taiping revolutionaries destroyed them. Elsewhere, in some cases, the rolls on which tax bills were calculated dated back to 1713.[13]

The situation was not everywhere quite so disastrous, but it was common knowledge in the smallest districts that many a field cultivated for generations had never been registered and had escaped taxation. Conversely, fields made impossible to cultivate because a watercourse had moved its channel, or fields carried away by floods or erosion, or fields encroached on by the widening of paths or roads were still being taxed. A well-known saying ran: "There are untaxed estates and also people paying land tax without owning any land" (*you chan wu liang, you liang wu chan*). Although the saying struck a balance between the two phenomena, the first case was decidedly more widespread than the second. For every phantom field on the cadastre, how many "black fields," estates not registered and not taxed, were still being cultivated every year! They might be alluvial land created after floods, progressively cultivated slopes, polders reclaimed from the sea or from lakes, or formerly salty or marshy stretches of land long since improved.[14] The improvement of lightly taxed parcels of land was rarely taken into account, because magistrates had no interest in increasing tax quotas for their counties—that would make it more difficult to collect the taxes. The good magistrate was one who brought in the taxes and maintained public order, which was threatened by antitax riots. For the same reason, he would conceal or reduce the extent of "black fields" by converting several *mu* of newly identified fields into a single tax *mu* (Ho 1959, 104–16).

These practices dated back to imperial times, but the Republic went along with them.[15] However, the disparity between the true ownership of land, its area, and value, and its tax registration was the source of injustices and inequalities between taxpayers and of an enormous loss of earnings for the administration. When cultivated fields were not taxed, other landowners in the locality saw their own burden increased since the quota of tax due remained unchanged. Just as the magistrate, anxious not to increase his quota, was obliged to pile up surcharges on a land tax that was imposed only on duly registered estates, the unfortunate landowners with no "black fields" were left paying the surcharges, while their luckier, craftier, or more powerful neighbors escaped them.

Officially, the administration had undertaken the review of the register in order to distribute taxation more fairly and even to lighten the tax burden on each registered *mu*, but as we have seen, its primary aim was to increase the revenue to the Treasury. That was the guiding purpose behind the two main land surveys embarked upon under the Republic, first by Yuan Shikai and later by the Nationalist government (Li 2005, Chapter 11). Since the creation of a new cadastre on a national scale was a very costly and long-drawn-out affair, the authorities tried to introduce it first at the local and regional level. Alternatively, they were content with a registration process designed to track the "black fields," which the owners were required to register in their entirety. Progress with these two tasks was slow, partly because of the expense (modest in the case of mere registration) and mostly because of landowners' obstructiveness.

This last problem, combined with the local authorities' lack of zeal, explains how little success was achieved by successive campaigns to register the "black fields." Not only did magistrates see more drawbacks than advantages in widening the tax base in their electoral districts, they also deemed it imprudent to compromise their good relations with the notables who owned the largest areas of "black land." These two considerations lost some of their force under the Nationalist administration, in that the county governments held on to part of the land tax revenue and were less dependent on cooperation from the local elite. But above all it was the government's more effective control at the subcounty level of the ward that explains its success—though relative—in detecting "black land" during the 1930s. I may speak of the Guomindang's "success" only while comparing it with the manifest failure of its predecessors; in fact, its own achievements were slight (Li 2005, 248–50). Its offensive against "black fields" was further impeded by widespread corruption among its local agents and by village solidarity. This deterred village heads from reporting honestly to their superiors the full extent of "black land" and other villagers from claiming the rewards offered to informers.

In the absence of reliable statistics on the (small) percentage of "black fields" detected before and especially during the Nationalist time in government, here are a few indications as to how the review of the register progressed. In 1936, only six provinces could pride themselves on some modest results, four of them restricted to a very small number of counties. The other two were Yunnan, which updated the register for one-third of its counties (37 out of 110), and Jiangsu, which carried out either the first or the second of its two tasks in half its counties: revising the register in 18 and registering landed properties in 14 out of a total of 63 counties (Tien 1972, 160). The government was nonetheless justified in pointing out that wherever they did manage to complete the cadastral survey, everyone benefited: the tax rate per *mu* fell considerably, most taxpayers paid less, and the Treasury's take went up.[16]

Everyone benefited, except for the owners of large stretches of "black land." It was often they who were behind the main instances of violent resistance—as contrasted with the nonviolent resistance mentioned earlier—to the government's attempts to detect "black land" or review land registers. According to the administration, the rich were exploiting the poor by fabricating rumors intended to mobilize them. There is no doubt that big landowners set the pace for tax evasion. The proportion of unregistered land was higher on their estates than on land cultivated by small farmers, higher also on land cultivated by village heads than by the other villagers (Duara 1988, 23; *Jacqueries*, 309). Having said that, everyone knew about it and did their utmost to prevent land from being registered. Resistance to the surveying and registering of land was an eminently popular cause and proved victorious. With those exceptions mentioned above, the Nationalist government's efforts on this front had pretty well collapsed by the time war became imminent and put an end to them. An end, let us be clear, in "free" China: in some areas of North China occupied by the Japanese, the cadastral surveys were promptly carried out. They were reported to have doubled the taxable land areas in eastern Hebei (Duara 1988, 233–34). So this was an indispensable reform that could be pushed through only by the occupying power.

Fierce resistance to field surveys (*qinzhang tudi*) and land registration (*tudi chenbao*), starting from the end of the Empire, was often led by big landowners but regularly drew support from a large majority of small taxpayers.[17] It went ahead under the Republic, its two peak outbreaks coinciding with the two main campaigns (see above) to detect "black fields." The first was during the last two years of Yuan Shikai's dictatorship; the second, still more significant, swelled to dozens of riots during the Nanjing decade. Most episodes in the first outbreak occurred in North China, where Yuan exerted most authority;[18] almost every incident in the second was in the area most tightly controlled by the Nationalists: the lower reaches of the Yangzi, including a harshly repressed riot that shook the city of Yangzhou, Jiangsu, in 1932 (see Box 5.4).[19]

The impact of the Jiangdu affair, as is confirmed by the numbers of people involved and the authorities' harsh response, was greater than most of those mentioned in this book. However, in the opening typology, I did not set impact or seriousness as distinguishing criteria between the different categories of rural unrest and I do not propose doing so now. All its other features mark Jiangdu as a typical antitax riot. In its beginnings it was spontaneous rather than premeditated, fed by rumors, then it gathered pace and took a new turn as the authorities reacted clumsily and with disproportionate cruelty to the challenge it posed: too many arrests, too many killed on 23 October. The peasants' actions did not exceed the usual repertoire: manhandling officials and surveyors, breaking up their camps, blocking traffic, and most of all, burning down houses. As with most other affairs we have no precise indications about the social composition of the rioters (peasant taxpayers), beyond the fact that they burned down the homes of 24 big landowners. Equally, we know nothing of the social adherence or identity of the ringleaders. The administration, which did not bring accusations against the big landowners, was content to rail against these "stupid peasants" (*yumin*) for opposing a measure that would benefit them.[20]

The Jiangdu riot was a classic case, then, in the way it developed, in the social composition of the participants, and also in its causes: as

Box 5.4   Resistance to the Cadastral Review: Jiangdu, Jiangsu, 1932

In 1931, the Jiangsu provincial parliament decided to undertake a fiscal survey, followed by the registration of newly surveyed estates. In September 1932, the Finance Bureau of the provincial government ordered all counties to complete these two operations. Although they encountered resistance elsewhere, they stirred up the most serious disorders in an area of Jiangdu county close to the city of Yangzhou. Jiangdu magistrate Yang Zhuomao nevertheless took care to call in various legal organizations (*fa tuan*) to ensure they would not obstruct the progress of the inquiry, but they were made up mostly of notables. Among the peasants, still ill-informed, rumors flew around. One story stated that the official units of measurement were smaller than the local ones and that all the extra land "discovered" by the survey would be confiscated.* In reality, surplus parcels of land could have been discovered using any unit of measurement, so numerous were the estates whose cultivated areas exceeded those written in the registers. According to some accounts, it was possible to "buy back" these extra parcels for 60 *yuan* per *mu*. Others say they would be taxed at 2 *yuan* per *mu*.

At first, the disturbances were not very significant. On 27 September, villagers in the east of the county threatened to attack magistrate Yang and his team of cadastral and tax officials. The magistrate backed off at once, closed the gates of Yangzhou, and suspended the land inventory. Calm restored, he announced on 18 October that the survey must resume. The very next day, the surveyors sent out on their duties were welcomed by dozens of women brandishing spades, hoes, and other farm implements. They destroyed the surveyors' instruments, so the next day the police escorted the surveyors into the villages. They were immediately surrounded by hundreds of peasants; and made 242 arrests (192 women and 50 men) according to one source, fewer according to others. Those held were transferred to the county jail, and in the classic manner, the ensuing riot was aimed at securing their release.

On 22 October, several thousand peasants—one source says 20,000—marched on Yangzhou. Its gates swung shut at their approach, but they broke them down, using a tree trunk as a battering ram. They invaded the city, freed the prisoners, and then ransacked the offices of the county government and the tax authorities. They burned the paperwork—tax and registration documents—and carried away any papers they had not burned. They blocked the traffic on the roads and the Grand Canal but did not prevent the magistrate from making his escape and phoning the garrison, which dispatched two companies. The soldiers resecured the city gates and made 200 new arrests.

The next day, 23 October, the peasants returned in greater numbers. According to different sources, more than 10,000 or even tens of thousands came back. Marching in three columns and armed with clubs, knives, farm tools, dry straw, and several guns, they arrived before dawn at the east, south, and west gates of Yangzhou. But this time, the police and soldiers were waiting for them outside the gates. According to the official report by two high-ranking investigators (sent to the spot by the provincial government and present in Yangzhou by 25 October), the peasants clashed with two officers and a dozen soldiers. They tried to grab the soldiers' bayonets and succeeded in seizing pistols, rifles, and four daggers—so the troops fired in the air to frighten the demonstrators. They aimed lower as well, since seven demonstrators were killed and about ten wounded. According to the American Consul-General in Nanjing, who happened to be visiting the city on a Sunday and arrived on the spot a few hours after the killings, they need not have fired on the peasants, mostly quite old. Rather, they could have forced them back with their rifle butts.

A delegation of three or four notables, led by the president of the county Chamber of Commerce, Wang Jingting, was sent outside the walls to negotiate with the peasants. There were four rebel demands: release the detained demonstrators, give up once and for all the inventorying of land, provide medical treatment for the wounded rioters and compensation for the families of those killed, and bring their killers to justice. Eight peasant delegates accompanied Wang into the city. They obtained satisfaction on points one and three: most of those arrested were freed by the following morning, with the exception of nineteen alleged ringleaders; and those seriously wounded were taken to a hospital in Zhenjiang, with support to be provided for the families of the victims. On the other hand, not one soldier was disciplined and the land inventory was only deferred until after a public information campaign, beginning in the villages from 25 October.

Even though no incident was reported comparable to the bloody battle of 23 October, the disturbances persisted for several days. From 23 to 27 October, crowds of armed peasants, variously estimated at between 6,000 and 7,000, or around 10,000, or several tens of thousands, gathered in a tavern, a temple, or near a bridge, and then went in for looting and burning down houses—the homes of peasants who had refused to join the movement; the homes of around a dozen ward, township, and village heads, deputy heads, or secretaries; the house of a member of the city's Defense Committee who opposed their first foray; and houses belonging to rich landowners. In all, 24 houses were reported burned down. The peasants also insisted that some landowners hand over their "self-defense guns," which, in one case, drove a landlord called Liu to kill a rioter. On 26 October, peasants attacked a group of four information officers who had come to explain the reasons and procedures for registering land. They beat one of them, threatening to burn him alive, after tying him to a pile of wood and setting it alight. These were no more than the final convulsions of the revolt. The shops opened their doors again, and communications were reestablished on roads and waterways.

Several dozen policemen speaking the Yangzhou dialect dressed themselves as villagers and mingled with them. They arrested ten suspected ringleaders (another source says thirteen). At dawn on 29 October, six of them (another source says twelve) were shot. Magistrate Yang, at his own request, was transferred to another post from 1 November. The suspension of the registration process, still provisional, was extended for two years. When surveying resumed in December 1934, it aroused some resistance, but no rioting. Suspended again, resumed in 1935, it dragged on for a while before being declared "completed" at the end of the year.

---

* The authorities had indeed contemplated this measure, designed to induce owners of "black fields" to declare them. The idea was to set two deadlines, imposing a modest tax if the lands were declared before the first, a heavier one before the second—and simply to confiscate them if both time limits were ignored.
SOURCES: *ZD2LDG*, file 2/2/973. The last (no. 16712) of the four documents in this file is the most detailed by far, but one-sided. Then, USDS, 893.00/12198, 25 October 1932; 893.00 PR Nanking/57 (5 November 1932) and /58 (21 December 1932); *Zhongyang ribao*, 23, 24, 25, 27, 28, 29, and 30 October 1932; *Dagong bao*, 27, 30, 31 October and 3 November 1932; Feng 1933, 534 (reprints a report in *Xinye bao*, 24 October 1932); *ZLN*, vol. 2, 1932, part 2, 99–100; *Hanjiang WSZL*, vol. 2, undated, 42–45; Stross 1982, 79–86; Bianco 1986, 280–82.

---

usual, it was something new that set it going. It is precisely this new development (the land survey, a prelude to the inventorying of land holdings) that defined this affair, as it did in all those cases cited in this third section. By their resistance (both nonviolent and violent) the taxpayers were as responsible as the administration for the disparity between the cadastre and the real distribution of land ownership. They did have some excuse for mistrusting innovations, however well intentioned. In Jiangdu, where the land tax had remained more or less stable between 1916 and 1927, it shot up from 1.6 *yuan* to 4.25 *yuan* per *mu* during the four years preceding the October 1932 riot (Stross 1982, 80). This sharp rise predisposed taxpayers to see in the surveying and registration of land the instrument and the pretext for a further increase. In themselves, even the false rumors were not implausible. The one suggesting there might be a tax on registering land was founded on the current practice of making taxpayers pay surveying expenses. The one about different units of measurement echoed the prevailing disparities between units of measurement in the Chinese countryside. During an operation to update the land inventory 30 months later in He Xian, Anhui, the villagers were to point out that the large bow used locally made their *mu* one- to two-tenths bigger than the *mu* in Jiangnan. So they feared the new survey would create bigger land areas and higher tax rates, a belief fuelled by former tax employees sacked by the magistrate (*Zhongyang ribao*, 15 April 1935).

A reduction in the rate of tax per *mu* was widely applied following new surveys of landed properties, but it was not automatic. In Xianju, Zhejiang, where taxable cultivated areas more than doubled after the July 1930 survey—the total area rose from 280,520 *mu* to 622,809 *mu*—it seems that the tax demanded per *mu* did not diminish, even though taxpayers also had to pay the surveying expenses. In any case, after the taxpayers had repeatedly and vainly requested some relief of their tax burden, they rebelled, "to fight the increase in taxes resulting from the survey" (*Xianju XZ*, 1987, 480). Similarly, villagers were sometimes required to buy the previously unregistered land; this provoked serious incidents in four coastal villages in northern Yuyao, Zhejiang, on 4 July 1935. Local peasants could not afford to buy the sandy parcels of land that they or their parents had reclaimed without precise measurements being specified, and thousands of them, having already paid the surveying expenses, attacked the survey teams, destroyed their equipment, and burned their files (Zhejiang provincial archives, file no. 1556).[21]

However far the gaps in the information accessible to taxpayers and the usual behavior of the tax collectors went toward explaining villagers' behavior, it was essential to distinguish this latter category of antitax riots (prefiguring Chapters 6 and 7) from disturbances provoked by higher taxes and the collectors' abuses.

The Social Component of Antifiscal Resistance

In principle, the tax was neither progressive nor regressive.[22] It was simply proportionate to the income, or more often, to the capital of each taxpayer. Someone with ten fiscal *mu* (in surface area adjusted according to the estimated productivity of the field) had to pay ten times more land tax than the owner of one *mu*. In reality, small taxpayers paid a little more than their share, because of fixed supplements, unrelated to the taxable area, demanded by many collectors, including so much for "collection and travel expenses" (charged to people who paid in small installments, obliging the collector to come back several times) and so much for an official receipt of payment.[23]

And then, more importantly, there was the gap between fiscal equality prescribed in law and the collectors' behavior. When dealing with the great families (*dahu*), locally influential and in direct contact with the county government, they tended to ask for less than what was owing. Under the Qing, it was not just the tax collectors but government officials themselves who in many counties classed taxpayers under two headings, *dahu* and *xiaohu* ("small families"), applying a preferential tax tariff to some *dahu* households.[24] Under the Republic, tax collectors did not always dare to step inside the mansions of the great families, who might keep them waiting outside the estate walls to intimidate them and deter them from being too fussy. Some families related to high-ranking officials considered it beneath themselves to pay taxes—and the collectors went along with them (Wan, Zhuang, and Wu 1934, 68).

Taking together those whose "face" exempted them from the common fate, those who delayed paying to gain time and money, those who pressured the tax agents, those who tricked them or bought them, there were many big landowners who paid less, even much less, than they owed.[25] Tax evasion, however democratically spread among all social categories, was practiced on such a scale by big landowners that—unlike taxation—we might agree it was progressive. Not only did the great families own a higher proportion of "black fields" than the small families, but they got away with far more unpaid tax. In 1933, the great families of Nantong, Jiangsu, were liable for one-third of the 700,000 *yuan* in unpaid tax (an enormous sum on the county scale) that the authorities despaired of recovering. A man called Wang, head of the salt transport organization, owed more than 10,000 *yuan* to the Treasury, something close to 1.5 percent of the total arrears owing from all the county's taxpayers (Wan, Zhuang, and Wu 1934, 167). Admittedly, the manager of a big estate might occasionally divert for himself the money owed to tax authorities, without the knowledge of the big absentee landlord (Ho 1934, 9–10), but even in such cases the beneficiary was a fairly well-off taxpayer. The poor often paid more than their share. When the administration was unable to bring in the taxes owed by the big landlords, it would increase tax rates for the smallholders (Yang

1959, 57). In sum then, unfair taxation was not only geographic, it was also social—mainly because of tax evasion.

If the poor did pay a greater share of their incomes in tax than the rich, one might easily infer that they took the lead in antitax resistance. But this was not the case, although several arguments could be advanced in favor of this thesis. Some antitax riots were led by authentically poor peasants, such as He Yongxi, tortured and executed for having led 3,000 rebel peasants in Heshui, Gansu, in 1924 (*Gansu WSZLXJ*, vol. 13, 1982, 130–33). In a neighboring province, Gao Yanfa, who instigated and led a peasant revolt in Yang Xian, Shaanxi, in January 1897, was a farm laborer and porter (Xibei daxue lishixi 1984, 93–94). In the same province ten years later, the leaders of a *jiaonong* movement were all poor peasants except for one first degree graduate (*xiucai*), whom the magistrate attempted to persuade to abandon his companions (Xibei daxue lishixi 1984, 163). Another man executed was scarcely less poor. Xu Fali was dismembered in 1927 for having led the antitax resistance in Shiquan county, Shaanxi, over the previous three years. He had a three-room house and three *mu* of land, but had sold two *mu* because his tax burden was too great for him to feed properly the four people in his family. According to communist criteria, Xu was a lower middle-class peasant; on the other hand, though, he had been elected *xiangyue* of his village in 1921 and reelected in 1923, to a post of control and arbitration implying public esteem quite rare among villagers of his condition.(*Shiquan XZ*, 1991, 700–702).[26]

Irrespective of the social identity of its leaders, antitax resistance could acquire a social component when it was targeted at some rich people or at rich people in general. It must be said, such targets were never exclusive; but alongside administrative buildings, public officials, police officers, and tax collectors, it was significant when rich people as such were also targeted. One of the seven houses set alight in Yangzhong in 1932 belonged to the island's biggest landlord (as discussed in Box 1.1). This detail is less meaningful, however, than the social coloration of an antitax revolt that took place seven or eight years before, a short distance to the east of Yangzhong: in Hengxiang, Taixing county (Box 5.5). The Hengxiang revolt was not a classic social conflict. Huang Picheng and his fellow notables were not fought as exploiters of their

Box 5.5   Targeting the Powerful, More Than the Rich:
Hengxiang, Jiangsu, Winter 1924–25

About fifteen miles to the northeast of Taixing, Huangqiao was considered the richest town in the county; its wealth was eclipsed, however, by that of Hengxiang township, a few miles away. Hengxiang was where the rich lived, eight great families in particular, all named Huang. But the rest of Hengxiang's inhabitants (including many of the Huangs' tenants) were mainly poor, even very poor. This social polarization was not unconnected with the fact that the successive targets of the revolt were, first, a primary school where the eight families' offspring were pupils, and second, the mansion owned by Huang Picheng, the richest of the eight.

However, even in the Hengxiang revolt, the social struggle was closely linked to the struggle against political oppression. The township's wealthy citizens were not just wealthy, they also exerted or simply assumed political responsibilities. It was they who had imposed the tax that triggered the revolt. In the warlord era, Huang Picheng was a legislator in the National Parliament. At the time of the revolt, one of the eight Huangs was a member of Jiangsu provincial assembly and two others were members of Taixing county council. After the 1911 Revolution, the Huangs gave the name "Zhendong City" to an area comprising 108 villages around Hengxiang. They governed it by decree, acting almost independently of the state, controlling the courts, the police, and the collection of taxes.

In Hengxiang, as in many other localities, a slaughter tax (*tuzai shui*) had to be paid on oxen, buffaloes, horses, and pigs. At the end of 1924, "Zhendong City" added on its own initiative a tax on pigs. It was to be paid on transactions involving live animals: buying piglets and then selling the fattened-up pigs. Practically every rural family was affected. It was axiomatic in Taixing that every farm has as many pigs as human beings and that every *mu* must feed a pig. Taixing was one of the more important, perhaps the most important, pig producers among all Jiangsu counties. The soil, which was largely sandy, suited little else than growing groundnuts, corn, and sorghum, so that the county produced mainly groundnut oil, sorghum-based wine, and pigs fed on sorghum and corn scraps. These pigs were bred for their precious manure and brought in hardly any profit. According to the peasants, the income drawn from them barely balanced the expenditure. So they will be unable to continue breeding pigs, they said, if they had to pay for each pig purchased and sold a tax equivalent to the purchase price of over 50 pounds of barley.

The breeders were so angry that 100 ransacked, demolished, and burned the primary school at Dingqiaohe (east of Hengxiang), which was reserved for the children of the eight great families. The authors of this "crime" were aware that they would not be forgiven, so they formed a secret alliance with the nearby village of Yucaizhuang to resist the new tax and forestall the inevitable repression—which began just after the burning of the school, on 11 February 1925. About 100 militiamen and police arrived, surrounded the village of Yucaizhuang, and arrested seven villagers. At dawn the following day, a crowd armed with sticks, pitchforks, and hammers attacked the well-guarded home of Huang Picheng. The villagers were easily repulsed after losing several men during the fight. Their leader, Yu Xuexian, a man of about 50 nicknamed Yu the Taoist, was arrested and thrown into the Huang mansion's private jail.

The following night (12–13 February), under a new leader, a second attack was made on Huang Picheng's home. Protected by the darkness, the assailants broke down a section of the outside wall, invaded the inner courtyard, and set fire to the buildings. Unluckily for the former chief they sought to rescue, they came across some gold, silver, and jewels hidden in the rubble of the wall and fell out over the booty. This enabled the Taixing magistrate, there to provide support to the defenders, and Huang Picheng himself with his wife and concubines to escape under police protection. They took Yu the Taoist with them and locked him up in Taixing prison.

During the following weeks, the younger villagers practiced their boxing and combat skills and pooled their resources to buy weapons. The practicalities of acquiring these weapons were to be decided at a clandestine meeting on the evening of 18 March, but the venue was betrayed. The Taixing magistrate led more than 200 soldiers to surround the meeting. This successful coup de main enabled the authorities to apply the traditional policy, combining repression with compromise: the original leader, Yu the Taoist, was executed and his successor jailed. In all, more than 20 villagers were reported dead and more than 80 wounded during or after successive battles. At the same time, the new tax on pigs was discreetly put aside and in Hengxiang was never heard of again.

SOURCES: *ZLN*, vol. 1, 1928, section 2, 466; Jiang 1988b. *ZLN* gives 1924 in dating this affair, and Jiang early 1925. I have, generally speaking, followed this second source, which is hagiographic but longer at nine pages, and more detailed.

---

tenants or even as moneylenders or grain traders. They were fought because they had acquired or usurped certain powers, using them to impose new taxes including the tax on pigs. A dozen years earlier, in Siyugang (Box 5.1), the political background emerged just as plainly behind the social rivalries. The rebels had slaughtered the rich and destroyed their houses: not the rich in general but those belonging to the *dangquanpai* ("the faction in power") in the "four ports"; in other words, they opposed those who had acquired or increased their influence thanks to the New Policies, managing the enterprise—costly for taxpayers but lucrative for themselves—of shoring up the banks of the Yangzi.[27]

This social and political concurrence was particularly in evidence in the time of the New Policies. The peasant rioters preferred to attack that section of the elite promoting or applying the reforms, especially when it profited dishonestly by them. Those were the circumstances in Laiyang, Shandong, where a significant antitax riot broke out in 1910, attracting support from 50,000 to 60,000 people, 1,600 of whom lost their lives. This episode has been well documented and studied;[28] and my account here will be focused on the social composition of this antitax movement.

At first sight, the Laiyang rebels' slogan "Hate the scholar gentry, not the officials!" (*chou shen, bu chou guan*) called attention to social rather than to political considerations. In fact, these "bad scholar gentry" (*lieshen*) were not exactly, at least not only, scholars. They were the clique of notables (among them tradesmen with no academic qualifications) who dominated local politics. Their rise, beginning in the late nineteenth century, had been greatly favored by two episodes: in 1902, the Laiyang magistrate gave them responsibility for land tax collection; and from 1906, the New Policies gave them many openings for greater influence. So, quite simply, as at the root of many other revolts, it was the notables' powers of taxation and coercion, acquired thanks to their bureaucratic acquaintances, that made people fear, hate, and fight them.

To this we may add the corruption found among some of them. It was blindingly apparent when, after the big freeze of spring 1910, peasants were obliged to call upon the reserves of cereals kept for hard times. The public granary (*shecang*) was empty, because the notables who had assumed management of it had sold its contents and deposited the profits in their own pawnshops. At the start of their movement in May 1910, the peasants put forward five claims: the last, expressed very moderately, concerned specifically the "public granary." Another demand was for all the corrupt people to be replaced, whether they belonged to the scholar gentry, to the lower ranks of the administration (*shendong*, scholar notables with local responsibilities, and *xiangzhang*), or to the para-administration (guards at the yamen and messengers). The other three claims related exclusively to tax: abolition of the head tax, reduction of the tax on theater, and lastly, a better rate for converting copper coins into silver money (the copper money was used by small taxpayers for paying their land tax; and the existing conversion rate undervalued it). So there was no specifically social element in these claims, framed during a movement noted for its opposition to a clique of rich men.

As this group allied the powerful with the gentry and the rich (merchants, financiers, and businessmen), we cannot possibly deny the social element in the Laiyang revolt. For all that, the leaders of these rebels who burned down the houses of the rich were not ordinary peasants. Qu Shiwen, the supreme leader and guiding spirit of the uprising (whose fate was to be executed in 1914), was indeed poor. But two of his four top lieutenants were landlords' sons. And one was, as Qu's father had been, *shezhang*, that is, the head of a small rural area (*shè*), half-way between township and village. Not all *shezhang* were necessarily well-off (they were chosen by virtue of wealth, capacities, or status in the village), but they were something more than ordinary villagers. Many *shezhang* and *cunzhang* (village heads) took part in the Laiyang revolt, but some supported the clique in power. The majority of *shezhang* helped to train and speak for the villagers as a whole. The Laiyang antitax movement, like the others, involved the great majority of the population.

In resisting oppression—fiscal and political, rather than economic—the Laiyang *shezhang* relied on another traditional organization: the *lianzhuanghui* (federations or "leagues" of villages). In many regions, the *lianzhuanghui* looked after the self-defense needs of threatened communities, which included protecting the property of the rich, generally against bandits and on occasion against tax collectors (*Jacqueries*, 169–71). Roxann Prazniak (1999, 51–58) rightly stresses the "secular" character of the *lianzhuanghui* (and of the *shezhang*), in contrast with the secret societies and other heterodox organizations, never mentioned in the numerous accounts of the Laiyang revolt. The Laiyang *shezhang* did not invoke support from these clandestine organizations (far less belong to them, like the leaders of other antitax revolts); they seem to have acted in the community's name as its accredited representatives. In this they recall the mayors and priests in pre-revolutionary France who demonstrated against taxation at the head of their parishioners, and in extreme cases, led them in unanimous resistance (Bercé 1991, 125–27 and 267–68).

Once we see an entire village resisting oppressive taxation under the leadership of its acknowledged leaders, we cannot accept that social conflict was the primary setting for the drama. Fairly often, indeed, villagers not involved in farming joined the antitax revolts, especially those aimed at the land tax and other taxes. Sometimes another social category profits from the success of the peasants' antitax unrest to make their own claims. Such was the case in Laiyang, where about 1,000 monks and priests demonstrated on 3 May 1910 outside the county yamen to demand the abolition of the tax on temples, which had soared from 10 percent of temple property values in 1909 to 30 percent in 1910 (Prazniak 1999, 71). Lastly, sometimes another social category mobilized peasants against tax, creating a wide, unified front against fiscal oppression. Far from creating what the CCP would have extolled as a "class alliance," this often amounted to sheer manipulation, as in Liuqiao in 1928 (see Box 5.6). More usually, it was not as in Liuqiao the Taoist or Buddhist clergy but simply a group of landlords who manipulated smallholders by invoking the idea of mutual defense among taxpayers. This occurred frequently whenever an antitax revolt was provoked by land surveys and cadastral reviews.

Yet, we must acknowledge that we know very little about the social identity of rebel leaders. The sources are not generally very forthcoming on this point. Hence our interest in the exceptions, none being so detailed as in Siyugang at the start of the Republic (Box 5.1)—detailed, in this case, because the administration undertook an inventory of the possessions of the "bandits" (the leaders of the revolt), which it confiscated and auctioned off. But the inventory was less instructive than one might have wished, since it mixed up different measurements, different kinds of property, and various categories of land; and since neither the figures nor even the names of localities matched each other in the two sources that list the estates owned or exploited (Yangzhou shifan xueyuan lishixi 1961, 229; Jiang 1988a, 5).

Let us linger a moment over the case of Lin Men, the most complex, probably because Lin was the richest of the condemned "bandits." The area of his fields is indicated sometimes in paces (*bu*), sometimes in *mu*. The inventory lists higgledy-piggledy the land he rented, the estates of which he is identified as owner of surface and subsoil, and other

Box 5.6   Peasants Manipulated in Other People's Interests:
Liuqiao, Jiangsu, 1928

The revolt that occurred in Liuqiao township, about twelve miles northwest of Nantong, Jiangsu, in April 1928, has features in common with the Daishan uprising (Box 5.2). Neither can be understood if we disregard the rigorous fiscal controls aimed at preventing or unmasking frauds. But in Liuqiao the discontent of peasant taxpayers (winegrowers, as it happens) was exploited by other taxpayers: monks and priests. At the start of 1928, the local Education Bureau introduced a tax on temples and monasteries. Taoist priests and Buddhist bonzes spread rumors designed to mobilize as many taxpayers as possible. When the faithful came on the 25th day of the second lunar month (16 March 1928) to burn incense at the Temple of the Sacred Mountain of the East (east of Liuqiao), the Taoist priests told them that ten new taxes had just been imposed. They cited various occupations (so as to rally craftsmen and shopkeepers) and stated that Yang Xingyuan, the unpopular collector of taxes on wines and spirits, had been charged with collecting them.

Implicating Yang was the best way of mobilizing the many winegrowers living in villages around Liuqiao. As the boss of the most important distillery in the region, he was envied for his wealth and hated for the fines and prison sentences imposed on winegrowers by the collectors he dispatched across the countryside. In principle, those producing less than five bushels (about 320 pints) of wine per year were presumed to be drinking it themselves and thus exempted from tax (see p. 8). Those winegrowers who had exceeded the legal quota of five bushels without declaring the fact were terrified of Yang's agents. These collectors ferreted around everywhere, even in women's bedrooms, imposing fines of several dozen *yuan* or even several hundred, and arresting anyone who dared to protest. It was widely accepted that Yang had enriched himself on the fines exacted by his agents. As it happens, Yang was not pocketing the fines; instead, he authorized his collectors to keep modest amounts before handing the rest over to the police—that way, he would pay them less himself.

On 14 April, several hundred peasants, duly emboldened by the priests, set off for Liuqiao township. Once there, they were joined by tailors, carpenters, and other craftsmen in a demonstration outside the Public Security Bureau. They asked Yang Xingyuan for exemption from the ten new taxes, then dispersed very quickly after several notables came to assure them they would win their case. For his part, Yang put up notices denying that he had been commissioned to collect any new taxes at all, offering also to resign his job as collector of taxes on wines and spirits. Since the resignation was slow in coming, another notice—anonymous but posted by villagers—called for a new demonstration on 29 April. Bigger than before, it ended badly, with the authorities having sent in nine policemen from Nantong and their chief forbidding the thousands of demonstrators to advance. The order was misunderstood and eventually the crowd surrounded the little squad of frightened policemen, who opened fire on the unarmed demonstrators. The casualty list included one demonstrator killed (a peasant), two seriously wounded (a Taoist priest and a florist), and two slightly hurt. The next day, the villagers carried the dead peasant's corpse into Yang's distillery. They got drunk on his wine and ransacked the distillery without the police daring to intervene.

SOURCES: See especially *Tonghai xinbao* (The New Nantong Newspaper), 2, 4, 6, and 8 May 1928. The article on 6 May is the most shallow, the one on 8 May the most substantial. The 4 May article is very hostile to Yang, while the one on 8 May finds too many excuses for him. It cites the detailed report by the two investigators sent in by the Guomindang Committee of Nantong county. See also *Nantong Xian WSZL*, vol. 1, 1987, 126–28, where the not very reliable recollections of a former Liuqiao policeman suggests communists were behind the incident.

property about which we learn nothing. The parcels Lin owned in entirety (subsoil and surface) were mostly sandy (*shatian*), but also included some rice paddies (*liangtian*). Some of the areas indicated in the newspaper *Tongbao* of 23 August (included in Jiang 1988a) are far more extensive than those given in the *Xinhai geming Jiangsu diqu shiliao* (Yangzhou shifan xueyuan lishixi 1961). The lower figures recorded on the official list (in the latter source) could be explained by the wish to show that the bandits' property would not be enough to compensate the victims of the revolt. In the end, because place-names are not reliably recorded, it is not easy to determine which source is likely to be more exact when the figures reported by one or the other are markedly divergent. In sum, Lin Men must have owned over 100 *mu*, making him a very rich peasant.[29] Leaving out double counting, both sources attribute to him ten or more parcels of land scattered across half a dozen localities and even in two different wards (*qu*). As these localities are more or less all *yu* (pieces of land surrounded by water) or *wan* (bays) belonging to *gang* (ports), it is easy to understand why he led the resistance to a tax that hit hard his multiple properties positioned at intervals along the Yangzi.

The other leaders of the revolt were far less well-off. One of them, Lin Men's nephew, was a carpenter who farmed 5 *mu* of rented land; another was a former soldier turned tenant farmer. However, a third owned 45 *mu* of sandy terrain and was a former *xiangzhang*, a local post of responsibility just like those detained by the rebels' opponents, the leading figures in the Society for Protection Against the Collapse of the River Banks. As for the top man, the "Commander in Chief" Zhu Tianrong or Zheng Jianrong, he had only 12 *mu* of sandy soil, but after his flight his wife employed several dozen women, farm laborers, to harvest the rice in their field. She paid each laborer 0.2 *yuan* a day, but this significant expense may perhaps be explained by her haste to bring the grain into a safe place before the authorities could confiscate it. In any case, the output from his 12 *mu* must have been no more than a sideline for Zhu Tianrong, salt trafficker and member of the Hongbang (Red Band). It is quite probable that the mass of Siyugang rebels formed a representative sample of potential taxpayers, given that each village and hamlet had been invited to provide its contingent of fighters. But we can identify, among the leaders and instigators of the revolt, individuals who were better-off (a big taxpayer likely to be hit worse than anyone else by the new tax) or a little more influential (a former *xiangzhang*, a member of a secret society) than the average villager.

So it seems consistent with a fairly common pattern. Some antitax revolts were led by well-off peasants, such as Yang Tonghai, whose "family owned quite a lot of irrigated fields and mountain land" (*Xianju XZ*, 1987, 480–81). More often, it was landlords who stirred up resistance, or even organized the revolt against taxation. As we have seen, in 1932, that was the case in Yangzhong, Jiangsu, where the initial leaders of the antitax revolt were two landlords who represented their respective constituencies in the county council (Box 1.1). Before the 1911 Revolution, it was not unusual for people with academic qualifications, from whom until 1905 were recruited the imperial administrators, to take the lead in resistance movements. In April 1906, in Luoning county, Henan, which had been stricken by a natural disaster, it was a provincial graduate (*juren*) who called for a massive handover of farm tools (*jiaonong*) to fight the collection of a special tax contribution.[30] Nearly 10,000 demonstrators took part in the movement he launched, which ended in failure and the deaths of three peasants (*Luoning WSZL*, vol. 2–3, 1988, 148–51). A few years later (in May 1909, in Zhenyuan, Yunnan), four mandarins started a petition against the *lijin*, while declining to assume personal leadership of the protest movement to which it led (*Zhenyuan WSZL*, vol. 3, 1989, 37–38). Sometimes—though very rarely—we need hardly ask who benefited by an antitax riot. The one that broke out in Leibo, Sichuan, in October 1934, was in response to the arrest of seven members of rich families (*Dagongbao*, 29 October 1934, cited in *ZJNSZ*, vol. 3, 1020).

Lastly, though strictly speaking it falls outside the present subject, we should remember the predominant part played by the rural elite in peaceful resistance to taxation (Li 2005, Chapter 9). The various forms it took (pressure, petitions, negotiations, bargaining), which Li Huaiyin has examined under the overall heading of "elite activism," were, as we have seen, more effective than most of the revolts described in this chapter. This was so at least until the formation of the Nanjing government, which hastened to dissolve the county councils where the elite had been able to express their objections and classed recalcitrant members of this elite as *tuhao lieshen*.

Even so, we should recognize that despite the considerable role played by the rural elite in leading resistance (occasionally violent, but more often peaceful), antitax riots were too numerous and diverse for us to catalogue them under a uniform "social" heading. Alongside those where the big landowners manipulated the small farmers, we must recall the more frequent cases of landlords and rural gentry naturally taking the lead in unanimous movements, as did mayors and even numerous minor nobles in sixteenth and seventeenth century France. Even when ordinary people controlled movements, as in Daishan (Box 5.2), it was not unusual (as with the salt workers and the fishermen) for insurgents to act in defense of prerogatives (in Daishan, the fishermen's right to acquire unlimited quantities of lightly taxed salt and the salt workers' right to sell freely to the fishermen) and also against measures deemed excessive (the salt dyed red for the fishermen and the compulsory salt piles for the salt workers). The Daishan rebels were no more likely than other antitax rioters to plan or even to envisage "offensive" claims. It took the rise of the communists, a few years later, to put into their heads such preposterous ideas as redistributing wealth among residents of the same village.

The avowed objective of many antitax revolts was to provide protection for rich people's property. However inappropriate the term "rich" might be to define the social condition of most small taxpayers living in dire poverty, that was nevertheless the explicit aim of numerous branches of the Hongqianghui (Red Spears) or the Huangqianghui (Yellow Spears) in Henan and Shandong in the 1920s, as it was also of the *lianzhuanghui*: they intended to protect their estates against the exactions of tax collectors, soldiers, and brigands. There is no need to conceal the indigence of many peasant families oppressed by taxation to distinguish their revolts from those of tenant farmers against the yearly rent (*PWP*, Chapter 7) or still less, uprisings of farm laborers against their employers—if any took place! Consider the instructive contrast between the near-absence of farm laborers' strikes—apart from those instigated by the communists—and the frequency of horizontal conflicts pitting camps of similar social composition (villages or lineages) against one another (*PWP*, Chapter 9).

SIX

Reforms

Resistance to taxation was ubiquitous, an active force in many revolts or riots that I have defined by other grievances, such as reforms or conscription. Because the latter sources of grievance are the subjects of this chapter and the next, my focus will be on them—not omitting, however, the connections between antitax revolts and other forms of resistance.

Just like—or even more than—the resistance to poppy eradication (*PWP*, Chapter 6) and military service (Chapter 7 here), resistance to reform delayed the modernization of the country. Bearing in mind that the Japanese invasion and the war interrupted the implementation of profound and urgently needed reforms, this chapter is restricted to the period between 1900 and 1937. The first part will concentrate on the final project of a moribund dynasty: the New Policies (*xinzheng*). These proved more innovative than the revolution they precipitated, and also more than a good many later undertakings (Ichiko 1980; Reynolds 1993 on the Japanese role). After the fall of the Empire, the reformers had to start from scratch. At first, they aroused villagers' anger pursuing causes that were often not worth the trouble. Then, when they attempted to improve the quality and competitiveness of a farm product vital for exports, silk production in this instance, they provoked resistance among those concerned.

Resistance to the New Policies

In some respects, such as the creation of a "New Army," the New Policies hardly affected the peasants. Similarly, the timid steps toward a constitutional monarchy, with the election of provincial consultative parliaments (in 1909), and then a national parlia-ment, also consultative (in 1910), did not mean much to them. By contrast, peasants felt directly affected by the almost simultaneous creation (starting in the summer of 1909) of the local autonomy offices, if only because the offices increased the surcharges on the land tax. In the same way, fiscal grievances—and others too—explain peasants' hostility to the creation of a modern police force and to the "new schools" (*xin xue*) springing up everywhere in the townships and sometimes even the villages of rural China. Education was at the heart of the New Policies.

And it was primarily by attacking the new schools, where the teaching of mathematics and science supplanted the classics, that the villagers vented their wrath, especially between 1905 and 1911. They also destroyed the homes of teachers, school heads, and directors of local and regional education offices. Close behind the schools came the police, rivalled as targets toward the end of the period (1910–11) by the offices of the local "self-governing" authorities (*zizhi gongsuo*).

Before 1905, attacks on schools were very infrequent, and even in 1905 resistance was expressed chiefly in peaceful demonstrations, as in Daning, Shanxi, where it was led by a scholar. The Daning magistrate had ordered that 1,730 cedar trees were to be cut down and sold to help finance the new schools, with the interest on the capital raised to provide working expenses. The scholar Liu Ruigen, who was against the idea, mobilized the villagers, who demonstrated outside the county yamen. Liu was arrested and died later in prison, but the plan for new schools was postponed (*Daning XZ*, 1990, 541). From 1906 onward, however, attacks became more frequent and more violent. We can find records of eighteen, across nine provinces from the north to the south of the country. The schools, sometimes even the county government, and in one case (in Chaoyang, Fengtian) the prefecture itself, were ransacked or destroyed (*Chaoyang WSZL*, vol. 1, 1986, 1–6). The movement continued in 1907 without any particular development and even subsided briefly in 1908 (seven incidents only by my count), acquiring fresh impetus in 1909. During those years, the most significant attacks were often led by religious sects, as in Kaijiang, Sichuan, in June 1907, where several thousand members of the Red Lanterns (Hongdengjiao) invaded the county capital. They demolished the school and a tax office, then killed dozens of militiamen. Once the militia reinforcements arrived the Red Lantern force lost over 100 lives. However, the uprising had lasted for at least a month, which would not have been possible with villagers alone—in other words, if the resistance had not been led by a broader-based organization such as the Red Lanterns (*Kaijiang XZ*, 1989, 470–71; Duara 1991, 77 on the sects' role).[1] All the same, a few serious riots were run without help from sects or secret societies. For example in Yichun, Jiangxi, in September 1909, ten to twenty demonstrators were killed by gunfire, and thousands of peasants surrounded the county capital for four days. The siege was finally raised only when the police were reinforced and in response to a public announcement that collection of the tax dedicated to the new schools was suspended and the project to create the schools was itself deferred (*XGQSJMDS*, 1985, 352–57; also Sheel 1989, 125–26; *Yichun shizhi*, 1990, 10; and *QMN*, no. 50, 1983, 84).

The resistance movement reached its peak in the spring of 1910, when attacks on schools reached epidemic proportions. In Jiangsu province alone, there is evidence of about 50 schools destroyed over the first five months of the year: 10 of them in March and April in Yixing county and 13 in April and May in Rugao (Wang 1977, 319–20, and Wang 1985, 205–6; *QMN*, no. 50, 1983, 91, 94–95, and 97; *NCH*, 29 April 1910, 235; Faure 1976, 473–96, whence come the later references to *NCH*). We should add a score of schools demolished in the neighboring province of Zhejiang (*DFZZ*, vol. 7, 1910, no. 5, 17451 and 17481–82; vol. 7, no. 6, 17666 and 17668–69; vol. 7, no. 7, 17839; vol. 7, no. 10, 18479; Prazniak 1999, 252*n*35; *Qing'an WSZL*, vol. 1, undated, 22–23; *Shangyu XZ*, 1990, 13–14; Shen 1981, 43–44; *QMN*, no. 50, 88, 94, 97, 100, 102, and 107; Zhejiang sheng zhengxie wenshi ziliao weiyuanhui 1990, 117) and a dozen in the rest of the country. The most important of this wave of revolts broke out in August 1911 in Zhuanghe, Fengtian and was described by Chinese historian Li Shiyue as "an armed uprising on a great scale." Though no schools were demolished, to my knowledge, what set it off were undoubtedly the taxes linked to new schools and police. Thousands of peasants invaded the county town, killed the president of the local self-government assembly, and destroyed its administrative headquarters. Reinforced by members of the Red Beards (Honghuzi) rushing in from across the region, they became a force formidable enough for the government to dispatch 1,000 mounted men to confront it. It took them ten days of fighting to defeat the insurgents and arrest their leader (Li 1959, 56–70 [quotation 57]; see also *QMN*, no. 50, 119).

In the preceding affair, the taxes imposed to fund schools and police were jointly targeted. And that was so in several of the incidents mentioned above. More often, the police—or the tax for the police—was the sole or main target of the riot. In Zunhua, Zhili, the villagers protested simultaneously against the new police station set up in the Temple of the Golden Mountain, by forcing out the police chief in 1909, and against the tax, which was resisted in 1910 by thousands of peasants from 28 villages (Prazniak 1999, 109–16).[2] In April of 1910, in Wukang, Zhejiang, the peasants demolished the county government building, two police stations, and a policeman's house. They injured several policemen and also the county magistrate, whom they threw into the river (Shen 1981, 43; also *QMN*, no. 50, 1983, 92 and Zhejiang sheng zhengxie wenshi ziliao weiyuanhui 1990, 117).

At least as much as the police, the local self-governing administrations, also very expensive, came under attack along with the schools—and sometimes by themselves. The new local administrations were set up in province after province from 1909 onward, which explains why the destruction of their offices and headquarters became so frequent in 1911. In March, 18 local self-government offices were destroyed in Chuansha, Jiangsu, along with more than 50 schools; in April came further such attacks, again including schools, in Jiashan, Zhejiang; and still others during the seventh lunar month (24 August to 21 September) in Wu Xian, Jiangsu; another in Shimen, Zhejiang, together with a police station, 9 May; another, together with the homes of *shendong* (members of the gentry charged with various local responsibilities) in the township of Tongli, Jiangsu, on 19 September (Prazniak 1999, Chapter 6; *QMN*, no. 50, 1983, 114 and 119–20; Wang 1985, 213–14).

Why the schools? Why the police? And why the local administration? Firstly, as we have already suggested, for fiscal reasons. The primary motivation behind the burning and destruction of schools, police stations, and local self-government offices was the outrage provoked by the taxes and surtaxes that financed the buildings and their upkeep. However, given the inflation rate, the tax burden had diminished during the two decades before 1905. That downward trend was reversed after 1905, but at least until 1908 or 1909, the overall tax burden was lower than it had been in the early 1880s (Wang 1973, 116–17).³ Few taxpayers had memories that long: what they noted, what infuriated them, was the sharp increase in taxes in the space of a few years. Seen from this perspective, the closing years of the Empire presented them with even nastier surprises. Between 1908 and 1911, "temporary" surtaxes multiplied, to the point of swelling considerably the overall tax burden (Wang 1973, 121 and 123). Since these surtaxes were introduced explicitly "for the school," "for the police," or "for the local administration," it is understandable that taxpayers' hostility became focused on the tangible objects for which they were intended.

A quite different surtax had been put in place in many counties from the beginning of the decade. It was to help pay the enormous sum in reparations (450,000,000 taels) imposed by the Great Powers in 1901, to recover the losses they had suffered during the Boxer Uprising, which by the end had become a war between China and the imperialists (Wang 1973, 62–64). That indemnity is often referred to in accounts of disturbances that took place during the Empire's closing decade; more often, indeed, than warranted, given the discontent caused by more specific surtaxes. We have seen that rural resistance was very weak at the start of the decade, and the surtaxes imposed to pay the indemnity to the Powers aroused little opposition. Things looked quite different by the very end of the decade, especially after the introduction of local self-government. The imperial rulers had granted autonomy without providing funding, which was to cost village taxpayers dear. No sooner were the new administrations established than they rushed to impose the taxes and surtaxes needed to realize their plans. And, as a rule, these were to include building modern schools and strengthening the police.

To be clear, however, if we were concerned here only with taxes, the riots listed would naturally have belonged in Chapter 5. In common with so many others, these riots would have confirmed the predominance of antitax disturbances, which is a recurrent theme of this book. However, on top of the fiscal surcharges, the villagers became angry with the new local administrations for taking over their temples and setting up their headquarters inside them. Other local temples were converted into modern schools, and others into, for instance, police stations, barracks, and post offices. Starting in 1904, local officials commandeered not just the temples but also their property—or else it was their new occupants who seized it—and quite often the income from landed estates entrusted to the temples. This accorded with the slogan *miaochan banxue* (build schools with temple property), itself a refinement of *pomiao banxue* (destroy temples to build schools).[4] As we have seen, it was immediately following that date (1905) that the peasants began resisting the reforms, in protest against acts of plunder perpetrated in the name of modernity. Yet, this does not (for the present) take us any further from antitax unrest than did those categories within our typology classed as special levies (see Chapter 1).

What is more, nearly all the proponents and beneficiaries of the reforms—in whose name the villagers were shut out of their temples—were privileged people. Many of the modern schools were located in urban areas; those in the countryside did not attract the peasants' children, who were ill prepared to assimilate an unfamiliar curriculum and discomfited by the new teaching methods and the style adopted in pupil-teacher relations. The abolition of the examination system, by contrast, quickly persuaded many members of the gentry of the new schools' advantages. Just sending their children to them was not enough. They founded them, administered them, and financed them out of their own pockets or those of the community, thanks to their stranglehold over the new authorities. They converted many of their *sishu* (traditional private schools) into "new schools."[5] So, perhaps to put it more plainly, local autonomy was a godsend to the traditional gentry.[6] They controlled the elections and monopolized the administrative posts, thus increasing their grasp over local finances and their power vis-à-vis the imperial bureaucracy. There were other well-off people in the countryside, though not formally members of the gentry, who also profited by a reform that provided a "new" education for their offspring, and for themselves, new access to local power.

In this light, it is legitimate to attribute a social coloration to the Chinese peasants' resistance to the New Policies—which they financed, which dispossessed them, and which profited other people. Nevertheless, things were not always so clear cut. Those directly dispossessed and driven into the street, such as Buddhist monks from their temples and nuns from their convents, often incited the peasants to rebellion.[7] In other cases, low-grade agents of the administration, stripped by the new local authorities of their monopoly over tax collection and the legal or illegal perks that went with it, fuelled the peasants' anger, and even led their revolts. More frequently, traditionalist scholar gentry—who were in no way resigned to the abandonment of, or lower status of, the teaching of the Classics—stirred up peasant hostility to an education system that had strayed from or lost its national and Confucian roots. Inspired by these scholars, conservative notables criticized and fought the New Policies in all their aspects. Other notables, who would not have opposed the new self-governing authorities had they controlled them, fought it because rival cliques had won power within it (Prazniak 1999, 226, on rivalries within the local elite). For them, this was reason enough to whip up the anger of the "ignorant" masses against the new administration.

We are left with numerous cases where peasants rebelled without being manipulated by anyone. They needed no one's encouragement in nicknaming the modern schools "foreign schools" (*yang xue* or *yang xuetang*) and in being indignant at the secularization of their temples and other religious meeting places where they had been accustomed to attend ceremonies. Admittedly, their mistrust of innovations from abroad and their protest at the profaning of sacred places only strengthened their resentment that "their" temples were being confiscated and their taxes spent on projects that did not touch their lives. In the short term, modernization benefits only those in a position to profit by it—and, for the peasants, that was not the case. Furthermore, "local self-government" meant only one thing for the peasants: the power to oppress them was being transferred from one privileged circle to another, from the bureaucracy to the gentry, who were supported by or in competition with a small group of local notables. The fusion of material considerations, vital to so poor a social class, with ideological resentment was just as incendiary even when tax was not a concern. One such instance was when local authority leaders diverted to the new school the funds earmarked for stockpiling grain. A simpler case was when the price of rice went up. The consumers' despair (the Lower Yangzi was given over to cash crops and grain was in short supply) found an outlet in attacking the modern schools, which were concrete symbols of the detested innovations. Shortages of food led to a fresh upsurge of arson attacks on schools and of pillage. Although the tax increases and the introduction of local autonomy during the closing years of the Empire did contribute greatly to the wave of destruction of schools and administrative headquarters in spring 1910, the accompanying rise in looting was no coincidence. The destruction of buildings had been accompanied before, in 1906 and 1907, by record outbreaks of looting (on the two peak periods of looting, 1906–7 and 1910, see *PWP*, 154–56).

The events of July 1910 in Yi Xian, Zhili, illustrate the concurrence of causes described above, to which was added another, also very common: corruption among those members of the gentry responsible for implementing the New Policies. As it had not rained for a long time, peasants from different parts of the county who had come to the county capital to pray for rain took the opportunity to ask that no new tax introduced by the local administration should be imposed until circumstances improved. The demonstrators received no answer. In addition, they noted that the local authority had installed itself inside a temple where it had destroyed the statue of Buddha. Thus, they attributed the drought to the anger of the deities. So they attacked the supposed source of their misfortunes (the New Policies) or more exactly its works (schools and local self-government) and its agents—specifically, the homes of the leading officials and the police chiefs (*DFZZ*, vol. 7, no. 8, September 1910, 18071–72; Prazniak 1999, 117–18; *XGQSJMDS*, 63–64; *QMN*, no. 50, 1983, 102–3).

Nevertheless, there was one last episode during which the prevailing emphasis on material (rather than mental) concerns was not so apparent. This was the determined opposition to the census (*diaocha hukou*) undertaken in the last years of the Empire and chiefly implemented in 1910. The enumeration procedures were linked to the introduction of local autonomy, in that they were designed to identify citizens with the right to vote and those with the necessary qualifications to exercise responsibilities in the new local administrations. It is not surprising that most of the riots sparked off by the census (71 out of 83) date from 1910. Like the attacks on schools and local authority offices, they reached their peak in spring 1910: 46 riots between April and July. This parallelism is largely due to the overlap between two categories of riot, with schools and teachers as the preferred targets (though by no means the only ones) of riots against the census. These disturbances—again, a real epidemic—spread through many regions of the country, from Zhili to Guangdong and Sichuan, although once again our documentation is particularly detailed for Jiangsu, northern Zhejiang, and southern Anhui.

Box 6.1	Opposition to the Census and House Number Plates: Lian Xian, Guangdong, 1910

On 31 August 1910, between 600 and 700 villagers meeting in Lian Xian county, Guangdong, convinced themselves that attaching the number plates foreshadowed the imposition of yet another new tax to fund schools. So on 15 September they attacked the secondary school and several primary schools. They also destroyed two shops and the homes of several individuals identified with the reform policy and with the building of school facilities. This destruction (eleven houses and buildings demolished or burned down) was only the first outbreak in a wave of unrest that continued throughout most of the autumn. In December, 2,000 to 3,000 peasants blocked traffic on the river Lianjiang, south of the town, killing three soldiers. This led to official repression.

SOURCES: Prazniak 1999, Chapter 5; *DFZZ*, vol. 7, nos. 10 and 11; Messant/Yun 1982, 56–57; *SB*, 4 October, 12 November, and 14 December 1910; *QMN*, no. 50, 105.

It would be wrong to claim that taxation was never involved in census procedures. In Qian'an and Lengkou counties (northeastern Zhili) in early September 1909, the census was accompanied by the imposition of *tanpai* (allotments) according to the number of inhabitants and animals enumerated (*QMN*, no. 50, 1983, 83). This concurrence was, however, the exception rather than the rule. More frequent but still in the minority were cases where those enumerated had to contribute to funding the census operations.[8]

Even when they had nothing to pay (which, again, was the general rule), many peasants were convinced that the census had been introduced purely with extra taxes in view—that the state, or the new local authorities, were planning to impose a head tax by stealth. The avalanche of taxes and surtaxes paid to fund the New Policies would have sufficed to explain this fear, along with scare stories being put about by opponents. Should the administration take it into its head, as often happened, to number houses by fixing a plate on every door (*menpai*), the villagers would immediately read this intrusion as proof of tax plans, that they are going to impose a new tax on every home visited. During a riot directed against the number plates in Dabu, Guangdong, on 18 August 1910, four soldiers and many peasants were killed (*DFZZ*, vol. 7, no. 8, 18064). In the following month, a similar riot—not more serious but better known—broke out in the same province (Box 6.1).

Similar revolts broke out the same year in several counties in southern Jiangsu. The rebels sometimes expressed the additional fear that the census was a prelude to conscripting more soldiers (Wang 1985, 208; Prazniak 1999, 250*n*33). But the dread that haunted everyone was taxation. A copy of the enumerators' manual was seized giving details of their pay as one *yuan* for each 1,000 households checked. It was taken as proof of the authorities' fiscal plans in August 1910 in Changxing county, Zhejiang (*SB*, 3 September 1910). So, usually, the peasants attacked the enumerators. Sometimes they were content to demand their registers and destroy them. At other times, they beat the officials, injured them, kidnapped them, or tied them up and sent them back to town. Those living in villages were likely to find their houses flattened.[9] Most of the enumerators were teachers, a fact that led to a second category of targets: primary teachers, schools, education authorities, and societies formed with the aim of promoting education.[10] A third range of targets, also foreseeable, was the offices and headquarters of the local authorities.[11] After that came the leaders of the new administrations and the old, from the lowest ranking (village head, local administration agent) to the highest (magistrate). Then, of course, there were a certain number of scholar gentry who backed the reforms or joined the new administrations. With few exceptions (a magistrate taken hostage, another beaten to death), the rioters attacked people less than their houses, which they regularly burned down.[12] Not forgetting the police, we should mention a last target, occasional, but significant: the Christian churches.[13]

The churches embodied, in common with the modern schools, the foreigners' stranglehold on China. People suspected foreigners of being the instigators and ultimate beneficiaries of the census. In Weiyuan county, Sichuan, in January 1910, in the eyes of more than 50,000 demonstrators, the points and lines inscribed on the plates fixed to their doors meant that their homes had been handed over to foreigners and that they would be forced to become Christians (Prazniak 1999, 143–44). In June of the same year, in Gujiatang, Jiangsu, a persistent rumor had it that the school had sold to foreigners three people's identities (*shengcheng ren bazi*: the characters standing for their names, birthplaces, and dates of birth), thus causing their deaths. These three people, members of the same family, did indeed grow sick and die (*DFZZ*, vol. 7, no. 8, 18062). Two months later, in Changxing, Zhejiang, the rumor became more specific. After the census takers had called, the enumerated person would be sold to foreigners and his body used for building dikes. Delivery date was to be September 3, and he would be put to death two days later. Here it was a sorceress who started the rumor; a few months earlier, in May in Nanling, Anhui, it had been a doctor. His version confirmed the inevitable death that people checked for the census should expect, but it differed as to the purpose: their bodies would be used for building railways, not dikes.[14]

The part played by the doctor is unexpected, though no more so than in those failed death plots in June 2007, in London and Glasgow. The more usual rumormongers were sorcerers and sorceresses, nuns and monks, members of sects, and even bandits, together with members of the gentry who were hostile to the reforms (Wang 1985, 209; *SB*, 1 October 1910). The enumerators or the authorities were sometimes able to explain away these rumors, but not always, so then they had to suspend the census process for a while. In other cases, the explanations provided did not prevent the revolt. The day will come, there is no doubt of it, when a historian of the 1911 Revolution (a Chinese Georges Lefebvre) will be able to disentangle the "original panics," trace the "propagation of panics," identify the "connections," and follow the "currents of the Great Fear."[15] Behind the rumors and panics of 1910 in China, one finds, like in the France of 1789, hunger, to which Lefebvre devoted his introductory chapter. The year 1910 was, I repeat, a year of serious and protracted natural disasters. The anti-census riots, just like the epidemic of arson attacks on schools and local self-government headquarters, attracted less attention at the time than did the other epidemic of looting. The year 1910, we should also remember, was that half-century's record year for looting (*PWP*, Chapter 8). Its reached its peak (as with school-burnings and anti-census disturbances) in spring and early summer, from March to July. During those months, looting was almost a daily activity, at least in our sample, and in reality it was even more prevalent. It was no coincidence that some revolts combined looting with protests against the census (for example in Taixing, Jiangsu, in April 1910: *QMN*, no. 50, 1983, 95; *NCH*, 29 April 29, 254) or that others were originally sparked off by soaring rice prices (for example in Rugao, in the same province and region, in May 1910; *DFZZ*, vol. 7, no. 5, 17459). Nor was it by chance that one of the peasants' most persistent fears was of the fresh upsurge of banditry, as always in periods of drought.

Again I am reminded of Lefebvre's portrait of prerevolutionary France, where a chapter is devoted to "The Fear of Brigands," and of Ernest Labrousse's emphasis on the immediate economic and social causes of the Revolution. Here, we need not call for a future Chinese authority: a great historian, Cai Shaoqing, has already made the connection between the spread of peasant struggles in 1910 and the early success of the 1911 Revolution (Prazniak 1999, 20). However, we should not exaggerate: yes, revolution did break out the following year under the combined pressure of natural disasters (the Yangzi floods) and intensified rural hardship; but there were other causes, less appealing ones, that set it off, such as the provincialism and self-interest of the Sichuan notables. And it is generally admitted that the New Policies hastened the demise of the dynasty they were intended to save. The New Army and the Japanese universities (including the military academies) were the seedbeds of radical nationalists, even of revolutionaries opposed to a dynasty of foreign origin. The revolutionaries were isolated and had little influence at the start of the decade, but became much more vigorous by the end, in a period when "parliamentary" opposition was being openly expressed in newly elected parliaments.

This is no excuse for underestimating the extent of the reforms, still less for forgetting how much they were needed. Had they been implemented one or two generations earlier, even incomplete as they were, and obstructed as they were by conservative Manchus, they would perhaps have changed the course of events. Seen from this perspective, peasant resistance to the New Policies represented a brake on the indispensable modernization of a backward country. To simplify the point, we should put aside the fiscal element in the peasants' rebellion—however essential it was. In this chapter, I have as far as possible excluded "pure" antitax revolts and focused on damage to property, including the destruction of schools, police stations, local authority headquarters, and the homes of the prime movers and beneficiaries of the reforms.[16] These attacks, it must be admitted, were motivated by the surtaxes that financed the reforms or by the expropriation of temples; but the accompanying motive was mistrust of innovations. Against the census, the "objective" reasons for rebellion were much flimsier, so much so that we have had to seek out further causes and circumstances, such as rumors and panic.

The violent opposition to the 1910 census is a little reminiscent of the Boxers' movement. A detour via the work of three sinologists ought to explain this viewpoint. First, Joseph Esherick. I have myself no quarrel with the standard view of the Boxers as a traditionalist and xenophobic reaction; however, this overall assessment cannot blind us to the tangle of causes (economic, religious, and social in particular) that account for the emergence and development of the Boxers' movement in Shandong and Zhili (Esherick 1987). Similarly, Esherick's critique of the elitist character of the reforms introduced under the New Policies, which benefited city-dwellers and privileged people and added to the burden on the rural masses, seems to me very well founded (Esherick 1976, 106–17). We might even generalize and assert that modernization offered the greatest benefits to those well placed to take advantage of it, while harming the destitute and most vulnerable. In nineteenth-century Europe, for example, the railways put grooms out of work and enriched financiers. The 1911 Revolution happened before there was time for the beneficial long-term effects of the New Policies to extend to the peasants themselves. For them, at the time, the balance sheet for the enterprise was in deficit.

The second work is by Roxann Prazniak (1999), who has consulted the same sources I have—and, to tell the truth, has read far more. Where I disagree with her is not in her diagnosis (I appreciated the expressive subtitle "Rural Rebels Against Modernity"), but with her implied value judgment in condemning modernity—or this particular modernity. Taking care myself not to express a hostile value judgment on the birth of modernity (painful but in the long term beneficial), I recall only that the primary cause of the Communist Revolution (which Prazniak regards more positively than I do) was China's backwardness. I am not convinced that some other form of modernization, for which Prazniak is nostalgic, was really practicable. The ruralism that she ascribes to the dissidents (a term she applies to the rioters and rebel peasants) seems to me to be a utopia no less vague than Rousseau's reveries on the state of nature and the natural goodness of man. By contrast, when I read Prazniak, I feel she might subscribe to my interpretation of the "patriotic" movement for protecting the railways. In their support for it, Sichuan's richest and most powerful people applied the usual forms of pressure: they stopped paying taxes and mobilized peasant support. As a result, everyone had to wait until the Communist Revolution before a single mile of railway track was laid in Sichuan. In 1911, it is true, the peasants would no more have travelled on trains than they would have sent their children to the new schools.[17] Today, it is they who fill the trains travelling to work in the towns and spend every last penny on their children's schooling. The peasants' descendents have come eventually to benefit from modernity.

Lastly, Prasenjit Duara (1991 and 1995, Chapter 3) analyses the interconnections of knowledge with power relationships (as well as conflicts of interest) in the modernist discourse. Once the apostles of modernization sought to impose their ideas they became engaged in a battle that served—or prejudiced—interests not explicitly identified in their propaganda. What is more, their program required administrative and political reorganization. In the twentieth century (and not only in China), a considerable expansion of state power was achieved or pursued in the name of modernization. At the local level, it may have represented an unbearable intrusion to most villagers, who had learned by experience to see through fine words and not to trust them.

Without subscribing to all of Duara's ideas—I agree more with him than with Prazniak but less than with Esherick—I nevertheless regard his thinking as healthy, quite simply because it strives to do full justice to the peasants.[18] We can excuse ourselves from ascribing a "ruralist" ideology to them, but not from seeking to understand their motivation. Were that not so, we should have to question the entire purpose of this chapter (and the next). If we permit ourselves the slightest value judgment, if we claim to decide or picture ourselves reaching decisions in the name of a universal truth impervious to influence from political ideals, we will at once invalidate the more modest task of working out whether (and in this case in what measure) rural revolts held back the modernization of the country.

Under the Republic

The change of government did not put a stop to the census. In January 1913 in Wudu, Gansu, this process was coupled with the payment of a light tax for each door number plate—the combination provoking an uprising that was in turn severely repressed, with some 500 peasants killed (*Wudu WSZLXJ*, vol. 1, 1986, 6–8). The rumors continued as well. In Zhejiang in 1914, natural disasters brought them out in profusion: flooding in May, which destroyed the spring harvest of cotton, and drought from late June onward, which ruined the autumn harvest. Just then, an epidemic arose, a sickness that carried off numerous babies and led to rumors that the children were dying because the administration was using their civil registration certificates to build a bridge. Two revolts broke out. The first was at Jinhua on 8 August, when a thousand and then several thousand fighters from numerous villages across Jinhua and Yiwu counties, on the initiative of a secret society (Longhuahui, the Society of the Dragon's Flower), resisted provincial security forces for a few days before being crushed. Many rebels were arrested and killed, while others committed suicide (*Jinhua XZ*, 1992, 527–28). In Yuyao on 20 August, it was the census registration of schoolchildren that sparked off the riot in which peasants seeking to retrieve the registers by force had injured or killed a dozen policemen. Their leaders were shot (*DFZZ*, vol. 11, no. 4, October 1914, 27121; Zhejiang sheng zhengxie wenshi ziliao weiyuanhui 1990, 136, which backdates the incident to June).

TEMPLES CONFISCATED

Apart from the census and its accompanying rumors, the confiscating of temples or their property also went on after the fall of the Empire. On 5 February 1912, this practice and the corruption of local despots provoked a riot in Xin Xian, Shanxi. At the outset, the rioters intended to set fire to the school, but finished by burning the homes of 48 local despots. The ringleaders were arrested, tortured, and killed (*Xin Xian WSZL*, vol. 2, 1986, 44–60). Ten years later, the installation of an upper elementary school in a temple led to a riot in Qinshui in the same province. In the course of renovation work, the village head and his deputy had a big tree and a copse on a nearby hill cut down, with disastrous effects on the local fengshui, according to the village's former head. The latter led about 1,000 peasants on a punitive expedition against his successors, each of whom lost an eye in the battle. The village head died of his wounds (*Qinshui XZ*, 1987, 598–99).

Yet, to be accurate, the setting up of schools or other public services in the temples was a little less frequent under the Republic than during the last decade of the Empire. On the other hand, the expropriation of temple land went ahead and was accompanied under the Nationalists by the partial seizure, for various motives or under various pretexts, of several great monastery estates. The administration would undertake, for example, to locate an experimental reforestation area or to protect a historic or touristic site within or on the margins of the monastery. Having abandoned agrarian reform, the government found that diminishing some immense monastic estates was a handy pretense of reform. These encroachments led more usually to lawsuits, petitions, and endless litigation than to real revolts. An important exception was the attack launched on 13 February 1929 by the Xiaodaohui (Small Knives) against the Suqian county capital, in northern Jiangsu. Militiamen and troops took three months to put down this complex uprising, driven also by other motives including resistance to taxation (Nedostup 2001, 340–70, with other references listed on 345*n*158).

TEMPLES DESTROYED

More frequent after 1927 was the straightforward destruction of temples or statues or other symbols of worship inside the temples, as well as the banning of festivals or religious processions. Many Guomindang militants, mostly recruited among teachers and their pupils, were imbued with the iconoclasm of the May Fourth Movement. In their eyes, the creation of a modern society, enlightened by science, required the eradication of superstitions (Geisert 2001, 148–63; Goossaert 2003, 432; and also Duara 1991 and 1995; Nedostup 2001). During the Second Revolution (1925–27), the slogan *pochu mixin* ("Eradicate superstitions!") accompanied the classic *dadao junfa* ("Down with the warlords!") and *dadao diguozhuyi* ("Down with imperialism!"). The route followed by the Northern Expedition is studded with ransacked temples. In 1927, a crowd led by young Guomindang members destroyed the temple of Baoshan, Jiangsu, and decapitated the statue of the city god. The inhabitants recovered the head from the gutter, and once the temple was restored, replaced it on the statue (Yang 1991, 366). That same year, Dong Minxin, a veteran of the 1911 Revolution who founded and headed a college in Gaochun, Jiangsu, led his pupils in demolishing a local temple.

Box 6.2　　　　　　　　　　　　　Maneuvers by Priests and Monks: 1928–29

On 4 October 1928, the temple of the city god of Yancheng, Jiangsu, was plundered and threatened with conversion into a local meeting hall. The temple had been providing the monk in charge, Pan, with an annual income of several thousand *yuan*. His associate, magistrate Li, was accused of corruption by the local Guomindang. On 8 October, the two partners instigated a riot, with the help of the police chief, who had also been involved in embezzlement. The rioters destroyed the Guomindang headquarters, the education offices, and several schools, before sacrificing an iconoclastic schoolboy.

Five months later (12 March 1929), a Taoist priest assembled a crowd of 10,000 men, mostly members of religious sects: Small Knives, Red Spears, and in particular, followers of the Way Without End (Wujidao). They demonstrated against the ban of the Association of the Temple of the City God, a religious association in Teng Xian, Shandong. Led by the Taoist priest, the rebels besieged the city, but were blown away by artillery fire. Casualties included over 1,000 rioters killed or wounded.

SOURCES: For the Yancheng episode, Geisert 2001, 150–54 and *Yancheng WSZL*, vol. 2, 1984, 47–53; for Teng Xian, *Teng XZ*, 1989, 16.

The villagers were so infuriated that Dong fled his native county and went to take up other administrative duties north of the river (*Gaochun XZ*, 1988, 801).[19]

The "masses," rural or urban, who protested and occasionally destroyed the Guomindang's local headquarters and the homes of its leading activists, were fairly often manipulated by the monks or by the traditionalist local elite, who were outraged (or pretended to be) by the attacks on religion.[20] Box 6.2 reports two riots whipped up by such manipulators, whose only purpose was to defend their interests against threats from politicians or rivals.

Resistance to the destruction of temples or to antireligious measures and campaigns was intrinsically different from burning schools and opposing the census when it was believed to kill babies. Indeed, such resistance also obstructed modernization and was sometimes specifically aimed at the symbols of modernity, but in the main it was the defensive reaction of a community under attack.[21] It strongly expressed the community's sense of belonging, as suggested by the fact that such riots were often triggered by attacks on the temple of the city god. For the most part, these two behavior patterns encompass all the movements studied in this book, though less specifically those that are the subject of this chapter. Replacing a people's religion—deemed superstition—with the cult of Sun Yat-sen (as happened in Gaoyou in 1931), and even secularizing a temple by converting it into a meeting hall (as in Yancheng in 1928), represented a less urgent progression toward modernity than establishing "modern" schools. The villagers' reaction being in both cases foreseeable, it would have been better to confront them over the schools that shortage of funding and urgency obliged the authorities to locate in the temples. Similarly, campaigns to stop sick people consulting Taoist priests, mediums, or sorcerers would ideally have followed, and not preceded, the building of hospitals, which over half the counties still lacked in 1936 (Nedostup 2001, 526).

The iconoclasm of the May Fourth Movement inspired both these latter measures, aimed at "reforming people's behavior" (*fensu gaige*) and the fury against the temples. Taoist temples were more often targeted. While the richest of the Buddhist monasteries might well have attracted envy by reason of their vast land holdings, the Guomindang activists did not destroy them "gratuitously." Buddhism was reputed a "legitimate" religion and on that count was often spared. By contrast, even more than Taoism, the innumerable local cults, not organized into national churches and bereft of any "noble" written tradition, were reputed to be pure superstition and therefore open to persecution. They embodied the old society organized into cult groups (lineages, clans, villages, cultural associations) and were viewed as being obstacles to the emergence of a modern society (Goossaert 2003, 432–36).

The archaic society that the iconoclasts intended to purge of its temples, cults, and superstitious customs was primarily a rural society. Once the Nationalists were securely in power, they did not always burden themselves with considerations of prudence and it was quite simply the police who took over from the Guomindang militants in the fight against superstition. When in November 1931 the inhabitants of Xiwan (the Western Bay) went in procession to Nanqiao (the Southern Bridge), in Fengxian county, near Shanghai, to "greet and thank the gods," the police opened fire to force them back. The marchers, now furious, destroyed the police station (*Fengxian XZ*, 1987, 29). Another scenario, scarcely any different, occurred in the same locality (Nanqiao) in the evening of 13 March 1946. This time, 1,000 peasants from the four corners of the county and two townships were on their way to participate in the Dragon's Lantern festival. The police threatened to fire, but did not, and instead beat the marchers, who went to demonstrate outside the county office. The magistrate slipped out by the rear entrance (*Fengxian XZ*, 1987, 35). Sometimes, the police were not content with obstructing festivals or "idolatrous" processions and blatantly extorted money from pilgrims coming to attend a religious ceremony. So it happened at the Dongyue Temple, in Junshan, Jiangyin county, Jiangsu, on 22 April 1914. The peasants surrounded the county offices, but their demonstration was dispersed (*Jiangyin shizhi*, 1992, 20).

QUEUES AND PRAYERS FOR RAIN

In the same way, the ban on prayers for rain and the cutting of queues were regarded by the authorities quite differently than by the peasants. From the authorities' point of view, there was no doubt that the banning of prayers for rain was part of the fight against superstition that we have described above. For the peasants, a vital question was at stake, drought being a recurrent and deadly scourge. The authorities were often very clumsy in interrupting or dispersing many processions it might have been expedient to overlook—for reasons applying equally to exorcists or healing sorcerers—until they found themselves able to provide irrigation and health care. There were times when they had to intervene, if only to prevent suicides by drowning in the pond where the dragon who controlled rainfall was supposed to reside (these sacrificial offerings were intended to prompt him to kindlier feelings). By comparison with this tragic confrontation, the affair of the queues seems almost harmless. The peasants had become fond of them but it was not a question of life or death. For the government, however, the cutting of queues symbolized the liberation of the Han from Manchu domination—a Nationalist manifesto rather than a modernist undertaking. Paradoxically, the Nationalist government was not in the avant-garde of this enterprise, quite simply because the requirement to wear queues had been abolished before they took power. It was at the very start of the Republic that it led to incidents; since the problem was less difficult, though, it was sorted out by the 1920s. By contrast, the conflict over prayers for rain lasted throughout the period.

Box 6.3   Resistance to the Cutting of Queues: Ankang, Shaanxi, 1913

Guards posted since the winter at the gates of Ankang were cutting the queues of people coming into the city. This aroused sharp displeasure among the peasants. In Jianshanzhai, an elementary school teacher who had two pupils shorn of their queues was sworn at by their parents. Three militiamen who came to bring these insulting parents to justice were killed by the villagers (17 February 1913). Conscious of what awaited them, the peasants hastily organized a self-defense force and placed themselves under the leadership of Yang Wenhan, a former militiaman in the time of Emperor Guanxu.

The first bloody encounters (15, 16, and 19 March) led to systematic killings and burnings. At their height (late March and early April), the forces commanded by Yang numbered several thousand men, supported by the villagers of three counties (in addition to Ankang, Hanyin, and Ziyang) working night and day making ammunition for the rebels. The militia gave no quarter, wiping out during a single raid more than 100 of Yang's supporters. Most of the peasant leaders were arrested and summarily shot, their homes burned, and their property confiscated.

SOURCE: *Ankang XZ*, 1989, 631–33.

Queues

From 1912 onwards, the new government set about banishing this symbol of subjection imposed by the Manchu conquerors. The task was so unpopular, at least in the countryside, that the authorities were quite often forced to defer its application.[22] When the police did insist and acted with brutality, they were likely to incite a revolt.[23] The most serious affair was the bloody confrontation that occurred in Jianshanzhai, in Ankang county, Shaanxi, from February to April 1913 (Box 6.3).

Prayers for rain

In a single county (Shehong, Sichuan), the authorities' intolerance and lack of understanding and the villagers' obstinate adherence to any saint just to survive provoked three riots in thirteen years (Box 6.4).

In the same region of Sichuan (around Nanchong), a riot broke out in Yingshan during the drought of summer 1943. It was triggered by the ban on sacrificing cattle during prayers for rain (*Yingshan XZ*,

Box 6.4 Fighting the Ban on Praying for Rain:
Shehong, Sichuan, 1928, 1936, and 1941

Following several periods of drought since 1926 and a still more severe drought in spring 1928, thousands of peasants in Fuxing Zhen gathered outside the county offices asking the magistrate to conduct a ceremony of prayers for rain addressed to the King Dragon (Longwang). The magistrate did not show himself, so the peasants invaded his residence, broke his opium pipe, and eventually obtained from a member of the administration the promise that a prayer service would be organized, that an emergency fund to help the hungry would be released, and that they would be exempted from some very heavy military dues. Outside the city walls, other peasants also numbering in thousands knew nothing of these latest concessions and attempted to force their way into the city. Troops killed five of them and wounded twelve others.

During the terrible famine of spring and early summer 1936 (*PWP*, 231–32), about 1,000 peasants marching in a score of processions forced the magistrate to accompany them, his head bare and bare-footed, to the Dragon Temple. The magistrate's son ordered the guards to fire on those who had stayed outside his father's office. One peasant was killed and a dozen wounded (22 June 1936).

A similar scenario unfolded on 28 and 30 May 1941. Believers in two processions praying for rain caused damage to the county offices and a *xiang* office. Two peasants were killed and sixteen arrested, of which five were later executed.

SOURCE: *Shehong XZ*, 1990, 9, 653 and 660.

1989, 18). In summer 1934, northern Zhejiang was stricken by drought. On orders from the Chongde magistrate, peasants praying for rain were slaughtered (*SB*, 16 August 1934, 9). On 12 August 1934, in Yuyao county (same province), peasants beat to death a 60-year-old school head, a member of the local Guomindang Committee. He had been attempting to dissuade them from praying for rain. They threw his body in the river. Later, when the body was fished out, his skull was found to be smashed and his throat cut (*SB*, 16 August 1934, 11).

SPRING SILKWORMS

To shift to a different perspective, let us borrow from Mao Dun the title of his famous story "Chuncan" ("Spring Silkworms") to introduce the series of riots sparked off by the provision of new, improved strains of silkworm eggs in several Zhejiang counties in spring 1933 (Box 6.5).

Box 6.5   Spring Silkworms: Zhejiang, 1933

The switch to new silkworm eggs was aimed at boosting the competitiveness of Chinese silk production in its heartland. The opposition of silkworm raisers delayed its application.

Zhejiang, enjoying climatic and pedological conditions favoring the cultivation of the mulberry, produced by itself one-third of all China's output of raw silk. Sericulture was practiced in more than three-quarters of the province's counties, but concentrated in the north: south of Lake Tai, around the capital Hangzhou, and a little further east, south of Hangzhou Bay. For centuries it had contributed to the region's prosperity, as an indispensable second source of income, after rice. Now came a catastrophic crisis, during which the value of Chinese silk exports fell by two-thirds in five years (from 282 million dollars in 1928 to 93 million in 1933). The slump in sales of Chinese silk owed much to the arrival on the market of artificial silk and the shrinking appetite for luxury imports induced by the global depression. However, world purchases of silk did not fall by nearly as much proportionately as did China's silk exports. So we must consider other factors in the declining competitiveness of Chinese silk, which for several decades had faced competition from Japanese silk of higher quality that was more cheaply produced thanks to mechanization and less conducive to losses thanks to the more "scientific" raising of silkworms. In 1909, for the first time, Japanese silk exports exceeded China's. As the China Year Book insists, "The most urgent need is for healthy silkworm eggs." In the absence of preventive measures, once disease took hold of a number of worms, it was transmitted from generation to generation by contact between the cocoons and the eggs. And as the sick or dead worms collected around the feet of the mulberry trees as a plant food, the germs came back to the farm with the mulberry leaves. So losses were considerable. The surviving worms were raised with more devotion than technical knowledge. Their environment was not properly ventilated, the temperature and humidity not controlled, and the cocoons not classified according to levels of quality. The threads, being drawn from several cocoons at a time, were of variable fineness. The end product was sometimes very good but its extreme irregularity discouraged importers.

Taking some helpful advice from a League of Nations expert, the Nationalist authorities sent a group of specialists to study the Japanese methods of raising silkworms and producing silk and directed significant funding into agronomic research in China. Provincial research centers opened numerous sericulture courses to students with elementary school diplomas or above. A Silk Regulation Office banned sales of poor-quality silk while subsidizing the production it judged correct. By 1932, a three-part program for reforming the traditional silk production techniques was in place: silk farms were to be disinfected, to stop infections of the silkworms; there would be technical regulation of the processes for raising the worms; and higher-quality eggs would be produced in experimental incubators, leading to better worms than those previously produced by the peasants themselves.

None of these three prescriptions for reform were well received by the silk raisers. Many of those in Lin'an county, to the southwest of Hangzhou, were convinced that disinfection would harm their health and that of their silkworms. They would not allow the government's agents through the door. Even in the outskirts of Hangzhou, where a team of reform inspectors had been providing extensive explanations and pressuring local notables into supporting the reforms, the agents succeeded in disinfecting only 46 percent of the houses where silkworms were being raised. Regulating the raising of the worms posed an even thornier problem, because it involved transferring them to temperature-controlled areas under expert supervision. Few peasants were prepared to give up raising silkworms by themselves and in their own homes. They were afraid that the proximity of other people's worms in a collective silk farm would contaminate their own. So they refused, or were forced into cooperating.

The first two elements in the reform aroused only passive resistance, nothing more extreme than nonviolent foot-dragging. It was the third element that set off the revolt, but not immediately. The administration was at first content to encourage raisers to buy better-quality eggs produced in experimental incubators, but when no one bought any, it resolved to forbid the use of lower-quality eggs produced by the raisers or bought cheaply from local tradesmen. It was this ban that enraged the raisers.

In Xiaoshan county, the location for several "model" sericulture centers, the order went out to collect and destroy all local silkworm eggs (*tuchan canzhong*, shortened to *tuzhong*, "strain of silkworm produced locally") before 20 February 1933. In compensation, the raisers were to receive a subsidy, not in money but in the form of reduced prices for the improved egg strains. A month later (20 March), 1,000 peasants attacked the experimental center that was producing the higher-quality eggs, ransacked the offices of the Farm Association (an official body) and several elementary schools, and injured a policeman and threw him in the water.

A few days later (24 March) in Lin'an county, several thousand peasants, called in by the Association of Silkworm Raisers (another official body), set fire to an experimental center for improving egg strains. A second center was destroyed soon afterward, followed by a government cocoon workshop.

On 25 March, the Office for Eliminating Local Silkworm Strains, in Yuhang county, gave the order for the proscribed strains to be destroyed and called for a meeting of raisers in the afternoon. The same day, a brigade of soldiers was dispatched to the meeting place, in order to prevent the outbreak of such riots as those that had just disturbed the two neighboring counties. In addition, the authorities decided to organize a new clarification session. Summoned on 30 March to the headquarters of Yuhang county, thousands of silkworm raisers were addressed by two representatives of the Provincial Bureau of Rural Reconstruction, who extolled the advantages of the improved strains. After the meeting, the two delegates prepared to leave Yuhang, but they found the road blocked by peasants on their knees imploring them not to destroy their home-produced silkworm eggs (*tuzhong*). The delegates' car moved forward, injuring the legs of two peasants.

On 5 April, a further incident occurred in which some peasants believed that petitioners from nearby villages en route for the county town were arrested by members of the Office for Eliminating Local Silkworm Strains. They sounded the gong to rescue them. The magistrate talked to the rescuers and thought he had calmed them down. But the petitioners moved onto the Sericulture Research Bureau to drive out the employees of the Office for Eliminating Local Silkworm Strains, whom the peasants considered to have no business in an office funded by their taxes. Peasants clashed with the office guards, soon reinforced by 30 or so policemen from their quarters east of the town. The newcomers opened fire, wounding three petitioners—whose comrades, now furious, ransacked the Research Bureau. The gongs had been sounding since midday, mobilizing 5,000 to 6,000 peasants who reached town by the evening. Since the guards had gone off to hide in a nearby village, the disturbances continued until midnight. One source tells a different story: the police, still on the spot, opened fire, killing or wounding five people, including a child. This provoked a general strike, a protest, by shopkeepers in the county town. On 7 April, the authorities beat a retreat, announcing the suspension of measures to eliminate the local strains of silkworm eggs. Calm was restored.

The incidents in Yuhang, Lin'an, and Xiaoshan broke out in the heart of the silk-producing area, in a region where almost two out of three farming families (62 percent in Xiaoshan and 64 percent in Lin'an), or even five out of six (83 percent in Yuhang), raised silkworms. What is more, Yuhang was the production center for the most widespread strain of *tuzhong*, sold beyond the county borders, and Xiaoshan was where the most important "model center" had been located by the Association for Improving the Raising of Silkworms and Cultivating Mulberries. By comparison, a very small proportion (less than 10 percent) of Yuyao farmers raised silkworms, which did not prevent more than 5,000 peasants from the east of the county from coming to demonstrate outside the county offices against the eradication of "local" silkworms. The army and the police opened fire and wounded three demonstrators, which impelled the others to destroy the Office for Eliminating Local Silkworm Strains.

SOURCES: On the reforms and the background, Weidner 1983 and 1980, 32–51; Miner 1973, 221–28; Kirby 2000, 143–44. See also Bell 1999 for comparison purposes with sericulture improvement and experiment stations in Wuxi, Jiangsu. The most detailed account of the revolts may be found in "Zhejiang sheng Xiaoshan Yuhang Lin'an Yuyao Cixi dengxian cuishou dijia jingguo qingxing" (The struggle by the peasants of Xiaoshan, Yuhang, Lin'an, Yuyao, and Cixi counties of Zhejiang province against the improved silkworms and against the surveying of sandy areas), a 40-page file kept in *ZD2LDG*, shelf 721/1/1556. See also *Lin'an WSZL*, vol. 1, 1988, 45–56; USDS 893.00 PR Shanghai/57 (monthly report, April 1933) and 893.00/12371 (Cunningham Dispatch, May 1933); *Yuhang XZ*, 1992, 11; "Zhejiang erwan nongmin baodong" (Rebellion of 20,000 peasants in Zhejiang), a three-page manuscript kept in the Hoover Institution, pro-communist and unreliable; Zhejiang sheng zhengxie wenshi ziliao weiyuanhui 1990, 258–59.

Among those counties mentioned in Box 6.5, Yuyao was a frequent focus for disturbances. No other county in the province—and indeed in the whole country—features so often in our record of revolts. That was not the case with Lin'an, which before the riot in spring 1933 was remarkably calm. In Xiaoshan county, a key location for implementing the reforms, the good results obtained using the improved egg strains distributed in 1928 encouraged so many raisers to buy eggs the following year from the model incubators that demand outstripped supply. The authorities had to encourage the establishment of private incubators conforming to the required technological standards. So one can identify even in the abortive attempt to improve silkworm eggs some elements that justified Fei Xiaotong's measured optimism: "The suspicion of novelty went hand-in-hand with the readiness to accept reform when, by demonstration, the new technique could be proved useful." (Fei 1939, 212). Sadly, the rapid progress in the production of improved egg strains during 1929 and 1930 caused prices to fall in 1931. That same year, the catastrophic floods in Jiangsu and Zhejiang ruined the harvest of mulberry leaves, which meant fewer worms could be raised, and the demand for eggs was thus much reduced. Still worse, during the season for fattening up the silkworms, bad weather led to a poor production of cocoons. At a stroke, the confidence of the raisers in the improved egg strains evaporated (*China Industrial Handbooks, Kiangsu*, 280–83; also *China Year Book*, 1934, 775).[24]

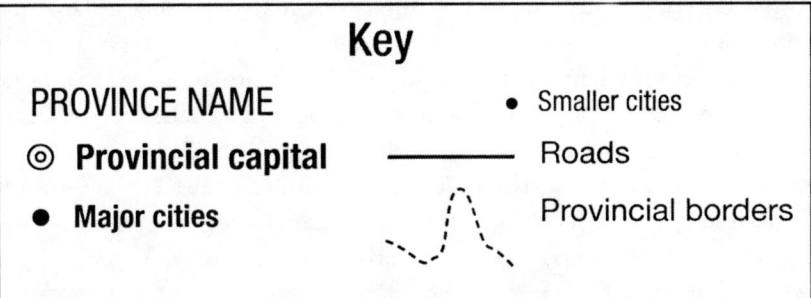

Map 6.1 Northern Zhejiang

These episodes enable us to define a little more closely the mentality and conduct of most Chinese peasants. They were far from irrational; indeed, they were fundamentally pragmatic. But they were prudent, and inclined to reach decisions by consulting their immediate interests. Such prudence and near-sightedness were supported by the peasants' incapacity to control the longer term or the repeated "blows of fate." How, then, could they not attribute to "fate" anything that did not depend on themselves: meteorological fluctuations and natural calamities, sharp jumps in currency rates, economic fluctuations, visits from predatory soldiers, or raids by bandits?

The silkworm raisers' extreme poverty, exacerbated by the collapsing export market, played a large part in their reluctance to give up using the local silkworm eggs raised at home or cheap to buy, in favor of improved strains costing a lot more. The subsidies granted in compensation for destroying the local strains were inadequate. Even when the administration backed the subsidies by selling the improved strains at cost and making cheaper credit available to customers, the sums did not add up. If the available funds (admittedly in short supply) provided from provincial or national budgets had permitted raisers freely to exchange local strains for an equivalent quantity of improved strains, the reforms would have had a better chance of success.

And even then, they would have had to be more amply and more patiently explained. Sometimes they were, though often too late, once the administration had grasped the full extent of peasant resistance. After the incident of 30 March in Lin'an, the Guomindang and the county government sent emissaries each day to the villages to explain to the raisers the advantages that the reforms would bring. Elsewhere, and in other circumstances, explanations were too summary and the reforms were implemented too quickly. The information officers—and there were never enough of them—were often inexperienced students borrowed from the provincial sericulture schools. Spokesmen recruited from within village society would have been invaluable. The reform officials tended to behave like technocrats, not taking the time beforehand to persuade enough local notables to act as spokesmen for the reforms among the "ignorant masses." In Yuhang, when delegates from the Rural Reconstruction Bureau suddenly announced that no cocoon produced from local silkworm strains would be permitted to survive, the village and township heads and members of local associations suggested they should advance prudently, take more time, and explain more—steps without which they would be risking serious misunderstandings.

We cannot then fully absolve an administration that relied too much on coercion, and not enough on persuasion. Moreover, the authorities did not plan the campaign more carefully. Supposing it had been welcomed, they would not have been in a position to satisfy the demand for the improved strains. In Xiaoshan, in 1933, they had in stock scarcely one-third of local requirements. That same year, in Wuxi, Jiangsu (quite a distance from the epicenter of the riots), the silk producers followed the example of their Zhejiang fellows in setting fire to the installations of the model silk center, because the staff had destroyed their "local eggs" when they had no more improved ones to sell.

Even so, the administration's task was not easy. Eliminating the low-quality silkworm eggs was absolutely necessary because their continued use would have undermined the effectiveness of all their other improvements to silk production. The raisers suspected the administration of seeking to dispossess them and establish its own monopoly. But, as a first step, a government monopoly of egg production, accompanied by tight regulation of operations before (mulberry cultivation) and after (raising of worms, production, sale and pricing of different quality cocoons) represented the least harmful solution. A man as heedful as Fei Xiaotong of the peasants' well-being acknowledged that the indispensable participation of a specialist, using equipment that individual raisers could never afford, required that eggs be produced collectively. This would have implied, not a financial dispossession (since the cooperative would have transferred the profits to them), but the loss of control over some phases of the work that formerly they had carried out as it suited them (Fei 1939, 213).

"As it suited them" is just a form of words. These people were slaves to their dear, voracious little creatures, which demanded to be fed night and day for six weeks and which, in addition, were playthings of the market's fads and foibles. All that effort, all that care, were in some years thrown away, when the sale price of the cocoons fell below the cost of production. And then again, the production cost was underestimated, because the peasants would never have included their own efforts. When, as prosperity revived in the West, world silk prices began to recover, cocoon prices did not follow suit. The silk filatures had pocketed the difference, partly to repay the interest on investments they had been forced into making, to survive the crisis, and to adapt. The breeding of higher-quality silkworm eggs was a technical and partial reform, one that might have fixed some problems (it began to do so in 1935), but not those of the silk market. That same market forced Mao Dun's hero to sell his cocoons at a loss. Having broken his back working through the spring, he ended up still poorer than before.

Nevertheless, let us return to those half-dozen schools ransacked at Xiaoshan in spring 1933. Schools were not responsible for eliminating the local strains of silkworm eggs. The fact that they were chosen as targets makes a connection between the 1933 movement and its predecessor in 1910. It suggests resentment of educated people, those with knowledge, those who oppress ignorant people. That resentment is part of the peasant revolt against modernization. Hu Shi was right to place ignorance among the "five great enemies" to be fought and eradicated as a matter of urgency. The peasants were its first casualties, while those people classed as educated—including some of the local elite's offspring with a superficial veneer of classical culture—mostly used and abused their "cultural capital," however meager, to exploit those deprived of it.

The exactions and corruption that the implementation of the reforms unleashed were enough by themselves to explain why the peasants eventually perceived any reform, any innovation, as a further means to exploit them. Such exploitation was often associated with contempt: the official who instructed his driver to advance on the kneeling crowd was prompted by fear perhaps, and perhaps also by arrogance.

However, we must appreciate the effects of ignorance, not just on ignorant people themselves, but also on society as a whole. We must be careful not to treat any of the superstitions cited in this chapter, still less any innocent religious ceremonies elsewhere regarded as folklore, as obstacles to the modernization of a backward country.[25] By contrast, other incidents mentioned in this chapter did effectively hold back modernization, firstly the countless arson attacks on schools perpetrated during the closing years of the Empire. Other episodes, such as the 1933 silk riots, obstructed it only a little, though they did complicate the task of the reformers. And many others, mentioned here or not (examples in Bianco 1986, 288; Geisert 2001, 155; Kirby 2000, 145–46), had no lasting effect but did have a comparable symbolic significance. At a wider level, the impact of ignorance, superstitions, and peasant traditions still today acts as a brake on the modernization of the country.

SEVEN

Conscription

Revolts targeted at the army were very rare before 1937 because they were too dangerous. But they became far more numerous during the Sino-Japanese War. More precisely, attacks were aimed less often at the army itself than at the institution that fed it: military service.[1] Introduced in 1933, conscription was hardly implemented anywhere outside the semi-autonomous province of Guangxi, until the time when resistance to the invaders called for millions of soldiers. It was from then on enforceable throughout the country, from autumn 1938 onward mainly in the unoccupied provinces of the southwest. The peasants could ill accept conscription and often fought it, since they constituted the overwhelming majority of recruits. At the outset, they found themselves dealing less directly with the army than with the civil administrators in charge of recruitment, against whom, in consequence, they directed their resistance. As it happened, "administrators" is rather a grand word for the multitude of *bao* and village heads who were responsible for visiting peasant households, preferably by night and accompanied by militiamen, to seize conscripts selected according to a more or less opaque, if not rigged, lottery system.

Between 1937 and 1945, conscription almost became the primary target for peasant unrest, even for the first time surpassing taxes in that distinction. I add the qualifier "almost" because the two motives were often linked in mixed affairs, which brought some further grievance (usually taxes) to bear against conscription. Furthermore, among the rare occasions when riots directed against the army did not specifically target military service, most were provoked by military taxes—or parafiscal exactions by the military. On top of the taxes raised by or for the army, various contributions and requisitions were demanded by army units stationed locally.

Let us first examine the revolts provoked by resistance to military service; after that, mixed cases, also very numerous, directed against military service and something else; and lastly, those far less frequent revolts directed against the army but not involving military service. A special paragraph at the end of the chapter will introduce those revolts of exceptional significance that were provoked by military service and one or several other causes. Even if they had originally been sparked off by a single cause, these uprisings could not have failed to draw in other grievances along the way, for the simple reason that they had acquired weight and momentum never previously encountered in this book.

Military Service

For those close to him, "a conscript's life usually ended on the day he disappeared down the road, shackled to his fellows" (Peck 1950, 226), unless he succeeded in deserting within a few days. But the army took care he should not. On an occasion when a Japanese warplane divebombed a train, the passengers succeeded in escaping—except for the conscripts, shackled to their seats and burned alive (*Weinan XZ*, 1987, 14). On a cold night in February 1945, an American military doctor was astonished to see 40 or 50 soldiers piled up naked in a filthy, freezing loft, while the ground floor, more spacious and less cold, was unoccupied. Upon asking about them, he was told that the soldiers could not be bedded down on the ground floor because they might escape, and that they were stripped of their clothes and shoes to stop them from getting out through the roof, which happened sometimes, despite the sentries posted around the building (Eastman 1984, 150).

These are extreme cases, certainly, but also revealing. It is not at all uncommon to read accounts of soldiers chained together, hands tied behind their backs, dragged hundreds of miles away from their homes. They were known to have drunk water from puddles, thereby contracting chronic diarrhea, to have been beaten to death, even shot down if they became too exhausted or ill to walk any further. This first march toward the front or wherever they were to be quartered was so harsh an experience that it reportedly cost the lives of more than a million conscripts over the eight years of the war.

This drain on manpower was still modest, when compared with the numbers lost through desertion. According to James Scott, desertion represented, along with tax evasion, the most formidable of the "weapons of the weak," which seriously eroded the effectiveness of Russia's Provisional Government forces in 1917, contributing thereby to the Bolshevik victory (1985, 293–94). If we return to the Chinese case and add to the deserters those abandoned as casualties or stragglers by the roadside, something like eight million soldiers disappeared into thin air between 1937 and 1945, about half of all those enlisted. Everyday resistance to conscription, or put another way, the flight of young peasants of draft age and the manipulation of their civil status by their families to make them older or younger, gives us the material for a prelude to our analysis of violent resistance.

DRAFT DODGING AND DESERTION

There were far more draft dodgers (*duo zhuangding*) than deserters. Some escaped military service through an absolutely legal route, by changing jobs. Workers in coal mines and salt works were exempted from military service, and so a considerable number of young Sichuanese peasants switched to these occupations. Others went to the cities, where for meager wages they swelled the numbers of rickshaw pullers, laborers, and domestic servants ("Beipei shehui gaikuang diaocha" 1942, 59 and 73; cited in Fu 2007, 168). As with running away, the rural exodus moved them into the margins of illegality and exposed to reprisals their families back in the village. Other families avoided the risk by fleeing all together, under the pretext of doing some business elsewhere. Other young men cut off their own index fingers so they could not pull triggers or put out their own eye so they could not aim. More numerous were the draft evaders who hid in isolated regions or joined sects or secret societies to secure protection. In many villages in southern Shaanxi, by 1944, a visitor would see only children, women, and old men (Guofangbu shizheng bianyiju bingyi dang'an, Taipei, file 370.3/7280: "Bingyi jiantao yü gaijin yijian huiji" [source provided by Fu]).

By way of a transition to violent resistance, I should mention an incident arising out of desertion. In southwestern Anhui in September

1942, 100 conscripts just enlisted were lying on the ground. They were ill fed and regularly beaten for nothing at all. One of them threw lime into the guard's eyes and shouted, "Let's get out!" They all ran for it, but being unfamiliar with the area, about 40 took an alley in the darkness that led down to a lake. They plunged in and hid under some water lily leaves, but were seen by the mistress of a company commander, who had the lake machine-gunned. The next morning, 24 bodies were fished out (*Taihu WSZL*, vol. 1, 1985, 34–36).

The transition to violent collective action becomes more apparent when we come to groups of draft dodgers or deserters surviving by hijacking salt convoys or pillaging grain stores, sometimes in alliance with bands of robbers. After 1939, rural society in Sichuan was destabilized and there was chronic brigandage in neighboring Hunan and Guizhou. Meanwhile, army units at the front deployed no more than two-thirds or three-quarters of their nominal strength, although it is true that desertion was not the only cause. Many officers put off declaring troop shortages (due to desertion, sickness, or death), keeping for themselves the missing soldiers' pay, food rations, clothing, and ammunition (Fu 2007, 66). These racketeers mocked their few honest colleagues for being unable to feed their families. By 1944, inflation had reduced their pay to one-eighth of its real value in 1937.

THE LOTTERY

Peasants often expressed their dissatisfaction when those eligible were subjected to selection by lottery. At the start of the Sino-Japanese War, the authorities hardly ever used this method. They preferred, and so did the public, to take a contribution from each household in rice or money, enabling them to pay a volunteer. This practice of "buying a volunteer" (*mai ziyuanbing*) was particularly widespread in densely populated Sichuan. Quite soon, however, manpower needs burgeoned and there were insufficient volunteers to fill the growing quotas assigned to each village or district. In autumn 1938, the first attempts were made at selection by lottery, arousing hostility and suspicion among those liable. Draftees were hostile because drawing lots involved greater obligations compared with the system of voluntary recruitment, and they were suspicious because they feared, often justifiably, that the dice were loaded and that parents, friends, and clients of local leaders were exempt from the draft, along with those who had paid to draw the right numbers.

The November 1938 incident in Xindu, Sichuan (Box 1.5), was one of the very first triggered by the practice of drawing lots. A few months later, in February 1939, a more lethal riot broke out in Ziyang, in the same province, in response to cheating by the *lianbao* chiefs during the draft lottery.[2] The draftees used axes and other farm tools to slaughter seventeen of the eighteen *lianbao* chiefs who had gathered to organize recruitment. The county magistrate restored order by calling out the militia, who killed or wounded 700 to 800 of the 2,000 to 3,000 conscripts active in the revolt (*ZD2LDG*, file 2/1863).

From 1939 onwards, recruitment was intensified in Sichuan and across the whole of southwest China. Responsibility was now passed to the county magistrates, who had been further promoted to the command of the local militias. The authorities hoped that this fusion of civil and military duties would encourage magistrates to prioritize the task of mobilization. In 1940, Guanghan county was the scene of a significant revolt, provoked by the lottery procedures and other causes also linked to conscription (Box 7.1).

LOTTERY RIGGING

The Guanghan revolt was emblematic of incidents arising from the lottery system—and something more. It threw light also on other recurring motives for resistance to conscription, beginning with corrupttion and lottery rigging. In Guanghan, admittedly, the riggers joined the revolt, but this was not usually the case. Elsewhere, they became targets for uprisings provoked by their misdeeds, as with the seventeen *lianbao* heads of Ziyang county mentioned above.

Far from being limited to the lottery, chicanery and extortion were common at every stage of recruitment. Some young men did not take part in the lottery, because village heads or *bao* chiefs had granted them, for a fee, authorization of absence. Others, who had drawn unlucky numbers, could still escape military service. In Fengjie county, Sichuan, the leader of the conscription service organized a network of corrupt officials who deputized *bao* heads to negotiate with the families of conscripts who had already drawn wrong numbers. These families could

Box 7.1   Opposition to the Draft Lottery:
Guanghan, Sichuan, 31 May–4 June 1940

The Guanghan revolt had several causes, of which the first and foremost was the draft lottery. One could escape military service by paying 200 *yuan* to be exempted from the lottery. This transaction even has an official name: *najin huanyi*, "spend money to obtain deferment" until the next draw. In addition, the young men discovered on the day of the lottery that it worked in an indirect way: instead of pulling out the conscripts' names, the officials drew bamboo slips with figures written on them. Those concerned had no knowledge of the figures assigned to them. Even after the draw, the list of conscripts was not made public so that those selected would not make a run for it. "Drawing lots" was renamed "drawing black" (*chou heiqian*) by the public, who mistrusted and protested this new form of recruitment. This was the main source of unrest among the 3,000 young men summoned to the lottery ceremony on 31 May in Guanghan.

The second cause was the increase in quotas. Many local youths had already fled the county in order to escape military service. Others, still more numerous, were content to purchase the cooperation of the *lianbao* heads, who left their names off the register of able-bodied men. Those who were actually listed noticed that the quota of 220 men to be recruited each month out of a population of 250,000 inhabitants was higher than that for neighboring counties. Yet, the quota was still theoretical, since the recruiting shortfall had become pronounced: in the eighteen months between November 1938 and April 1940, 1,494 fewer men had been recruited than the quota demanded. Perhaps that is what induced the magistrate in January 1940 to raise the monthly quota to 250 men.

The rigging of the lottery and the revolt of those behind it were a third cause. An official inquiry, carried out in spring 1940, put at over 20,000 the number of able-bodied men in the county aged between 18 and 36, instead of the 7,714 registered by the *bao* and *jia* heads. So these "little chiefs" left unregistered nearly two-thirds of those liable for the draft lottery, their purpose being to protect them, often in exchange for monetary considerations. Having been unmasked, they attempted to escape legal proceedings by encouraging the conscripts to rebel. The clumsiness, arrogance, and greed of the officers made things easier for them. On 30 May, the army unit responsible for delivering supplies to the conscripts in Lianshan township demanded a sum of 30 *yuan* per conscript, calling this an "induction expense" (*huanyingfei*). The head of the 20th *bao* refused to part with this sum. On his own authority, he reduced it to 10 *yuan*, being careful to pay the rest to the conscripts' hostel to win some popularity. The commander, who did not see it that way, placed the *bao* head in detention and also seized the conscripts (who were supposed to be on their way elsewhere) to secure "what is owed to him." This prompted unanimous protests from conscripts and *bao* heads, under the slogan "Not satisfied with claiming our men, the army also wants our money" (*bujin yaoren erqie yaoqian*).

The next day, 31 May, the lottery procedure was interrupted by a dozen armed militiamen from the 20th *bao*, who demanded that their chief be released. The young men summoned for the draw took advantage of the interruption to cause disturbances, and others came running in from outside. Caught unprepared, the commander and the district inspector, who were jointly presiding over the lottery, arrested three ringleaders, unleashing the "anger of the masses." Crowds surrounded the encampment of a company of the regiment garrisoned in Lianshan and called on the magistrate (who had come to witness events for himself) to move the entire regiment out. The magistrate played for time, but by the afternoon he was confronted with the siege of the Guanghan county capital by 2,000 to 3,000 peasants. A squad of armed police was dispatched to deal with them. The peasants attempted to block the road. The local people joined the protest, shouting slogans denouncing the rigging of the lottery system. The crowds started ransacking public buildings. The police opened fire, killing one rioter and wounding another. Violent clashes continued until the early hours.

The next day, 1 June, the disturbances spread to other parts of the county, fueled by the news that another township in the county would go ahead with the lottery as though nothing had happened. The rioters stormed through a *lianbao* office, destroying its registers and looting arms and ammunition. More peasants arrived from the four corners of the county, wielding knives, pickaxes, and guns. They joined forces with the besiegers of Guanghan, where shopkeepers went on strike. The police resorted again to gunfire, wounding several dozen of the besiegers.

On 2 June, the rebels, their numbers now swelled to 5,000, cut all communications. The magistrate finally yielded to the unanimous advice of local notables and canceled the current census operations, but this belated concession satisfied no one. Clashes became more violent, and the troops killed or wounded a large number of insurgents. The following day, 30 more were killed attempting to seize an arms depot. Confronted by an inrush of forces of repression (a whole division of troops was sent as reinforcements), the rebels finally lifted their siege on 4 June. Thanks to the intervention of a Guanghan notable, an influential member of a secret society, they nevertheless imposed their own conditions. The county government drew a line under the conscription shortfall (the accumulated deficit of 1,494 men since 1938), it quashed the results of the lottery, it renounced any damages claims against the rioters, and made no demand for the stolen weapons to be returned or replaced. Order was restored after five days of mayhem, during which seventeen *lianbao* offices were demolished and 130 militiamen and local people were killed.

SOURCES: Liu and Ran 1985; *ZD2LDG*, file 2/1863; *Deyang WSZLXJ*, vol. 6, 1987, 39; *Guanghan XZ*, 1992, 16.

buy dispensation of service for their sons, and the local authorities undertook to enlist other conscripts to fill the gaps. This traffic, which was discovered in 1942 after it had led to a riot, had possibly been going on for several years (*ZMDZH*, series no. 5, part 2, vol. 5, 1988, 203; source provided by Fu).

There were others who were ordered to pay for the local authorities to acknowledge the exemption from service to which the law entitled them. Though salt workers were exempted, as we have seen, from all military service, the mayor of Zigong, Sichuan, saw fit to demand preliminary payments of 200 *yuan* per man before accepting the exemption. He applied the measure by forcibly enlisting six salt workers on 2 August 1939, which set off a major riot (Fu 2007, 201–2).

Lastly, there were those who paid nothing, such as the son of the district head of Lanshui, Jiangxi, the only young man in his village to escape service in August 1937. The villagers took revenge on his father, whom they killed during the night of the Festival of the Moon. For their crime, especially since they went on to attack the district office and disarmed the militiamen, they paid dearly: their leaders were arrested and executed (*Yihuang WSZLXJ*, vol. 2, 1989, 35–38).

QUOTAS INCREASED OR DEMANDED IN ADVANCE

As in Guanghan, sudden or arbitrary increases in quotas were often sources of unrest. A village of 200 residents, to which had been applied a quota of 7 conscripts during the winter of 1937, had to face a demand a few months later for 5 extra conscripts. It was the village head of Gaopei, Sanjiang county, Guangxi, who made this demand with the single purpose of extorting 5,000 *yuan* from the villagers, which worked out to 1,000 *yuan* per extra conscript not recruited. When the militiamen arrived to pick up the recruits in March 1938, they were disarmed and chased off by the villagers (*Guangxi WSZLXJ*, vol. 28, 1988, 22–25). On a larger scale, Langdai county, Guizhou, saw its quota of conscripts increased without explanation from 692 in 1941 to 984 in 1942—and the quota was more than filled, with 1,140 soldiers actually recruited (*Liuzhi WSZLXJ*, vol. 3, 1988, 1–46). Such circumstances (quotas exceeded) usually were not achieved, because of huge difficulty in recruitment, because of chicanery—or both at once.

In the absence of reliable demographic data, recruitment officials were supposed to follow two simple rules, not always observed. In accordance with the first (*yijia yibing, yibao shubing*), they had to recruit one conscript per *jia* of 10 families and several conscripts per *bao* of 100 families. The second was intended to protect families with only one adult son from being deprived of minimal manpower: a family of five sons must provide two conscripts, a family of three one conscript, and only sons are exempted from military service (*wuding chou er, sanding chou yi, duzi miancheng*). This was a rule that *bao* heads broke quite often, if only to make up for exemptions granted to the rich. Thus it was in 1939 on the borders of Hunan and Guizou where failure to observe the rule exempting an only son provoked a deadly revolt (*Zhenyuan WSZL*, vol. 1, 1986, 146–51; *Guizhou WSZLXJ*, vol. 22, 1986, 96–104; both sources are by the same author, Wang Guohua).

Favors and corruption were not the only reasons why the rule was not always observed. In the closing stages of the civil war, the urgent need to close the gaps due to defeats and desertions induced a district head on Gouqi Island (Zhoushan Archipelago, Zhejiang) to recruit all the able-bodied men aged between 18 and 38, only sons included. He did not succeed; many of the fishermen made themselves scarce, and about 100 others resisted at harpoon point the recruiting force of militiamen (*Shengsi WSZLXJ*, vol. 1, 1989, 45–49).

Another practice not always tainted by corruption was the recruitment of soldiers according to future quotas. Just like collecting taxes in advance, this procedure could arouse dissatisfaction and resistance, as in Dashiban, Shaanxi, where the *bao* heads sought to recruit in 1945 the troops required for 1946 and 1947 (*Tongchuan WSZLXJ*, vol. 3, 1984, 43–47).

ZHUADING AND LADING

The forcible enlisting of designated conscripts (*zhua zhuangding* or *zhuading*) was legal in cases where the conscripts had not presented themselves willingly. It was a different matter with the illegal abduction (*lading*) of able-bodied men to make up for a shortage of recruits. Both practices aroused resistance, and whether civilians or soldiers, the recruitment officers risked being killed. Most often, villagers would take joint action to free the conscripts either by attacking at night the recruitment centers or by ambushing a convoy of conscripts. Thus, on 21 May 1939, the villagers of Luopi, Jiangxi, mounted a successful nighttime ambush of a convoy on the only road out of their village (*Shicheng WSZLXJ*, vol. 2, 1987, 89–98).[3] Solidarity between villages was also possible. During the recruitment campaigns of 1947 and 1948, Jiaoyuan and Xiaobu villages (in Ningdu county, Jiangxi) coordinated their efforts and gathered several hundred strong to rescue the conscripts (*Ningdu XZ*, 1986, 35).

As sketched briefly in Chapter 1, *lading* aroused greater indignation than the sudden seizure of designated conscripts. We have mentioned the case of salt workers, legally exempt from conscription, who had to pay 200 *yuan* to have that right acknowledged. Still more numerous were salt workers who were simply abducted and recruited by force.[4] From boatmen to peddlers to harvest workers selling their labor from farm to farm, those who moved about were more vulnerable than others to abductions or raids. The authorities hoped that enlisting them would not arouse so much resistance on the part of local people who might not know them so well. Even so, recruitment officers did come up against the solidarity of fellow workers, even that of villagers themselves. Needless to say, such raids did not always spare the local peasants.[5]

Whether the rules were observed or flouted, the primary victims of conscription were, as always, poor peasants. This was particularly true when the rules were flouted, given the corruption of local officials who sold exemptions to families able to afford them. It was true even when rules were observed: students and "professionals" being exempt from service, and substitutes, having to be paid, being drawn from families too poor to pay their share of the indemnity. This is a consideration that lends a social ingredient to the resistance to conscription. And the army's treatment of recruits was even worse than the usual treatment of peasants by the civil administration.

ILL-TREATMENT OF CONSCRIPTS

In 1938, a battalion of conscripts was crossing the Zhongjiang market in Sichuan, gaunt, dressed in rags, their hands tied behind their backs (Zhongguo guomindang dangshihui dang'an, file 493/160: Zhongjiang shibian jingguo wenjian; cited in Fu 2007, 510). In the ethnic minority regions, recruits were even worse treated, even more despised, and beaten for almost no reason, for example because they did not speak Mandarin. Being half-starved and denied access to hygiene, many fell ill. When the soldiers from eastern Guizhou (mostly members of ethnic minorities) were sent as reinforcements to Hunan, the sick and the dead were left behind on the roadside. It happened even that sergeants would shoot conscripts at their last gasp, so that they could grab their uniforms (*Guizhou WSZLXJ*, vol. 22, 1986, 96–97). In eastern Gansu, soldiers who were practicing Muslims (Hui) had to eat pork like the Han. At the start of the 1937 war, members of a charity visited a makeshift barracks and discovered there about 100 conscripts, all in a bad way or ill, lying on the ground among dead bodies and filth. Four years later, in October 1941, 2,000 conscripts were sent from Tianshui, in southeastern Gansu, to Lanzhou, the capital. When they reached Dingxi (a little over half-way there), there were only 800 left. Most of the others had died of hunger or cold, their officers having helped themselves to the money for their food rations and pay. The bodies had been abandoned under tufts of grass or in cesspits (*Gansu WSZLXJ*, vol. 1, 1963, 142–43; *Lanzhou WSZLXJ*, vol. 3, 1985, 112–13).

Ill-treatment and suffering provided further incentive to desert. When deserters were recaptured, they risked being shot or tortured to death, while recidivists could be buried alive. In testimony to a case of such brutality in 1941 in Santai, Sichuan, people declared the Chinese army "more inhumane than the Japanese enemy." Two years later in the same county, a conscript—it is not known if he had attempted to desert—was executed in public. The spectators vented their indignation, and the commanding officer ordered his men to fire on the crowd. Four demonstrators were killed and about ten were wounded. The furious locals surrounded the troops, who in turn became scared, thinking they would be prosecuted later for killing civilians. They deserted en masse (He 1986, 291 [source provided by Fu]).

MILITARY TRAINING FOR CIVILIANS

The male population was quickly learning about the condition of the soldiers and acquiring first-hand experience of military life. Indeed, military training courses were compulsory for all able-bodied men. In addition, the youngest (at first those aged between 18 and 30 and, from 1941 onwards, between 18 and 45) were required to serve in the local militia. On the short courses, men were supposed to bring their own food. They were frequently bullied, even brutalized—all the more so when they belonged to ethnic minorities. A contingent of Miao cadets from the borders of Hunan and Guizhou was driven beyond endurance, when during the night of 27 September 1939, the trainees cut the throats of several dozen military instructors. The reprisals fit the crime, with villages flattened and more than 100 peasants shot (*Zhijiang WSZLXJ*, vol. 1, 1987, 31–36; *Huaihua WSZLXJ*, vol. 2, 1988, 53–96).

The revolts mentioned above were chiefly concentrated in a single province: Sichuan. Indeed, it was there that resistance to conscription was most common and most intense. Sichuan was then (and is still now) China's most populous province, but there were circumstances other than demography to explain why Sichuan provided by itself three million of China's approximately 15 million soldiers enlisted during the Sino-Japanese War. In 1937 and 1938, more recruits were drawn from Henan and Guangxi, though their populations were smaller. In 1938, Chiang Kai-shek took refuge in Chongqing, where there followed a sudden rise in recruitment from a province in which local authorities were obliged more than elsewhere to apply the national government's directives. Thus, Sichuan's predominant role in resisting conscription lasted less than seven years, from November 1938 to August 1945. It was nowhere near the top of the list between 1900 and 1937, nor during the first fifteen months of war, nor between August 1945 and September 1949.

The resistance to conscription was at its height during the period from 1938 to 1945. The civil war years trailed far behind, with a few riots recorded between 1933 and 1937, and almost none between 1900 and 1932. During the war against the Japanese, unrest, already simmering between 1937 and 1940, became particularly intense from 1941 onward. The peak period was between 1942 and 1943, concurrent also with the most significant uprisings during the first half of the twentieth century (see below pp. 176–89).

Mixed Cases: Conscription and Something Else

During the war, cases of resistance to conscription, although numerous, were slightly outnumbered by mixed cases, provoked by conscription and some further cause. This extra element of dissatisfaction and unrest arose most often from taxes or something similar (charges and requisitions of all kinds imposed on villagers by the military). It might also arise from the ill-treatment, violence, and cruelty inflicted by the soldiery on the civil population. Or, lastly, it could happen (as in a minority of cases) that conscription was not a factor, that the army's demands and the bad behavior of the troops were enough to inflame the peasants against it.

TAXATION

Once again, taxes caused the most disaffection (see Box 7.2). The terms *kangding* (resist conscription) and *kangjuan* (resist taxes) are very often associated in our sources. The concurrence of these two "resistances" is becoming a cliche in many local monographs, compilations, or memoirs published in the PRC.[6] Sometimes the terms refer to a slogan of the time, but it is plausible that the leaders of the revolt were simply appealing to a wider public by invoking two subjects for complaint.[7] We should recall that the tax burden rose appreciably during the war (see Chapter 5). On top of "civilian" taxes were added those imposed by the administration for military needs and those the army took upon itself to demand without considering existing tax levels or taxpayers' ability to pay. And, worst of all, conscription itself often implied a new tax, heavier still than the land tax: namely, the share that everyone had to pay toward compensating substitutes, whether volunteers or selected by lottery.

BINGCHAI AND JUNLIANG

These two terms cover the multitude of charges by which the army bore down on the villagers. We have already encountered *bingchai* (see Chapter 1), the range of requisitions—including food, draft animals and fodder, wood, machinery, and corvée labor—imposed by or to the benefit of the army. *Junliang* was, more specifically, the army's grain, in other words the cereals destined for feeding the soldiers, and considered as a wartime priority. This grain was sometimes requisitioned and sometimes purchased at rock-bottom prices.

Box 7.2   Resistance to Tax and Conscription:
Zhongjiang, Sichuan, December 1938

The total land tax revenue for Zhongjiang had been fixed at 120,000 *yuan*, but this amount was not coming in well. By early 1938, the arrears reached 700,000 *yuan*. After several years of drought, the 1938 harvest promised to be good. The magistrate took the opportunity to pay off a good proportion of the arrears: 500,000 *yuan*, which was added to the 120,000 take for the year. The peasants' discontent increased when the tax office hired as collectors some thugs who conspired with the ward and *bao* chiefs to extort travel expenses and file charges from the taxpayers. They granted deferment of contributions to those who paid up, imposing lateness penalties on the others; and they even arrested some defaulters and marched them through the streets wearing asses' heads with "tax debtor" written on them.

The magistrate followed the same policy with conscription. To recover the deficit, he added to the quota of two conscripts per *bao* another two conscripts "in reserve." This meant calling up 4,296 men for the 1,074 *bao* in the county. Despite the fact that only sons were, as we have seen, exempt from service, local officials extorted from their parents payment for substitutes or cash allowances for conscripts' families, money that they often kept for themselves. They also abducted young men to fill the conscription quota and they poured into *xindou* (new bushels) the allocation of cereals for conscripts' families, whereas they themselves had collected the grain contributions in *laodou* (traditional bushels), with each of the latter holding the equivalent of 2.67 *xindou*.

The resentment aroused by taxes, the draft, and the corruption triggered a whole series of demonstrations and riots, to shouts of "Refuse military service, defer payment of land tax, punish corrupt officials!" As early as 24 November, the peasants destroyed a tax office. The next day they smeared with excrement the director of a tax office. On 5 December, a protest against unfair selection of conscripts turned nasty: a *bao* head was denounced, his son fired on the crowd, they responded by tearing down his father's house. In a township nearby, the rioters surrounded the *lianbao* offices demanding that the lottery results be cancelled. When the magistrate prevaricated, they destroyed the offices, then threw stones and bricks at the magistrate. He was saved from a worse fate by the arrival of a score of militiamen, several of whom were killed by the rioters.

Even after a state of siege was declared, the disturbances spread quickly. Twenty-three townships and villages joined the uprising between 7 and 9 December. In several of these localities, the peasants demolished *lianbao* and tax offices, burning the homes of *lianbao* heads, beating officials to death, ransacking schools, and thrashing schoolchildren guilty of having spread pro-conscription publicity. Ten thousand insurgents—the peasant rioters had been infiltrated by brigands—besieged the Zhongjiang county capital. By 14 December, a regiment of security police had put an end to the revolt, at the cost of significant concessions. The magistrate and several ward heads were dismissed, 200 jailed tax defaulters were released, tax payments were deferred, and the method and rate of recruitment were adjusted to 537 conscripts a month (one per *bao* every two months). Nevertheless, two accused "conspirators" were summarily shot to pay the price for a revolt that resulted in the homes of 800 *bao* and *jia* heads torched and a score of officials killed—not to mention about 100 dead rioters.

SOURCES: Guomindang Archives, file 493/160, reports by Wang Yuanhui and Wu Di (provided by Fu); ZMDZH, 1988, series 5, part 2, report by Cheng Defang, 160–64 (provided by Fu); *Zhongjiang WSZLXJ*, vol. 4, 1986, 60–67.

The army did not worry about whether the regions it crossed or occupied could afford the contributions. It was content simply to express its needs. So these "military" charges (as opposed to the "civilian" charges described in the previous paragraph that themselves partly fed into the army budget) varied enormously from one region to the next, according to the army's movements and the number of troops stationed in any one place. Of course, they were heavier in "war zones," such as the Guanzhong region east of Shaanxi, where the two armies stationed in 1938 had been strengthened to fourteen by 1943—not so much to contain any possible Japanese advance as to encircle the main communist base. In all, there were more than 300,000 soldiers who had to be fed at the region's expense. It is no surprise that those 30 or so counties were far more grievously stretched than those in neighboring provinces, whose cereal harvests were more abundant. (Wang 1996, 76 and 88 [source provided by Fu]; Zhang 1996, 504 and 506–7).

It was common for the army to requisition coolies, who were, as we have seen, part of the *bingchai*. Still more common was the insistence that the food produced in the region for feeding the soldiers (this being a *junliang* element) should be delivered to the troop emplacements. In 1939 and 1940, in the southern Shaanxi mountains, the peasants were obliged to deliver their corn four times a year to the army. Anyone who forgot to grease the palms of the staff taking delivery was likely to be kept hanging about for a week or more, and to have their contributions weighed on rigged scales. Being unable to meet the expenditure incurred during that delay, the unlucky ones sold their carts or their donkeys and returned home beggars (Fan 1998, 377 [source provided by Fu]). In other cases, the grain brought in by the producer was not strictly speaking a war contribution, since the army did indeed pay, at prices varying from one-half to one-fifth of the normal rate. And the sale was not voluntary. The army fixed the rates for its low-priced purchases, offering a foretaste of the grain quotas at official prices that were later demanded by the communist government. Sometimes the army bought more than it needed, so it stockpiled the surpluses and sold them at better prices during the off-season (Hu 1995, 3 and 6). In Henan in 1942, the army did not have to wait until the off-season. The persistent drought caused a food shortage, so that the officers were able to seize the rice as soon as it arrived and resell it to anyone who could still afford it. In the stricken regions (Henan was an extreme case, but not a unique one), the peasants hid their food. If the army discovered it, there were some who preferred suicide rather than seeing their families die of hunger.

Not So Much Conscription, Just the Army

These disturbances were provoked by the army, and rarely by conscripttion. Almost everywhere in "free" China, public respect for the army had sunk to its lowest point since the time of the warlords. In 1944–45, the peasants in northern Hubei and southern Henan refused to deliver the food that the army was demanding. They massed in huge numbers and prevented the retreating armies from crossing their region. Further to the west, at the approach of the 9th Army en route between Shaanxi and Sichuan (in December 1944), the shops closed. The soldiers were exhausted, ill fed, and short of water, spending freezing nights on the bare ground, even the sick and the wounded. Some deserted, to become "soldier-bandits" (*bingfei*), surviving by pillaging food, cattle, and any articles of value that could be resold (Tang 1988, 437 [source provided by Fu]). The regulars were behaving no better. During that same winter, as the 93rd Army was withdrawing southward from Hunan, its 25,000 soldiers lived off the country, pillaging farms, slaughtering cattle, and demanding food. The local peasants, chiefly members of the Yao and Miao ethnic minorities, organized resistance to the army in Rongshui, northern Guangxi (Zhang 1992, 34–38 [source provided by Fu]). Incidents of this kind became very common by the end of the war, and some of them became serious confrontations (see Box 7.3).

Box 7.3   Resistance to the Army, Not Conscription: Tianhekou, Hubei, June 1944

After the fall of Wuhan in October 1938, Nationalist army units withdrew to the north of Hubei province, a region already disputed between Guomindang (GMD) and communist guerrillas, not counting some Chinese forces collaborating with the Japanese. Since 1941, the Second GMD Army Corps based its "headquarters of guerrilla columns from the Henan-Hubei borders" in Tianhekou, to block infiltration by communist guerrillas based in the Tongbai mountains, on the other side of the provincial frontier.

The local villages in the region had been picked bare by these troops, who numbered 200,000 men in all, not counting some 50,000 civil servants and students on the run. Their inhabitants suffered three bad harvests in a row (1940, 1941, and 1942) followed by a mediocre one in 1943. That did not stop the army demanding cheap grain sales and requisitioning fodder, cattle, equipment, and corvée labor. Units with not a single horse demanded cash contributions to their purchases of fodder. Other units exaggerated their needs and sold off the surpluses. The 29th Army Corps, numbering 20,000 men, demanded food for 40,000. Caught short by an order to evacuate the region, the soldiers could neither carry off their grain stocks nor sell them quickly or profitably to the impoverished local population. So they bribed officers in the army headquarters into putting off their departure. They hastily requisitioned a labor force of local villagers, who were set to building barracks, cutting down trees, and dragging them for miles, while transporting the officers' stocks of salt and other contraband merchandise.

By autumn 1943, food shortages had pushed up the price of rice. Most of the peasants by now were eating wild edible herbs and aquatic plants. For all that, the troops' exactions and requisitions continued undiminished. Even if the peasants were to hand over their entire meager harvest (without eating or selling any of it), it would not satisfy the army's demands.

Despite a three-month drought (in spring 1944), followed by an invasion of locusts, army requisitions persisted, with demands for wood, rice, oil, and salt, along with mushrooms and other regional specialities that they could sell at a profit. In desperation, the peasants mobilized the secret society of the Huangqianghui (Yellow Spears) in resistance. On 17 June, 3,000 Huangqianghui members attacked the guerrilla headquarters at Tianhekou, killing 25 soldiers and capturing 50 others, among them the commanding officer. The army reacted swiftly, torching about 40 villages and killing and wounding about 1,000 villagers.

SOURCE: Fu 2007, 286–95.

Other incidents, in response neither to conscription nor to the army's theoretically legal charges and demands, were provoked by the bad behavior or violence of the soldiers and militiamen. This could range from buying goods on credit, without ever paying, to pilfering food from villagers' vegetable plots, from stealing a buffalo to pillage, rape, and murder. These misdeeds, endlessly repeated, eventually aroused resistance or revolt, such as the Marrow War, which for ten days (16 to 27 July 1943) pitted marauding soldiers of the 76th Army against members of the Dadaohui (Big Knives Society), on the outskirts of Yibin, Sichuan (Bianco 1986, 292; Fu 2007, 279–80).

The involvement of religious sects (such as the Dadaohui or the Huangqianghui of Tianhekou) in resistance to the army was quite common, if only because of their capacity to raise more significant forces—which were much appreciated in enterprises that, on the face of it, were more dangerous than attacking a tax office or a school.[8] Some sects and secret societies joined in preparing and carrying out major revolts, which rocked the Chinese countryside in the early 1940s. Their role was not negligible in Gansu, and in Guizhou it was decisive.

Major Revolts

Major revolts bring us back to mixed cases, whose progress was aided by the alliance of taxpayers with disaffected conscripts. Even if the usual two grievances (tax and conscription) had not been joined from the outset by others (including corvée, official corruption, army brutality, and the ban on poppy growing), the revolt would have been very likely to draw them in along the way. Movements that grew to exceptional size attracted new allies, who directed the struggle toward new targets.

The unusual success of the revolts described below is further explained by incidental factors: firstly, the participation—in Guizhou one might almost say the conspiracy—of religious sects. We have seen (as in Chapter 2) that while the sects (and the secret societies) were not easily controlled, they did provide a reservoir of forces far beyond those usually available in spontaneous riots.

Secondly, these big revolts broke out in provinces numbered among the poorest in the country: Guizhou and Gansu. These two provinces generally relegated to the western periphery of the country acquired some strategic importance at that time by virtue of their proximity to

Sichuan, where Chiang Kai-shek established his wartime government. Gansu was also close to those communist rivals whom Chiang intended to contain, which increased the strategic significance, even the danger, represented by the disturbances there, with Sichuan nearby to the south and Shaan-Gan-Ning, the strongest of the communist bases, to the east.

Lastly and most importantly, the major revolts broke out in regions where there were large communities of ethnic minorities, who were even less eager than the Han peasants to serve in the army of a largely unknown and faraway government.[9] These communities added to conscription their own specific grievances (against Han chauvinism and the discrimination to which they were subjected) and even new aims (the claim to self-government). In one case, however, the Han peasants themselves joined the uprising alongside representatives of the ethnic minorities. Thus, the insurgents made an explicit virtue of this inter-community cooperation between ethnic groups in the struggle against oppression (by the government) and the Japanese invaders.

THE REVOLT IN EASTERN GUIZHOU

At first sight, the great uprising of August 1942 to June 1943 that mobilized 20,000 insurgents, setting alight for several months fourteen counties of eastern Guizhou, should not concern us here.[10] It was the work of a secret society, which planned and led it, and it expressed the political claims of ethnic minorities who were unhappy with government policy. Nevertheless, the other causes of discontent, beginning with military service and tax, were exactly those that mobilized so many (Han) Chinese peasants during the war, though usually without the intervention of a secret society.

In this region of ethnic minority populations, mainly the Miao and Tong along the Hunan-Guizou border, the administration disregarded even more than elsewhere the rule of military service "one conscript per family with three boys, two per family with five"; here, it was rather "two per family with three" (*san chou er*). The only sons of poor families did not always escape conscription, while the offspring of the few rich families easily secured exemption. The obligation to serve their country increased the tension between the Miao minority and the administration,

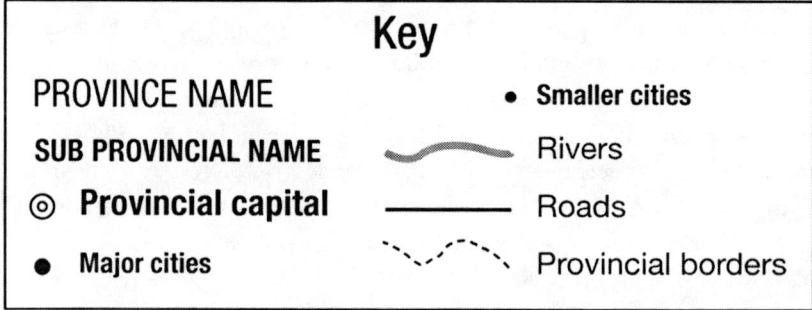

Map 7.1 Eastern Guizhou

all the more so since Miao conscripts were bullied and often ill-treated. To escape service, many Miao youngsters sought refuge in the mountains. Their fathers were jailed or sentenced to heavy fines, which they could not pay. This in turn forced the sons to come back and enlist. In 1939, a revolt against military service brought together thousands of members of the Tong and Miao communities from both sides of the

Hunan-Guizhou frontier. It was repressed after a few months, but since the burden of conscription was not eased, the tension persisted.

To maintain so many soldiers at the front, special taxes were raised. In one village in Zhenyuan county, the tax burden in the early 1940s was over 700 *yuan* a year per household (*Qiandongnan WSZL*, vol. 6, 1987, 304). Though the exact date is not certain—and in inflationary times this might have been significant—the sum represented for most people an almost unbearable burden that was much heavier than it had been in the late 1930s. To evaluate the growing tax burden in real terms, we can look at taxes in kind, which becomes possible from the moment (1941) when the land tax became payable in grain. In the space of one year, the total demand for cereals more than doubled across the whole of the province, rising from 1.2 million to 2.9 million *dan* (Zhou et al. 1987, 365). These grain exactions were imposed in a province where cultivated land made up less than 9 percent of the total area and where farming methods were still backward. Every year, Guizhou had to buy cereals from neighboring provinces.

In compensation, Guizhou sold—or had been selling—opium, which was produced across 60 percent of the province's cultivated land during the 1920s and early 1930s (when the warlords were encouraging poppy growing) and which accounted for 57 percent of the province's income in 1935. The warlords, as well as the peasants, took their share of the profits. During the war, when the national government took refuge in the neighboring province, it controlled the region more rigorously, applying its policy of suppressing opium production. Once opium was banned, prices soared, making it still more profitable—but more dangerous—to continue growing it in secret. The police forces responsible for eradicating poppies hunted down the growers or were killed by them. Several incidents known as *kang chanyan* (against the eradication of poppies) brought violence and bloodshed to Miao and Tong villages in 1941, then in spring 1942, before the outbreak of the great eastern Guizhou rebellion.

The army put down these disturbances with maximum cruelty. The 28th Division under Liu Bolong's command was not content with repression. It took peasants hostage and held them to ransom, established tolls along the roads, killed, pillaged, and terrified the local people, who fled their villages at its approach. In December 1940, General Liu summoned the heads of influential clans, and killed them, perhaps because their small private forces made them potential rivals. One of these groups, the Pan clan, revenged itself by killing several dozen soldiers and officers of the 28th Division, including Liu's chief of staff. Liu struck back by burning the villages involved in the attack and massacring their inhabitants. This incident (January 1941) was not the end of it. Liu ordered the slaughter of hundreds of poppy growers in 1942. So the villagers' hatred for the army was fairly general by the time the great revolt broke out.

The army, military service, tax, and opium were prime factors in the revolts on which this chapter is focused. The presence of ethnic minorities who, as we have said, were the majority populations in this region, was more unusual. The Miao leadership's resistance to the growth of the central power brought an already tense situation to a critical level. Added to the grievances of the "peasant masses" were those, more political, of their traditional leaders, who had been supplanted by Han newcomers. By 1935, Chiang Kai-shek's armies were embedded in the region with the mission of pursuing the communists on their Long March. On their heels, the propagandists of the New Life Movement, designed to regenerate the country and its soul, claimed to be ridding the Miao of various barriers to progress, beginning with their mother tongue, their clothing, and their customs. Zealous officials cut the women's hair or tore up their "native" costume accessories. In 1936, some demobilized servicemen of Tong and Miao origin launched a revolt, expelling some magistrates, forming an indigenous force of several thousand men, and demanding to be reintegrated into the national army. But it was above all the war that accelerated the hegemony of the central government and the dominance of the Han over the Miao. The governor of the province installed quite a number of graduates of the Nationalist Party's Central School as heads of counties and important administrative services. Gradually, indigenous people found themselves replaced in many posts of authority by refugees from the "lower end of the river," people who were better educated, better sponsored, and considered as loyalists.[11] We should not be surprised that Miao particularism and a form of xenophobia (against Han people and "outsiders") should have colored a revolt whose first slogans began with the ritual appeals "Resist taxes, military service, and poppy eradication" and concluded with the injunction "Kill people from the lower end of the river!" (*sha xiajiangren*).

What distinguishes still more plainly the eastern Guizhou revolt from most other revolts studied in this book is the decisive role of a secret society: the Tongshanshe (Society of Universal Goodness). It had been banned in 1927, being accused both of attempting to restore the monarchy and colluding with the Northern Warlords. It disguised its now clandestine activities beneath the banners of other religious sects, such as the *shenbing* ("divine soldiers"), Dadaohui (Big Knives), Hongqianghui (Red Spears), and Yiguandao (Way of Basic Unity). During the Sino-Japanese War, the Tongshanshe did, in fact, call for the restoration of the monarchy and attempted to overthrow the Nationalist government. It fomented several uprisings in various provinces (Sichuan, Hubei, Anhui, Fujian) by mobilizing the peasants against conscription and taxation.

In the region that concerns us, the frontier area between eastern Guizhou and western Hunan, the society exploited the popularity of a sect, Tiaoxianhui (Society of the Dance of the Entranced Sorcerers), which since 1941 had been conveying Miao aspirations to independence. In their trances, the sorcerers maintained that the king of the Miao had been born, that the people should help this infant prodigy ascend the throne, and to that end, should begin by killing high-ranking government officials. Even so, it was such tried and tested slogans as *kangbing kangjuan* ("resist conscription and taxes") that rallied the peasants behind the sorcerers and spread their movement along both sides of the provincial frontier. The movement was deliberately exploited by the local leaders of the Tongshanshe, who met in March 1942 in order to launch an insurrection. After a further meeting in June, two months later they launched their revolt, one they had undoubtedly prepared for and now led.

Are we able to say that political aims were driving the revolt? In their posters, its leaders denounced the "rebel," even the "traitor" Chiang Kai-shek and freely accused him of using resistance to Japan as a pretext for raising troops and money from the southwestern populace. Citing secret talks in Shaoyang, Hunan, between Tongshanshe delegates and emissaries of the Nanjing collaborationist government, some sources suspect this secret society of "anti-patriotic" collusion, or at the very least, of letting themselves be manipulated by the real "traitors."[12] To my knowledge, no proof has been offered that Nanjing provided funding or arms to the Guizhou insurgents. On the other hand, the facility with which the rebellion recruited among the peasants and renewed its numbers after each reverse confirms how popular were their classic watchwords appealing for public support: "No to military service and taxes" and "Yes to free poppy cultivation."

Nonetheless, this revolt was less "spontaneous," more carefully planned, than most of the other revolts and mini-revolts studied in this book. The near-concurrence of the seven uprisings, mustering nearly 7,000 men in four different counties between 19 October and 8 November 1942, attests to the coordination not only within the Tongshanshe, but also between different secret societies, in that some of the revolt leaders were at the same time local Tongshanshe chiefs and Hongbang members. And it was precisely in November 1942 that the second, more ambitious, phase of the movement began. After the initial uprising launched at the end of August in Songtao, northeast Guizhou, the movement consolidated itself in the border counties of Hunan and Guizhou populated by Tong and Miao communities. From November onwards, the rebellion won over the southeast, in the valley of the river Qingshui, while holding on to its positions in the northeast. It controlled, partly or wholly, fourteen counties in the east of the province, from Songtao in the northeast to Leishan in the southwest. It repulsed quite easily militia attacks, though not all its own offensive operations against cities were successful. Eventually, however, in early 1943, Chongqing became alarmed and sent in the regular army (the 19th Infantry Division) to annihilate the rebels. From that moment, the war changed its nature and fortune changed sides. Nevertheless, it took the troops several months to liquidate the last concentrations of rebels, who had taken refuge in the mountains, and then to secure the surrender of their leaders.

Taking account of the more or less simultaneous revolt on the Xilu shibian, or the "road to the west" (*Jacqueries*, 154–55; Fu 2007, 347–55), and another the following year that set ablaze nineteen counties in the south of the province (*Jiefang ribao*, 29 July 1945), only central and northern Guizhou escaped the great rebellions of 1942–44, which coincided with the peak of resistance to conscription in China as a whole.

GANSU REVOLTS

All three Guizhou revolts put together probably did not match the scale of the Gannan rebellion in southern Gansu, itself preceded by three significant revolts among the Hui minorities in the east of the province.[13]

Quotas for conscripts and taxes were fixed per *bao*. In principle, each *bao* comprised 100 households, but in the two sparsely populated counties of Haiyuan and Guyuan (eastern Gansu, today southern Ningxia) they averaged only 50 to 60 Hui households. Each had to provide as many conscripts and as much grain as any nearby Han *bao* sometimes comprising 150 households. Originally, the quota was fixed at three conscripts per *bao* per year, but as requirements increased, the authorities sometimes imposed additional quotas of one conscript per *bao* per month. When deserters came home, they complained to the imams of being ill-treated by the army, accusing the Han soldiers of pillage and brutality, even of raping Hui women. In May 1938, the Great Imam Ma Guorui voiced the complaints of the Hui community to the provincial government, which arrested him on the basis of accusations trumped up by the ward and *lianbao* heads.

This arrest fanned the flames of rebellion. The provincial authorities released Ma quite quickly, but at the local level, the clumsiness (putting it euphemistically) of the Haiyuan magistrate rekindled public outrage. He likened Ma Guorui to the famous Muslim rebel Ma Hualong, who had fought the Manchus in the same region. To the Hui, this man was a hero; the magistrate called him a traitor. And on a less symbolic level, he sent armed police to disarm two Hui districts. They searched every house for arms and ammunition, imposing heavy fines on anyone in possession of a gun, unless that person had declared and handed over the weapon to the police. They arrested and tortured suspects, extorting money from them in the absence of weapons. Hundreds of villagers then prepared to attack the magistrate, who had wind of it and fled in the middle of the night. The attack turned into a revolt. While this was the first and least important of the three Hui revolts, it nevertheless mobilized 3,000 men before being put down in late January 1939.

Each of the next two revolts (May–June 1939 and April–May 1941) rallied 20,000 men, but the shortage of guns obliged them to confront

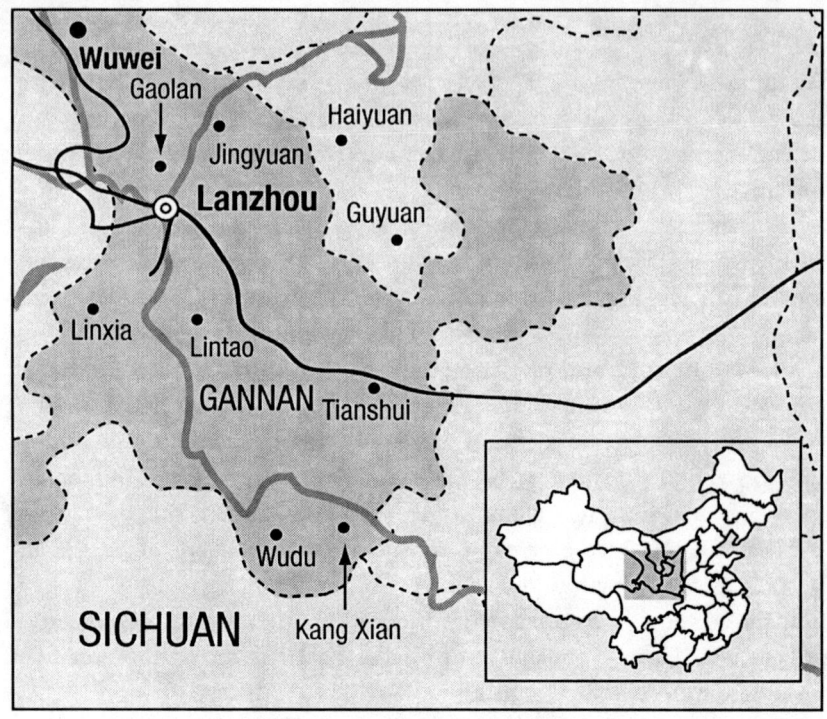

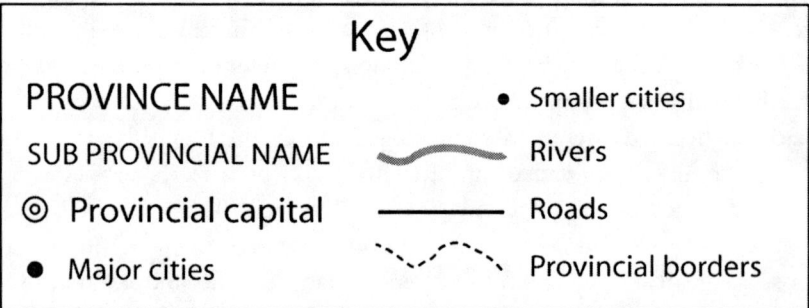

Map 7.2 Southern Gansu

the troops with only axes, swords, and spears. They did kill many soldiers all the same, but were themselves slaughtered by artillery and air attacks. The last of the rebels, managing to break out of encirclement, joined in May 1941 the communist base of Shaan-Gan-Ning where Mao and the Yan'an leadership were quartered.

We come now to the great uprising that set ablaze more than 20 counties (even 30, according to one source) in southern Gansu between December 1942 and July 1943. Not just 20,000 but 70,000 to 80,000 men rallied to its cause, while other estimates varied between 50,000 and 100,000 men.[14] Including skirmishes and surprise attacks, they rioters fought 100 or more battles with the security forces who, by the end, numbered 60,000 armed police as well as soldiers drawn from the forces surrounding the Shaan-Gan-Ning base under General Hu Zongnan's command. As a result, the attack on Yan'an and its capture, originally planned for 1943, had to be put off until 1947 at the height of the civil war.

The revolt was launched in December in Lintao county, on the right bank of the Tao He, a tributary of the Yellow River. It developed very quickly, especially after mid-February 1943, when it spread across to the left bank of the same river. Up until the end of March, by which time several hundred peasants were enrolling every day alongside the rebels, progress was spectacular. The battles extended even into the outskirts of Lanzhou, the provincial capital, and the police in disarray became the insurgents' main source of arms and ammunition. At the beginning of April, the rebel leaders meeting in Mapo, Gaolan county, to the north of Lanzhou—which confirms how far the rebel-controlled territory had expanded—appointed themselves a commander-in-chief (Wang Zhongjia) and a "regular" structure. The rebel army was reorganized into ten *lu* (columns), each subdivided into brigades, regiments, battalions, and companies. All the combatants now wore red chevrons with the character *yi* ("justice") in the middle.

Paradoxically, this reorganization coincided with the ebbing of the rebel movement's fortunes between April and July 1943, precipitated by the arrival of significant reinforcements to the opposing camp. In addition to those troops drawn from General Hu's army, others were sent from Qinghai province. After a three-month delay, the government had now taken measure of the danger and replaced the ineffective police and other local militia with regular army forces, increasing still further their numbers over the following months. The troops finally crushed the rebels, slaughtering the bulk of their forces in a series of bloody battles beginning on 6 June. By the end of the month, the army announced officially that it had killed 14,000 rebels and taken 18,000 prisoners. Raids and killings persisted into July, the victims now being simple villagers as often as they were rebels hiding among them.

What led to the rebels' defeat? More particularly, how can we explain their earlier successes? The first question needs no very lengthy answers. Sources published in the PRC point to divisions among the leadership, opportunism and indiscipline among some commanders, too-frequent changes of organization and command, strategic mistakes (the insurgents could not call upon the CCP's "enlightened leadership"), and the absence (despite the decisions made at Mapo) of any unified strategy. We should emphasize this last point, which ties in to others: the disagreements and rivalries among leaders and the clumsiness and errors in command. However, let us not overlook the most important cause, the unequal balance of forces and firepower. Though the rebels did manage to seize arms and ammunition from the police, they had only one gun for every fifteen men even at the height of the movement. From the moment when the government took the decision to send in whole regular army divisions, the rebels' days were numbered.

Far more surprising than the final defeat were how extensive and long-lasting were the earlier successes. Many sources and studies published in the PRC adduce the will to resist the Japanese invader—though the evidence for this is hardly convincing. Yes, the Mapo conference did officially give the ten columns the overall name "Army of the Gansu peasants Volunteering to Resist Japan and Save the Country," but that aim was trumpeted at that time by all rebel forces of any significance. Already before the war Chiang Kai-shek's warlord rivals were wrapping themselves in the flag, claiming they were worried about his policy of appeasing the insatiable Japan. As for the hackneyed descriptions, usually reserved for the Red Army, of rebel soldiers distributing grain to the poor and treating civilians kindly, they are hardly more believable.

The preceding account is based on communist sources. The official (Nationalist) sources raise the question: were the communists involved in this great peasant insurrection? Wang Zhongjia had fought in the Red Army and several leaders who survived the defeat were to join the communist guerrillas in 1945 and 1946. Yet, their allegiance after the rebellion had been put down proves nothing, and we cannot infer from the available documents anything more than a community of interests among those sharing the same enemy. The communists could not object to a revolt that destabilized the government in a province close to their main base and obliged it to withdraw encirclement troops from its southern flank. On the rebel side, an important strategic discussion on which route to take (eastward, toward the communist areas, or south) ended in April with the second option being picked—with Wang Zongjia himself pushing it through. We should be careful not to exaggerate the communists' role in a peasant revolt distinguished from others chiefly by its successes.

All the same, one can identify some of the causes of this exceptional achievement. Firstly, the divisions among opponents and their initial underestimate of the scale of the revolt. Well before it broke out, there was notorious rivalry between two fellow graduates of the Tōkyō Shinbu Gakkō (the Tokyo Military Academy): the Governor of Gansu, Gu Zhenlun, and the commanding officer of the Eighth War Zone (himself a former Governor of Gansu), Zhu Shaoliang. At first, Zhu seems to have allowed the revolt to spread with the purpose of tarnishing Gu's administration. Surprised by the expansion of a revolt that neither had taken seriously, to the point of relying on local forces (police and militia) to end it, Zhu and Gu then asked Chiang Kai-shek for reinforcements—whereupon Chiang called to the rescue his faithful Hu Zongnan. Throughout the first three months of 1943, the rebels had had the leisure to build up their forces, and after easy victories, to replace with captured arms (rifles, machine guns, grenades) the knives, axes, spears, pick-axes, sticks, and bamboo poles employed during their early battles.

Secondly, sects and secret societies played a role, though one more modest than in eastern Guizhou. Wang Zhongjia was a member of the Hongbang, while other rebel leaders belonged either to the Hongbang or the Qingbang (Green Band). From inside Lanzhou, Qingbang spies were transmitting information about the movements and intentions of the urban garrison, and others were sticking up posters and distributing pamphlets equally hostile to the two rivals Gu and Zhu. In all, however, there was nothing comparable with what had been seen a few months earlier in eastern Guizhou.

On the other hand, ethnic minorities did play a role comparable with that of the Miao and the Tong on the borderlands between Guizhou and Hunan. What is more, the different communities were united both among themselves and with the Han in their joint struggle against the provincial government. Originally, in late 1942, more or less simultaneous revolts broke out among the Hui, whose target was conscription, and the Han, who rebelled against taxes. They were promptly reinforced by contingents belonging to the Dongxiang ethnic minority, and in particular, the Tibetan army of Leba, the "living Buddha." On this occasion, at least, the different ethnic groups did get on well. Their leaders meeting in Mapo took care to round off their program with Point Eight, a call for unity: "Peoples of Gansu, do not allow corrupt officials to sow discord between you and cause you to kill each other" (Gansu shifan daxue lishixi 1960, no. 3, 30).

Returning to the main issue, the Gansu revolt was, like the others, born of discontent arising from military service and tax. One original feature of that region where Muslim horsemen were plentiful was that a horse could be handed over to the army in exchange for a conscript (*ma dai ding*), a practice that was no worse than what could be seen elsewhere. What was perhaps worse was the fate of the soldiers. This is the region in which occurred the aforementioned death march of 2,000 conscripts, from which only 800 lived even to approach their destination. Readers will recall that the bodies of those who did not make it were thrown into cesspits, while survivors slept on the bare earth surrounded by corpses and filth. In addition to military service and taxes, a further grievance was the *junliang*, the forced deliveries of low-priced grain to the army, to feed troops including those stationed in Shaanxi. And although this was nothing unusual, we should not forget the endemic corruption of administrators and petty officials of the public services—or, quite simply, the destitution of the area. People were, indeed, poorer there than elsewhere, and the province remains today one of the poorest in China. The unusually bad harvest of 1942 made things worse. It was still more difficult, even impossible, to pay the land tax (its rate was not eased) or the countless surtaxes (on animals, wool, *baojia* expenses, and other stamp duties) that the army required the local authorities to collect.

Is coverage of these great rebellions justified in a book that is not a work of general history?[15] Any revolt on an exceptionally large scale spills over from social to military history. Our sources have provided infinite detail on each ambush and surprise attack, on the amount of captured arms and the quality, on the losses on each side and on the towns besieged, taken, lost, and retaken. If this handful of revolts had not developed so far, the question of whether they belong to our subject would not need to be asked; it is so apparent that the rebels they mobilized in such great numbers were reacting to conscription, taxes, and the other traditional grievances.

In addition to these great rebellions, many other revolts were significant and savagely fought. Resistance to conscription was widespread in the Chinese countryside during World War II, and the revolts it provoked were in general more serious than those against taxes or land rent. Perhaps more worrying for the government was the ubiquitous brigandage. Even before the war, it had been a familiar scourge in rural China (Billingsley 1988), and during the war, men rushing to escape conscription swelled the bandits' ranks. This was firstly because the bands of draft dodgers and deserters haunting the forests, caves, mountains, and borderlands between provinces and counties could survive only by dint of plunder, pillaging of salt convoys, or raids on isolated villages.[16] And then it was because the "professional bandits," who were in reality poor wretches themselves who had dropped out from village life, were never slow in resorting to demagogic or particularist slogans (such as "Let's defend our homeland; let's refuse to serve under the flag or be sent to the front") with the single aim of recruiting peasants rebelling against conscription. As time passed, it became difficult to distinguish between rebels and bandits, except that the bandits could muster even greater numbers, up to tens of thousands of men. But these ragged armies survived or prospered to shouts of *kangliang kangbing* ("Resist taxes and military service!"), just like mere draft dodgers, who themselves eventually recognized no imperative other than solidarity among outlaws.

EIGHT

Permanencies

In France Long Ago, but Yesterday in China

When I read Yves-Marie Bercé's book *Histoire des Croquants* (1986), or his more general study (1991) devoted to peasant uprisings in France from the sixteenth to the nineteenth century, I feel I am in familiar territory. It is not so much that the Croquants and the Nu-Pieds are my compatriots, but that they resemble like siblings the Chinese peasants of the twentieth century.[1] Those in China were as poor as Molière's *manants* (yokels) and as wretched as La Bruyère's *animaux farouches* ("wild creatures") who were "tethered to the soil which they dig and till with unconquerable tenacity" (La Bruyère 1913, 428). True, their revolts mustered more considerable numbers than in France and were generally more bloody—though that difference was more striking in France in the eighteenth century, and even more so in the nineteenth century, than it was in the century of Louis XIV. This is no accident, and the resemblances confirm this time lag. The Chinese peasant movements in the first half of the twentieth century recall in many respects those of past centuries in France, but much more often those of the seventeenth, even of the sixteenth, than of the nineteenth century.

DIFFERENCES

The contrasting dimensions and population densities of the two countries make differences in numbers less surprising. The numbers of those resisting the tax policies of the French monarchy in the sixteenth and seventeenth centuries were impressive enough: at least 10,000 armed peasants were mobilized against the salt tax in 1548 (the "Pitauts" revolt in southwestern France); the "Croquant" revolt mobilized even greater numbers in 1636–37; and, in the interim, the Norman "Gautiers" assembled no fewer than 16,000 men. However, these were exceptional revolts, nearly as well known in France as the Taiping, the Nian, or the Boxers in China. Between the Boxers' Uprising and the Communist Revolution in China, many revolts known only to specialists mobilized peasant armies that were as numerous or more so.

In France, "peasant wars" on this scale faded from the scene in around 1675. Over the following two centuries, the numbers of rioters, insurgents, or rebels were generally far more modest. So modest, indeed, that a classic work on French rebellions in the late seventeenth century and the eighteenth century fixed at 50 participants the threshold beyond which one might be dealing with a very significant revolt (Nicolas 2002, 120 and 154–55). If we kept to that criterion, nearly all the Chinese disturbances in the first half of the twentieth century would belong to the category that Nicolas rated as "maximum intensity." The same author suggests the threshold number of participants in an incident to be four individuals not belonging to the same family. This same threshold is confirmed by another author, who recognizes unequivocally that the 50-participant threshold would probably disqualify most of the episodes listed in his study of food disturbances in France during the first half of the nineteenth century (Bourguinat 2002, 346). We are decidedly not working to the same scale; in China, an incident bringing together only four or even ten or twenty participants rarely comes to our attention. A last example from France: during the food crises of 1812, 1817, and 1847, the bands of beggars wandering across Touraine, Berry, and other French provinces tended to swell to several dozen members (Bourguinat 2002, 258). Such small groups would have passed unnoticed in China, where bands of starving people (*jimin tuan*) commonly numbered hundreds, and sometimes over a thousand pillaging beggars.

The comparison with France is still more revealing when we consider the loss of human lives. Here again, the difference is less stark between the Chinese twentieth century and the French sixteenth and seventeenth centuries. Deaths by the hundred in combat, leaders of uprisings beheaded if they were noble, burned alive if they were clergymen, hanged or broken on the wheel if commoners—these were the regular casualties for the great revolts, from the Pitauts to the Croquants. The rebels themselves were less well armed and killed fewer people, but were not outdone in terms of the agonies they inflicted on salt tax collectors and other tax officials. By contrast, from the eighteenth century onward, peasant violence cooled down dramatically, especially north and east of a line from Saint-Malo to Geneva, whereas "underdeveloped" France from Brittany to the Massif Central preserved until the end of the Ancien Régime its more traditional and more aggressive customs (Le Roy Ladurie 2002, 659). Both sides in disturbances, rebels and security forces, were killing each other in China more readily than in France. The macabre anthology in Nicolas (2002, 64–67) has little to shock hardened observers of the twentieth-century scene in China. In France, monarchic again in the first part of the nineteenth century, the contrast with China a century later becomes even more marked. In 1847, in Buzançais (Indre), three rioters were sentenced to death, but this was "the exception that proves the rule. Two landowners had been killed, a unique event in the annals of food disturbances since the start of the century" (Bourguinat 2002, 369–70). In half a century, only a single food riot ended in killings: the murder of two landowners and the execution of three rioters! Between 1800 and 1848 in France, "arson attacks were feared on a more significant level than stolen harvests" and "the arsonist had crossed an unacceptable line" (Bourguinat 2002, 343). A century later in China, nearly 1,000 of our 3,600 riots and revolts included one or more arson attacks, sometimes dozens. The Guerre des Farines (the "Flour War") in 1775, the most famous food riot in French history and the most intensively studied, was very far from having led to loss of life and damage comparable with those in the Subei flour mills in spring 1910 (*PWP*, 147–48). By themselves, these attacks and the ensuing repression killed more people in a month than all the subsistence looting and riots that occurred in France in half a century (between 1800 and 1850), perhaps even in two-thirds of a century, between the food crisis of 1709 and the Flour War. The episode in spring 1910 (from Changsha to Subei) was admittedly unusual, but there were also many other less well-known subsistence riots in our sample that caused many more deaths than their French (and European) counterparts.[2]

Although the Chinese state was more readily repressive than the European monarchs, it has preserved up until the present day its atavistic concern to feed its people. It has not always succeeded, particularly since the end of the eighteenth century, but has never questioned its obligation to feed the hungry. In Europe during the eighteenth century, as protectionism gradually gave way to the liberalization of the grain trade, the authorities tended—firstly in England and later in France—to put aside this traditional obligation, all the more so as growing productivity and the amelioration of rural living standards allowed the state to spare itself having to intervene against shortages. Hence the gulf that opened between those in power and the people, who remained faithful to the "moral economy" (Thompson 1971). In China, that gap did not exist, or if it did, only scarcely. The authorities, imperial and later republican, showed themselves to be no less inclined than the poorer classes to suspect the maneuvers of the wealthy. Accordingly, they would not hesitate to sell off rich people's stockpiles or to arrest their spokespeople (*PWP*, 160). And the Chinese equivalent of Thompson's moral economy implies duties as much as rights (*PWP*, 243–44).

Lastly, one difference is hardly surprising: acts of hostility toward nobles or the church or, more generally, religious conflicts (such as the revolt by the Protestant Camisards in southern France) had scarcely any equivalent in China.

SIMILARITIES

That concluding difference is in the targets of peasant movements and their typology, areas in which similarities are nevertheless decidedly more prevalent. In France during the sixteenth and seventeenth centuries, as in China in the twentieth, antitax revolts were indisputably the most common. In addition, food riots proliferated in France (and in England) during the eighteenth century, as did pillaging in twentieth-century China. To make a closer comparison of the percentages, let us take a look (though with some caution) at the above-mentioned survey in Nicolas (2002, 548–50), which covers Louis XIV's reign and the following century up until the French Revolution. This work of collective research, thanks to extensive archival access, lists more than 8,500 incidents in a country far smaller and less populous, but over a longer period than mine (130 years as against 50) and including urban riots, which represent 60 percent of the total—but only 40 percent if we place townships within rural society.

Antitax riots are ahead in both cases, constituting 32 percent of the Chinese sample and 39 percent of the French. Subsistence disturbances amount to 22 percent of all the Chinese incidents (but my estimate of the number of looting attacks is very uncertain; see Appendix) and 17.5 percent of the French total. The third category, grouping all other actions directed against the administration (that is, not including antitax incidents), represents 16.5 percent of all incidents occurring in France and 23 percent of the incidents in China.³ So altogether, the first three categories group around three-quarters of the recorded incidents (73 percent of the French and 77 percent of the Chinese).

In China—and in China alone—a fourth category of disturbance reaches significant levels at 10.6 percent of the total. These are conflicts between villages or clans (*xiedou*). Their equivalents are not unknown in France, but they are rare, one indication among others of the relative modernity of French society in the eighteenth century, and not the seventeenth century, compared with Chinese rural society in the first half of the twentieth century.⁴

We should not exaggerate the significance of these percentages, which are not necessarily representative, particularly where China is concerned (*PWP*, Chapter 4). The main point is still the preponderance of antitax unrest, and then at a lower level the frequency of food disturbances and non-tax actions directed against the civil and military administrations.

Let us take a more detailed look at these predominant categories. Two reasons help to account for the gap between the "achievements" of antitax resistance in France and in China. Firstly, I have dealt separately with mixed and complex affairs, almost all of which had a taxation component, as well as the resistance to corvée and to the New Policies at the end of the Qing Dynasty.⁵ Secondly, and more importantly, while salt smuggling is excluded from my category, it is included in the French sample where, along with clashes arising from tobacco trafficking, it represents by far the most important subdivision among affairs linked to taxation. These divergent choices among researchers explain a further difference between the two samples. In China, resistance to the salt tax is ranked in second place to resistance to land tax, whereas in France, it comes first, precisely because salt smuggling (the famous *faux-sauniers*) was much more frequent than resistance to the salt tax as such.

When we come to looting and food riots, the differences mentioned above (and several others, described in *PWP*, 242–47) are partly offset by some striking resemblances. In France and England during the eighteenth century, most of the rural looters were peasants who were never in trouble with the police (Rude 1956 and 1995, 201–3), which was exactly the case in Wuxi in 1932 (*PWP*, 150). They seldom attacked the persons of the wealthy, usually just their property. Pillage and riots were not as a rule coordinated, still less controlled by conspirators seeking to manipulate starving crowds (Rude 1956, 166–67; Kaplan 1982). They were almost always spontaneous incidents, progressing as in China by a process of contagion along the rivers or on the basis of rumors and stories peddled in township markets (Rude 1995, 24–29, 40–43, 111–14; Kaplan 1986, 138; and in particular Lefebvre 1932).

Looters resorted to forms of action that were similar in western Europe and China. First came the blocking of grain transportation (Nicolas 2002, 222; for the nineteenth century, Beliveau 1992, Chapter 3 and Bourguinat 2002, 352). Stopping a grain convoy could be, in France as in China, the prelude to other forms of protest (Bourguinat 2002, 353), mainly looting or "taxation by the people." The stolen grain was shared among the people, though it happened that poor consumers were content to force the tradesmen and the wealthy to sell their grain instead of stockpiling it. In such cases, they would generally demand that it should be sold at a price accepted as fair, affordable by the mass of consumers and thus lower than the rates charged after one or two poor harvests. The Chinese notions of "stable prices" (*pingjia*) and "reduced prices" or "reduced-price sales" (*pingtiao*) were paralleled by "taxation by the people" and "market taxation," which were common in Europe during the eighteenth century (Kaplan 1986, 143; Nicolas 2002, 222; Rude 1995, 23 and 28) and at the start of the nineteenth century (Beliveau 1992, Chapter 4; Bourguinat 2002, 355).

Thus, the looters had the feeling, not that they were flouting justice, but that they were restoring it by sharing among the needy the grain they had seized or selling it cheaply. In both countries, they were concerned not to be taken for robbers or bandits (Bourguinat 2002, 317;

on China, *PWP*, 152). Their mentality and motivation sprang from the same source, even if the "moral economy" that they claimed to represent did not have exactly the same meaning and influence in China as in Europe (*PWP*, 159–61).

When we look at non-tax actions against civil or military administrations, it was chiefly the army's demands and military service that provoked similar resistance in France and China. The food and the accommodation provided for servicemen aroused discontent as sharp and widespread in the French seventeenth century as did the institution of *junliang* (see Chapter 7) three centuries later in China. Louis XIV was often at war, but less permanently so than revolutionary France and the Empire, 100 to 150 years later. So it is more valuable to compare resistance to conscription (and to requisitions intended for the army) in France between 1792 and 1814 and in China between 1937 and 1949. In both cases there was only one year of peace (1802 to 1803 and 1945 to 1946). Allowing for differences in place, time, and civilization, juxtaposing Alan Forrest's classic study (1988) and Chapter 7 here brings to light the intimate connections between popular reactions to similar state measures.

In revolutionary and imperial France as in republican China, troops were mostly recruited from among peasants; accordingly, it was in the countryside that military service was most resented. The draft followed the same procedures of quotas, drawing lots, paying a substitute, or collective contributions to compensate "volunteers" who were sometimes picked against their will. This led to the same inequalities (social and regional) and to the same abuses, often in the form of incompetent and corrupt officials and recruiting sergeants. The effects on agriculture (shortage of manpower and higher pay) were aggravated by the requisitioning of food, cattle, and fodder for the army. Once recruited, the conscripts often had to make a long, lonely march, in France as in China, to join their units. Poorly fed, badly clothed, and ill-treated, the soldiers could glimpse no end to their torments other than the end of the war. No end, that is, unless they deserted. With 140 years between their campaigns, desertion—on top of losses due to draft-dodging, self-mutilation, and ambushes aimed at freeing recruits—caused the French and Chinese armies a veritable hemorrhage of frontline strength. Unlike deserters, who often had to steal to survive and sometimes in the end formed bands hardly less feared than the brigands, the draft-dodgers generally succeeded in hiding near their home villages, which sheltered, employed, and fed them. Rarely were they informed on. Indeed, local communities were not in any way hostile to the draft evaders, or even to the deserters, just so long as they restricted their robberies to public, rather than private, property. They held them to be victims of the state's interference with local affairs, or putting it another way, of the attack on the traditional way of life perpetrated by the agents of urban authority. Just as much as taxes, conscription aroused the unanimous resistance of rural society—with the exception of mayors in France and *bao* and *lianbao* heads in China. They were forced to carry out orders but were skilled in circumventing them by exempting their sons, close relatives and friends, and anyone else who greased their palms. The close correspondence between rural France and China in the practical application, effects, and rejection of conscription is all the more significant in that it occurs in the former as a postrevolutionary society (as portrayed by Alan Forrest) and in the latter as a pre-revolutionary society (as I have described) in which the abuses and failings of conscription and the army hastened the collapse of the old political system.

In terms of the repertoire of protest, even more than the targets and categories of peasant resistance, China in the early twentieth century recalls France of the seventeenth and eighteenth centuries, indeed of the first half of the nineteenth century, but never post-1850 France, the date around which Charles Tilly (1986) places the decisive change in the French repertoire. He detects an impressive continuity in forms of protest during the two preceding centuries, from the aftermath of the Fronde (1648–53) to the Revolution of 1848. The latter "put an end in practical terms to such forms of protest as the seizing of grain or tax revolts while promoting others, such as meetings, demonstrations and strikes" (Tilly 1986, 54, also 107, and 426). More importantly, "The repertoire in force during the seventeenth century was played out in a communal setting by local actors or the representatives of national actors." By comparison, the available repertoire since 1850 is "more national in scope; . . . it lends itself to easy coordination between different localities" (Tilly 1986, 543). The Chinese repertoire described in Chapter 3 might be considered more colorful (cutting the throat of a cock or pig, swearing an oath while drinking the animal's blood) or perhaps more folkloric (a chicken's feather stuck to a letter) and more traditional (there was no equivalent of *jiaonong* in France), but these actions were related in many respects to those maintained across two centuries before 1850 in France. And not only in France: we can discern a longstanding pattern of peasant disturbances linked to the "old, pre-industrial, multisecular world" (Bercé 1991), a world to which France and the great majority of nations belonged before 1850, and China up until 1950 and even later.

In France as in China, anger and hatreds built up (mostly against the tax collectors) until the day when an incident no more serious than many another, a mere rumor perhaps, set a spark to the tinderbox. The gong or the alarm bell would be sounded to summon the local people, who would come running from the four corners of the village or *xiang* in China, and of the parish in France. Neighboring villages would be alerted, in China by "chicken feathers" and in France by *mandements* and *lettres de sommation* (mandates and warning notices), and their people would come to lend a hand. If needed, they might be forced to join the revolt, under threat (in France) of their village being sacked, of villagers being mutilated, and/or (in China) of their houses being burned. Threats of this kind would be uttered firstly within the village where the movement began, because solidarity remained primarily local. In rare cases when the revolt spread further, mobilization was based on locality rather than on class, as in Guizhou and Gansu in the 1940s or in the bocage, the hedged farmlands of Normandy, in the seventeenth century (Le Roy Ladurie 2002, 457–58). The freeing of prisoners, who were generally arrested during an earlier riot or at an earlier stage of the same revolt, was part of the repertoire common to both countries, but a specifically Chinese practice was the carrying of coffins or even the dead body of a demonstrator. In both countries, rebels would declare themselves ready to face death, in often similar terms—perhaps there was more boastfulness in France, where the risks were smaller.[6]

Despite these differences, of degree rather than kind, the rebels' meager weaponry made the struggle very one-sided in both countries, with the peasants' only advantage being in numbers. The essential character of such collective action by the peasantry can still be identified across the two or three intervening centuries. These actions were essentially local, being the expression of near-unanimous populations, in which the entire village community made demands, demonstrated, or rebelled. It protected itself as a group against any threat or hostile encroachment embodied, for example, by the installation of a government agent in the village.[7] This primacy of vertical and local solidarity, so evident in cases of *xiedou* (*PWP*, Chapters 9 and 10), was present also in most other riots, antitax riots in particular, in France and China. It was accompanied by two associated features. Firstly, localism: participants intended to resolve the problem for their own community without worrying too much about any other peasants living further away. They were willing, in a pinch, to defend their country, but at home—not by traveling to places tens of leagues (or hundreds of *li*) away to take on the quarrels of city-dwellers. Rather than being conscious of belonging to a nation shared with city-dwellers, peasants resented any intrusion by a greedy state acting on behalf of those predatory cities. Above all else, the Chinese peasants of the twentieth century and the French peasants of the seventeenth century (in the time of the notorious *crue des tailles*, or increased tax, and the growing powers of the centralized monarchy) were rebelling against the state and its agents.

While the *crue des tailles* was deeply resented, the principle of a royal tax was not challenged. And so it was in China three centuries later, where villagers rebelled not against the principle of taxation but against massive increases or newly imposed taxes (see Chapters 1 and 5). It was the newness that aroused the anger, the unprecedented abuse, the "inventions" of the salt tax collectors in France, or the "wicked" Chinese tax collectors whose behavior departed from the standards legitimized by time.

Peasant rebellion, being dedicated to the defense of the status quo, remained essentially reactive, until about 1850 in France (Tilly 1986, 425–26 and 542–43) and well into the twentieth century in China. This attribute—defensive, and by that very fact, limited—leaves us light years away from the revolutionaries' offensive strategy. It undermines their assumptions when they assert the peasants' revolutionary capacity and exalt their class consciousness. This brings us to the second corollary of the primacy of vertical and local solidarity: the low levels of class consciousness among peasants, who were more inclined to defend their group (parish, village, guild, or clan) than their class. Their demands were concrete and locally based, not abstract or universal. A tenant felt he had more in common with the well-off peasants in his village than with the tenants of the neighboring village, whom he perceived first of all as rivals, because land to rent was not plentiful and competition from "outsiders" was unwelcome. As for the farm laborer who almost never went on strike (see Chapter 4) or the farmhand, respectful (outwardly at least) toward the landowner who provides him with shelter, he behaved exactly like the servants and other dependants of the Sire de Gouberville, the Norman gentleman of the Cotentin four centuries before (Foisil 2001).[8]

It was necessary to wait until the very end of the twentieth century to see how class consciousness had progressed among Chinese peasants subjected to 30 years of Maoist propaganda (Perry 1995). To witness a change of repertoire as decisive as that which French protesters adopted in the 1850s, the wait had to be still longer. At the dawn of the third millennium, the change has hardly begun.

Today in China

Changes are taking place too swiftly in China today for rural society and peasant resistance not to be affected themselves. The scale and the seemingly unrestrained tone of peasant demands has been striking.

THE NEW

The accelerated modernization of the country has increased the privileges of the cities, the first Chinese communities to open up and enrich themselves. City-dwellers despise those rustics whose honesty, toil, and poverty were glorified by Maoist ideology. The reversal of the peasants' status (Murphy 2002, 45) has led to their being perceived as obstacles to modernization, unable to share in the values, skills, and manners of modern civilization. These are the forgotten victims of the growing inequality of contemporary society and the casualties of authoritarian governance. Although intellectuals and the middle classes might be thought to suffer more than others from the absence of democracy—which, moreover, has been less absent in the countryside since the government announced then imposed elections to the village committees—in reality, no one is more bullied, ill-treated, and exposed to the arbitrary power of local officials than the villagers.

Those disadvantages notwithstanding, the "positive" effects of recent modernization have eventually reached the countryside itself, beginning with the loosening grip of poverty, which explains the most noteworthy change since the rural unrest of pre-revolutionary China: today there is very little evidence of food riots or looting. And a further significant development directly affecting peasant resistance is that peasants today are better informed and therefore less resigned. They are no longer isolated and shut away in their villages; instead, the twin policies of reform and openness have opened the floodgates to information and mobility, and economic development and technology have swelled the flow into a torrent. Today's peasants can compare their local authority's performance with the official policy in the capital, and their local living standards with those in Chinese cities and, indeed, with prevailing conditions in Hong Kong, Taiwan, Japan, and the West.

Two phenomena have speeded these changes, especially the first: the exodus of more than 100,000 young workers (*mingong*), who traveled to the cities to build skyscrapers and expressways for rock-bottom wages that were nevertheless a great improvement on peasant incomes. The *mingong* come home to their villages with a little capital, some new experiences, some much-respected savoir-faire, broader horizons, and aspirations that would before have been inconceivable. They create new enterprises and even new towns (Murphy, 2002, 191–94). Moreover, they inspire those who hear and see them with new perspectives and new aims. The other phenomenon, already mentioned, plays a lesser role in accelerating changes: village elections. They are a little less tightly controlled, a little more "democratic" than twenty or even ten years ago. While the village committees still quite often clash with the authority of the appointed Party Secretary and have no say over tax rates, some have come to exert a modest influence over the allocation of income and control of the budget. And when they cannot, their elected representatives are well placed if necessary to lead the resistance, which is also something new.

As a result of these new experiences, this greater mobility, this less-controlled access to information, and for a few, of this access to better education, peasant resistance has been intensified and transformed. Firstly, intensified: ten times more collective incidents were recorded in 2005 (87,000 incidents) than in 1993 (8,706 incidents), of which

35,000 were in the countryside. The increasing spread and scale of demonstrations, complaints, and riots by the Chinese peasantry have become so apparent that they are being reported in the media across the planet. And secondly, transformed: resistance is adopting new tactics and is less often confined within the village perimeter. One researcher of repute was maintaining as early as 2003 that, since 1998, movements had been cooperating more in their activity, and that peasant representatives were even beginning to organize associations linking numbers of villages with each other—though we should bear in mind that the survey was based on a single Hunan county. The new-style, unofficial "Peasant Unions" broadcast via loudspeakers the government proclamations and measures favoring the peasantry (Yu 2003a, 4). From now on they are holding society as witness, exposing injustices on the Internet, communicating by email and mobile phones, and calling on lawyers to present their claims (Thireau and Hua eds. 2007, 10; O'Brien and Li 2006, 85*n*15). A little more often now, from one incident to another, we see the same leaders and activists involved, and successfully prolonging some resistance campaigns.[9]

More seasoned now, the organizers of resistance are also becoming more professional and more sophisticated in their conduct of the movement. Some of them express more radical, more generalized demands. We are now hearing and reading political slogans, no longer just complaints, no longer just concrete and specific demands.[10] The relatively "modern" tone (economic and political) of the slogans, comparable with those current in other latitudes, suggests that the contemporary peasant movement is also beginning to free itself from traditional religiosity and messianic eschatology (Rocca 2006, 254).

What is more, those collective actions that turn to violence are no more than the tip of the iceberg. As in Mao's time, they are still eclipsed by the daily forms of resistance, because of the very limited tolerance shown by communist regimes to any other form of opposition (Scott 1985 and 1989, 15). And far more than under Mao, the less coercive character of the system has enabled both violent and peaceful resistance to progress in concert. For the past ten years or so, peaceful resistance, basing itself on the law and, barring accidents, staying within it, has become the most widespread form of peasant action (Unger 2002, 214). It includes legal complaints, mainly against local officials (O'Brien and Li 1995; Bernstein and Lü 2003, 190–96); communications to local and regional newspapers and to the Farmers' Daily; and lastly and most importantly those famous letters and visits to official bodies set up for that purpose (Letters and Visits Offices). In their various forms, these protests are on the increase year on year. The letters, least expensive, are seldom effective. Unless visits are paid to higher-ranking officials, the local authorities ignore problems and demands. The visits themselves, preferably collective, must be repeated dozens of times to be heard—and even then, the administration temporizes in the hope that complainants will simply give up for lack of funds. They often have no other recourse than to go to Beijing, where they are likely to be picked up straight off the train by agents sent by the local authorities, or to cause trouble (*naoshi*) and thus to break the law. The difficulty of being heard and obtaining redress is such that a complainant, a petitioner, even an elected member of the village committee is tempted into civil disobedience, the skill being to walk the tightrope without falling.

The "Rightful Resistance" leaders themselves have to perform with equal artistry. Rightful Resistance is a new strategy, devised by contemporary activists on the basis of legal, nonviolent forms of action (the theory is set out in O'Brien and Li 2006), that is less risky than violent action, and less limited in its effectiveness than everyday resistance. It consists in defending rights already granted, yet often denied by local officials, such as the limitation of the tax burden to 5 percent of in-come, when in reality it reaches or often exceeds 15 percent. The proponents have amplified the strategy into a legitimating ideology supposed to guarantee for peasants a whole series of rights that, because they are not precisely defined, can be interpreted very loosely. Some end by venturing "boundary-spanning claims" sitting close to the "fuzzy boundary" between official politics and forbidden ones, "in a middle ground that is neither clearly transgressive nor clearly contained" (O'Brien and Li 2006, 52).

Being bold theorists but conscientious researchers, O'Brien and Li acknowledge the "local and parochial focus" of most contemporary peasant actions (108; also 113*n*19). Moreover they remember that "rightful resisters know that they exist at the sufferance of higher levels and that the 'rights' they act on are conditional." Having warned from the outset that, "in today's China, rightful resisters seldom win the day uncontested" (11), they conclude soberly: "Rightful resisters (and other villagers) are best thought of as occupying a position between subjects and citizens" (122). In short, the germs of change are visible, but are only just starting to undermine inveterate permanencies. Yet I concede that perhaps it would be right—and soon, given the rapid pace of change—to update my restrictive approach by inverting the terms and say that while permanencies prevailed until the dawn of the twenty-first century, they are in the process of being overtaken by the transformation of modern Chinese society.

THE OLD AND THE TRADITIONAL

Targets

The permanencies are, firstly, the motives and targets of peasant unrest. Right up until 2002, the primary cause of discontent and revolt was the overall burden and the multiplicity of taxes, exactly as it was under the Nationalist government (see Chapters 1 and 5).[11] In the mid-2000s, requisitions or "expropriations" of land have succeeded *sanluan* ("three disorders," the name given to taxes, fines, and contributions raised on anything or nothing) in heading the grievances list, at least along the most developed fringe of the Chinese mainland.[12] They are part of a second category of grievances, also very common under the Nationalists: those attributed by peasants to the administration, and not just to the tax authorities. Today as before 1949, the corruption among officials, the arbitrary authority and contempt with which they treat the peasants, the blows, even killings, that they inflict on them—or which others inflict on their orders—arouse recurring outrage and rebellion (Chen and Chun 2003, Chapters 1 and 2; Chen and Wu 2006). Among the administration's abuses, the requisitioning of land certainly was not invented by communist officials; on the contrary, the practice follows a venerable tradition (see Chapters 1 and 4).

The new predominance of resistance to land requisitioning, now that the latter has become so widespread, illustrates how it has been the constant scourge of the moment that most outrages and mobilizes the peasants. Thus, conscription temporarily equalled or supplanted taxation as the villagers' primary target, at a time (1938 to 1945) when they suffered less from taxation than from taxation in blood (see Chapter 7).

Resistance to innovations

On the face of it, one grievance seems radically new, since no previous government ever troubled to rein in demographic growth: the One-Child Policy, with its accompanying controls, fines, compensations, and imposed sterilizations. It is new, as were in their time the ban on poppy cultivation in the closing years of the Empire, or two decades later, the "anti-superstition" campaigns insensitively enforced by the Guomindang activists. The peasants' resistance to innovation is another traditional feature of their movements, where villagers will fight a newly imposed tax or surtax rather than taxation as such, and they will resist a sudden increase in the tax burden (for example in 1926–28) rather than a still heavier tax that has been imposed for years or decades.

The rejection of innovations feeds the nostalgia for the golden age, always in the past, even when that past, in this case not so long ago, was in its day terrifying in its newness. The communists had to overcome enormous difficulties in mobilizing the peasants in the service of that ultimate symbol of newness, the Revolution (*res nova* in Latin). The Cultural Revolution—revolution against the Revolution—was a still more radical, if not inconceivable, innovation. Many villagers idealize it today, as a pure, altruistic, and egalitarian revolution. Admittedly, what inspires this strange reconstruction of an episode that terrorized them, is a sincere reaction to the withdrawal of social welfare provision, to the thirst for wealth and consumption, and even to the "loss of moral values" complained of by elderly villagers (Friedman, Pickowicz, and Selden 2005, 278). In particular, the egalitarian values vaunted under Mao encouraged them to count on services (education, health care, help for the elderly) as if entitled to them, which is not at all the case since the start of the reforms. All the same, the villagers who eulogize the old times under Mao would not for anything go back to the Maoist era and collectivization, which they remember only as "panic, hunger, and chaos" (Ku 2003, 77, 123, 132, 147–48, 231).

Local unanimity

There are further connections between contemporary peasant unrest and the tradition that it has adapted yet perpetuated. On the identity of leaders and participants, for example, recent developments do not invalidate the long-term continuity. Of these recent developments, we should recall the progress of education and the new choice of leaders from among educated villagers, returning *mingong*, former officials (even incumbent officials), and veterans of the People's Liberation Army.[13] Under successive former governments, county magistrates sabotaged the eradication of the poppy decreed by imperial edict, and then leaders of the Guomindang and the administration stirred up riots, sometimes against each other (*Jacqueries*, 186–90). The other features of past leaders were deceptively similar to those of present-day leaders: mostly male, better educated or experienced than the average villager, and including quite a high proportion of former soldiers, militia commanders, or practitioners and masters in the martial arts. Among the peasants themselves, those who had dabbled in other professions and worked outside farming were proportionately better represented among rebel leaders than those with only farming experience (*Jacqueries*, Chapter 5).

Those who took part, almost all of them peasants, were generally of one mind with the whole community, rich and poor alike. And, as today, those in disagreement were quite often forced into taking part. Today they are cajoled, threatened, and sometimes beaten into defending the common interests of the village. Persuasion is not always needed. Just the fear of being the object of gossip, of being accused of lacking solidarity with one's fellow villagers, is often enough to bring the timid into line (Ku 2003, 181).[14] Enforced—or almost enforced—participation was, as we have seen (as in Chapter 3), already a feature of peasant movements before 1949.

Local actions (and reactions): the paradoxical alliance

A fourth feature common to contemporary and past peasant actions is their local, limited character. They are directed against such and such a measure introduced by the local authorities, not against the government; they are limited to concrete claims, and when these are satisfied or satisfaction is promised, the demonstrators or rioters disperse. As during the first half of the twentieth century, peasant revolts are usually directed against a particular abuse, which they denounce and want abolished. When the authorities redress this local injustice (and if necessary punish the responsible officials), calm is restored.

These actions, or more precisely these local reactions, are—despite the recent progress we have mentioned on p. 202—rarely coordinated one with another. The authorities are faced with a string of separate riots, rather than an organized peasant movement. At most one might observe something like a chain reaction, just as outbreaks of looting could spread along the waterways a century or three-quarters of a century ago (*PWP*, 162). When movements become diffused in this way, it is seldom in any concerted or prearranged way. Rioters or rebels are unable or unwilling to seek prior understandings with their counterparts in other regions—and still less with striking workers. For example, the peasants made no attempt to establish any links with the 30,000 demonstrators who were protesting in March 2002 in Liaoyang over the huge numbers of workers made redundant from state enterprises and the long delays in paying their wages and pensions.

Paradoxically, we can observe an alliance between impoverished peasants and the central government, united in protest against the abuses and corruption of the local authorities. Appealing to higher authorities to remedy the misdeeds of local officials limits the spread of movements that hold back from challenging the government itself. And the central government is usually eager—except when it fears rural unrest might threaten the sacred concept of social stability—to fulfill its contractual role as legal arbiter, righter of wrongs and punisher of the corrupt, and as kindly protector, recommending and sometimes imposing reductions in the tax burden.

This alliance, still intact after a fashion, is based not only on the shared wish to put an end to the abuses of countless petty tyrants and to implement Beijing's well-intentioned directives rather than avoiding or sabotaging them. The local authorities, against whom the peasants wage their ceaseless struggle, are at once responsible for the scourges besetting them and scapegoats for the government's own abuses and shortcomings: their growing numbers, their sumptuous lifestyle given such limited local resources, their chronic indebtedness (and therefore their excessive recourse yesterday to taxation and today to land requisitions), their frequent corruption, their embezzlement of public funds, the unjustified arrests they order, their violence, their lies and denials of proven facts when taken to court or questioned by the media. These and so many further abuses (amply documented in Chen and Chun 2003 and Chen and Wu, 2006) unendingly fuel the villagers' anger. At the same time, the peasants' alliance with the central government against that government's local subordinates rests upon a misunderstanding. So long as it does not challenge Beijing itself, the peasant movement will find it difficult to overcome the ambiguity that constricts and limits its action.

Rather than "central government" it would be more exact for us to speak of the various levels of higher authority (Beijing, province, and even county) to whom the delegates, petitioners, or demonstrators address their complaints about the local authorities (ranging from the village to the township). Only the local administration has tangible reality for the peasants, being in regular or permanent contact with them. It is they who make exorbitant tax demands or seize their land, often because they are corrupt, often also because central policies (in the sense of the state's withdrawal of public education and health) or county directives cannot be applied in any other way, especially in the Chinese interior where farm taxation still provides the bulk of the slender resources available to the *xiang* and village administrations. In almost all the poor *xiang* of Henan, primary and secondary teachers' pay is by far the major item on the budget. A well-intentioned measure such as nine years' compulsory schooling triggers at the local level a series of financial and fiscal catastrophes that its promoters do not really care about (Cao 2005).

The higher authorities impose many other quotas and obligations on local governments. Mao limited or forbade commercial farming, but today numerous CCP county committees insist on it, even when the climatic and pedological conditions are unfavorable and the results uncertain. It is the same story with rural industries, which local officials were absolutely required fifteen to twenty years ago to set up, even when funding, technical knowledge, and qualified manpower were all lacking. Hence the factory closures, the bankruptcies, the wasting of time and money—all at the villagers' expense and for which they hold the local authorities responsible. Other factories, which would have survived, have to be shut down because they are polluting the environment. The "higher authorities" (again in the wider sense, meaning all those giving orders to the *xiang* and the village) decree that polluting factories (which they had ordered to be built) must be closed, without a thought for the now useless equipment, the workers whose jobs are gone, and the bank loans that the local authorities have to repay. All that the village victims know and remember is that it was these same local authorities who dragged them into this disastrous venture.

In addition to the creation of rural enterprises, birth control became in the 1990s an absolute priority in many counties. Moreover, the local authority leader who did not achieve the targets in these areas, whatever his overall record, would come in for public censure. Of those departments controlled from Beijing, the Family Planning offices embody better than most the intrusion of central government. Their staffing has grown swiftly: from one woman employed in Chenliu, southeast of Kaifeng, in 1983, to 10 in 1990, and to 32 by 1996. And among all such departments, the Family Planning offices are the most active and most dreaded because of the tasks they assign to local officials, the fines they impose (if only to pay their own salaries), and the ever-increasing tours of inspection they order. Families blame the local officials who collect these fines, and if need be, revenge themselves on the officials' children for the forced abortion of male fetuses.[15] Nevertheless, the One-Child Policy is as unpopular among local officials as among the villagers. But the frequent collusion between them to conceal "illegal" births does not lead to any change of allegiance, because the local officials, daily and in all departments, ill-treat the peasants—if only to impose policies of which they disapprove and achieve targets they know to be unrealistic.

In the long run, Rightful Resistance itself could suffer from the very circumstances that have enabled it to take root, or it at best might turn out unstable. The divisions within a "multilayered state [with] formidable principal-agents problems" (O'Brien and Li 2006, 65) make Rightful Resistance possible. Thanks to such divisions, rightful resisters can attempt to fight the local authorities' abuses and injustices by finding allies or patrons at higher levels of the administrative hierarchy, even within the central government. Some of them are becoming aware of the gulf between Beijing's declared intentions and its capacity, even willingness, to have them honored (Li 2004, 229 and 237–38; O'Brien and Li 2006, Chapters 5 and 6). In the short term, "successful rightful resistance probably enhances regime legitimacy" (O'Brien and Li 2006, 126), but what of the longer term? A slide into politics and into opposition to the regime, despite the highly unequal balance of power?

A concluding thought

In comparing peasant revolts in twentieth-century China and today, I have found myself returning to some of the themes addressed in the earlier comparison with the French Ancien Régime. Naturally, I would not foolishly gloss over contrasts as obvious as those between China today and France in the seventeenth century. But I think I should now underline some constant features that may well apply to a very large number of peasant actions in different ages and latitudes: their reactive nature (reactions to intrusions—fiscal above all—by the state and the predatory city); their rejection of whatever is new (the scourge of the moment) rather than of the status quo (although the latter is usually contrary to peasant interests); the barrier they may represent to some of these innovations, modernization for instance, whose short-term effects may be still more unfavorable to peasant interests than the status quo; their achievement in uniting local people; their primacy of local solidarity; their parochialism; the frequent assumption of leadership by men unconnected with farming or by villagers distinguished by education or experience; the notions of justice, fairness, and mutual obligation that underlie the defense of peasant interests; their overall weakness (due to the inferior weaponry available to villagers, to their poor grasp of strategy, and their usual lack of organization); and (up to the present) the disproportion between their limited political influence and the numbers of people involved in these actions, as well as the monstrous injustices they seek to redress.

Appendix

The appreciable increase in the recorded number of rural disturbances compared with *PWP* (64) may be partly ascribed to the new cases (375 incidents) discovered between 2001 and 2008, but mostly to the inclusion of 806 pillages and food riots in the new total. In terms of scientific accuracy, my decision in 2001 was the right one: to count the food riots (few in number), but not the far more frequent pillages. My only justification for including the latter at this point is my wish to compare (as in Chapter 8) the incidents in France (drawing on Nicolas 2002) with those in China.

I still need to explain to the reader how I set about estimating what could not be counted. When pillaging becomes endemic, there is no way of counting individual incidents. "There have been so many looting attacks, there is no means of counting them" (*ZJNSZ*, vol. 3, 1032–33). This remark by Zhang Youyi refers to summer 1934 and the early months of 1935. There is one report of 26 pillaging incidents recorded between July and September 1934, 14 of which took place in Zhejiang province alone and 6 of those in Jiaxing county. This record is itself a considerable underestimate since another source refers to 40 pillaging incidents in less than three weeks (between 22 July and 8 August) in a single township (Wangdian) in Jiaxing county. To be clear in my own mind, I went in November 2003 to Wangdian and Jiaxing, where the local archives office freely opened up its sources (research in China has become easier). The result was new cases recorded in Wangdian, but still far short of 40. There were others elsewhere in Jiaxing county (many more, by contrast, than the 6 mentioned above), and still more in five neighboring counties, most unknown to me! I resolved nothing at all: my visit merely confirmed that my figures were wrong or incomplete, just like the corrected ones.

It is obvious that, when different sources do tally, one cannot be content simply to add up their figures. I even suspect, sometimes, that a single incident is, from one source to the next, dated in different seasons or years and that consequently I may have registered it more than once. An added complication is that one frequently finds pillages mentioned as having broken out several times over in the same place, the same county, or the same province. Or one reads of "numerous," "multiple," "repeated," or "daily" pillages—or even, with no other details, that "there were some *chi dahu*" (literally, "eating at the homes of the great families"). At my wits' end, I counted two pillages when the context seems to suggest a plural; three when "several" are mentioned; four for "many, repeated, frequent"; five for "daily"; and six for "pillages in six localities" numbered in a single source.

Let me illustrate with one last example the uncertainties underlying my estimates. This one comes from Wuxi county (Jiangsu) in spring 1932 (*PWP*, 148–52). I have good reasons for believing that more than 100 incidents took place there in the space of a month (11 May to 10 June 1932). I have identified 35 and chosen to record 70 (double that)! So, is the reader at last warned how arbitrary is my "counting" of pillages? Not quite yet, because one might have counted as one the entire episode (the pillaging epidemic of May–June 1932 in Wuxi), as I have done for this or that antitax revolt or secret society insurrection that dragged on for one or several months. I did not risk it, because that would have meant favoring the least well-known, the most isolated, or most dispersed incidents. The legitimacy of my argument (that pillages were far more frequent than tenants' revolts) is weakened by it, since I counted as one the big revolt by tenant farmers in Wu Xian (*PWP*, 127), which went on, with some slack periods, from November 1935 to June 1936.

This latter discrepancy does not only affect pillages: it applies to all the categories of incidents that I have listed. Fairly often, I have found myself counting as one a long-extended affair that seemed to me to

Appendix

Table A.1
The Various Categories of Rural Disturbances

Target of resistance	Number of incidents
Antitax movements	
Land tax	703
Salt tax	239
Poppy tax	51
Taxes on cattle and slaughtering	45
Taxes on alcohol and tobacco	29
Taxes on fish and fishing	16
Various	75
TOTAL ANTITAX	1,158
Other movements directed against the administration	
Corvée labor	48
Late Qing New Policies	163
Opium eradication	149
Other administrative measures	137
Conscription and the army	346
TOTAL OTHER MOVEMENTS	843
Social movements within society	
Vertical movements	
Pillages and food riots	806
Resistance to land rent	155
Other social movements	60
Subtotal vertical social movements	1,021
Horizontal movements	
xiedou	382
TOTAL SOCIAL MOVEMENTS	1,403
Miscellaneous	
Baohuang and *naohuang*	17
Mixed and complex	92
Religious sects and secret societies	135
TOTAL MISCELLANEOUS	244
GRAND TOTAL:	3,648

NOTE: These statistics include incidents of looting. I have excluded four "indeterminate" incidents, not knowing what form they took or what provoked them.

have been too unified to be split up, whereas I counted separately two or three minor incidents I knew little about. If I had known them better or if I had discovered incidents linking them together, I might perhaps have been moved to group them as one incident.

In other words, estimating the number of pillages is not the only thing at issue. I cannot in any way claim that the rest of my figures are soundly based. I have set out their imperfections and approximations in Chapter 4 of *PWP*. Let me add (or repeat) that this picture does not do justice to the overwhelming predominance of antitax resistance. Here is just one example: adding the 382 *xiedou* to the 346 actions directed against military service and the army (two categories that admittedly are as different as apples and oranges) would give a higher total than the 703 incidents provoked by land tax—but that result would be entirely deceptive. The 382 *xiedou* owe much to a survey carried out in southern Fujian once the pioneering studies of Harry Lamley had awakened my interest in what I had called up till then horizontal movements. In addition to the fact that the 222 cases of resistance to the army and conscription listed in *PWP* became 306 in *Jacqueries* and 346 here, thanks largely to Fu Hung-chung's dissertation, I repeat that many of these incidents targeting the army or conscription were in reality mixed affairs also involving resistance to tax. The same applies to many other categories, beginning with the resistance to the New Policies.

Reference Matter

Notes

Chapter One

1. These other uses of bamboo are celebrated in Benton 1999, 17–18.

2. Agricultural tools were at the center of peasant resistance in Gansu in 1914 and 1915; a tax on boats was opposed in Zhangxing, Zhejiang, on 21 April 1910 (*QMN*, no. 50, 1983, 94); when resisting the tax on manure in September 1920, the peasants of a suburb of Nanyang, Henan, demolished the transit tax offices (*Nanyang XZ*, 1990, 24).

3. For examples from the Ming Dynasty, see Beattie 1979, 12 and 57–60; on labor services (*yi*) under the Empire, see also Elvin 1973; on the resistance by corvée draftees, see Naquin 1981, 183–84.

4. On *baojia*, see Chapter 7, note 1.

5. In 1942, 200,000 men were recruited to build Xinjin airport in Sichuan (*Xinjin XZ*, 1989, 27). On a more modest scale, dozens of local monographs speak of hundreds (and more often thousands) of draftees being rounded up for building roads, army posts, and airstrips. For example, on two occasions in October 1937 and December 1938 in Guangan, eastern Sichuan; three occasions in December 1937, 1938, and November 1939 in Shifang, in northern Sichuan; and three more occasions in July 1938, November 1939, and spring 1944 in Jiajiang, western Sichuan, where the inhabitants had already been called out in 1935 to build army posts in mountain passes to hold back the communists. There were similar examples in May and November 1944 in Pingtang, in the south of neighboring Guizhou (*Guang'an XZ*, 1992, 15; *Shifang XZ*, 1988, 28–29 of section I; *Jiajiang XZ*, 1989, 6; *Pingtang XZ*, 1992, 35).

6. The Funing magistrate recruited over 40,000 draftees to work on the river Huai in 1935. Although the corvée period lasted until September 1936, the draftees received not the slightest compensation (*Funing XZ*, 1992, 12).

7. This expression was coined by James Sheridan (1966, 14–16) to apply to warlords who hung onto regional power after 1928.

8. I am referring to the "basic type" and the "secondary type" as defined by Jean Nicolas (2002, 548). He considers, for example, that a mixed affair is basically antitax when taxation is the rioters' main grievance. If it is only a subsidiary target, Nicolas considers antitax resistance to be the secondary type behind the incident.

9. To the sources indicated in Bianco 1986, 299, note 68, add *ZLN*, vol. 2, 1932, 186–87 and *Fujian WSZLXJ*, vol. 2, 1963, 156–63. *Jacqueries* (100–101) modifies the 1986 version by taking account of these new sources but does not adopt the (erroneous) dates indicated in *Fujian WSZLXJ*.

10. Following an official inquiry, the administration rejected the public's accusations against Han.

11. A good presentation of the New Policies appears in Ichiko 1980. See also Chapter 6 of the present study.

Chapter Two

1. One author makes a simple distinction between looting and looting with violence (Wang 1981, 149–50). See also *PWP*, Chapter 8.

2. In South China, for example, the notable responsible for renting out clan properties often agreed to lower rates for clan members.

3. Ownby 2001 makes the point about recent Chinese production. See also, among others, Ownby 1993, 3–15 and Park 2002.

4. Dai Xuanzhi puts at over a million the forces of the Red Spears in alliance with Wu Peifu in 1926 (Tai 1985, 113). He is probably referring to members of the sect and therefore only potential fighters. The same is true of the 400,000 Tianmenhui followers mentioned in Box 2.3 and the 400,000 to 500,000 members of the Gelaohui counted (or estimated) at the end of the 1930s in the (thinly populated) province of Gansu (Park 2002, 91).

5. Here are some examples: more than 500 Hongqianghui members and villagers killed in March 1929 in Laixi, Shandong (*Laixi XZ*, 1990, 666); more than 1,000 Hongqianghui members massacred in the space of a few days between the end of August and the beginning of September 1927 in Anyang, Henan (*Anyang XZ*, 1990, 733); more than 1,600 members of the Xiaoyihui (Society of Filial Piety and Equity) killed in Dazhu, Sichuan, in January 1915 (*Dazhu XZ*, 1992, 4); more than 2,000 Dadaohui (Big Knives) members and civilians over twelve years old killed in Tonghua, Jilin, in January 1928 (Bianco

1972, 218); 7,000 to 8,000 killed in the ranks of the Red Spears (and also among villagers) during a revolt against a small warlord in Xi Xian and Sui Xian, Henan, during the winter of 1926–27 (*Zhongguo nongmin wenti*, January 1927).

6. An example taken from Jiangsu: half a company of the communist New Fourth Army were massacred on 3 August 1940 near Lishui by 20,000 Big Knives (*Lishui XZ*, 1990, 491); and three examples from Henan: more than 100 soldiers in the Fengtian Army massacred by the Tianmenhui in Yuecheng in January 1927 (*Xiangdao Zhoubao*, no. 188, 16 February 1927); 1,000 warlord soldiers killed or wounded during an antitax revolt in Xin'an early in 1927 (*Dagongbao*, Tianjin, 3 May 1927); in the west of the province, in spring 1926, the Red Spears are said to have exterminated tens of thousands of soldiers in the army of Governor Yue Weiling (Dai 1973, 192).

7. We should mention the Red Spears' operation in Henan in 1926–27 (Dai 1973 and Tai 1985, for Ronald Suleski's translation; Slawinski 1975) and the essential role of the Tongshanshe (Society of Universal Goodness) in sparking off the great revolt that shook east Guizhou in 1942–43 (see Chapter 7, 181–82, of the present study). The secret societies feature infrequently among the smaller episodes in our sample, but much more often among the large-scale revolts.

Chapter Three

1. That, at least, is what was claimed by peasant "strikers" (since they "handed over" their tools with the avowed intention to stop working the land). They were not always wrong, and this was despite the fact that the average level of land tax in China was low. Given the considerable variations in the overall burden of taxation—even within a single province—we find many a case where fiscal oppression became unbearable, to the point of forcing taxpayers to give up, either their ownership of land, conspicuously handing the deeds over to the authorities, or an occupation that no longer provided them with a living. That was the argument cited by farmers who turned in their tools en masse to magistrates or ward heads. The authorities carried out thirteen tax collections in a single year in two Shaanxi counties: in 1931 in Baoji (*Baoji WSZL*, vol. 2, 1984, 18) and in 1932 in Qishan (*Qishan WSZL*, vol. 4, 1989, 59). In 1932, in Shaanxi as a whole, the total revenue from taxes and surtaxes (3 *yuan* per *mu*) was greater than the average farm income, estimated at 1.7 *yuan* per *mu* (at least according to Feng 1935, 413). As with taxation so with credit: average interest rates were far from reaching the levels often cited in the secondary literature—though, here and there, money certainly was lent at wildly excessive rates.

2. That is suggested by another label for *jiaonong*, more worrying for the authorities: this was *yongtang*, "surging in a mass into the hall" of the county yamen (*Pucheng WSZL*, vol. 1, 1985, 11). The peasants' confidence in the ef-

fectiveness of *jiaonong* was shown by a slogan that seems an early draft of Mao's famous formula "political power grows out of the barrel of a gun": "If we follow the order to hand over our tools, power will be at the point of the steel" (*jiaonong weiling, tiequan wei zheng*, *Shaanxi WSZL*, vol. 9, 1981, 229).

3. In July 1931, peasants from across the county broke through the west and north gates of Chengcheng, Shaanxi, and won a partial suspension of taxation (*Chengcheng WSZL*, vol. 2, 1987, 20). A few months earlier, 10,000 peasants had thrown stones and bricks and, after the police killed a "striker," burned down the gate into Baishui, Shaanxi to storm the town. The magistrate was frightened into granting them three years' tax exemption, from 1930 to 1932 (*Baishui WSZL*, vol. 1, 1986, 80).

4. Or variants such as *jiaonong kang kuan*: "Let's hand over our tools to resist the special contribution," or again, *jiaonong bageng*: "handover of tools and strike."

5. Dating back to antiquity, as one of our sources assures us, while limiting herself to citing three *jiaonong* movements that took place in Pucheng under the Qing Dynasty: in 1646, 1674, and 1877. At the end of the last of these, sparked off by the collection of the usual taxes in mid-famine, several dozen peasants were executed (*Pucheng WSZL*, vol. 1, 1985, 11–12). This same famine gave rise to a *jiaonong* movement in Daying, in the neighboring province of Henan (*Shaanxi WSZL*, vol. 3, 1963, 55–56). And another *jiaonong* movement in Luoyang in 1890 (*Yiyang WSZL*, vol. 3, 1987, 31–34) confirmed that, in Henan too, this form of action had long been known.

6. For example, in July 1932, 70 counties in Shaanxi (out of less than 100) are recorded as affected by a *jiaonong* movement (Feng 1935, 413).

7. The other eleven occurred only in provinces adjacent to Shaanxi: four in Gansu (two of them in 1914, then one each in 1915 and 1926), two in Shanxi (in 1900 and 1903), and five in Henan (1903, 1906, 1910, 1913, and 1936). References are available to interested readers.

8. For example, in Pucheng in 1927, 1928, 1930, 1931, and 1932 (*Pucheng WSZL*, vol. 1, 1985, 14–18); in Chengcheng in 1931 and 1932 (*Chengcheng WSZL*, vol. 2, 1987, 19–20); in Baishui in 1931 (*Baishui WSZL*, vol. 1, 1986, 76–81); in Qishan in 1932 (*Qishan WSZL*, vol. 4, 1989, 57–62); and in Bin Xian in 1936 (*Bin Xian WSZL*, vol. 1, 1987, 74–77). All these counties are in Shaanxi.

9. For example, in 1909 and 1910, a succession of disasters (floods, droughts, and damaging gales) struck 56 Anhui prefectures and counties. In He Zhou prefecture, stricken from the outset, prices rose because shopkeepers and gentry landlords refused to sell their rice. In spring 1909, anonymous letters calling on people to loot the homes of rich families were distributed almost everywhere, leading to looting on 6 June (Weng Fei et al. 1990, 361).

10. For example, in Sanjiang, Guangxi, in March 1938, 300 members of the Miao ethnic minority sacrificed a cock, drank its blood, and swore to resist taxation and military service (*Guangxi WSZLXJ*, vol. 28, 1988, 23).

11. For example, in Heng Xian, Guangxi, in December 1909, 800 delegates meeting in the Temple of Culture solemnly pledged "unanimously to resist taxation" (*jixin kangjuan*) and chose a master of martial arts as leader (*Heng XZ*, 1989, 196).

12. A chicken feather stuck to a letter was enough to signal an urgent message. In Lantian, Shaanxi, in September 1915, a message calling on everyone to meet at dawn on 20 August of the lunar calendar (28 September of the Gregorian calendar) reached all the county's villages in a single night. The message was very short, but specified, "This letter, as soon as you get it, must be copied and sent on." An old peasant some 47 years later still remembered it, likening the swift circulation of messages to "that of children nowadays" (*Shaanxi WSZL*, vol. 2, 1962, 114).

13. This was so in Ankang, Shaanxi, in 1913, during an uprising against the order for queues to be cut off. Although this social discrimination seemed to penalize the poor (who did the fighting while the rich were content with making contributions), most well-off villagers supported the revolt under duress, inwardly disapproving of this "disorderliness." The peasant masses, on the other hand, wholeheartedly backed the revolt, being eager to defend the right to wear queues, and more generally, the duty to observe their ancestral traditions (*Ankang XZ*, 1989, 631–33 and Chapter 6). During a big antitax revolt (directed against the land clearance tax) in northern Dongtai county, Jiangsu, in 1922, the rule was slightly altered. Each house had to supply as many fighters as it had chimneys: several chimneys denoted a numerous family, with married brothers living under the same roof (*Jiangsu WSZLXJ*, vol. 18, 1986, 170–71).

14. During an emergency meeting called on 2 July 1906 in Ji'an county, Jiangxi, to prepare for resistance to taxation, the organizers pointed out that villages not represented would be penalized. All able-bodied men aged between 16 and 60 had to be ready to fight on 7 July (*XGQSJMDS*, 300–301). At the same time, people in the mountains of Liaoyang prefecture, Fengtian, who were resisting taxes on oxen and horses were content at first to eat and lodge overnight with those refusing to join the movement (like the doctors three-quarters of a century afterwards whom the communist authorities sent to stay with village women refusing to be sterilized). But later on, they tied up those still not cooperating and even took away the fourteen-year-old son of one who had fled his house (*Liaoyang WSZL*, vol. 5, 1990, 79–80). In Lantian, Shaanxi, in 1915, those who did not join the movement were warned that their houses would be demolished (*Shaanxi WSZL*, vol. 2, 1962, 114). The same

kind of warning was given in Zhongjiang, Sichuan, in 1938: "We'll set fire to the houses of those who do not come"(*bulai shaofangzi*; Fu 2007, 505). In Weinan, Shaanxi, in 1923, any family refusing to send someone to hand over farm tools at the county yamen was threatened with "punishment." The warning stated that "Poor or rich, all families must play their part" (*jiajia douqu, pinfu buguan*; Shaanxi *WSZL*, vol. 9, 1981, 226). In 1926, peasants in southeastern Ning Xian, Gansu, en route to the county capital to hand in tools, forced those working in their fields to join them, threatening otherwise to break their tools (*Ning XZ*, 1988, 404). During the celebrated Luddite movement of 1830 in England, the rural poor likewise visited each farm, "for the purpose of compelling the laborers to unite with them" (Hobsbawm and Rude 1970, 135).

15. As was done by the *tunmin* in 78 villages in Yingkou county, Fengtian, in autumn 1906 (*Lishi yanjiu*, no. 6, 1959, 56). The *tunmin* were descended from the peasant-soldiers whom the imperial authorities had sent to colonize and protect strategic areas. They enjoyed privileged tax status.

16. This was even the case when this "cause" was limited to more generous compensation for land expropriated to make space for an airport in the Chongqing area in September 1941. The procession of coffins succeeded a petition, which had ended with the person who wrote it being arrested. The government had offered to reimburse only 450 *yuan* per *mu* for fields that were worth, because of inflation, 3,000 to 4,000 *yuan* per *mu*. The demonstrators won their case (*Chongqing XZ*, 1991, 17).

17. In Lantian, Shaanxi, in October 1915, villagers escorted as far as the county yamen their four leaders, who had decided to turn themselves in to save the lives of a dozen peasants already arrested. They made their own funeral preparations, in case they were sentenced to death: coffins in heavy wood and mourning clothes worn by the heads of the fifteen villages that had taken part in the movement. In the end, no one was executed (*Shaanxi WSZL*, vol. 2, 1962, 118). In Nantong county, Jiangsu, on two occasions the bodies of demonstrators killed by the security forces were carried through the streets: Liuqiao in 1928 and Pingchao in 1933 (*ZLN*, vol. 4, 1934, 66).

18. These eight characters (*guanfu hai min, baixing chu hai*) were printed in black on the red background of a triangular flag brandished in December 1909 by peasants in Heng Xian, Guangxi. Soldiers had earlier been sent to the peasants' village to enforce tax payments. They had arrested taxpayers and looted their homes (*Heng XZ*, 1989, 196).

19. An example of the first case: the "Regiment of Those Forced to Rebel" (Bifantuan) in Nanfeng Xiang, Jiangxi, in December 1942 (*Dayu XZ*, 1990, 27). Second case: since the plans were generally aimed at lowering taxation levels, the "Antitax Armies" (Kangjuanjun) that were raised in southern Sichuan in

1933 (*ZLN*, vol. 4, 1934, 69–70). Others called themselves "Peasant Army of Resistance to Taxation" (Nongmin kangshuijun) or again "Peasant Self-Defense Army" (Nongmin ziweijun), as in Laifeng, Hubei, in 1927 (*Laifeng XZ*, 1990, 568).

20. An example of a legally inspired name: the "Army of Justice" (Yijun), which opened up the granaries and distributed grain to the poor in Sanmen, Zhejiang, in 1881 (*Sanmen XZ*, 1992, 10). Two social examples: the Qiongrenhui (Society of the Poor) who resisted taxation in Ji county, Hebei, in 1935; and the Qiongguangdanhui (Poor Bare Egg Society), whose members looted rice along the borders separating Henan, Hebei, and Anhui in 1934–35 (*ZJNSZ*, vol. 3, 1033).

21. Examples: the Hongjinjun (Army of the Red Headband) raised in 1900 on the border between Zhejiang and Jiangxi (*Jiangshan XZ*, 1990, 420–21 and *Yushan XZ*, 1985, 204); the Qingqihui (Green Flag Society), which mustered 600 to 700 armed peasants in resistance to the exactions of a warlord in Wulian county, Shandong, in 1930 (*Wulian XZ*, 1992, 10).

22. For example: the Aiyingjun (Army That Loves Babies). Its members attributed the abnormally high death rate among babies brought about by natural disasters to the ill effects of civil registration on the fate of new-born babies. To save them, they destroyed the births, marriage, and death registers in Jinhua county, Zhejiang, in 1914 (see Chapter 6).

23. Cf. the slogan printed on the banner of a Mintuanjun (People's Army) resisting military requisitions in Zhouzhi, Shaanxi, in November 1929: "Let's go and destroy the provincial capital!" (*Ta shengcheng qu!*). The interesting point about this slogan, rarely seen, is that it expresses peasant hostility to the cities, the seat of power (Feng 1936, 388–89).

24. Ploux 2002 refers to France in the nineteenth century, but see as well Hobsbawm and Rude 1970, 97–102, 130, 146, 152, 165–68 for England in 1830–31 and Viola 1996, 121–24 for the Soviet Union a century later.

25. Gates reopened: in Danyang, Jiangsu, in September 1909 during a revolt provoked by the increase in the tax burden (*XGQSJMDS*, 283). Taxes suspended: in Pucheng, Shaanxi, in spring 1928 (*Pucheng WSZL*, vol. 1, 1985, 16).

26. Seven houses were burned in July 1941 in two villages of Sha county, Fujian, which had resisted the imposition of a special contribution (*Sha XZ*, 1992, 20). In May 1926, the burning of a township in "resistance" could be seen 100 *li* away in Qi county, Henan (*Xiangdao*, no. 158, 16 June 1926, 1545–46).

27. In September 1937, it was not certain that most villagers in Ziyang county, Shaanxi, were aware of the invasion of eastern China by the Japanese

"dwarfs" (as they were called). For them, even more than the foreign invader, the scourge was Wang Sanchun, a bandit who systematically burned all the houses in his path, whose progress could be traced from many miles away by the smoke. For most of the region's villagers, that terrible summer recalls just one event, in no way imperialist: the destruction wrought by another bandit in 1929 (*Ziyang XZ*, 1989, 548).

28. For example, in November 1931, in Changle, Fujian, soldiers occupying a temple suddenly found themselves surrounded, and then were slaughtered by peasants who had lain in ambush behind a hill overlooking the temple (*ZLN*, vol. 2, 1932, 187).

29. Still in Changle, there was no need to persuade the militia commander Lin Guru to assume leadership of the revolt: he had launched it. But he took care to enlist several graduates of the Baoding Military Academy to complete the rebels' training.

30. Among many other sects reputed "invulnerable," the Yingduhui (Society of Hard Bellies) took this name to signify that enemy bullets bounced harmlessly off members' armor-plated bellies.

31. Rain, for example: on 10 June 1919, in Haiyang, Shandong, the magistrate was unable to repress a riot provoked by the salt tax and the brutalities of the collectors. Heaven came to his aid: it began raining, and the marchers dispersed spontaneously, everyone eager to get home and sow the autumn wheat (*Haiyang XZ*, 1988, 704).

32. Qiang Yuncheng was the hated magistrate who, in his desire to promote Hu from third-class county status to second-class, increased the tax burden and ordered taxpayers in arrears to be whipped, and later tortured (*Hu Xian WSZL*, vol. 1, 1985, 50–51). Similarly, two or three months earlier, the magistrate of Anyang, Henan had been forced to parade in a big hat labelled, "I am a corrupt official" (*Anyang Shi jiaoqu WSZL*, vol. 1, 1986, 85). Yet, we should point out that while many peasants joined these two revolts, one had been organized by students and schoolchildren, the other by teachers. These badges— or rather hats—of infamy were not yet part of the usual repertoire of peasant actions.

33. Examples: in 1910, peasants seized and tied up the commander of a squad of policemen sent to collect a special contribution for the police in a village in Zunhua county, Hebei (*Zunhua XZ*, 1990, 656); tax collectors were beaten in three villages in Wanzai county, Jiangxi, in 1921 (*Wanzai XZ*, 1988, 18); a tax collector was beaten and another killed in two villages in Wenjiang county, Sichuan, in 1926 (*Wenjiang XZ*, 1990, 19); a tax collector was knocked about until he died in a village in Dazhu county, Sichuan, in August 1927 (*Dazhu XZ*, 1992, 6).

34. Four policemen were stoned and their bodies thrown into the sea in Haiyang county, Shandong, in June 1919 (*Haiyang XZ*, 1988, 704); 20 tax inspectors killed in a single village (Xiachu Xiang) in Rushan county, Shandong, between August and October 1928 (*Weihai WSZL*, vol. 4, 1989, 89); a dozen officials killed in Ninyang, Fujian, in 1943 (*Zhangping WSZLXJ*, vol. 1, 1982, 29–34); and in Ziyang, Shaanxi, in 1931, tax officials were killed "right across the county" (*quan xian ge di*; *Ziyang XZ*, 1989, 551).

35. Aimed in this case not at the usual targets (tax collectors and policemen) but at the target of the moment: teachers, during the campaign of resistance to the creation of modern schools. Peasants in Sheng county, Zhejiang, had rebelled in spring 1910 against the switching of temple land revenues to fund schools. The arrest of two leaders exacerbated the unrest and eventually provoked this incitement to murder (*DFZZ*, vol. 7, no. 6, 1910, 17 and 668).

36. During an antitax uprising in Duyun county, Guizhou, in April 1906, because the target (the *zongbao*, a Miao official who understood Chinese and acted as intermediary between the administration and two Miao-inhabited districts) had fled, the rebel peasants solemnly sacrificed his son (*Duyun WSZLXJ*, vol. 5, 1986, 68). At the same time, in the same province (in Caoguan, Baiyun county), the rebels wiped out the entire family of a local despot, demolished the tombs of his ancestors, and emptied the pond, so as to destroy the *fengshui* of the family (*Baiyun WSZL*, vol. 5, 1988, 111–13).

37. The year before, five emissaries and junior officials sent out by the same county government (Shiquan) had been decapitated by peasants rebelling against excessive taxation (*Shiquan XZ*, 1991, 701). See also what befell the policemen fleeing their burning headquarters in Daishan, Zhejiang, in July 1936 (Box 5.2).

38. The Dadaohui (Big Knives Society), Dadaohui (Great Way Society), Yühuangtan (Emperor Yü's Word), Shentuan (Heavenly Militia), Hongqianghui (Red Spears Society), and the Mudaohui (Wooden Knives Society) were among the groups active in Ziyang in the 1930s (*Ziyang XZ*, 1989, 551).

39. The five emissaries and junior officials decapitated in Shiquan in autumn 1925 were part of a group of nine officials sent by the county government who, under the pretext of collecting taxes, had extorted money from taxpayers, beaten others, and shot the village head (*Shiquan XZ*, 1991, 701). The year before, the peasants had also looted the home of a man called Chen Licheng and killed two of his family, failing to catch Chen himself. Chen, who was responsible for collecting taxes on wine and slaughtering, was known to expose defaulting taxpayers to the sun with barrels hung round their necks (*Shiquan XZ*, 1991, 700–701).

40. When it came to the regular army, there is no end to examples of villages burned and peasants massacred by soldiers. To take one example, a score were killed in Heshangping, Jiangxi, in 1914 (*Qianshan WSZL*, vol. 3, 1989, 3). See further cases in Chapter 7 and in Rowe 2007, 273–75, 297, and passim. On the warlords' armies, cf. among a hundred other examples the exactions, tortures, and rapes perpetrated by rival bands in Xingping county, Shaanxi, in 1916 (*Xingping WSZL*, vol. 1, 1983, 181–82) or the scholars hanged in Liping in 1925 on the orders of Sichuanese troops (*Liping XZ*, 1989, 17). Cf. also Lary 1985; McCord 2001; and Zhang Tianyi's (1985) short story "Chouhen" (Hatred).

41. Yang was defeated by the militia in 1931 and forced to flee. He was to be rehabilitated by Liu Zhidan's Red Army and would end up (like Wang Zuo and Yuan Wencai, the famous Jinggangshan brigands enrolled and later killed by Mao and Zhu De) being shot in Heshui, Gansu, on Liu's orders because Liu judged him beyond redemption (*Baishui XZ*, 1989, 499).

42. This environment also affected their capacity for feeling. The American consul in Nanjing, who was visiting Yangzhou the day soldiers had just killed seven or eight peasants, was surprised to see people coming and going, "chatting and laughing just as usual" (USDS, SD 893.00/12198, Peck's dispatch 25 October 1932). On the Yangzhou riot, see Box 5.4.

43. Such resistance was less rare, of course, among salt workers (in Zigong, Sichuan, for example) or other workers adopting the same forms of struggle as the industrial proletariat.

Chapter Four

1. Rural people owning no land at all were far more numerous. They were even more destitute than the farm laborers, many of them (tramps wandering from village to village, disabled and otherwise disadvantaged people subsisting on handouts or the occasional job offered by charitable people) belonging to the subproletariat rather than the proletariat.

2. The typical wage was 0.34 *yuan* with a meal, as against 0.51 *yuan* without (survey carried out by the Zhongshan Centre for Cultural Education, cited in Xue Muqiao 1937, 52–53).

3. For example, the farmhands in Fuling, Sichuan, who roughly drove off some jobless day-workers who had sneaked in to work in "their" rice field hoping to be paid in the evening (*ZGNC*, vol. 2, no. 4, 1936, 75).

4. There are more details, though still not enough, in *Jacqueries*, 249–51.

5. For example, the transporters of fine china (as in Ci Xian, Hebei, in 1932; Thaxton 1989, 258–60) or the coolies mobilized by the authorities to work on big projects (such as dredging a coastal river in northern Jiangsu in 1936;

Guanyun WSZL, vol. 2, 1985, 138–40). The great majority of these coolies and transporters were villagers, often peasants as poor as many of the farm laborers. All the same, they were not farm laborers and their actions come under different headings. For example, the Guanyun revolt that we have just mentioned (far more than a simple strike) arose from resistance to corvée labor, described in the first chapter.

6. In particular, natural disasters forced a heightened need for credit: in Jiangnan in 1931, after the Yangzi floods, credit increased by a third. The Yellow River floods in 1935 caused a famine during which monthly interest rates reached 10 percent at the start of 1936 in the west of Shandong (Li 1991, 497).

7. An example of alleged dishonesty: on 30 June 1940, in Nanchong, Sichuan, the county capital was sacked during a riot directed against "dishonest shopkeepers," one of whom, a butcher, was beaten and injured by the rioters. The archived file does not tell us in what respect the shopkeepers were dishonest. It is true that it consists of a dispatch from the provincial government to the Executive Yuan giving an account of demands for reinforcements addressed by the local authorities and a petition signed by representatives of the local gentry asking authorization for using force in the event of new disturbances. The first document is dry and official, but the signatories of the second are too concerned with giving an apocalyptic description of the damage to dwell on the rioters' grievances (*ZD2LDG*, file 2/1865). Allegations of dishonesty, probably justified, relating to the conversion of the copper coins used by villagers into accounting currency: in May 1909, peasants considering themselves swindled destroyed several shops in Huating, Zhejiang, and a bureau de change in Fengxian, Jiangsu (today Shanghai) (*QMN*, no. 50, 1983, 79–80). An example of proven dishonesty: the management of a pawnshop looted by troops in 1924 in Lücheng, Jiangsu, claimed that garments deposited as pledges by peasants had been stolen and that it could not therefore return them to the depositors. An "Association of Depositors" formed on the initiative of a member of the Guomindang obtained compensation (Geisert 2001, 58–59).

8. Up until then (usually), those resisting were mainly lumberjacks, salt workers, or fishermen—even though their families generally farmed a patch of land. Here is a case where peasants resisted in their capacity as farmers: 3,000 of them, on 30 June 1925, marched through the county town of Yin Xian, Zhejiang, and destroyed the headquarters of the monopoly fertilizer company (Zhejiang sheng zhengxie wenshi ziliao weiyuanhui 1990, 199–200).

9. For example, the monopolization by scholar gentry and landowners of the bulk of the subsidies granted to 27 villages in Fangshan county, Hebei,

between the start of the Republic and 1914 (*Fangshan WSZL*, vol. 3, 1990, 30–31). Giving to the scholars more than their share was already a long-standing tradition with the imperial administration, as observed when food was being distributed to the starving in Shanxi in 1878 (Janku 2004).

10. *Qingpu XZ*, 1991, 16–18 and 537–38; *Xiangdao zhoubao*, no. 179, 25 October 1926 (article written by Mao Zedong). Where the two sources are in contradiction, I have favored Mao's version as more reliable. See a similar example from quite close by (in Songjiang) in 1926–27 in Geizert 2001, 60–61.

11. See for example the Henan case in Alitto 1979, 240–41 and the Hebei case in Huang 1985, 41–42, 269–70, 273–74 and Huang 1996, 68–70.

12. In 1912, a new revolt (also put down) brought together in the same way about 1,000 shepherds, but this time the political element outweighed the social: the rebels contested the obligation on all families with two or more sons to send one to serve in the *qinwang* cavalry—and to supply his own horse (*Xinjiang WSZLXJ*, vol. 13, 1985, 51–57).

13. For example, the *tulie* in Su Xian, Anhui (*PWP*, 81–83). On these political and, incidentally, sociological developments, see Alitto 1979, Duara 1988, and especially Kuhn 1975.

Chapter Five

1. Yet, some of the special contributions (*tankuan*) demanded by quite a number of counties were imposed equally on all village households, including those possessing no land. It was the same with the head tax and a few other taxes. With some exceptions, these deductions were less onerous than the land tax and the surcharges on the land tax, which by definition were restricted to owners of land. It was rare for the authorities, as in Siyugang (Box 5.1), to step outside that restriction.

2. From the start of our period, we should recall the revolt that broke out in May 1901 in Anping, Hebei, against the imposition of a new *mujuan* (*XGQSJMDS*, 1), followed in the second half of the same decade by many riots directed against the imposition of a *xuejuan* (school tax).

3. Here are some examples of surtaxes linked to national defense and the maintenance of public order: surtax for defense, surtax for public security, surtax for building blockhouses, surtax for armament and ammunition, surtax for the police, surtax for exterminating the red bandits, surtax for resisting Japan, surtax for voluntary contribution toward planes intended for fighting the Japanese (Sun Zuoqi 1935, 156–57).

4. Outside Jiangsu, we can find equivalent cases in Sichuan and Hunan, and more extreme cases in Hubei (Duan 1935, 53–54; Sun Xiaocun 1935, 19). Even where the burden of surtaxes was far more modest, it nevertheless went up

considerably between the start of the Republic and the 1930s. An example from a Hebei county: surtaxes measured in proportion to regular taxation rose from 11 percent in 1912 to 103 percent in 1934 (Li 2005, 36–37).

5. In Wujin, Jiangsu, where one *mu* of land was worth 60 *yuan*, the authorities arbitrarily fixed the price at 80 *yuan*, so as to maintain the land tax within the 1 percent limit (Wan, Zhuang, and Wu 1934, 100).

6. This section is concerned on one hand with the abuses and frauds committed by agents of the revenue collectors and the administration, on the other with frauds practiced by taxpayers themselves. When it comes to the latter, we shall deal more briefly with tax evasion than with action to prevent it; and likewise we shall look more quickly at smuggling than at repressing it, for it was official action (fiscal inquisition and repression) that gave rise to resistance and revolts.

7. The gentry nevertheless maintained, even increased, its share in the creation—in the absence of collection—of taxes and local surtaxes (*tankuan* rather than surcharges on the land tax) at the end of the Empire and under the Republic, to the point where they obliged the administration to reclaim its authority during the years preceding the Japanese invasion. The suppression of surtaxes enacted in 1935 had this end in mind, rather than providing relief to taxpayers (Kuhn 1979, 100–36).

8. On the collection of the land tax, the best source relates to the imperial period: Wang 1973, 39–47. For an earlier period, cf. Huang 1974, 40 and 145. For the Republican period, cf. among others Duara 1988, 218–21 and 226–34; Wan, Zhuang, and Wu 1934, 53–87 and 154–67; Sun Xiaocun 1935, 17–26.

9. When the peasants paid in copper coins a tax where silver money was stipulated, quite a number of collectors overvalued the silver dollar while performing the conversion (Sun Zuoqi 1935, 365). See a similar case (converting taels into silver dollars) in Anxiang, Hunan, in 1931 in Wu Zhongdao 1935, 71–72.

10. "To fabricate a good or a bad harvest" (*nie shu huang*) is a synonymous expression (Weng 1936, 240).

11. Salt is partly produced by boiling, partly by evaporation—which does not need a furnace and costs less but is subject to climatic hazards. Rain, even the absence of sunshine, impedes the collection of brine.

12. During the closing years of the Empire alone, a few dozen cases (9 for the single year of 1907 and 11 in 1908) fall within one or another of these categories—sometimes within several at once.

13. An imperial edict of 1713 stating "Never increase the amount of land tax" (*yong bu jiafu*) was generally interpreted by officials as implying a freeze on taxable cultivated areas (Wang, 1973, 29).

14. Compare the case in Zhili, Hebei, examined by Li 2005, 234–35.

15. In the 1930s, most of the villages in northern China kept two land registers: one, intended for the administration, in which only half the cultivated fields were registered, and the other, more exact, being kept strictly for local use (Duara 1988, 222).

16. Compare three instructive cases: Jiangdu, Jiangsu, where surveying was interrupted by the 1932 revolt and finally completed in 1935; Xiao Xian, Jiangsu (today in Anhui); and Dangtu, Anhui (Bianco 1986, 284).

17. Examples in Xiaoshan, Zhejiang, in December 1907, April 1908, and May 1909 (*QMN*, no. 49, 1982, 170; no. 50, 1983, 78 and 79), Hankou, Hubei, 1 June 1908, and Dantu, Jiangsu, 23 August 1910 (*QMN*, no. 49, 1982, 175 and no. 50, 104).

18. Examples in the counties of Binxian, Acheng, Yucheng, and then Wuchang, Heilongjiang; 15 and 29 December 1915 (*DFZZ*, 30146 and 30378; *Wuchang XZ*, 1989, 7); Xinmin and Xiuyan, Fengtian, 13 January 1915 and 24 May 1916 (*DFZZ*, vol. 12, no. 3, March 1915, 28134; *Xiuyan XZ*, 1989, 11 in the chronology); Zhuoxian, Yixian, and Laishui, Zhili, in June 1915 and May 1916 (*DFZZ*, 31217 and 31424); Feicheng, Shandong, 22 March 1916, then in the four neighboring counties of Dong'e, Pingyin, Dongping, and Xintai (*DFZZ*, 31107; also Young 1977, 248 and Li 2005, 240).

19. Among dozens and dozens of examples, we should mention those in Jiangsu, including such counties as Xinchang (18 August 1929; Zhejiang sheng zhengxie wenshi ziliao weiyuanhui 1990, 234), Dinghai (Liuheng Island, 30 January 1930; *Zhoushan shizhi*, 1992, 16; Zhejiang sheng zhengxie wenshi ziliao weiyuanhui 1990, 237), Yongkang (January 1930; *Yongkang XZ*, 1991, 79), Xianju (26–27 July 1930; *Xianju XZ*, 1987, 7 and 480–81), Yuyao (4 July 1935; Zhejiang provincial archives, file no. 1556; *ZJNSZ*, vol. 3, 1025); those in the two Jiangsu counties of Zhenjiang (November 1929 and July 1934; Stross 1982, 78–79) and Tongshan (October 1936; *ZJNSZ*, vol. 3, 1026); and one in Hexian county, Anhui (April 1935; *Zhongguo ribao*, 15 April 1935).

20. "It is distressing to note such stupidity on the part of the villagers," was the comment from the Governor of Jiangsu in his first official report on the Jiangdu riot (Dispatch from Gu Zhutong to Song Ziwen, 26 October 1932, in *ZD2LDG*, no. 2/2/973).

21. The most important part of this file is the report dated 14 August 1935 addressed by the Permanent Committee of the Guomindang Executive Committee for Zhejiang to the Committee in charge of Mass Movements within the Guomindang Central Executive Committee (Zhejiang provincial archives, file no. 10784/2369).

22. However, there did exist some rare surtaxes exclusively for the rich, particularly in Jiangxi. The competition there from the communists induced the Nationalist administration to impart a "social" tinge to the taxes—but in practice everybody paid them.

23. I have left out something often mentioned but seldom substantiated: the landlords' practice of offloading to their tenants the duty of paying their taxes. Among the rare cases established, we shall cite those of Hunan tenants forced to pay the land tax owed by their absentee landlord (Zhuang 1936, 300) and tenants in Lanxi, Heilongjiang, ordered to pay 60 percent of the land tax while the landlord contented himself with paying the remaining 40 percent (Li 1932, 130). More often, the administration would make tenants pay tax owed by a defaulting or recalcitrant landlord, but reduce by the same sum the rent payable to the landlord (Chen 1966, 262). See also Box 5.1.

24. In the last decade of the Empire, the difference between the two "tariffs" was far from negligible (Wang 1973, 40–41).

25. Examples abounded in all regions. In Hexi, Gansu, in 1936, most of the estates of the *da hu* escaped land tax (*Dagongbao*, 7 April 1936, cited in Chen 1966, 243). See less flagrant cases in Shaanxi, Suiyuan, the three Manchurian provinces on the eve of their occupation by Japan, and the north of Jiangsu (*Shishi xinbao*, 1 April 1931, cited in Li 1932, 129–30); in Zhejiang: *Shenbao*, 10 August, 1929; *Minguo ribao*, 12 May 1932, cited in Li 1932, 130). The Buddhist monastery Jilean, which owned 1,000,000 *mu* of land in northern Jiangsu, paid land tax on 250,000 *mu*, so three-quarters of its land was not taxed (Li 1932, 129). In Shaoxing, Zhejiang, a former governor of Jiangxi never paid a penny in tax; in Jiaxing, in the same province, another notable named Zhu enjoyed the same freedom: Ho 1934, 10.

26. Responsible under the Empire for control of policing and ideology, the *xiangyue* also acted as mediator of disputes. In a Shandong village under the Republic, he was further charged with collecting taxes (Yang 1945, 173).

27. One of them, a man called Shao, had advised his son when bringing him into the enterprise, "This'll be like a bowl of rice." (Jiang 1988b, 1).

28. See especially Prazniak 1999, Chapter 2; Prazniak 1980, 41–71; and Wang 1954, 209–21. See also *DFZZ*, vol. 7, no. 6, July 1910, 17637–40, no. 7, August 1910, 17836–37, no. 8, September 1910, 18053–55, no. 9 (October 1910), 18290–91; Messant-Yun 1982, 53–54; *Shibao* (Shanghai), 16, 17, 18, 19 August 1910; *QMN*, no. 50, 1983, 97; Zhang Yufa, second edition, 1987, 462–67.

29. Kathy Le Mons Walker (1999, 163) gives him 141 *mu*, which is about 23 acres.

30. We should specify, nevertheless, that this admirer of the industrial revolution had sold some of his estate to invest in a factory and that the venture had collapsed.

Chapter Six

1. In April 1909, a new attack by the Red Lanterns destroyed a school in another Sichuan county, An Xian (*QMN*, no. 50, 1983, 79).

2. According to *Zunhua XZ* (1990, 10), more than 50 villages were mobilized, whereas 28 had been involved in the revolt against the tax on orchards that occurred in Shangdian (in the same county) two years earlier. On this latter episode, see Prazniak 1999, 97–100.

3. The analysis by Wang Yeh-chien here relates to Chuansha (and, a little further away, Suzhou), but that was precisely the region where we can note the greatest number of incidents. It is the abundance and relative reliability of the available documentation that encourages us to favor the study of this region—which, incidentally, was much more highly taxed than the rest of the country (Wang 1973, 89 and 126).

4. On this movement, see Goossaert 2000, 98 and 100 and especially 2003, 431–32; see also interesting details on Jiangsu in Wang 1985, 210–13. The seizure of temple buildings to establish a new school provoked a revolt in Sheng Xian, Zhejiang, 2 June 1910 (*DFZZ*, vol. 7, no. 6, 17667–68).

5. In Jingning county, Zhejiang, the Liu family started up two schools reserved for its own children, but all the residents had paid the tax on salt and bamboo that funded them, which provoked a revolt in late April or early May 1910 (*DFZZ*, vol. 7, no. 5, 17482).

6. Local autonomy was welcomed by the traditional—but not traditionalist—gentry. The following paragraph describes the case of the traditionalist members of the gentry who refused to countenance the withdrawal of the classics from the schools.

7. In Shunjiangzhou, Jiangsu, a Taoist priest led 2,000 to 3,000 monks in an attack on a school opened up in a Confucian temple that he was renting (Xiao-Planes 2001, 228–29). Two leaders of the Chuansha revolt (March 1911) were running rural temples (Prazniak 1999, 234).

8. See examples in several counties in southern Jiangsu and two north of the river in *QMN*, no. 50, 1983, 91 and Wang 1985, 208; in two Yunnan counties in May 1910 (*QMN*, no. 50, 1983, 95 and *DFZZ*, vol. 7, no. 5, 17484); and in 25 villages in Laiyang county, Shandong (Prazniak 1999, 70).

9. Registers were demanded from the enumerator under threat of burning down his house in Jiayuan Xiang, Jiangsu, 14 August 1910 (*SB*, 1 September 1910) and torn up in Nantong, Jiangsu, on 17 April 1910 (*QMN*, no. 50, 1983,

93). Enumerators were beaten in Jintan, Jiangsu, between April and May 1905 (*QMN*, no. 50, 96) and wounded in Nanling, Anhui, 19 May 1910 (*QMN*, no. 50, 97; *DFZZ*, vol. 7, no. 6, 17669–70); Shazhou, Wujin county, Jiangsu, 25 December 1910 (*QMN*, no. 50, 109), tied up and beaten in Yancheng, Jiangsu, on 25 and 26 April 1910 (*DFZZ*, vol.7, no. 5, 17479), and tied up and sent back in Yangzhou prefecture, Jiangsu, 22 May 1910 (*DFZZ*, vol. 7, no. 5, 17479). The enumerator and his family were attacked and their home destroyed and pillaged in Yaojiaqiao, Zhejiang, 23 August 1910 (*SB*, 3 September 1910 and *DFZZ*, vol. 7, no. 8, 18068). Among the numerous other cases of census takers' homes being demolished and pillaged is the incident in Nanling, Anhui, in the summer of 1910 (Weng Fei et al. 1990, 360).

10. Teachers (and sometimes pupils) were beaten, injured, and their houses demolished in Heqiao, Jiangsu, in February 1910 and Sima Zhen, Jiangsu, in March 1910 (interview with Xiaohong Xiao-Planes, who obligingly transmitted as well the two sources—*Jiaoyu zazhi* and *Jiangsu xuewu zonghui wendu*—cited below). Among large numbers of other cases, we should recall that between one and several dozen schools were burned down in six Jiangsu counties or prefectures and seven Zhejiang counties (*Jiaoyu zazhi*, 1933, t. 3/1, 2427). Arson attacks on education offices included a case in Yancheng, Jiangsu, April 1910 (*DFZZ*, vol. 7, no. 5, 17479). A case of burning and looting of the home of the Director of Education occurred in Dongtai, Jiangsu (*Jiangsu xuewu zonghui wendu*, vol. 1, section 2, 47–48).

11. Local autonomy offices were attacked or destroyed in Jintan, Jiangsu, in April and May 1910 (*QMN*, no. 50, 1983, 96) and in Zhuanghe, Fengtian, 10 September 1911 (*QMN*, no. 50, 1983, 119).

12. A magistrate was taken hostage in Changxing, Zhejiang, 22 August 1910 (*SB*, 3 September 1910 and *DFZZ*, vol. 7, no. 8, 18067–68); another was beaten to death in Nandan, Guangxi, in March 1910 (*QMN*, no. 50, 91); a prefect was attacked in Quanzhou, Guangxi, 11 October 1910 (*DFZZ*, vol. 7, no. 10, 18527); the houses of various local officials were burned down or demolished, for example in Caonianchang, Jiangsu, 24 April 1910 (*DFZZ*, vol. 7, no. 5, 17479), in Xincheng Zhen, Jiangsu, 24 May 1910 (*DFZZ*, vol. 7, no. 5, 17479), in Yangcheng, Jiangsu, 25 April 1910 (*QMN*, no. 50, 94), in Ludian and En'an, Yunnan, 4 May 1910 (*QMN*, no. 50, 95), and in Jiading, Jiangsu, late May 1910 (*DFZZ*, vol. 7, no. 5, 17479; *QMN*, no. 50, 98). Rather than extend this wearisome list, I would recommend two tables in Prazniak 1999, 236–37 and 240.

13. A police station was destroyed in Zhuanghe, Fengtian, 10 September 1911 (*QMN*, no. 50, 1983, 119) and a police station and the police chief's home were destroyed in Si'an Zhen, Zhejiang, in August 1910. In this same township, rebels destroyed the church, two schools, and the home of two school heads, as

well as notables' homes, in all about ten buildings (*SB*, 3 September 1910; *DFZZ*, vol. 7, no. 8, 18068). Numerous churches were demolished in 1910 in Jurong, Jiangsu (*DFZZ*, vol. 7, no. 8, 18165), in Ningxiang and Anhua in Hunan (*QMN*, no. 50, 95 and 99), and also in several Zhejiang counties (Shen 1981, 44).

14. On the rumor that bodies would be used to build dikes, see *SB*, 3 September 1910. A similar fear was expressed in Taixing, Jiangsu, in April: the souls of those involved in the census and condemned to an early death would be used for the pillars of a great bridge over the Yellow River (*NCH*, 29 April 1910, 254). On the rumor about laying of railway tracks, see *DFZZ*, vol. 7, no. 5, 17459. In He Xian (a little further north in eastern Anhui, the site of the riot of 25 June 1910), it was rumored that people checked for the census would be used to build a railway bridge (*DFZZ*, vol. 7, no. 5, 17460) or as railway ties (Prazniak 1999, 143 and 222).

15. These expressions are borrowed from chapter headings in Lefebvre 1932, which was translated into English as *The Great Fear of 1789: Rural Panic in Revolutionary France* and published by Pantheon Books in 1973.

16. Revolts targeted exclusively against taxation were particularly numerous at first, at a time when the destruction of schools and police stations was still rare. Examples of riots and demonstrations against the taxes for schools, not accompanied by destruction of schools, appear in Xinping, Shaanxi, in 1904 (Xibei daxue lishixi 1984, 140–42); in Xinye, Henan, 19 April 1905 (*Xinye XZ*, 1991, 19) and 27 June 1905 (*QMN*, no. 49, 1982, 136); and in Rugao, Jiangsu, 17 August 1905 (*QMN*, no. 49, 1982, 137–38). A similar situation occurred with police: no attack on the police station, just the refusal to pay the tax for the police (*jingcha juan* or more simply *jingjuan* or *jingshui*) in Fushun, Sichuan, in 1905 (*QMN*, no. 49, 135), as well as in Lingshou and Ji Xian, Zhili, in 1907 (Li 1980, 123). Again in July 1910, in Changge, Henan, 10,000 demonstrators ransacked the county yamen, and distributed pamphlets attacking the magistrate, who attempted suicide. It was his taxation measures that they opposed, in particular a tax per *mu* (in reality a surcharge on the land tax) intended to fund expenditure on the police (Prazniak 1999, 123; *DFZZ*, vol. 7, no. 7, 17839–40 and no. 8, 18055–56; Liu 1994, 82; *QMN*, no. 50, 102).

17. Between 1905 and 1907, fourteen riots (in my records; many more, in fact) broke out in Shaanxi against the "tax for the railway" (*lujuan*), a railway that was not built at that time and that the taxpaying peasants would not have used, except to walk along the track and get themselves run over by a train. This was the fate of a blind man killed 450 miles to the east (in Shandong, 1905), which provoked a demonstration by more than 2,000 blind people against the German driver of the train (*Zichuan WSZLXJ*, vol. 3, 1990, 236–38). And 600 miles to the southeast and five years later, this was a fate shared by two

villagers (not blind), who were run over in the same conditions in Xinfeng, near Zhenjiang, Jiangsu, after which the villagers blocked rail traffic for a few hours (*SB*, 19 December 1910).

18. I have expressed a few disagreements with Duara's *Rescuing History from the Nation* in Bianco 2007, 505–6.

19. Elected head of the Dong clan after his retirement, the same individual later had a young burglar drowned in a pond (*Gaochun XZ*, 1988, 801), which shows how tradition (here, clan law) can continue to dictate the attitudes of a revolutionary iconoclast.

20. Apart from rare exceptions, I have left out urban riots, such as those in Fogang, Guangdong, in 1928 (*Fogang WSZL*, vol. 2, 1985, 56–57) and in Gaoyou, Jiangsu, in 1931 (Geisert 2001, 159; Nedostup 2001, 392–93). The motivation of urban and rural protesters being quite close, I have allowed myself occasionally to venture beyond the rural restrictions imposed by my subject, especially when suburban peasants have joined forces with city rioters.

21. In the second incident described in Box 6.2, the rebels tried to tear up the railway track south of Teng.

22. In Yongshou, Shaanxi, an association formed in October 1912 and charged with cutting queues ordered all male inhabitants to get rid of their queues within a month. As no one complied, the association decided to wait for better times. Then, in 1921, a new magistrate dispatched militiamen to every village with the task of going from house to house and cutting queues. Their mission was accomplished, this time without resistance (*Yongshou XZ*, 1991, 17).

23. For example, west of Hunyuan county, Shanxi, 2,000 and later 6,000 to 7,000 members of a "Peasant Army" rose up in June 1912 against the cutting of queues. As usual, the casualties were particularly high among the ranks of the peasants (*Shanxi WSZL*, vol. 34, 1984, 111–13).

24. Similarly, the silk production cooperative set up in the village where Fei Xiaotong carried out his research enrolled only 21 homes at first. Then, quite quickly, the entire village joined up once the overwhelming advantages of modern methods of raising silkworms had been demonstrated. But when raw silk prices fell, including prices for the high-quality silk produced by the cooperative, half the village members stopped paying their annual subscriptions (Fei 1939, 210–12 and 229–30).

25. According to the historian Gu Jiegang, the greater ignorance was sometimes on the side of the iconoclasts, who sought to eradicate a religion and a popular culture without perceiving their richness and vitality (Schneider 1971, 13, 123–24; see also 148–51 on Gu's criticism of the "anti-superstition" campaign launched by the Nationalist government).

Chapter Seven

1. I wish to repeat at the outset of this chapter what I emphasized in the preface, namely the debt of the teacher to his student. The first draft of this chapter was less substantial; it has been greatly enriched by the fascinating archival and other material from Taiwan made available to me by Dr. Fu Hung-chung, as well as by his own research. Subsequent references to sources discovered and read by Dr. Fu (and not by myself) are so noted. Interested readers may refer to his dissertation (Fu 2007), which contains and reveals much more than what was possible to compress within this chapter.

2. A legacy of the Qing, the *baojia* system was reinvigorated by the Nationalist government. During the war it served as a basis for recruiting soldiers, with one conscript per *jia*, which amounted to anything from six to fifteen families (ten, in principle). Even more than the *jia* heads, the *bao* heads (one *bao* = ten *jia*) played a central role in selecting conscripts. The *lianbao*, group of *bao*, was the next level up in the hierarchy of local authorities.

3. There were comparable incidents in Guizhou between 1943 and 1944 and in 1948 (*Qianxi XZ*, 1990, 219–20 and 667–68; *Huishui XZ*, 1989, 24).

4. There are examples, all within the single province of Sichuan and the single year of 1940, in Taihe, Yangxi, Pengxi, and Yanting. In each case, the practice led to resistance or to the release of the abducted recruits (Fu 2007, 202–3).

5. In August 1942, 200 boatmen broke down the door into the Chengxiang warehouse, in Sichuan, to free a colleague drafted by force. While they were at it, they freed 40 other conscripts (*Kai XZ*, 1990, 14). Still in 1942, about 100 villagers broke into an administrative office in Xujia, Sichuan, to rescue some peddlers abducted by recruiting sergeants. The attempt failed because the victims had already been escorted to the county town. The villagers assuaged their wrath by pillaging the *bao* head's house (*Guan XZ*, 1991, 804). Two further examples: the forcible drafting of 20 young peasants by a detachment of 600 armed police in Luopi, Jiangxi, in 1939 (*Shicheng WSZLXJ*, vol. 2, 1987, 89–98; *Shicheng XZ*, 1990, 154) and the abduction of villagers attending a fair in Shangyuanpu, Shaanxi, in 1945. In the latter case, the peasants were unable to free their comrades, so they killed two officials, including the one who had ordered the raid (*Xixiang XZ*, 1991, 245).

6. The following examples are variations on this stock phrase: *kangding* (or *kangbing*) *kangliang*, "Resist conscription and grain deliveries" (examples in *Dazhu XZ*, 1992, 12; *Yongdeng XZ*, 1997, 22), two phrases that became particularly frequent during the second half of the war, once inflation had brought the government to collect the land tax in kind, but here *liang* can mean either this

tax or the compulsory deliveries of grain to the army, at low prices fixed by the army; *kangding kangkuan*, "Resist conscription and contributions" (see example in *Peng XZ*, 1989, 18); *bu dangbing bu naliang*, "No to conscription, no to taxes in kind" (example in *Jiefang ribao*, 29 July 1945); *fandui zhuading he kejuan zashui*, "Fight against the capture of conscripts and multiple taxes" (example in *Shicheng XZ*, 1990, 683); and *fandui zhengbing nashui zhengce*, "Fight the policy on recruiting soldiers and raising taxes" (example in *Hefeng XZ*, 1990, 8).

7. For example, *fan zhengbing fan juanshui*, "Let's fight military service and taxation" was the slogan used by 200 demonstrators in Qingliu, Fujian, on 18 July 1938. As it turned out, the revolt, which was to last two months and cause the deaths of sixteen peasants in bloody clashes on 17 and 20 September, was apparently aimed at protecting the guerrillas hiding in the mountains to escape military service (*Sanming WSZL*, vol. 7, 1989, 71–72). At other times, one comes across a saying, then popular, *shengxia erzi shi lao Jiang de, daxia liangshi shi baozhangde*, "The son we've raised is for old Jiang [Chiang Kai-shek], and the grain we've harvested is for the *bao* head [who collected the taxes]" (*Henan WSZLXJ*, vol. 14, 1985, 101).

8. Let me mention just two other examples. In February 1942, the Hongqianghui launched a revolt in Jiujiawan, Shaanxi, against military service, corvée labor, taxes, and soldiers' misdeeds (a rape attack by a militiaman). After the revolt was crushed, ten members of the society were shot (*Shanyang WSZLXJ*, vol. 1, 1985, 19–35; *ZMDZH*, series 5, part 2, vol. 5, 203–6; latter source provided by Fu). In 1943–44, the Niujiaohui (Buffalo's Horn Society) organized resistance to military service in Qianxi county, Guizhou. At the recruiting agents' approach, a member of the society would sound the horn and all the young men took flight. After the society's leader was executed in May 1944, the organization collapsed (*Qianxi XZ*, 1990, 19, 219–20, and 667–68; *Shuixi WSZLXJ*, vol. 1, 1983, 21–24).

9. The Jinuo, who lived in the mountains of southern Yunnan, near China's border with Burma, rose up in 1941 against military service and taxation, declaring war on the Emperor of Peking and sending him an ultimatum (Fu 2007, 296–97).

10. Whole volumes of *WSZL* are devoted to the eastern Guizhou revolt. The richest source is *Qiandongnan WSZL*, vol. 6, 1987. See also *Guizhou WSZLXJ*, vol. 2, 1983, 183–219; vol. 15, 1984, 107–19; vol. 22, 1986, 96–104; *Guizhou Qiandong WSZL*, vol. 3, 1985, 57–81; *Jinping WSZLXJ*, vol. 2, 1988, 1–4; *Shibing WSZL*, vol. 3, 1987, 1–33; *Songtao WSZL*, vol. 6, 1988, 38–44 and 56–59; *Tongren diqu WSZL*, vol. 1, 1990, 1–5, 127–32, 147–51, and 177–202; *Yunyuan WSZLXJ*, vol. 5, 1987, 28–38; *Zhenyuan WSZL*, vol. 1, 1986, 152–57 and 169–72. Besides

the *WSZL* series, see also *Bingyi xunkan*, nos. 2–3, 1939–40; Dai 1983, 119–24; Zhou et al. 1987, 302–3 and 365–72.

11. In other words, the lower stretch of the "long river" (the Yangzi), which flows through Jiangsu. There were also educated newcomers from neighboring Zhejiang, the homeland of Chiang Kai-shek and equally well supplied with graduates.

12. See in particular *Qiandongnan WSZL*, vol. 6, 1987, 142; secondarily, the whole account of a former member of the Tongshanshe, 141–46; and that of a higher-ranking member of the same society, 159–64. Also USDS, 893.00/15024 and /15095.

13. On the three Hui revolts, see Ma 1958; Xie 1981, 7–15 and 94–98; and Fu 2007, 300–301.

14. On the Gannan (southern Gansu) revolt in 1942–43, see in particular *Lanzhou WSZLXJ*, vol. 3, 1985, 111–37 and Gansu shifan daxue lishixi, *Lishi jiaoxue yu yanjiu*, no. 3, 1960, 26–35. See also *Gansu WSZLXJ*, vol. 1, 1963, 142–43; *Lanzhou WSZLXJ*, vol. 1, 1983, 58–73; *Linxia WZLXJ*, vol. 5, 1989, 39–64; Meng 1983, 12–15; and Sheng 1989 (cited in Fu 2007, 320, 322, and 323). More sources are mentioned in Fu 2007, 311–21.

15. Nevertheless, from this point of view, the preceding account does add a brick to the building, because these revolts have not been accorded the coverage they deserve in Western histories of the period. A partial exception is, as so often, Eastman 1984, 68–69.

16. Some of these bands numbered up to 1,000 men, young and relatively well-armed (when the deserters were able to bring their own guns). They called themselves the Kangzhengtuan (Brigade Resisting Military Service), or more descriptively, the Nongmin taoshengtuan (Corps of Peasants Seeking Salvation in Flight) or Jiushengtuan (Brigade Bringing Help to Conscripts). These three examples are all from Jiangxi: in the same order, *Dongxiang* XZ, 1989, 351; *Xingan* XZ, 1990, 30; *Jishui* XZ, 1992, 304–5.

Chapter Eight

1. The Croquant Uprisings (1636–37) in and around the Périgord region and the Revolt of the Nu-Pieds (1639) in Normandy were among the most significant antitax rebellions in France during the seventeenth century. On the Croquants, see in particular Bercé 1986; on the Nu-Pieds, see Foisil 1970.

2. Casualties were higher in China, especially when revolts were being repressed—which was done heedless of legalities. In two locations in Yifeng county, Jiangxi, the local militia killed 61 looters in 1906 (*Yifeng* XZ, 1989, 14). There were executions, less numerous but systematic, in the countryside around Changsha, Hunan, in April 1910 (Messant-Yun 1982, 44–46), in Qi-

jiang, Sichuan, in April 1926 (*Qijiang XZ*, 1991, 19), and Guang'an, Sichuan, in 1947 (*Guang'an XZ*, 1992, 16).

3. Sections 1 (rejection of the state's reform initiatives), 3 (resistance to the state's legal, military, or police apparatus), and 8 (challenge to municipal authority) in Nicolas 2002, 548–49.

4. We are reminded of *xiedou* by section 12 ("regional particularism") of the Nicolas typology, as well as by parts of section 13 ("rivalry between districts and parishes" and "rivalries between nobles degenerating into collective confrontations"; Nicolas 2002, 550). These categories comprise smaller numbers of incidents but, in the body of the book, the paragraph on "bravado and brawling" (452–56) confirms that situations and feelings likely to generate *xiedou* or something like them were not exclusive to China.

5. Nicolas (2002, 548) lists the (very few) refusals to comply with corvée under resistance to taxation and surcharges, which is at least as reasonable as my choice of listing them under special levies, as a transition from antitax resistance (see Chapter 1).

6. Examples of such declarations in China: "To die fighting is better than dying of hunger" (*Pucheng WSZL*, vol. 1, 1985, 17) and "Better to break the law than die of hunger" (*Tonglu XZ*, 1991, 12). The year (1934) when these looters thus justified their actions, 100,000 of the county's inhabitants were reduced to eating grass and earth. In France, the Ancenis rioters of the late seventeenth century declared that they would "prefer to be hanged than die of starvation" (Nicolas 2002, 281; cf. many other similar declarations, 282).

7. Fairly often, mayors and priests marched at the head of their parishioners when they rose up against the *taille* (Bercé 1991, 125–27). In 1910, the *shezhang* in Laiyang, Shandong, played similar roles in the service of their community.

8. A further indication of how seldom the peasants' collective actions were motivated by class consciousness: their leaders were more usually well-off peasants or landowners than peasants known to be poor or of average means. And more frequently they were not peasants—and some in France were even nobles (in China: *Jacqueries*, 162 and Chapter 5; in France: Le Roy Ladurie 2002, 432, 444, 452, 454–55 for the sixteenth century; 458–60, 464, 467, and 663 for the seventeenth century; 672–74 for the eighteenth century).

9. In one village in Yuntang county, Jiangxi, the tax boycott lasted for three years, from 1998 to 2001 (Lü 2003, 11).

10. Examples: "Down with the bureaucratic Communist Party!" (in Hebei in 1998, where the peasants formed a short-lived "people's autonomous government"; *Dongxiang*, June 1998, 15); "All the wealth produced from the land must go to the peasants!" (Bernstein and Lü 2003, 142); "Free the slaves of

today, the peasants!" (Yu 2003a, 9); "We're citizens—return us our citizenship rights!" (O'Brien and Li 2006, 116–17).

11. As attested by, among many other sources, the famous survey carried out in about 50 villages and townships in Anhui by husband-and-wife partnership Chen Guidi and Wu Chuntao (Chen and Chun 2003; partial translation in Chen and Wu 2006).

12. *Sanluan* recall the surtaxes, *mujuan*, and other *tanpai* (allotments) of the 1920s and 1930s (Chapter 5). See Bernstein and Lü 2003, 53–58.

13. This summary represents a compromise between the analyses and surveys by Yu (2003a and 2003b) and by O'Brien and Li (2006, 136).

14. But the other villagers can be both numerous and enthusiastic. It is far more difficult for a local official to collect taxes than it is for the peasant leader to collect money for presenting a petition or complaint to the higher levels of the administration (*shangfang*). When a leader is interviewed, a number of peasants go along to support him, displaying their obedience, eagerly "learning" from him. He can travel and eat for free, as restaurant owners will not accept his money (Duan, Tan, and Chen 2002, 9–10).

15. The details provided in these last two paragraphs are all drawn from Cao 2005. We should acknowledge that Professor Cao Jinqing's excellent survey dates back a dozen years (1996) and that, the author having interviewed more local officials (at village or *xiang* level) than county leaders, he is mainly giving us the local version. The fact remains that it really is the top-down, authoritarian, regime that is challenged by the comments he records and the abuses that he has identified. The system is still monolithic, the central government being mainly responsible and the main beneficiary.

Works Cited

Adshead, S. A. M. 1970. *The Modernization of the Chinese Salt Administration, 1900–1920*. Cambridge, MA: Harvard University Press.

———. 1983. "Un cycle bureaucratique: l'administration du sel en Orient et en Occident." *Annales ESC*, 38ème année no. 2 (March–April): 221–33.

Alitto, Guy S. 1979. "Rural Elites in Transition: China's Cultural Crisis and the Problem of Legitimacy." In *Select Papers from the Center for Far Eastern Studies*, no. 3. Ed. Susan Mann Jones. Chicago, IL: University of Chicago, 218–75.

Ankang XZ, Shaanxi, 1989. Xi'an: Shaanxi renmin.

Anyang Shi jiaoqu WSZL, Henan, vol. 1, 1986.

Anyang XZ, Henan, 1990. Beijing: Zhongguo qingnian.

Ash, Robert. 1976. *Land Tenure in Pre-Revolutionary China: Kiangsu Province in the 1920s and 1930s*. London: Contemporary China Institute, SOAS.

Baishui WSZL, Shaanxi, vol. 1, 1986; vol. 2, 1987.

Baishui XZ, Shaanxi, 1989. Xi'an: Xi'an ditu.

Baiyun WSZL, Guizhou, vol. 5, 1988.

Baoji WSZL, Shaanxi, vol. 2, 1984.

Baoji Xian WSZL, Shaanxi, vol. 6, 1988.

Beattie, Hilary, J. 1979. *Land and Lineage in China: A Study of T'ung-ch'eng County, Anhwei, in the Ming and Ch'ing Dynasties*. Cambridge, UK: Cambridge University Press.

"Beipei shehui gaikuang diaocha" (Investigation of social conditions in Beipei). 1942. In *Shehui diaocha yü tongji* (Social sueveys and statistics). Chongqing: Publications of the Ministry of Social Affairs, 1–159.

Beliveau, Denis. 1992. "Les révolutions frumentaires en France dans la première moitié du XIXe siècle." Ph. D. diss., École des Hautes Études en Sciences Sociales, Paris.

Bell, Lynda. 1999. *One Industry, Two Chinas: Silk Filatures and Peasant Family Production in Wuxi County, 1865–1937*. Stanford, CA: Stanford University Press.
Benton, Gregor. 1999. *New Fourth Army: Communist Resistance Along the Yangtze and the Huai, 1938–1941*. Richmond, Surrey, UK: Curzon Press.
Bercé, Yves-Marie. 1986. *Histoire des Croquants*. Paris: Seuil.
———. 1991. *Croquants et nu-pieds*. Paris: Gallimard.
Bergere, Marie-Claire. 1986. *L'âge d'or de la bourgeoisie chinoise, 1911–1937*. Paris: Flammarion.
Bergere, Marie-Claire, Lucien Bianco, and Jürgen Domes, eds. 1989. *La Chine au XXe siècle*. Vol. 1, *D'une révolution à l'autre (1895–1949)*; 1990. Vol. 2, *De 1949 à aujourd'hui*. Paris: Fayard.
Bernstein, Thomas, and Xiaobo Lü. 2003. *Taxation without Representation in Contemporary Rural China*. Cambridge, UK: Cambridge University Press.
Bianco, Lucien. 1972. "Secret Societies and Peasant Self-Defense, 1921–1933." In *Popular Movements and Secret Societies in China, 1840–1950*, ed. Jean Chesneaux. Stanford, CA: Stanford University Press, 213–24.
———. 1986. "Peasant Movements." In *The Cambridge History of China*, vol. 13: *Republican China*, ed. J. K. Fairbank and A. Feuerwerker. Cambridge, UK: Cambridge University Press, 270–328.
———. 2001. *Peasants Without the Party: Grass-roots Movements in Twentieth-Century China*. Armonk, NY: M. E. Sharpe.
———. 2005. *Jacqueries et révolution dans la Chine du XXe siècle*. Paris: La Martinière.
———. 2007. *Les origines de la révolution chinoise*. Fourth updated and expanded edition. Paris: Gallimard.
Bianco, Lucien, and Yves Chevrier, eds. 1985. *Dictionnaire biographique du mouvement ouvrier international: la Chine*. Paris: Editions Ouvrières and Presses de la Fondation Nationale des Sciences politiques.
Billingsley, Phil. 1988. *Bandits in Republican China*. Stanford, CA: Stanford University Press.
Bingyi xunkan (Periodical on conscription). 1939–40. Nos. 2–3. Guiyang: Gui Xing shiqu.
Bin Xian WSZL, Shaanxi, vol. 1, 1987.
Bourguinat, Nicolas. 2002. *Les grains du désordre: L'Etat face aux violences frumentaires dans la première moitié du XIXe siècle*. Paris: Editions de l'École des Hautes Études en Sciences Sociales.
Cao Jinqing. 2005. *China Along the Yellow River: Reflections on Rural Society*. Translated by Nicky Harman and Huang Ruhua. London and New York: RoutledgeCurzon [originally published as *Huang He biande Zhongguo*. Shanghai: Wenyi, 2000].
Chaoyang WSZL, Liaoning, vol. 1, 1986.

Chen Dengyuan. 1966. *Zhongguo tianfu shi* (History of the land tax in China). Taipei: Shangwu.
Chen Guidi and Chun Tao. 2003. *Zhongguo nongmin diaocha* (An investigative report on the Chinese peasantry). Beijing: Renmin wenxue.
Chen Guidi and Wu Chuntao. 2006. *Will the Boat Sink the Water? The Life of China's Peasants.* Translated by Zhu Hong. New York: Public Affairs.
Chengcheng WSZL, Shaanxi, vol. 2, 1987.
Chifeng Shijiaoqu WSZL, Liaoning, vol. 2, 1990.
China Industrial Handbooks: Kiangsu. 1933. Compiled and published by Bureau of Foreign Trade, Ministry of Industry, Shanghai.
China Year Book. 1921–30. Ed. H. G. W. Woodhead. Tianjin; 1931–39. Shanghai.
Chongqing XZ, Sichuan, 1991. Chengdu: Sichuan renmin.
Chuansha XZ, Jiangsu, 1990. Shanghai: Shanghai renmin.
Cixi XZ, Zhejiang, 1992. Hangzhou: Zhejiang renmin.
Cochran, Sherman. 1996. "A Guide to Memoirs in Chinese Periodical Literature: A Review of a New Bibliography." *Republican China*, vol. 21, no. 2 (April): 91–93.
Cochran, Sherman, and Andrew C. K. Hsieh, eds., with Janis Cochran. 1983. *One Day in China: May 21, 1936.* New Haven, CT: Yale University Press.
Dagong bao (daily). 1902– (Tianjin); 1935– (Shanghai).
Dai Gaoxiang. 1983. *Gaoxiang wencun* (Collection of Gaoxiang's works). Taipei: Chuan-Kang-Yu wenwuguan.
Dai Wen. 1957. *Jiangzhou huoan* (Jiangzhou fire). Nanjing: Jiangsu renmin.
Dai Xuanzhi. 1973. *Hongqianghui, 1916–1949* (Red Spears Society from 1916 to 1949). Taipei: Shihuo.
Daning XZ, Shanxi, 1990. Beijing: Haichao.
Danyang XZ, Jiangsu, 1992. Nanjing: Jiangsu renmin.
Daozhen Xilaozu Miaozu zizhi XZ, Guizhou, 1992. Guiyang: Guizhou renmin.
Daye WSZL, Hubei, vol. 2, 1987.
Dayu XZ, Jiangxi, 1990. Haikou: Zhongguo sanhuan.
Dazhu XZ, Sichuan, 1992. Chongqing: Chongqing chubanshe.
Deqing XZ, Zhejiang, 1992. Hangzhou: Zhejiang renmin.
DeVido, Elise A. 1995. "The Making of the Communist Party-state in Shandong Province, 1927–1952." Ph.D. diss., Harvard University.
———. 2000. "The Survival of the Shandong Base Area, 1937–1943: External Influences and Internal Conflicts." In *North China at War: The Social Ecology of Revolution, 1937–1945*, ed. Feng Chongyi and David S. G. Goodman. Lanham, MD: Rowman and Littlefield, 173–88.
Deyang WSZLXJ, Sichuan, vol. 6, 1987.

Ding Changqing, ed. 1990. *Minguo yanwu shigao* (Historical survey of salt affairs). Beijing: Renmin.

Dongfang zazhi (*The Eastern Miscellany*; monthly). 1904– (Shanghai). Pagination is as a rule indicated by sections within each issue, which makes it difficult to locate texts. Whenever possible references mention only numbers given on each page of the Taiwan reprint (1967–90; Taipei: Dongfang zazhishe). Most run through the 17,000 and 18,000 range (corresponding to the years 1910 through early 1911), a few through the 27,000 to 31,000 (1914–16), very few above 66,000 (from 1926 on).

Dongxiang (bimonthly). Currently published (Hong Kong).

Dongxiang XZ, Jiangxi, 1989. Nanchang: Jiangxi renmin.

Duan Xianju, Tan Jian, and Chen Bin. 2000. "'Yingxiong' haishi 'diaomin'?" ("Heroes" or "wily"?). *Banyuetan* (neibuban), no. 2 (February): 8–13.

Duan Zhongrong. 1935. "Sichuan tianfu zhi zhengli" (Land tax reorganization in Sichuan). *Sichuan yuebao*, vol. 7, no. 1 (January): 49–61.

Duara, Prasenjit. 1988. *Culture, Power, and the State: Rural North China, 1900–1942*. Stanford, CA: Stanford University Press.

———. 1991. "Knowledge and Power in the Discourse of Modernity: The Campaigns against Popular Religion in Early Twentieth-Century China." *Journal of Asian Studies*, vol. 50, no. 1 (February): 67–83.

———. 1995. *Rescuing History from the Nation: Questioning Narratives of Modern China*. Chicago, IL: University of Chicago Press.

Duyun WSZLXJ, Guizhou, vol. 5, 1986.

Eastman, Lloyd E. 1974. *The Abortive Revolution. China Under Nationalist Rule, 1927–1937*, Cambridge, MA: Harvard University Press.

———. 1984. *Seeds of Destruction: Nationalist China in War and Revolution, 1937–1949*. Stanford, CA: Stanford University Press.

Elvin, Mark. 1973. *The Pattern of the Chinese Past*. Stanford, CA: Stanford University Press.

Esherick, Joseph W. 1976. *Reform and Revolution in China: The 1911 Revolution in Hunan and Hubei*. Berkeley, CA: University of California Press.

———. 1987. *The Origins of the Boxer Uprising*. Berkeley, CA: University of California Press.

———. 1994. "Deconstructing the Party-state: Guilin County in the Shaan-Gan-Ning Border Region." *China Quarterly*, no. 140 (December): 1052–79.

———. 1995. "Ten Theses on the Chinese Revolution." *Modern China*, vol. 21, no. 1 (January): 45–76.

———. 2000. "Revolution in a "feudal fortress": Yangjiagou, Mizhi County, Shaanxi, 1937–1948." In *North China at War: The Social Ecology of Revolution*,

1937–1945, ed. Feng Chongyi and David S. G. Goodman. Lanham, MD: Rowman and Littlefield, 59–91.

Fan Songfu. 1998. *Longtou jiangjun chenfulu* (Autobiography of General Dragonhead, Red Band leader). Shanghai: Shanghai shudian.

Fangshan WSZL, Hebei, vol. 3, 1990.

Fang XZ, Hubei, 1991. Beijing: Zhongguo wenshi.

Faure, David. 1976. "Local Political Disturbances in Kiangsu Province, China, 1870–1911." Ph.D. diss., Princeton University.

Fei Fanjiu. 1986. "Minchu Siyugang fankang mujuan fengchao" (Siyugang revolt against the per *mu* tax in the early Republic). *Nantong WSZLXJ*, vol. 6, 5–9.

Fei Hsiao-tung. 1939. *Peasant Life in China: A Field Study of Country Life in the Yangtze Valley*. London: Routledge and Kegan Paul.

Fei Hsiao-tung and Chang Chih-i. 1948, *Earthbound China. A Study of Rural Economy in Yunnan*. London: Routledge and Kegan Paul.

Feng Chongyi and David S. G. Goodman, eds. 2000. *North China at War: The Social Ecology of Revolution, 1937–1945*. Lanham, MD: Rowman and Littlefield.

Feng Hefa. 1933. *Zhongguo nongcun jingji ziliao huibian* (Documents on Chinese village economy). Shanghai: Liming shuju.

———. 1935. *Zhongguo nongcun jingji ziliao xubian* (Supplementary documents on Chinese village economy). Shanghai: Liming shuju.

———. 1936. *Zhongguo nongcun jingji lun* (On Chinese village economy). Shanghai: Liming shuju.

Feng Xian WSZL, Jiangsu, vol. 4, 1986.

Fengxian XZ, Jiangsu, 1987. Shanghai: Shanghai renmin.

Fogang WSZL, Guangdong, vol. 2, 1985.

Foisil, Madeleine. 1970. *La Révolte des Nu-Pieds et les Révoltes normandes de 1639*. Paris: Presses Universitaires de France.

———. 2001. *Le Sire de Gouberville*. Paris: Flammarion.

Forrest, Alan. 1988. *Déserteurs et insoumis sous la Révolution et l'Empire*. Paris: Perrin.

Friedman, Edward, Paul G. Pickowicz, and Mark Selden. 2005. *Revolution, Resistance, and Reform in Village China*. New Haven, CT: Yale University Press.

Fu, Hung-chung (Hongzhong). 2007. "Le service militaire en Chine à la veille de la Révolution chinoise." Ph. D. diss., École des Hautes Études en Sciences Sociales.

Fujian WSZLXJ, vol. 2, 1963.

Funing XZ, Jiangsu, 1992. Nanjing: Jiangsu kexue jishu.

Gansu shifan daxue lishixi (History department of Gansu Normal University). 1960. "Kang-Ri zhanzheng shiqide nongmin qiyi" (Peasant uprisings at the

time of the war of resistance against Japan). *Lishi jiaoxue yu yanjiu*, nos. 2–3: 26–35.
Gansu WSZLXJ, vol. 1, 1963; vol. 13, 1982.
Gaochun XZ, Jiangsu, 1988. Nanjing: Jiangsu guji.
Geisert, Bradley K. 2001. *Radicalism and Its Demise: The Chinese National Party, Factionalism, and Local Elites in Jiangsu Province, 1924–1931*. Ann Arbor, MI: Center for Chinese Studies, University of Michigan.
Gillin, Donald G. 1967. *Warlord: Yen Hsi-shan in Shansi Province, 1911–1949*. Princeton, NJ: Princeton University Press.
Gong Xian WSZL, Henan, vol. 7, 1990.
Goodman, David S. G. 1994. "JinJiLuYu in the Sino-Japanese War: The Border Region and the Border Region Government." *China Quarterly*, no. 140 (December): 1007–24.
———. 2000. *Social and Political Change in Revolutionary China*. Lanham, MD: Rowman and Littlefield.
Goossaert, Vincent. 2000. *Dans les temples de la Chine*. Paris: Albin Michel.
———. 2003. "Le destin de la religion chinoise au 20ème siècle." *Social Compass*, vol. 50, no. 4 (December): 429–40.
Guang'an XZ, Sichuan, 1992. Chengdu: Sichuan renmin.
Guanghan XZ, Sichuan, 1992. Chengdu: Sichuan renmin.
Guangxi WSZLXJ, vol. 28, 1988.
Guan XZ, Sichuan, 1991. Chengdu: Sichuan renmin.
Guanyun WSZL, Jiangsu, vol. 2, 1985.
Gucheng WSZL, Hubei, vol. 1, 1987.
Guizhou Qiandong WSZL, vol. 3, 1985.
Guizhou WSZLXJ, vol. 2, 1983; vol. 15, 1984; vol. 22, 1986.
Guofangbu shizheng bianyiju bingyi dang'an (Military Archives, Ministry of Defense, Historical Policies Redaction and Translation Bureau). Taipei.
Haicheng XZ, Liaoning, 1987. Ed. Xu Zhuangyou (internal publication).
Haiyang XZ, Shandong, 1988. Unknown publisher (chronology separately paginated).
Hancheng WSZL huibian, Shaanxi, vol. 2, 1983.
Hanjiang WSZL, Jiangsu, vol. 2, no date.
He Chengjun. 1986. *He Chengjun jiangjun zhanshi riji* (General He Chengjun wartime diary). Taipei: Zhuanji wenxue.
Hefeng XZ, Hubei, 1990. Wuhan: Hubei renmin.
Henan WSZLXJ, vol. 14, 1985.
Heng XZ, Guangxi, 1989. Nanning: Guangxi renmin.
Ho, Franklin L. 1934. "Land Tax in Chekiang." *Monthly Bulletin on Economic China*, vol. 7, no. 1 (January): 1–14.

Ho, Ping-ti. 1959. *Studies on the Population of China, 1368–1959*. Cambridge, MA: Harvard University Press.

Hobsbawm, Eric J., and George Rude. 1970. *Captain Swing*. London: Lawrence and Wishart.

Honghe XZ, Yunnan, 1991. Kunming: Yunnan renmin.

Honghu XZ, Hubei, 1992. Wuhan: Wuhan Daxue.

Hu Jianguo. 1996. "Kangzhan shiqi Ebei wuzhanqu junliang gongxu luelun" (Brief history of miltary grain supply in Northern Hubei Fifth War Zone during the War of Resistance). In *Kangzhan jianguo ji Taiwan guangfu Zhonghua minguoshi zhuanti disanjie taolunhui lunwen*. Taipei: Guoshiguan.

Hu Xian WSZL, Shaanxi, vol. 1, 1985.

Huaihua WSZLXJ, Hunan, vol. 2, 1988.

Huaiyin WSZL, Jiangsu, vol. 2, 1984; vol. 3, 1985.

Huang, Philip C. C. 1985. *The Peasant Economy and Social Change in North China*. Stanford, CA: Stanford University Press.

———. 1996. *Civil Justice in China: Representation and Practice in the Qing*. Stanford, CA: Stanford University Press.

Huang, Ray. 1974. *Taxation and Government Finance in Sixteenth-Century Ming China*. Cambridge, UK: Cambridge University Press.

Huishui XZ, Guizhou, 1989. Guiyang: Guizhou renmin.

Ichiko, Chuzo. 1980. "Political and Institutional Reform, 1901–1911." In *The Cambridge History of China*, vol. 11, ed. John K. Fairbank and Kwang-ching Liu. Cambridge, UK: Cambridge University Press, 375–415.

Institute of Pacific Relations, comp. 1939. *Agrarian China: Selected Source Materials from Chinese Authors*. Chicago, IL: University of Chicago Press.

Janku, Andrea. 2004. "Integrating the Body Politic: Official Perspectives on the Administration of Relief during the 'Great North China Famine.'" Paper presented at the annual meeting of the Association for Asian Studies, March 4–7, San Diego.

Jiajiang XZ, Sichuan, 1989. Chengdu: Sichuan renmin.

Jiangshan XZ, Zhejiang. 1990. Hangzhou: Zhejiang renmin.

Jiangsu jiaoyu zonghui wendu (Documents of Jiangsu Educational Society). 1907–11. Vols. 2–6.

Jiangsu sheng geming douzheng shibian weiyuanhui, jiangsu sheng dang'an ju, comp. 1981. *Jiangsu geming shiliao xuanji* (Collection of historical documents on revolution in Jiangsu). Nanjing: Jiangsu sheng dang'an guan.

"Jiangsu sheng nongmin yundong dashi nianbiao (yijiuerer yijiusansi nian)" (Chronology of the peasant movement in Jiangsu from 1922 to 1934). 1981. In *Jiangsu geming shiliao xuanji*, comp. Jiangsu sheng geming douzheng shibian weiyuanhui, jiangsu sheng dang'an ju. Nanjing: Jiangsu sheng dang'an guan, 429–63.

Jiangsu WSZLXJ, vol. 18, 1986.

Jiangsu xuewu zonghui wendu (Documents of the Jiangsu Educational Society). 1906. Vol. 1. Shanghai.

Jiangyin Shizhi, Jiangsu, 1992. Shanghai: Shanghai renmin.

Jiang Zhiliang. 1988a "Nantong yanjiang nongmin fankang mujuan fengchao" (Uprising of Nantong riverside peasants against the per *mu* tax). Lecture. Paris, École des Hautes Études en Sciences Sociales.

———. 1988b. "Huoshao Zhendongshi" (Fire on Zhendong city). Lecture. Paris, École des Hautes Études en Sciences Sociales.

———. 1988c "Subei huidang wuzhuang baodong" (Armed uprisings of Secret Societies in North Jiangsu). Lecture. Paris, École des Hautes Études en Sciences Sociales.

Jianwei XZ, Sichuan, 1991. Chengdu: Sichuan renmin.

Jiaoyu zazhi (monthly). 1909– (Shanghai).

Jiefang ribao (daily). 29 July 1945.

Jindaishi ziliao (bimonthly). 1954–59.

Jingchuan XZ, Gansu, 1996. Lanzhou: Gansu renmin.

JinhuaXZ, Zhejiang, 1992. Hangzhou: Zhejiang renmin.

Jinping WSZLXJ, Guizhou, vol. 2, 1988.

Jinshan XZ, Jiangsu, 1990. Shanghai: Shanghai renmin.

Jintian WSZL, Jiangxi, vol. 4, no date.

Jinxian XZ, Jiangxi, 1989. Nanchang: Jiangxi renmin.

Jishui XZ, Jiangxi, 1992. Beijing: Xinhua.

Kaijiang XZ, Sichuan, 1989. Chengdu: Sichuan renmin.

Kai XZ, Sichuan, 1990. Chengdu: Sichuan Daxue.

Kaiyuan WSZL, Liaoning, vol. 3, 1988.

Kang XZ, Gansu, 1989. Lanzhou: Gansu renmin.

Kaplan, Steven I. 1982. *Le complot de famine: histoire d'une rumeur au XVIIIe siècle.* Paris: Armand Colin.

Keating, Pauline B. 1994. "The Yan'an Way of Co-operativization." *China Quarterly*, no. 140 (December): 1025–51.

———. 1997. *Two Revolutions: Village Reconstruction and the Cooperative Movement in Northern Shaanxi, 1934–1945.* Stanford, CA: Stanford University Press.

Kirby, William C. 2000. "Engineering China: Birth of the Developmental State, 1928–1937." In *Becoming Chinese: Passages to Modernity and Beyond,* ed. Wen-Hsin Yeh. Berkeley, CA: University of California Press, 137–60.

Ku Hok Bun. 2003. *Moral Politics in a South Chinese Village: Responsibility, Reciprocity, and Resistance.* Lanham, MD: Rowman and Littlefield.

Kuhn, Philip A. 1975. "Local Self-Governement under the Republic: Problems of Control, Autonomy, and Mobilization." In *Conflict and Control in Late Imperial China*, ed. Frederic Wakeman, Jr., and Carolyn Grant. Berkeley, CA: University of California Press, 257–98.

———. 1979. "Local Taxation and Finance in Republican China." In *Select Papers from the Center for Far Eastern Studies*, no. 3. Ed. Susan Mann Jones. Chicago, IL: University of Chicago, 100–36.

La Bruyère, Jean de. 1913. *Les Caractères ou les Mœurs de ce Siècle*. Ed. Gaston Cayrou. Paris: Henri Didier.

Laifeng XZ, Hubei, 1990. Wuhan: Hubei renmin.

Laixi XZ, Shandong, 1990. Jinan: Shandong renmin.

Lanzhou WSZLXJ, Gansu, vol. 1, 1983; vol. 3, 1985.

Lefebvre, Georges. 1932. *La grande peur de 1789*. Paris: Armand Colin [new edition, 1970; English translation: New York, Pantheon Books, 1973].

Leping XZ, Jiangxi, 1987. Shanghai: Shanghai guci.

Le Roy Ladurie, Emmanuel. 2002. *Histoire des paysans français: de la peste noire à la Révolution*. Paris: Seuil.

Lianyungang Shi WSZL, Jiangsu, vol. 4, 1986.

Liaoyang WSZL, Liaoning, vol. 5, 1990.

Lichuan WSZL, Jiangxi, vol. 2, 1991.

Li Guoqi. 1982. *Zhongguo xiandaihua de quyu yanjiu: Min-Zhe Tai diqu, 1860–1916* (A regional study of China's modernization: Fujian, Zhejiang, and Taiwan, 1860 to 1916). Taipei: Zhongyang yanjiuyuan jindaishi yanjiusuo.

Li Huaiyin. 2005. *Village Governance in North China, 1875–1936*. Stanford, CA: Stanford University Press.

Li Lianjiang. 2004. "Political Trust in Rural China." *Modern China*, vol. 30 (2004): 228–58.

Li, Lillian. 1991. "Life and Death in a Chinese Famine: Infanticide as a Demographic Consequence of the 1935 Yellow River Flood." *Comparative Studies in Society and History*, vol. 33, no. 1 (July): 466–510.

Li Shiyue. 1959. "Xinhai geming shiqi dongsansheng geming yu fangeming de douzheng" (Struggle between revolution and counter-revolution in the three eastern provinces at the time of the 1911 revolution). *Lishi yanjiu*, no. 6 (November): 56–70.

Li Wenzhi, comp. 1957. *Zhongguo jindai nongye shi ziliao, di yi ji, 1840–1911* (Materials on Chinese modern agricultural history, vol. 1, 1840–1911). Beijing: Sanlian.

Li Zongyi. 1980. *Yuan Shikai zhuan* (Biography of Yuan Shikai). Beijing: Zhonghua shuju.

Li Zuozhou. 1932. "Zhongguo de tianfu yu nongmin" (Landtax and peasants in China). *Xin chuangzhao*, vol. 2, nos. 1–2 (July): 110–32.

Lin'an WSZL, Zhejiang, vol. 1, 1988.

Linxia WSZLXJ, Gansu, vol. 5, 1989.

Liping XZ, Guizhou, 1989. Guiyang: Bashu shushe.

Lishi yanjiu (bimonthly). 1959. No. 6.

Lishui XZ, 1990. Nanjing: Jiangsu renmin.

Liu Jun and Ran Guangrong. 1985. "Sichuan Guanghan shijian lüeshu" (Brief record of Guanghan incident, Sichuan province). In *Kang-Ri zhanzhengshi lunchong* (Collection of essays on the history of the war of resistance against Japan). Chengdu: Sichuan Daxue.

Liu Ping. 1994. "Guanyu Qingmo nongmin yundong de jige wenti" (A few questions concerning the peasant movement at the end of the Qing dynasty). *Jiangsu jiaoyu xueyuan xuebao*, no. 2 (April): 82–85.

Liuzhi WSZLXJ, Guizhou, vol. 3, 1988.

Longchang WSZL, Sichuan, vol. 4, 1986.

Long Xian WSZLXJ, Shaanxi, vol. 1, 1981; vol. 2, 1982.

Lü, Xiaobo. 2003. "Taxation, Protest, and (In)stability in Rural China." *Asia Program Special Report*, no. 108 (March): 8–13.

Luoning WSZL, Henan, vols. 2–3, 1988.

Ma Jun. 1958. "Kangzhan shiqi de sanci Huimin qiyi" (The three muslim uprisings at the time of the war of resistance). *Guangming ribao*, 1 September.

McCord, Edward A. 2001. "Burn, Kill, Rape, and Rob: Military Atrocities, Warlordism, and Anti-Warlordism in Republican China." In *Scars of War: The Impact of Warfare in Modern China*, ed. Diana Lary and Stephen McKinnon. Vancouver, BC: University of British Columbia Press, 18–47.

Mao Zedong (Mao Tsé-toung). 1933. See Schram 1995.

——. 1955. *Œuvres choisies*. Vol. 1 (1926–37). Paris: Éditions sociales.

Meng Qinghua. 1983. "Gannan minbian shimo chutan" (Preliminary study of the southern Gansu rebellion). *Shandong shida xuebao*, no. 1 (January): 12–15.

Meng Yu (pseudonym). 1936. "Daishan yanmin yumin fengchao de qianhou" (Before and after the uprising by Daishan saltmakers and fishermen). *Zhongguo nongcun*, vol. 2, no. 9 (September): 69–73.

Messant-Yun, David. 1982. "Les mouvements populaires avant la révolution chinoise (1906–1911)." M.A. diss., École des Hautes Études en Sciences Sociales.

Mianyang Shi WSZL, Sichuan, vol. 5, 1990.

Miner, Noël Ray. 1973. "Chekiang: The Nationalists' Effort in Agrarian Reform and Construction, 1927–1937." Ph.D. diss., Stanford University.

Mingshan XZ, Sichuan, 1992. Chengdu: Sichuan kexue jishu.

Minguo ribao. 12 May 1932.
Mingxi WSZL, Fujian, vol. 3, 1985; vol. 5, 1988.
Mingxi XZ, Fujian, 1997. Beijing: Fangzhi.
Mizhi WSZL, Shaanxi, vol. 1, 1964.
Muping WSZL, Shandong, vol. 3, 1990.
Murphy, Rachel. 2002. *How Migrant Labor Is Changing Rural China.* Cambridge, UK: Cambridge University Press.
Muscolino, Micah. 2005. "A Forest of Sails and Masts: Environment and Economy in an Early Twentieth-Century Chinese Fishery." *Twentieth-Century China*, vol. 31, no. 1 (November): 3–32.
Myers, Ramon H. 1970. *The Chinese Peasant Economy: Agricultural Development in Hopei and Shantung, 1890–1949.* Cambridge, MA: Harvard University Press.
Nantong WSZLXJ, Jiangsu, vol. 3, no date; vol. 6, 1986.
Nantong Xian WSZL, Jiangsu, vol. 1, 1987.
Nanyang XZ, Henan, 1990. Zhengzhou: Henan renmin.
Naquin, Susan. 1981. *Shantung Rebellion: The Wang Lun Uprising of 1774.* New Haven, CT: Yale University Press.
Nedostup, Rebecca Allyn. 2001. "Religion, Superstition, and Governing Society in Nationalist China." Ph.D. diss., Columbia University.
Ngo Thi Minh-hoang. 2003. "Les processus externes et internes de formation du système communiste chinois dans la société rurale de la province du Shanxi des années 1930 aux années 1950." 2 vols. Ph. D. diss., École des Hautes Études en Sciences Sociales.
Nicolas, Jean. 2002. *La Rébellion française: Mouvements populaires et conscience sociale (1661–1789).* Paris: Le Seuil.
Ning XZ, Gansu, 1988. Lanzhou: Gansu renmin.
Ningbo ribao (daily). July 1936.
Ningdu XZ, Jiangxi, 1986. Ningdu: Ningdu xianzhi bianji weiyuanhui.
North China Herald (weekly), Shanghai.
O'Brien, Kevin J., and Li Lianjiang. 1995. "The Politics of Lodging Complaints in Rural China." *China Quarterly*, no. 143 (September): 756–83.
——. 2006. *Rightful Resistance in Rural China.* Cambridge, UK: Cambridge University Press.
Overmeyer, Daniel L. 1976. *Folk Buddhist Religion: Dissenting Sects in Late Traditional China.* Cambridge, MA: Harvard University Press.
Ownby, David. 1993. "Introduction: Secret Societies Reconsidered." In *"Secret Societies" Reconsidered: Perspectives on the Social History of Early Modern South China and Southeast Asia*, ed. David Ownby and Mary Somers Heidues. Armonk, NY: M. E. Sharpe, 3–33.

———. 2001. "Recent Chinese Scholarship on the History of Chinese Secret Societies." *Late Imperial China*, vol. 22, no. 1 (June): 139–58.
Park, Sang-Soo. 2002. "La Révolution chinoise et les sociétés secrètes: l'exemple des Shaan-Gan-Ning et du nord Jiangsu (années 1930–1940)." 2 vols. Ph.D. diss., École des Hautes Études en Sciences Sociales.
Peck, Graham. 1950. *Two Kinds of Time*. Boston, MA: Houghton Mifflin.
Pei Xian WSZL, Jiangsu, vol. 3, 1985.
Peng XZ, Sichuan, 1989. Chengdu: Sichuan renmin.
Pingtang XZ, Guizhou, 1992. Guiyang: Guizhou renmin.
Ploux, François. 2002. *Guerres paysannes en Quercy: Violences, conciliations et répression pénale dans les campagnes du Lot (1810–1860)*. Paris: Boutique de l'histoire.
Prazniak, Roxann. 1980. "Tax Protest at Laiyang, Shandong, 1910: Commoner Organization Versus the Country Political Elite." *Modern China*, vol. 6, no. 1 (January): 41–71.
———. 1999. *Of Camel Kings and Other Things: Rural Rebels against Modernity in Late Imperial China*. Lanham, MD: Rowman and Littlefield.
Pubei Xian WSZL, Guangxi, vol. 2, 1988.
Pucheng WSZL, Shaanxi, vol. 1, 1985.
Qiandongnan WSZL, Guizhou, vol. 6, 1987.
Qianjiang WSZL, Hubei, vol. 1, 1986.
Qianshan WSZL, Jiangxi, vol. 3, 1989.
Qian Min. 1986. "Minchu Pingchao nongmin kangjuan baodong jishi" (Pingchao peasants' antitax uprising in the early Republic). *Nantong WSZLXJ*, vol. 6, 1986, 10–25.
Qianxi XZ, Guizhou, 1990. Guiyang: Guizhou renmin.
Qiao Peihua. 1993. *Tianmenhui yanjiu* (Research on the Society of the Heavenly Gate). Kaifeng: Henan jiaoyu.
Qihe XZ, Shandong, 1990. Beijing: Zhonghua shuju.
Qijiang XZ, Sichuan, 1991. Chengdu: Xinan Jiaotong Daxue.
Qing'an WSZL, Heilongjiang, vol. 1, no date.
Qingfeng XZ, Henan, 1990. Jinan: Shandong Daxue.
Qingpu XZ, Jiangsu, 1991. Shanghai: Shanghai shudian.
Qinhuangdao WSZL, Hebei, vol. 1, 1987.
Qinshui XZ, Shanxi, 1987. Taiyuan: Shanxi renmin.
Qin Xian WSZL, Shanxi, vol. 2, 1986.
Qishan WSZL, Shaanxi, vol. 3, 1988; vol. 4, 1989.
Rawski, Thomas G. 1989. *Economic Growth in Prewar China*. Berkeley, CA: University of California Press.
Redfield, Robert. 1956. *The Little Community and Peasant Society and Culture*. Chicago, IL: University of Chicago Press.

Reed, Bradly. W. 2000. *Talons and Teeth: County Clarks and Runners in the Qing Dynasty*. Stanford, CA: Stanford University Press.

Reynolds, Douglas R. 1993. *China, 1898–1912: The Xinzheng Revolution and Japan*. Cambridge, MA: Council on East Asian Studies, Harvard University.

Rocca, Jean-Louis. 2006. *La condition chinoise: la mise au travail capitaliste à l'âge des réformes (1978–2004)*. Paris: Éditions Karthala.

Romanus, Charles F., and Riley Sunderland. 1959. *Time Runs Out in CBI*. Washington, DC: Office of the Chief Military History, Department of the Army.

Rowe, William T. 2007. *Crimson Rain: Seven Centuries of Violence in a Chinese County*. Stanford, CA: Stanford University Press.

Rubinstein, Ivan. 1986. "Étude sur les réquisitions militaires en Chine (fin des années 20-début des années 30)." M.A. diss., École des Hautes Études en Sciences Sociales.

Rude, George E. 1956. "La taxation populaire de mai 1775 à Paris et dans la région parisienne." *Annales Historiques de la Révolution Française*, no. 143 (April–June): 139–79.

———. 1995. *The Crowd in History: A Study of Popular Disturbances in France and England, 1730–1848*. London: Serif [original edition, New York: Wiley, 1964].

Rudong XZ, Jiangsu, 1983. Nanjing: Jiangsu renmin.

Ruf, Gregory A. 1998. *Cadres and Kin: Making a Socialist Village in West China, 1921–1991*. Stanford, CA: Stanford University Press.

Saich, Tony, ed. 1996. *The Rise to Power of the Chinese Communist Party: Documents and Analysis*. Armonk, NY: M. E. Sharpe.

Saich, Tony, and Hans van de Ven, eds. 1995. *New Perspectives on the Chinese Communist Revolution*. Armonk, NY: M. E. Sharpe.

Sandu XZ, Guizhou, 1992. Guiyang: Guizhou renmin.

Sanmen XZ, 1992. Hangzhou: Zhejiang renmin.

Sanming WSZL, Fujian, vol. 7, 1989.

Schneider, Laurence A. 1971. *Ku Chieh-kang and China's New History: Nationalism and the Quest for Alternative Traditions*. Berkeley, CA: University of California Press.

Schram, Stuart, ed. 1994 and 1995. *Mao's Road to Power: Revolutionary Writings, 1912–1949*. Vols. 2 (1920–27) and 3 (1927–30). Armonk, NY: M. E. Sharpe.

Scott, James C. 1985. *Weapons of the Weak: Everyday Forms of Peasant Resistance*. New Haven, CT: Yale University Press.

———. 1989. "Everyday Forms of Peasant Resistance." In *Everyday Forms of Peasant Resistance*, ed. Forrest D. Colburn. Armonk, NY: M. E. Sharpe, 3–32.

Seckington, Ian. 2007. "County Leadership in China: A Baseline Survey." *China: An International Journal*, vol. 5, no. 2 (September): 204–27.

Selden, Mark. 1995. *China in Revolution: The Yenan Way Revisited.* Armonk, NY: M. E. Sharpe.
Shaanxi WSZLXJ, vol. 2, 1962; vol. 3, 1963; vol. 9, 1981.
Shangyu XZ, Zhejiang, 1990. Hangzhou: Zhejiang renmin.
Shanxi WSZL, vol. 34, 1984.
Shanyang WSZLXJ, Shaanxi, vol. 1, 1985.
Sha Xian WSZL, Fujian, vol. 2, 1983.
Sha XZ, Fujian, 1992. Nanjing: Zhongguo kexue jishu.
Sheel, Kamal. 1989. *Peasant Society and Marxist Intellectuals in China.* Princeton, NJ: Princeton University Press.
Shehong XZ, Sichuan, 1990. Chengdu: Sichuan Daxue.
Shen Yuwu. 1981. "Xinhai geming qianxi Zhejiang nongmin de fankang douzheng" (Resistance struggle of Zhejiang peasants on the eve of the 1911 revolution). *Zhejiang shifan xueyuan xuebao*, no. 4 (April): 40–46.
Shenbao (daily). 1872– (Shanghai).
Sheng Dan (pseudonym?). 1936. "Daishan de yuyanmin" (Daishan fishermen and saltmakers). *Guangming*, vol. 1, no. 8 (25 September): 514–17.
Sheng Wen. 1989. *Shengwen xiansheng fangwenjilu* (Oral memoirs of Mr. Sheng Wen). Koushu lishi congshu (Oral history series) 18. Taipei: Zhongyang yanjiuyuan jindaishi yanjiusuo.
Shengsi WSZL, Zhejiang, vol. 1, 1989.
Sheridan, James E. 1966. *Chinese Warlord: The Career of Feng Yü-hsiang.* Stanford, CA: Stanford University Press.
Shibao (daily). 1904– (Shanghai).
Shibing WSZL, Guizhou, vol. 3, 1987.
Shicheng WSZLXJ, Jiangxi, vol. 2, 1987.
Shicheng XZ, Jiangxi, 1990. Beijing: Shumu wenxian.
Shifang XZ, Sichuan, 1988. Chengdu: Sichuan Daxue.
Shiquan XZ, Shaanxi, 1991. Xi'an: Shaanxi renmin.
Shuixi WSZLXJ, Guizhou, vol. 1, 1983.
Sichuan WSZLXJ, vol. 3, 1962; vol. 13, 1964.
Slawinski, Roman. 1975. *La Société des Piques Rouges et le Mouvement Paysan en Chine en 1926–1927.* Warsaw: Wydawnictwa Uniwersytetu Warszawskiego.
Songming WSZL, Yunnan, vol. 1, 1989.
Songtao WSZL, Guizhou, vol. 6, 1988.
Stross, Randall Elliot. 1982. "A Hard Row to Hoe: The Political Economy of Chinese Agriculture in Western Jiangsu, 1911–1937." Ph.D. diss., Stanford University.
Sun Xiaocun. 1935. "Zhongguo tianfu de zhengshou" (Land tax collection in China). *Zhongguo nongcun*, vol. 1, no. 7 (July): 17–26.

Sun Zuoqi. 1935. *Zhongguo tianfu wenti* (The issue of the land tax in China). Shanghai: Xin shengming shuju.

Tai Hsüan-chih. 1985. *The Red Spears, 1916–1949*. Translated by Ronald Suleski, introduction by Elizabeth Perry. Ann Arbor, MI: Center for Chinese Studies, University of Michigan.

Taihu *WSZL, Anhui*, vol. 1, 1985.

Tang Zong. 1988. *Tangzong shiliao zai dalu de riji* (General Tang Zong's diary in mainland China). Taipei: Zhuanji wenxue.

Teng XZ, Shandong, 1989. Beijing: Zhonghua shuju.

Thaxton, Ralph A., Jr. 1989. "Peasants and Porcelain: Collective Action in China's Rural Trade and Transport Sector During the Republican Period." *Peasant Studies*, vol. 16, no. 4 (Summer): 251–65.

———. 1997. *Salt of the Earth: The Political Origins of Peasant Protest and Communist Revolution in China*. Berkeley, CA: University of California Press.

Thireau, Isabelle, and Hua Linshan. 2007. *D'une illégitimité à l'autre dans la Chine rurale contemporaine*. Vol. 179 of *Études rurales*. Paris: Éditions de l'École des Hautes Études en Sciences Sociales.

Thompson, E. P. 1971. "The Moral Economy of the English Crowd in the Eighteenth Century." *Past and Present*, no. 50 (February): 76–136.

Tien, Hung-mao. 1972. *Government and Politics in Kuomintang China, 1927–1937*. Stanford, CA: Stanford University Press.

Tilly, Charles. 1986. *La France conteste de 1600 à nos jours*. Paris: Fayard [originally published in English as *The Contentious French*. Cambridge, MA: Belknap Press, Harvard University Press, 1986]. References are to the French edition.

Tongchuan WSZLXJ, Shaanxi, vol. 3, 1984.

Tonghai xinbao (daily, Nantong). May 1928.

Tonglu XZ, Zhejiang, 1991. Hangzhou: Zhejiang renmin.

Tongren diqu WSZL, Guizhou, vol. 1, 1990.

Tongshan WSZL, Jiangsu, vol. 2, 1983.

Tongtong ribao (daily, Nantong). May 1928.

Unger, Jonathan. 2002. *The Transformation of Rural China*. Armonk, NY: M. E. Sharpe.

United States, Department of State (USDS). *Relationship Relating to the Internal Affairs of China, 1930–1939*. Microfilms, Series 893. Washington, DC: National Archives Publications.

Viola, Lynne. 1996. *Peasant Rebels under Stalin: Collectivization and the Culture of Peasant Resistance*. Oxford, UK: Oxford University Press.

Waldron, Arthur. 1990. *The Great Wall of China: From History to Myth*. Cambridge, UK: Cambridge University Press.

Walker, Kathy Le Mons. 1999. *Chinese Modernity and the Peasant Path: Semi-Colonialism and the Northern Yangzi Delta.* Stanford, CA: Stanford University Press.

Wan Guoding, Zhuang Qianghua, and Wu Yongming. 1934. *Jiangsu Wujin Nantong tianfu diaocha baogao* (Report on a survey of land tax in Wujin and Nantong, Jiangsu). Nanjing: n.p.

Wang, David Der-wei. 2004. *The Monster That Is History: History, Violence, and Fictional Writing in Twentieth-Century China.* Berkeley, CA: University of California Press.

Wang Shuhuai (Shu-Hwai). 1977. "Qingmo Jiangsu difang zizhi fengchao" (Late Qing local autonomous disturbances in Jiangsu). *Zhongyang yanjiuyuan jindaishi yanjiusuo jikan*, vol. 6 (June): 313–27.

———. 1981. "Qingmo minchu Jiangsu Sheng de zaihai" (Calamities in Jiangsu province in late Qing and early Republican times). *Zhongyang yanjiuyuan jindaishi yanjiusuo jikan*, vol. 10 (July): 141–86.

———. 1985. *Zhongguo xiandaihua de quyu yanjiu: Jiangsu sheng, 1860–1916* (A regional study of modernization in China: Jiangsu province, 1860–1916). Taipei: Zhongyang yanjiuyuan jindaishi yanjiusuo.

Wang Wei. 1996. *Wang Wei xiansheng fangwen jilu* (Oral memoirs of Mr. Wang Wei). Koushu lishi congshu (Oral history series) 60. Taipei: Zhongyang yanjiuyuan jindaishi yanjiusuo.

Wang, Yeh-chien. 1973. *Land Taxation in Imperial China, 1750–1911.* Cambridge, MA: Harvard University Press.

Wang Yingsheng, Shi Kaifu, and Xue Pinxuan. 1931. *Zhongguo beibu de bingchai yu nongmin* (Military requisitions and peasants in Northern China). Shanghai: Guoli zhongyang yanjiuyuan [republished as "Bingchai yu nongmin" in Feng 1933, 355–97; summarized in Institute of Pacific Relations 1939, 101–9; partially translated into French in Rubinstein 1986, 36–79].

Wang Zhong. 1954. "Yijiuyilingnian Shandong Laiyang qunzhong de kangjuan kangshui douzheng" (Antitax struggle by the masses in Laiyang, Shandong in 1910). *Zhongguo kexueyuan lishi yanjiusuo disansuo jikan*, vol. 1 (July): 209–21.

Wanzai XZ, Jiangxi, 1988. Nanchang: Jiangxi renmin.

Weidner, Terry M. 1980. "Rural Economy and Local Government in Nationalist China: Chekiang Province, 1927–1937." Ph.D. diss., University of California, Davis.

———. 1983. "Local Political Work under the Nationalists: The 1930's Silk Reform Campaign." *Illinois Papers in Asian Studies*, no. 2: 67–86.

Weihai WSZL, Shandong, vol. 1, 1989; vol. 4, 1989.

Weinan XZ, Shaanxi, 1987. Beijing: Sanlian.

Weng Fei et al. 1990. *Anhui jindaishi* (Modern history of Anhui). Hefei: Anhui renmin.

Weng Zhiyong. 1936. "Tianfu jibi tanzheng" (Research on land tax deep-rooted evils). *Dizheng yuekan*, vol. 4, no. 2–3 (March): 229–42.

Wenjiang XZ, Sichuan, 1990. Chengdu: Sichan renmin.

Wenshan Zhou WSZL, Yunnan, vol. 3, 1985.

Wou, Odoric Y. K. 1994. *Mobilizing the Masses: Building Revolution in Henan*. Stanford, CA: Stanford University Press.

———. 2004. "Social Cleavages and Sectarian Violence: Xinyang Red Spears during the Northern Expedition." Paper presented at the annual meeting of the Association for Asian Studies, March 4–7, San Diego.

Wu Xiaochen. 1935. "Zhejiang Ping Yan erxian yanhai yidai de yanmin" (Saltmakers in the costal area of Pinghu and Haiyan counties, Zhejiang). *Zhongguo nongcun*, vol. 1, no. 1 (January): 85–90.

Wu Zhongdao. 1935. "Hunan Anxiang xian nongcun de shuijuan he gaolidai" (Tax burden and usury in the villages of Anxiang county, Hunan). *Zhongguo nongcun*, vol. 1, no. 8 (August): 71–72.

Wuchang XZ, Heilongjiang, 1989. Harbin: Heilongjiang renmin.

Wuding XZ, Yunnan, 1990. Tianjin: Tianjin renmin.

Wudu WSZLXJ, Gansu, vol. 1, 1986; vol. 3, 1990.

Wulian XZ, Shandong, 1992. Beijing: Zhongguo Renmin Daxue.

Wushan XZ, Sichuan, 1991. Chengdu: Sichan renmin.

Wutai XZ, Shanxi, 1988, Taiyuan: Shanxi renmin.

Wuyishan shizhi, Fujian, 1994. Beijing: Zhongguo tongji.

Xiangdao (daily). 20 February 1924, 25 March, 16 June, and 25 October 1926.

Xiangdao zhoubao (weekly). 1922– (published by the CCP).

Xiangxi WSZL, Hunan, vol. 4, 1985; vol. 5, 1985.

Xianju XZ, Zhejiang, 1987. Hangzhou: Zhejiang renmin.

Xiao-Planes, Xiaohong. 2001. *Education et Politique en Chine: Le rôle des élites du Jiangsu, 1905–1914*. Paris: Editions de l'École des Hautes Études en Sciences Sociales.

Xiaoshan XZ, Zhejiang, 1987. Hangzhou: Zhejiang renmin.

Xibei daxue lishixi (Xibei University, History Department), ed. 1984. *Jiu minzhuzhuyi geming shiqi Shaanxi dashi jishu* (Important events in Shaanxi during the old democratic revolution). Xi'an: Shaanxi renmin.

Xie Shengzhong. 1981. "Hai Gu Huimin 1938–1941 nian sanci qiyi shimo" (The three Muslim usprisings in Haiyuan and Guyuan counties from beginning to end, 1938–1941). *Ningxia daxue xuebao*, no. 1 (January–March): 7–15.

Xingan XZ, Jiangxi, 1990. Beijing: Zhongguo shijieyu.

Xingping WSZL, Shaanxi, vol. 1, 1983.

Xingtang WSZL, Hebei, vol. 1, 1989.
Xinjiang WSZLXJ, Jiangxi, vol. 13, 1985.
Xinjin XZ, Sichuan, 1989. Chengdu: Sichuan renmin.
Xin Xian WSZL, Shanxi, vol. 2, 1986.
Xinye XZ, Henan, 1991. Zhengzhou: Zhengzhou guji.
Xiuning XZ, Anhui, 1990. Hefei: Anhui jiaoyü.
Xiuyan XZ, Liaoning, 1989. Shenyang: Liaoning Daxue.
Xixiang XZ, Shaanxi, 1991. Xi'an: Shaanxi renmin.
Xue Muqiao. 1937. *Zhongguo nongcun jingji changshi* (Basic facts on Chinese rural economy). Shanghai: Xinzhi shudian.
Yancheng WSZL, Jiangsu, vol. 2, 1984.
Yang, Benjamin. 1997. *Deng: A Political Biography*. Armonk, NY: M. E. Sharpe.
Yang, C. K. 1959. *A Chinese Village in Early Communist Transition*. Cambridge, MA: The MIT Press.
——. 1991. *Religion in Chinese Society: A Study of Contemporary Social Functions of Religion and Some of Their Historical Factors*. Berkeley, CA: University of California Press.
Yang, Martin C. 1945. *A Chinese Village: Taitou, Shantung Province*. New York: Columbia University Press.
Yangzhong XZ, Jiangsu, 1991. Beijing: Wenwu.
Yangzhou shifan xueyuan lishixi (Yangzhou Normal Institute, History Department). 1961. *Xinhai geming Jiangsu diqu shiliao* (Historical documents on the Jiangsu area during the 1911 revolution). Nanjing: Jiangsu renmin.
Yanshi WSZL, Henan, vol. 1, 1987.
Yantai WSZL, Shandong, vol. 3, 1984; vol. 7, 1987.
Yantai shifan xueyuan zhongguo jinxiandaishi shiliaoxue yanjiusuo (Research Institute on Historical Materials in Modern and Contemporary China, Yantai Teachers College) comp. 1992. *Quanguo geji zhengxie wenshi ziliao pianmu suoyin 1960–1990* (Index to literary and historical materials published by the People's Political Consultative Conference Nationwide at all Levels, 1960–1990). 5 vols. Beijing: Zhongguo wenshi.
Yi Chen. 1988. "Nongmin qiaodou dizhu" (Peasants' skillful ways of fighting landlords). *Kaiyuan WSZL*, vol. 3, 1988.
Yichun shizhi, Jiangxi, 1990. Haiku: Nanhai chuban gongsi.
Yifeng XZ, Jiangxi, 1989. Shanghai: Zhongguo dabaike quanshu.
Yihuang WSZL, Jiangxi, vol. 2, 1989 ; vol. 3, 1991.
Yingshan XZ, Sichuan, 1989. Chengdu: Sichuan cishu.
Yiyang WSZL, Hunan, vol. 3, 1987.
Yong'an XZ, Fujian, 1994. Beijing: Zhonghua shuju.
Yongdeng XZ, Gansu, 1997. Lanzhou: Gansu minzu.

Yongkang XZ, Zhejiang, 1991. Hangzhou: Zhejiang renmin (separately paginated chronology).
Yongsheng XZ, Yunnan, 1989. Kunming: Yunnan renmin.
Yongshou XZ, Shaanxi, 1991. Xi'an: Sanqin.
Young, Ernest P. 1977. *The Presidency of Yuan Shih-k'ai: Liberalism and Dictatorship in Early Republican China*. Ann Arbor, MI: Center for Chinese Studies, University of Michigan.
Yuan'an XZ, Hubei, 1990. Beijing: Zhongguo chengshi jingji shehui chubanshe.
Yuhang XZ, Zhejiang, 1990. Hangzhou: Zhejiang renmin.
Yü Jianrong. 2003a. "Nongmin you zhuzhi kangzheng ji qi zhengzhi fengyin?" (Evaluating peasants' organized resistance and its political impact). *Zhanlüe yu Guanli*, no. 3: 1–16.
———. 2003b. Lecture on the contemporary peasant movement in Hunan province. Fairbank Center for East Asian Research, Harvard University, 4 December.
Yunyuan WSZLXJ, Guizhou, vol. 5, 1987.
Yushan XZ, Jiangxi, 1985. Nanchang: Jiangxi renmin.
Yu Xian WSZL, Shanxi, vol. 1, 1985.
Yuyao WSZLXJ, Zhejiang, vol. 2, 1986; vol. 3, 1986.
Zhang Faqian. 1992. *Zhang Faqian xiansheng fangwen jilu* (Oral memoirs of Mr. Zhang Faqian). Koushu lishi congshu (Oral history series) 34. Taipei: Zhongyang yanjiuyuan jindaishi yanjiusuo.
Zhang Li. 1996. "Zushi yu zubing: zhanshi Shaanxishengde junshi dongyuan" (Enough supply and soldiers: wartime military mobilization in Shaanxi province). In *Qingzu kangzhan shengli wushizhounian liang'an xueshu yantaohui lunwenji* (Collection of essays submitted to the Conference commemorating the 50th anniversary of victory in the war of resistance). Taipei: Zhongguo jindaishi xuehui, 497–518.
Zhang Miao. 1935. "Jiangsu tianfu gaikuang" (General conditions of the land tax in Jiangsu). *Dizheng yuekan*, vol. 1, no. 7 (July): 927–74.
Zhang Tianyi. 1985. "Chouhen" (Hatred). In *Zhang Tianyi wenji* (Works of Zhang Tianyi), vol. 1. Shanghai: Wenyi, 311–34.
Zhang, Xin. 2000. *Social Transformation in Modern China: The State and Local Elites in Henan, 1900–1937*. Cambridge, UK: Cambridge University Press.
Zhang Youyi. 1957. *Zhongguo jindai nongye shi ziliao* (Documents on China's modern agricultural history). Vols. 2 (1912–27) and 3 (1927–37). Beijing: Sanlian.
Zhang Yufa. 1987. *Zhongguo xiandaihua de quyu yanjiu: Shandong sheng (1860–1916)* (Regional research on China's modernization: Shandong province, 1860–1916). Second edition. Taipei: Zhongyang yanjiuyuan jindaishi yanjiusuo.

Zhang Zhenhe. 1954. "Yijiulingse nian Jiangxi Leping qunzhong kangjuan yundong" (1904 tax resistance movement by the masses in Leping, Jiangxi). *Zhongguo kexueyuan lishi yanjiusuo disansuo jikan*, no. 1 (July): 188–97.

Zhang Zhenhe and Ding Yuanying. 1982–83. "Qingmo minbian nianbiao" (Annals of late Qing popular disturbances). *Jindaishi ziliao*, no. 49 (1982): 108–81 and no. 50 (1983): 77–121.

Zhangping WSZLXJ, Fujian, vol. 1, 1982.

"Zhejiang erwan nongmin baodong" (Twenty thousand peasants' uprising in Zhejiang). Three page manuscript, Hoover Institution, no. 4398, 29/3314.

Zhejiang sheng dang'an guan (Zhejiang provincial archives), Hangzhou.

Zhejiang sheng zhengxie wenshi ziliao weiyuanhui. 1990. *Xinbian Zhejiang bainian dashiji, 1840–1949* (One hundred year chronology of Zhejiang, 1840–1949). Hangzhou: Zhejiang renmin.

Zhenyuan WSZL, Guizhou, vol. 1, 1986; vol. 3, 1989.

Zhijiang WSZLXJ, Hunan, vol. 1, 1987.

Zhonggong rudong xianwei dangshi bangongshe ed. 1986. *Rudong renmin geming shi* (Revolutionary history of the people of Rudong). Shanghai: Shanghai renmin.

Zhongguo di'er lishi dang'an guan (China's Number Two Historical Archives).

———. 1988. *Zhonghua minguoshi dang'an ziliao huibian* (Collection of archival documents relating to the history of the Republic of China). Nanjing: Jiangsu guji.

Zhongguo diyi lishi dang'an guan (China's Number One Historical Archives). 1985. *Xinhai geming qian shinian jian minbian dang'an shiliao* (Archival documents on popular uprisings during the ten years preceding the 1911 Revolution). 2 vols. Beijing: Zhonghua shuju.

Zhongguo guomindang dangshihui dang'an (Archives of the Guomindang Committee of History), Taipei.

Zhongguo laodong nianjian (China's Labor Yearbook). 1928–34. Vols. 1–4. Comp. Tao Menghe. Beijing.

Zhongguo nongcun (monthly). 1935–37 (Shanghai).

Zhongguo nongmin wenti. 1927 (Guangzhou).

Zhongguo ribao (daily). 15 April 1935.

Zhonghua Minguo shishi jiyao (Chronology of the Republic of China). 1944. Taipei: Guoshiguan (Academia Historica).

Zhongjiang WSZLXJ, Sichuan, vol. 4, 1986.

Zhongyang ribao (daily). 1928– (Shanghai, then Nanjing).

Zhou Chunyuan, He Changfeng, and Zhang Xiangguang. 1987. *Guizhou jindaishi* (Modern history of Guizhou). Guiyang: Guizhou renmin.

Zhoushan shizhi (Gazetteer of Zhoushan archipelago). 1992. Hangzhou: Zhejiang renmin.
Zhouzhi WSZL, Shaanxi, vol. 4, 1989.
Zhuang Qianghua. 1936. "Yinian lai gesheng tianfu zhi xingge" (Land tax reform in varoius provinces during the past year). *Dizheng yuekan*, vol. 4, nos. 2–3 (January): 285–314.
Zichuan WSZLXJ, Shandong, vol. 3, 1990.
Ziyang XZ, Shaanxi, 1989. Xi'an: Sanqin.
Zunhua XZ, Hebei, 1990. Shijiazhuang: Hebei renmin.

Index

Administrative measures, resistance to, 28–30
Agricultural workers, 17. *See also* Farm laborers
Alcohol / wine tax, 8, 125–26, 213
Anhui, 101. *See also* Chen Guidi and Wu Chuntao; Shou Xian
Animals, 8, 52, 57, 67, 120, 213
Anticapitalist movements, 80–82
Antireligion campaigns, resistance to, 144–48
Antisuperstition campaigns, 145–47; resistance to, 147–50
Antitax resistance, 3, 91–96 *passim*, 113–23 *passim*, 133–34, 171, 194, 204, 213, 234nn16–17. *See also* Tax; Tax evasion; Tax increases; *and names of specific taxes such as* Land tax, Opium tax, Salt tax
Aoshang. See Yan ao
Arms, of rebels, 61, 104, 121, 187
Army and soldiery, 30–32; resistance to, 19–21, 30, 159, 171, 173–74, 180; treatment of soldiers, 169, 183

Arson, 61–62, 115
Associations, 53
Authorities: handling of protests, 55, 59, 115; concessions by, 95; repression by, 66, 116, 173, 193; divisions among, 187

Bandits, 48, 66, 189, 223–24n27
Banners displayed in revolts, 42, 57, 60, 78, 79, 222n18, 23n23
Baohuang (report of poor harvest), 213
Baojia (lowest tax and security unit), 236n2
Baozhang (head of *bao*), 159, 172
Battles, 62, 107, 185
Bercé, Yves-Marie, 190, 198
Biandanhui (Society of Yokes), 80
Bingchai (military requisitions), 19–21, 52, 171, 173, 175
Birth control, 205, 209
Black land. *See Heidi / Heitian*
Boxer indemnities, 5, 134
Boxers, 142
Bu na liang, bu dang bing ("no taxation, no military service"), 22

Cai Shaoqing, 141
Calamities, 53, 101, 144, 227*n*6
Cannibalism, 64
Cao Jinqing, 240*n*15
Casualties, 191–92, 218*n*5, 219*n*6, 238*n*2
CCP (Chinese Communist Party), 46, 80, 186–87
Census, resistance to, 137–39, 232*nn*8–9, 233*nn*10–13, 234*n*14
Changgong (long-term agricultural laborers), 70
Chen Guidi and Wu Chuntao, 240*n*11
Chi dahu ("eating at the homes of great families"), 212
Chiang Kai-shek, 15, 20, 33, 84, 89, 181, 237*n*7
Chimneys, 14
Chinese countryside, recent changes, 200–204. *See also under* PRC
Chuanxie ("wearing boots"), 101
Churches, 139
Class consciousness, 199–200
Coffins / corpses displayed during protest, 60, 198, 222*nn*16–17
Conscription, 32–33, 160–67 passim; resistance to, 32–35, 168, 196–97, 236*nn*3, 5, 6
Conscripts: army's treatment of, 160, 169, 188, 196; villagers' treatment of, 236*n*5
Contraband, 9, 175. *See also* Salt smuggling
Corruption, 23–26, 99–102
Corvée labor, 14–19. See also *Kang liyi*
Crafts, 11
Credit and usury, 72–78, 227*n*6

Croquants (uprising in seventeenth-century France), 190–91, 238*n*1
Cruelties: as reprisals, 65, 225*n*39; by rebels, 64, 104, 225*n*34, 36; by sects and secret societies, 65; by army and authorities, 65–66, 226*n*40; by bandits, 66
Cultural Revolution, nostalgia for, 205

Dadaohui (Big Knives Society), 31, 176, 181, 218*n*5
Dafu jipin ("hit the rich and help the poor"), 42, 78
Dahu (great families), 118–19
Daimao ("putting on a hat"), 101
Daishan, Zhejiang, 128
Daning, Shanxi, 131
Debtors, 76–77. *See also* Credit and usury
Debts, 73
Demonstrations, 54–55, 131
Desertions, 161–62, 189, 196–97, 238*n*16
Diannong (tenants), 38
Diding (head tax), 13
Dou (bushel), 13
Doujuan (tax on bushels), 13
Draft dodging, 161
Duara, Prasenjit, 143, 235*n*18

Eastman, Lloyd, 238*n*15
Eba (local despots), 24–25, 63, 69, 84–86
England, 193, 195
Escalation (from petition to riot), 54–55
Esherick, Joseph, 142
Ethnic minorities, 86; discrimination against conscripts, 169; instiga-

tion or participation in revolts, 177, 180–81, 183, 187–88, 237*n*9
Everyday forms of resistance, 52, 72, 76–77, 202–3
Evolution of repertoire, 67, 197–98
Exactions, resistance to, 24–26
Excesses. *See under* Cruelties
Expropriations, resistance to, 26, 204, 217*n*5

Family planning, 205, 209
Famine: 1877 in Shaanxi, 220*n*5; 1929 in Shaanxi, 22, 43, 57; 1936 in Sichuan, 150
Farm laborers, 69–72
Faux-sauniers (salt smugglers in monarchical France), 106, 195
Fei Xiaotong, 154, 157, 235*n*24
Fengshui (geomancy), 86, 144
Fengxiang, Shaanxi 5
Fires. *See under* Arson
Fishing and fishermen, 9, 103–6, 213
Flour war (in eighteenth-century France), 192
Food disturbances, 36–37, 195. *See also* Looting incidents
Food riots, 193–94
Forrest, Alan, 196–97
Fortified villages, 87
France, sixteenth to nineteenth century: similarities and differences between protests by French and Chinese peasants, 190–99; salt trade and salt smuggling in, 7, 106; surtaxes in, 97; local unanimity in protest, 123; hunger, brigands, and "Great Fear" in 1789, 140–41
Frauds and deception, 25, 78; related to tax, 99–102, 229*nn*6–7, 9–10, 12, 230*n*15; related to conscription, 163–67
Fu Hung-chung, 235–36*n*1
Fujian. *See* Mingxi
Fujiashui (surcharge to the land tax), 2
Fuling, Sichuan, 18, 226*n*3

Gannan revolt (1942–1993), 185–88
Gansu. *See* Gannan revolt, Guyuan, Hui minority revolts
Gelaohui (Elders and Ancients Society), 18, 47–48
Geomancy, 86, 144
Grain requisitions, 30. *See also Bingchai; Junliang*
Guangdong, 8, 9, 97
Guangxi, 9
Guanyan (official salt), 105
Guizhou, 177–82. *See also* Niujiaohui, Opium trade, *Xilu shibian*
Gu Jiegang, 235*n*25
Guyuan, Gansu (present-day Ningxia), 183
Gu Zhenlun, 187

Haicheng, Liaoning, 71
Haiyan, Gansu (present-day Ningxia) 183
Han ethnic group, relations with minority groups, 79, 180–81
Han Yuming, 49–50
Handicraft products, 11
Hebei, 102. *See also* Huailu, Shunde, Yi Xian
Heidi / Heitian ("black fields"), 110–12, 118
Henan: resistance to corvée in, 16; sects and secret societies in, 45, 49–51, 219*n*5, 7; financial strains

of local administration in the
1990s, 208
Hongqianghui (Red Spears Society),
129, 175, 181, 218n5, 237n8
Huailu, Hebei, 53
Huanyingfei (induction fee for conscripts), 164
Hui minority revolts, 183–84
Human life, value of, 66–67, 226n42
Hu Xian, Shaanxi, 20, 63, 224n32
Hu Zongnan, 185

Iconoclasm, 145, 147–48
Ignorance, as one of the "five great enemies," 58
Indigo, tax on, 10
Intellectuals, targets of riots, 158; exempted from conscription, 168
Invulnerability of sect members, 48, 62–63
Irrigation, 27, 42

Jiangdu, Jiangsu, 113, 116, 230nn16, 20
Jiangnan, 91
Jiangsu, 112, 132–33, 139. *See also* Jiangdu, Lücheng, Lujinggang, Nantong, Siyugang, Subei, Taixing, Wuxi, Xuzhou area, Yangzhong, Yangzhou
Jiangxi. *See* Leping, Yichun
Jiaonong ("the handing over of farm tools"), 17, 56–57, 127, 219–220n2, 220nn4–5
Jiaxing, Zhejiang, 211
Jimaoxin ("chicken-feather letter"), 58–59, 221n12
Jimintuan (bands of starving people), 191

Jingjuan (tax for the police), 2, 133
Jinhua, Zhejiang, 144
Jisidui (salt police), 104, 107
Junliang ("army's grain"), 171

Kangbao douzheng (struggle against oppression), 24, 83–86
Kangbing kangjuan, kangding kangjuan ("resist conscription and taxes"), 171, 181, 236–37n6
Kang chanyan ("resist the eradication of poppies"), 179
Kangjuan kangshui ("resist taxes and levies"), 1
Kang liyi (resistance to corvée labor), 16–19
Kenwu juan (clearance tax), 13, 83

Labing (picking up soldiers), 34
Labor requisitions, 175. *See also Bingchai*; Corvée labor
Labrousse, Ernest, 141
Lading (illegal abduction of recruits), 168
Laiyang, Shandong, 122–24
Lamley, Harry, 214
Land expropriation. *See* Expropriations
Land occupation and seizure, 42, 82
Land registration, resistance to, 112–13, 230nn15–19
Land rent, 38–42, 213
Land surveying, 112
Land tax, 2–4
Landlord courts, 41
Leaders, of revolts, 119, 121, 124, 126–27, 185–87, 205–6, 239nn7–8; social origins and conditions of, 3, 5–6, 119, 122–24, 126–28, 149
Lefebvre, Georges, 140–41

Leping, Jiangxi, 10
Lianbao chiefs, 163–64, 172
Lianbao offices, as targets of riots, 172
Liangfang (custodians of land registers), 100
Lianzhuanghui (federations of villages), 123, 129
Liaoning, *see* Haicheng
Li Huaiyin, 53, 128
Lijin (tax on goods in transit), 12, 54
Lin'an, Zhejiang, 152–53
Lin Men, 94, 124, 126
Lintao, Gansu, 185
Local actions and reactions, 206
Local administration: under the Republic, 88–89; as preferred target of rebels, 207–8
Local despots. See *Eba*
Local elite: resistance to tax, 3, 53, 124, 127; support of law and order, 58, 61
Localism, 45, 198–99
Local self-defense, 45
Local unanimity, 123–24; 198–99, 205–6, 239*n*7
Looters, 195–96
Looting incidents, 36–37, 195, 201, 211–13
Lottery rigging, 163–66
Lottery, selection of draftees by, and resistance to, 33, 162–66
Lücheng, Jiangsu, 81, 227*n*7
Lujinggang, Jiangsu, 93
Lujuan (tax for the railway), 234*n*17

Maizai ("sell a disaster"), 101
Mai ziyuanbing (buying a volunteer for military service), 162
Market calendar, 28

Martial arts masters, 5, 20, 206
Menbian juan (tax on door nameplates), 13
Military, resistance to. See *under* Army and soldiery
Military service. See *under* Conscription
Militias, 170
Mingong, 201, 206
Mingxi, Fujian, 30–31
Miscellaneous taxes and surtaxes, 96–98
Monks and priests, 87, 125–26, 135, 146
Moral economy, 193
Mujuan (land tax per *mu*), 2, 93
Muslims. See Hui minority revolts

Nantong, Jiangsu, 93–95, 118, 125, 222*n*17
Nationalist government, and local administration, 88–89
Natural calamities. See Calamities
New Policies, resistance to, 29, 122, 130, 213
Nicolas, Jean, 21, 191–93, 239*nn*3–6
Niujiaohui (Buffalo's Horn Society), 237*n*8
Nizai ("hide a disaster"), 101
Nonghui, (Farming Association), 53
Nonviolent resistance, 128
Novelties, resistance to, 199, 204–5
Nu-pieds (peasant revolt in seventeenth-century France), 190, 238*n*1

Oaths taken before revolt, 57, 59, 221*nn*10–11
O'Brien and Li, 203–4
One-child family policy, 205–9

Opium eradication, and resistance to, 28–29, 179, 213
Opium tax, 7
Opium trade (Guizhou), 179

Paoge ("Gowned Brothers"), 47–48
Para-administration, 98, 100, 102
Parochialism, 28. *See also under* Localism
Peasant protests, mixed and complex, 21–23, 213; defensive and reactive, 45, 123, 149, 206, 223*n*19; nonviolent, 56, 72, 77, 202–3; compulsory participation in, 59, 98, 221–22*n*14; against novelties, 199, 204–205; recent increase, 201–2; enduring characteristics, 210
Peasant rebels, discipline of, 45, 62, 95, 121; weakness of, 62, 198; coordination among, 202, 206–7
Peasants: manipulation of, 124–26 (*see also* Monks and priests); reversal of status (recently in PRC), 200
Permanent tenancy, 39–40
Petitions, 52–54, 128
Pingjia ("stable prices"), 195. *See also* Moral economy
Pitauts (peasant revolt in sixteenth-century France), 191
Pochu mixin ("eradicate superstition"), 145
Police as target of resistance, 27, 133, 233*n*13
Political oppression, 24, 83–86.
Pomiao banxue ("destroy temples to build schools"), 135
Poor versus rich, 42–43, 78–83
Poppy eradication. *See under* Opium eradication

Poppy tax. *See under* Opium tax
Poverty, national policy toward, 193
Prayers for rain, 148–50
Prazniak, Roxann, 142–43
PRC: peasant protests in, 200–209; recent changes, 200–204; continuities with pre-1949 protest, 204–9; center-peasant alliance, 206–9.
Priests. *See* Monks and priests
Producers vs. buyers, 80
Protest targets, 60–61, 63–65, 204, 207–8, 213

Qianjiang, Sichuan, 18
Qingyuan (petitions), 52
Qiongrenhui (Association of the Poor), 84, 223*n*20
Qu (ward), 88–89, 99, 111
Queues, 148–49, 235*nn*22, 23
Quzhang (ward head), 16–17, 25, 27–28, 63, 89, 115

Rain, 224
Raw materials, 11
Reactive revolts, 199, 206
"Ready to face death," 198, 239*n*6
Red Spears Society. *See* Hongqianghui
Reforms, resistance to, 28–30
Religion. *See under* Antireligion campaigns
Religious sects, 44. *See also* Tianmenhui
Rent. *See* Land rent
Repertoire: change, 67, 197–98; French and Chinese compared, 198
Repression. *See under* Authorities
Revenge, 65, 225*nn*37, 39

Revolt, 61; 176–89
Rich: as reluctant participants in rebellion, 221*n*13; rich versus poor, 42–43, 78–83
Rightful resistance, 203–4, 209
Riots, 57–61
Rong Desheng, 82
Rumors, 144, 234*n*14
Rural disturbances, reporting of incidents, 212, 214
Rural elite. *See under* Local elite

Salt, 4, 7
Salt smuggling, 105–9, 194–95
Salt tax, resistance to, 4–7, 103–6, 213
Salt workers, 103–6, 166
Sanluan (taxes, fines, and contributions), 204, 240*n*12
Santai, Sichuan, 169
Scholars: as targets of sect leader, 50; attempts to reason with rebels, 61; survival tactics under the Republic, 88; support of New Policies, 135; opposition to New Policies, 136
Schools, as targets of resistance, 131–132, 136, 139, 158
Scott, James, 52. *See also under* Everyday forms of resistance
Sects and secret societies, 20, 44, 62–63, 146, 181, 213, 225*n*38, 237*n*8. *See also* Dadaohui, Gelaohui, Hongqianghui, Paoge, Tianmenhui
Self-defense, 45–46, 123, 149, 223*n*19
Sericulture, 29–30, 150–57, 235*n*24
Shaanxi, 56–59. *See also* Fengxiang, Hu Xian, Zhouzhi

Shafu jipin ("kill the rich and help the poor"), 79
Shandong, 44–45, 108–9. *See also* Laiyang and Teng Xian
Shanxi, 11, 55, 62, 144. *See also* Daning
Sharecropping, 38–39
Shecang (public granary), 122
Shenbing ("divine soldiers," "Heavenly soldiers"), 18, 24, 181
Shezhang (head of *she*, small rural area), 123
Shiwei (demonstrations), 54
Shou Xian, Anhui, 31
Shunde, Hebei, 20
Sichuan, 163, 170. *See also* Fuling, Qianjiang, Santai, Zigong, Ziyang
Silkworm eggs, 151–53
Silkworm raising, 150–57
Single-child family campaign, 205, 209
Siyan ("private salt"), 105
Siyugang, Jiangsu, 121–22, 124, 126–27
Slogans, 19, 78–79, 86, 181, 188, 202, 204
Social exploitation, 69–70, 73–76, 80–83
Social movements: not correlated to severity of issues, 69–77; and class conflict, 119–22
Songming, Yunnan, 26
Songtao, Guizhou, 182
Sources, 95–96
Statistics, reliability of, 211–12, 214
Strikes: by labor draftees, 17; by farm laborers, 71–72, 200. See also *Jiaonong*
Sub-administration, 88–89. *See also* Para-administration

Subei, Jiangsu, 192. *See also* Xuzhou area
Suicides: by officials, 4; by debtors, 76; by rebels, 144; by peasants, 148
Sun Zuoqi, 102
Superstitions. *See* Antisuperstition campaigns
Surtaxes, 96–98, 228–29nn3–4

Taixing, Jiangsu, 120
Tangjuan (tax on sugar), 9
Tankuan (special contributions), 228n1, 229n7
Tanpai (tax allotments), 138, 240n12
Tax, 117
Tax arrears, 102
Tax evasion, 118, 231nn23, 25
Tax increases, 91–92, 133–34, 219n1, 229n13
Tax resistance. *See under* Antitax resistance
Teachers, 139, 233n10
Temples, 144–47. *See also under* Antireligion campaigns
Tenants, 38–42, 90
Teng Xian, Shandong, 146
Tianmenhui (Sect of the Heavenly Gate), 49–51, 219n4
Tilly, Charles, 52, 197
Tobacco, 10, 96, 194, 213
Tongshanshe (Society of Universal Goodness), 181–82
Tulie ("tuhao lieshen"), 88
Tusi (head of minority tribe in Yunnan), 82–83
Tuzai shui (slaughter tax), 8, 120
Tuzhong (home-produced silkworm eggs), 152–53

Usury. *See* Credit and Usury

Vendettas, 28
Village elections, 201
Violence, 64. *See also under* Cruelties

Wages of farm laborers, 70
Wangdian, Zhejiang, 211
Wang Zhongjia (rebel leader), 185–87
Water-related incidents, 26–27
Waterworks (along the Yangzi), 27, 93
Weakness of rioters and rebels. *See under* Peasant rebels
Wine. *See* Alcohol / wine tax
Women: participation in demonstrations, 55; in riots, 16, 114; avenging the deaths of their children, 65
Wuxi, Jiangsu, 15–16, 154, 157, 195, 212

Xiaomin ("nitrate people"), 109
Xiaoshan, Zhejiang, 152–54
Xiedou, 43–44, 48, 194, 213, 239n4
Xilu shibian ("road to the west" revolt), 182
Xuzhou area, North Jiangsu, 84–85, 87

Yan ao (licensed salt merchants), 103, 106
Yanbing (salt soldiers), 5, 103
Yancheng, Jiangsu, 146
Yangzhong, Jiangsu, 27
Yangzhou, Jiangsu, 114–16
Yanjing (salt police), 5

Yanshui, see Salt tax
Yanyong (salt guards), 5
Yichun, Jiangxi, 132
Yi Xian, Zhili (Hebei), 137
Yongdian (permanent tenancy), 39–40
Yuhang, Zhejiang, 152–53, 156
Yumin ("stupid peasants"), 113, 230n20
Yunnan, 112. *See also* Songming, Tusi
Yu Xuexian (or Yu Hu the Taoist), 121
Yuyao, Zhejiang, 80, 117, 144, 150, 153–54, 230n19
Yuzheng (advance recruitments of conscripts), 33

Zhang Jian, 80, 93–94
Zhang Xueliang, 50
Zhang Youyi, 211
Zhejiang: 132–33; 139; 150–58. *See also* Daishan, Jiaxing, Jinhua, Lin'an, Wangdian, Xiaoshan, Yuhang, Yuyao
Zhouzhi, Shaanxi, 20
Zhuading (forcible, yet legal, enlisting of designated conscripts), 167–68
Zhu juan (tax on pigs), 8, 120
Zhu Shaoliang, 187
Zigong, Sichuan, 166
Ziyang, Sichuan, 163
Zizhi gongsuo (self-governing local administration, 1909–11), 131, 133, 139

Harvard East Asian Monographs
(*out-of-print)

*1. Liang Fang-chung, *The Single-Whip Method of Taxation in China*
*2. Harold C. Hinton, *The Grain Tribute System of China, 1845–1911*
 3. Ellsworth C. Carlson, *The Kaiping Mines, 1877–1912*
*4. Chao Kuo-chün, *Agrarian Policies of Mainland China: A Documentary Study, 1949–1956*
*5. Edgar Snow, *Random Notes on Red China, 1936–1945*
*6. Edwin George Beal, Jr., *The Origin of Likin, 1835–1864*
 7. Chao Kuo-chün, *Economic Planning and Organization in Mainland China: A Documentary Study, 1949–1957*
*8. John K. Fairbank, *Ching Documents: An Introductory Syllabus*
*9. Helen Yin and Yi-chang Yin, *Economic Statistics of Mainland China, 1949–1957*
 10. Wolfgang Franke, *The Reform and Abolition of the Traditional Chinese Examination System*
 11. Albert Feuerwerker and S. Cheng, *Chinese Communist Studies of Modern Chinese History*
 12. C. John Stanley, *Late Ching Finance: Hu Kuang-yung as an Innovator*
 13. S. M. Meng, *The Tsungli Yamen: Its Organization and Functions*
*14. Ssu-yü Teng, *Historiography of the Taiping Rebellion*
 15. Chun-Jo Liu, *Controversies in Modern Chinese Intellectual History: An Analytic Bibliography of Periodical Articles, Mainly of the May Fourth and Post-May Fourth Era*
*16. Edward J. M. Rhoads, *The Chinese Red Army, 1927–1963: An Annotated Bibliography*
*17. Andrew J. Nathan, *A History of the China International Famine Relief Commission*
*18. Frank H. H. King (ed.) and Prescott Clarke, *A Research Guide to China-Coast Newspapers, 1822–1911*
*19. Ellis Joffe, *Party and Army: Professionalism and Political Control in the Chinese Officer Corps, 1949–1964*
*20. Toshio G. Tsukahira, *Feudal Control in Tokugawa Japan: The Sankin Kōtai System*
*21. Kwang-Ching Liu, ed., *American Missionaries in China: Papers from Harvard Seminars*
*22. George Moseley, *A Sino-Soviet Cultural Frontier: The Ili Kazakh Autonomous Chou*

Harvard East Asian Monographs

23. Carl F. Nathan, *Plague Prevention and Politics in Manchuria, 1910–1931*
*24. Adrian Arthur Bennett, *John Fryer: The Introduction of Western Science and Technology into Nineteenth-Century China*
*25. Donald J. Friedman, *The Road from Isolation: The Campaign of the American Committee for Non-Participation in Japanese Aggression, 1938–1941*
*26. Edward LeFevour, *Western Enterprise in Late Ching China: A Selective Survey of Jardine, Matheson and Company's Operations, 1842–1895*
27. Charles Neuhauser, *Third World Politics: China and the Afro-Asian People's Solidarity Organization, 1957–1967*
*28. Kungtu C. Sun, assisted by Ralph W. Huenemann, *The Economic Development of Manchuria in the First Half of the Twentieth Century*
*29. Shahid Javed Burki, *A Study of Chinese Communes, 1965*
30. John Carter Vincent, *The Extraterritorial System in China: Final Phase*
31. Madeleine Chi, *China Diplomacy, 1914–1918*
*32. Clifton Jackson Phillips, *Protestant America and the Pagan World: The First Half Century of the American Board of Commissioners for Foreign Missions, 1810–1860*
*33. James Pusey, *Wu Han: Attacking the Present Through the Past*
*34. Ying-wan Cheng, *Postal Communication in China and Its Modernization, 1860–1896*
35. Tuvia Blumenthal, *Saving in Postwar Japan*
36. Peter Frost, *The Bakumatsu Currency Crisis*
37. Stephen C. Lockwood, *Augustine Heard and Company, 1858–1862*
38. Robert R. Campbell, *James Duncan Campbell: A Memoir by His Son*
39. Jerome Alan Cohen, ed., *The Dynamics of China's Foreign Relations*
40. V. V. Vishnyakova-Akimova, *Two Years in Revolutionary China, 1925–1927*, trans. Steven L. Levine
41. Meron Medzini, *French Policy in Japan During the Closing Years of the Tokugawa Regime*
42. Ezra Vogel, Margie Sargent, Vivienne B. Shue, Thomas Jay Mathews, and Deborah S. Davis, *The Cultural Revolution in the Provinces*
43. Sidney A. Forsythe, *An American Missionary Community in China, 1895–1905*
*44. Benjamin I. Schwartz, ed., *Reflections on the May Fourth Movement.: A Symposium*
*45. Ching Young Choe, *The Rule of the Taewŏngun, 1864–1873: Restoration in Yi Korea*
46. W. P. J. Hall, *A Bibliographical Guide to Japanese Research on the Chinese Economy, 1958–1970*
47. Jack J. Gerson, *Horatio Nelson Lay and Sino-British Relations, 1854–1864*
48. Paul Richard Bohr, *Famine and the Missionary: Timothy Richard as Relief Administrator and Advocate of National Reform*
49. Endymion Wilkinson, *The History of Imperial China: A Research Guide*
50. Britten Dean, *China and Great Britain: The Diplomacy of Commercial Relations, 1860–1864*
51. Ellsworth C. Carlson, *The Foochow Missionaries, 1847–1880*
52. Yeh-chien Wang, *An Estimate of the Land-Tax Collection in China, 1753 and 1908*
53. Richard M. Pfeffer, *Understanding Business Contracts in China, 1949–1963*

Harvard East Asian Monographs

*54. Han-sheng Chuan and Richard Kraus, *Mid-Ching Rice Markets and Trade: An Essay in Price History*
 55. Ranbir Vohra, *Lao She and the Chinese Revolution*
 56. Liang-lin Hsiao, *China's Foreign Trade Statistics, 1864–1949*
*57. Lee-hsia Hsu Ting, *Government Control of the Press in Modern China, 1900–1949*
*58. Edward W. Wagner, *The Literati Purges: Political Conflict in Early Yi Korea*
*59. Joungwon A. Kim, *Divided Korea: The Politics of Development, 1945–1972*
 60. Noriko Kamachi, John K. Fairbank, and Chūzō Ichiko, *Japanese Studies of Modern China Since 1953: A Bibliographical Guide to Historical and Social-Science Research on the Nineteenth and Twentieth Centuries, Supplementary Volume for 1953–1969*
 61. Donald A. Gibbs and Yun-chen Li, *A Bibliography of Studies and Translations of Modern Chinese Literature, 1918–1942*
 62. Robert H. Silin, *Leadership and Values: The Organization of Large-Scale Taiwanese Enterprises*
 63. David Pong, *A Critical Guide to the Kwangtung Provincial Archives Deposited at the Public Record Office of London*
*64. Fred W. Drake, *China Charts the World: Hsu Chi-yü and His Geography of 1848*
*65. William A. Brown and Urgrunge Onon, translators and annotators, *History of the Mongolian People's Republic*
 66. Edward L. Farmer, *Early Ming Government: The Evolution of Dual Capitals*
*67. Ralph C. Croizier, *Koxinga and Chinese Nationalism: History, Myth, and the Hero*
*68. William J. Tyler, tr., *The Psychological World of Natsume Sōseki*, by Doi Takeo
 69. Eric Widmer, *The Russian Ecclesiastical Mission in Peking During the Eighteenth Century*
*70. Charlton M. Lewis, *Prologue to the Chinese Revolution: The Transformation of Ideas and Institutions in Hunan Province, 1891–1907*
 71. Preston Torbert, *The Ching Imperial Household Department: A Study of Its Organization and Principal Functions, 1662–1796*
 72. Paul A. Cohen and John E. Schrecker, eds., *Reform in Nineteenth-Century China*
 73. Jon Sigurdson, *Rural Industrialism in China*
 74. Kang Chao, *The Development of Cotton Textile Production in China*
 75. Valentin Rabe, *The Home Base of American China Missions, 1880–1920*
*76. Sarasin Viraphol, *Tribute and Profit: Sino-Siamese Trade, 1652–1853*
 77. Ch'i-ch'ing Hsiao, *The Military Establishment of the Yuan Dynasty*
 78. Meishi Tsai, *Contemporary Chinese Novels and Short Stories, 1949–1974: An Annotated Bibliography*
*79. Wellington K. K. Chan, *Merchants, Mandarins and Modern Enterprise in Late Ching China*
 80. Endymion Wilkinson, *Landlord and Labor in Late Imperial China: Case Studies from Shandong by Jing Su and Luo Lun*
*81. Barry Keenan, *The Dewey Experiment in China: Educational Reform and Political Power in the Early Republic*
*82. George A. Hayden, *Crime and Punishment in Medieval Chinese Drama: Three Judge Pao Plays*

Harvard East Asian Monographs

*83. Sang-Chul Suh, *Growth and Structural Changes in the Korean Economy, 1910–1940*
84. J. W. Dower, *Empire and Aftermath: Yoshida Shigeru and the Japanese Experience, 1878–1954*
85. Martin Collcutt, *Five Mountains: The Rinzai Zen Monastic Institution in Medieval Japan*
86. Kwang Suk Kim and Michael Roemer, *Growth and Structural Transformation*
87. Anne O. Krueger, *The Developmental Role of the Foreign Sector and Aid*
*88. Edwin S. Mills and Byung-Nak Song, *Urbanization and Urban Problems*
89. Sung Hwan Ban, Pal Yong Moon, and Dwight H. Perkins, *Rural Development*
*90. Noel F. McGinn, Donald R. Snodgrass, Yung Bong Kim, Shin-Bok Kim, and Quee-Young Kim, *Education and Development in Korea*
*91. Leroy P. Jones and Il SaKong, *Government, Business, and Entrepreneurship in Economic Development: The Korean Case*
92. Edward S. Mason, Dwight H. Perkins, Kwang Suk Kim, David C. Cole, Mahn Je Kim et al., *The Economic and Social Modernization of the Republic of Korea*
93. Robert Repetto, Tai Hwan Kwon, Son-Ung Kim, Dae Young Kim, John E. Sloboda, and Peter J. Donaldson, *Economic Development, Population Policy, and Demographic Transition in the Republic of Korea*
94. Parks M. Coble, Jr., *The Shanghai Capitalists and the Nationalist Government, 1927–1937*
95. Noriko Kamachi, *Reform in China: Huang Tsun-hsien and the Japanese Model*
96. Richard Wich, *Sino-Soviet Crisis Politics: A Study of Political Change and Communication*
97. Lillian M. Li, *China's Silk Trade: Traditional Industry in the Modern World, 1842–1937*
98. R. David Arkush, *Fei Xiaotong and Sociology in Revolutionary China*
*99. Kenneth Alan Grossberg, *Japan's Renaissance: The Politics of the Muromachi Bakufu*
100. James Reeve Pusey, *China and Charles Darwin*
101. Hoyt Cleveland Tillman, *Utilitarian Confucianism: Chen Liang's Challenge to Chu Hsi*
102. Thomas A. Stanley, *Ōsugi Sakae, Anarchist in Taishō Japan: The Creativity of the Ego*
103. Jonathan K. Ocko, *Bureaucratic Reform in Provincial China: Ting Jih-ch'ang in Restoration Kiangsu, 1867–1870*
104. James Reed, *The Missionary Mind and American East Asia Policy, 1911–1915*
105. Neil L. Waters, *Japan's Local Pragmatists: The Transition from Bakumatsu to Meiji in the Kawasaki Region*
106. David C. Cole and Yung Chul Park, *Financial Development in Korea, 1945–1978*
107. Roy Bahl, Chuk Kyo Kim, and Chong Kee Park, *Public Finances During the Korean Modernization Process*
108. William D. Wray, *Mitsubishi and the N.Y.K, 1870–1914: Business Strategy in the Japanese Shipping Industry*
109. Ralph William Huenemann, *The Dragon and the Iron Horse: The Economics of Railroads in China, 1876–1937*
*110. Benjamin A. Elman, *From Philosophy to Philology: Intellectual and Social Aspects of Change in Late Imperial China*
111. Jane Kate Leonard, *Wei Yüan and China's Rediscovery of the Maritime World*

Harvard East Asian Monographs

112. Luke S. K. Kwong, *A Mosaic of the Hundred Days:. Personalities, Politics, and Ideas of 1898*
*113. John E. Wills, Jr., *Embassies and Illusions: Dutch and Portuguese Envoys to K'ang-hsi, 1666–1687*
114. Joshua A. Fogel, *Politics and Sinology: The Case of Naitō Konan (1866–1934)*
*115. Jeffrey C. Kinkley, ed., *After Mao: Chinese Literature and Society, 1978–1981*
116. C. Andrew Gerstle, *Circles of Fantasy: Convention in the Plays of Chikamatsu*
117. Andrew Gordon, *The Evolution of Labor Relations in Japan: Heavy Industry, 1853–1955*
*118. Daniel K. Gardner, *Chu Hsi and the "Ta Hsueh": Neo-Confucian Reflection on the Confucian Canon*
119. Christine Guth Kanda, *Shinzō: Hachiman Imagery and Its Development*
*120. Robert Borgen, *Sugawara no Michizane and the Early Heian Court*
121. Chang-tai Hung, *Going to the People: Chinese Intellectual and Folk Literature, 1918–1937*
*122. Michael A. Cusumano, *The Japanese Automobile Industry: Technology and Management at Nissan and Toyota*
123. Richard von Glahn, *The Country of Streams and Grottoes: Expansion, Settlement, and the Civilizing of the Sichuan Frontier in Song Times*
124. Steven D. Carter, *The Road to Komatsubara: A Classical Reading of the Renga Hyakuin*
125. Katherine F. Bruner, John K. Fairbank, and Richard T. Smith, *Entering China's Service: Robert Hart's Journals, 1854–1863*
126. Bob Tadashi Wakabayashi, *Anti-Foreignism and Western Learning in Early-Modern Japan: The "New Theses" of 1825*
127. Atsuko Hirai, *Individualism and Socialism: The Life and Thought of Kawai Eijirō (1891–1944)*
128. Ellen Widmer, *The Margins of Utopia: "Shui-hu hou-chuan" and the Literature of Ming Loyalism*
129. R. Kent Guy, *The Emperor's Four Treasuries: Scholars and the State in the Late Chien-lung Era*
130. Peter C. Perdue, *Exhausting the Earth: State and Peasant in Hunan, 1500–1850*
131. Susan Chan Egan, *A Latterday Confucian: Reminiscences of William Hung (1893–1980)*
132. James T. C. Liu, *China Turning Inward: Intellectual-Political Changes in the Early Twelfth Century*
*133. Paul A. Cohen, *Between Tradition and Modernity: Wang T'ao and Reform in Late Ching China*
134. Kate Wildman Nakai, *Shogunal Politics: Arai Hakuseki and the Premises of Tokugawa Rule*
*135. Parks M. Coble, *Facing Japan: Chinese Politics and Japanese Imperialism, 1931–1937*
136. Jon L. Saari, *Legacies of Childhood: Growing Up Chinese in a Time of Crisis, 1890–1920*
137. Susan Downing Videen, *Tales of Heichū*
138. Heinz Morioka and Miyoko Sasaki, *Rakugo: The Popular Narrative Art of Japan*
139. Joshua A. Fogel, *Nakae Ushikichi in China: The Mourning of Spirit*

Harvard East Asian Monographs

140. Alexander Barton Woodside, *Vietnam and the Chinese Model: A Comparative Study of Vietnamese and Chinese Government in the First Half of the Nineteenth Century*
*141. George Elison, *Deus Destroyed: The Image of Christianity in Early Modern Japan*
142. William D. Wray, ed., *Managing Industrial Enterprise: Cases from Japan's Prewar Experience*
*143. T'ung-tsu Ch'ü, *Local Government in China Under the Ching*
144. Marie Anchordoguy, *Computers, Inc.: Japan's Challenge to IBM*
145. Barbara Molony, *Technology and Investment: The Prewar Japanese Chemical Industry*
146. Mary Elizabeth Berry, *Hideyoshi*
147. Laura E. Hein, *Fueling Growth: The Energy Revolution and Economic Policy in Postwar Japan*
148. Wen-hsin Yeh, *The Alienated Academy: Culture and Politics in Republican China, 1919–1937*
149. Dru C. Gladney, *Muslim Chinese: Ethnic Nationalism in the People's Republic*
150. Merle Goldman and Paul A. Cohen, eds., *Ideas Across Cultures: Essays on Chinese Thought in Honor of Benjamin L. Schwartz*
151. James M. Polachek, *The Inner Opium War*
152. Gail Lee Bernstein, *Japanese Marxist: A Portrait of Kawakami Hajime, 1879–1946*
*153. Lloyd E. Eastman, *The Abortive Revolution: China Under Nationalist Rule, 1927–1937*
154. Mark Mason, *American Multinationals and Japan: The Political Economy of Japanese Capital Controls, 1899–1980*
155. Richard J. Smith, John K. Fairbank, and Katherine F. Bruner, *Robert Hart and China's Early Modernization: His Journals, 1863–1866*
156. George J. Tanabe, Jr., *Myōe the Dreamkeeper: Fantasy and Knowledge in Kamakura Buddhism*
157. William Wayne Farris, *Heavenly Warriors: The Evolution of Japan's Military, 500–1300*
158. Yu-ming Shaw, *An American Missionary in China: John Leighton Stuart and Chinese-American Relations*
159. James B. Palais, *Politics and Policy in Traditional Korea*
*160. Douglas Reynolds, *China, 1898–1912: The Xinzheng Revolution and Japan*
161. Roger R. Thompson, *China's Local Councils in the Age of Constitutional Reform, 1898–1911*
162. William Johnston, *The Modern Epidemic: History of Tuberculosis in Japan*
163. Constantine Nomikos Vaporis, *Breaking Barriers: Travel and the State in Early Modern Japan*
164. Irmela Hijiya-Kirschnereit, *Rituals of Self-Revelation: Shishōsetsu as Literary Genre and Socio-Cultural Phenomenon*
165. James C. Baxter, *The Meiji Unification Through the Lens of Ishikawa Prefecture*
166. Thomas R. H. Havens, *Architects of Affluence: The Tsutsumi Family and the Seibu-Saison Enterprises in Twentieth-Century Japan*
167. Anthony Hood Chambers, *The Secret Window: Ideal Worlds in Tanizaki's Fiction*
168. Steven J. Ericson, *The Sound of the Whistle: Railroads and the State in Meiji Japan*
169. Andrew Edmund Goble, *Kenmu: Go-Daigo's Revolution*

Harvard East Asian Monographs

170. Denise Potrzeba Lett, *In Pursuit of Status: The Making of South Korea's "New" Urban Middle Class*
171. Mimi Hall Yiengpruksawan, *Hiraizumi: Buddhist Art and Regional Politics in Twelfth-Century Japan*
172. Charles Shirō Inouye, *The Similitude of Blossoms: A Critical Biography of Izumi Kyōka (1873–1939), Japanese Novelist and Playwright*
173. Aviad E. Raz, *Riding the Black Ship: Japan and Tokyo Disneyland*
174. Deborah J. Milly, *Poverty, Equality, and Growth: The Politics of Economic Need in Postwar Japan*
175. See Heng Teow, *Japan's Cultural Policy Toward China, 1918–1931: A Comparative Perspective*
176. Michael A. Fuller, *An Introduction to Literary Chinese*
177. Frederick R. Dickinson, *War and National Reinvention: Japan in the Great War, 1914–1919*
178. John Solt, *Shredding the Tapestry of Meaning: The Poetry and Poetics of Kitasono Katue (1902–1978)*
179. Edward Pratt, *Japan's Protoindustrial Elite: The Economic Foundations of the Gōnō*
180. Atsuko Sakaki, *Recontextualizing Texts: Narrative Performance in Modern Japanese Fiction*
181. Soon-Won Park, *Colonial Industrialization and Labor in Korea: The Onoda Cement Factory*
182. JaHyun Kim Haboush and Martina Deuchler, *Culture and the State in Late Chosŏn Korea*
183. John W. Chaffee, *Branches of Heaven: A History of the Imperial Clan of Sung China*
184. Gi-Wook Shin and Michael Robinson, eds., *Colonial Modernity in Korea*
185. Nam-lin Hur, *Prayer and Play in Late Tokugawa Japan: Asakusa Sensōji and Edo Society*
186. Kristin Stapleton, *Civilizing Chengdu: Chinese Urban Reform, 1895–1937*
187. Hyung Il Pai, *Constructing "Korean" Origins: A Critical Review of Archaeology, Historiography, and Racial Myth in Korean State-Formation Theories*
188. Brian D. Ruppert, *Jewel in the Ashes: Buddha Relics and Power in Early Medieval Japan*
189. Susan Daruvala, *Zhou Zuoren and an Alternative Chinese Response to Modernity*
*190. James Z. Lee, *The Political Economy of a Frontier: Southwest China, 1250–1850*
191. Kerry Smith, *A Time of Crisis: Japan, the Great Depression, and Rural Revitalization*
192. Michael Lewis, *Becoming Apart: National Power and Local Politics in Toyama, 1868–1945*
193. William C. Kirby, Man-houng Lin, James Chin Shih, and David A. Pietz, eds., *State and Economy in Republican China: A Handbook for Scholars*
194. Timothy S. George, *Minamata: Pollution and the Struggle for Democracy in Postwar Japan*
195. Billy K. L. So, *Prosperity, Region, and Institutions in Maritime China: The South Fukien Pattern, 946–1368*
196. Yoshihisa Tak Matsusaka, *The Making of Japanese Manchuria, 1904–1932*

Harvard East Asian Monographs

197. Maram Epstein, *Competing Discourses: Orthodoxy, Authenticity, and Engendered Meanings in Late Imperial Chinese Fiction*
198. Curtis J. Milhaupt, J. Mark Ramseyer, and Michael K. Young, eds. and comps., *Japanese Law in Context: Readings in Society, the Economy, and Politics*
199. Haruo Iguchi, *Unfinished Business: Ayukawa Yoshisuke and U.S.-Japan Relations, 1937–1952*
200. Scott Pearce, Audrey Spiro, and Patricia Ebrey, *Culture and Power in the Reconstitution of the Chinese Realm, 200–600*
201. Terry Kawashima, *Writing Margins: The Textual Construction of Gender in Heian and Kamakura Japan*
202. Martin W. Huang, *Desire and Fictional Narrative in Late Imperial China*
203. Robert S. Ross and Jiang Changbin, eds., *Re-examining the Cold War: U.S.-China Diplomacy, 1954–1973*
204. Guanhua Wang, *In Search of Justice: The 1905–1906 Chinese Anti-American Boycott*
205. David Schaberg, *A Patterned Past: Form and Thought in Early Chinese Historiography*
206. Christine Yano, *Tears of Longing: Nostalgia and the Nation in Japanese Popular Song*
207. Milena Doleželová-Velingerová and Oldřich Král, with Graham Sanders, eds., *The Appropriation of Cultural Capital: China's May Fourth Project*
208. Robert N. Huey, *The Making of 'Shinkokinshū'*
209. Lee Butler, *Emperor and Aristocracy in Japan, 1467–1680: Resilience and Renewal*
210. Suzanne Ogden, *Inklings of Democracy in China*
211. Kenneth J. Ruoff, *The People's Emperor: Democracy and the Japanese Monarchy, 1945–1995*
212. Haun Saussy, *Great Walls of Discourse and Other Adventures in Cultural China*
213. Aviad E. Raz, *Emotions at Work: Normative Control, Organizations, and Culture in Japan and America*
214. Rebecca E. Karl and Peter Zarrow, eds., *Rethinking the 1898 Reform Period: Political and Cultural Change in Late Qing China*
215. Kevin O'Rourke, *The Book of Korean Shijo*
216. Ezra F. Vogel, ed., *The Golden Age of the U.S.-China-Japan Triangle, 1972–1989*
217. Thomas A. Wilson, ed., *On Sacred Grounds: Culture, Society, Politics, and the Formation of the Cult of Confucius*
218. Donald S. Sutton, *Steps of Perfection: Exorcistic Performers and Chinese Religion in Twentieth-Century Taiwan*
219. Daqing Yang, *Technology of Empire: Telecommunications and Japanese Expansionism, 1895–1945*
220. Qianshen Bai, *Fu Shan's World: The Transformation of Chinese Calligraphy in the Seventeenth Century*
221. Paul Jakov Smith and Richard von Glahn, eds., *The Song-Yuan-Ming Transition in Chinese History*
222. Rania Huntington, *Alien Kind: Foxes and Late Imperial Chinese Narrative*
223. Jordan Sand, *House and Home in Modern Japan: Architecture, Domestic Space, and Bourgeois Culture, 1880–1930*

Harvard East Asian Monographs

224. Karl Gerth, *China Made: Consumer Culture and the Creation of the Nation*
225. Xiaoshan Yang, *Metamorphosis of the Private Sphere: Gardens and Objects in Tang-Song Poetry*
226. Barbara Mittler, *A Newspaper for China? Power, Identity, and Change in Shanghai's News Media, 1872–1912*
227. Joyce A. Madancy, *The Troublesome Legacy of Commissioner Lin: The Opium Trade and Opium Suppression in Fujian Province, 1820s to 1920s*
228. John Makeham, *Transmitters and Creators: Chinese Commentators and Commentaries on the Analects*
229. Elisabeth Köll, *From Cotton Mill to Business Empire: The Emergence of Regional Enterprises in Modern China*
230. Emma Teng, *Taiwan's Imagined Geography: Chinese Colonial Travel Writing and Pictures, 1683–1895*
231. Wilt Idema and Beata Grant, *The Red Brush: Writing Women of Imperial China*
232. Eric C. Rath, *The Ethos of Noh: Actors and Their Art*
233. Elizabeth Remick, *Building Local States: China During the Republican and Post-Mao Eras*
234. Lynn Struve, ed., *The Qing Formation in World-Historical Time*
235. D. Max Moerman, *Localizing Paradise: Kumano Pilgrimage and the Religious Landscape of Premodern Japan*
236. Antonia Finnane, *Speaking of Yangzhou: A Chinese City, 1550–1850*
237. Brian Platt, *Burning and Building: Schooling and State Formation in Japan, 1750–1890*
238. Gail Bernstein, Andrew Gordon, and Kate Wildman Nakai, eds., *Public Spheres, Private Lives in Modern Japan, 1600–1950: Essays in Honor of Albert Craig*
239. Wu Hung and Katherine R. Tsiang, *Body and Face in Chinese Visual Culture*
240. Stephen Dodd, *Writing Home: Representations of the Native Place in Modern Japanese Literature*
241. David Anthony Bello, *Opium and the Limits of Empire: Drug Prohibition in the Chinese Interior, 1729–1850*
242. Hosea Hirata, *Discourses of Seduction: History, Evil, Desire, and Modern Japanese Literature*
243. Kyung Moon Hwang, *Beyond Birth: Social Status in the Emergence of Modern Korea*
244. Brian R. Dott, *Identity Reflections: Pilgrimages to Mount Tai in Late Imperial China*
245. Mark McNally, *Proving the Way: Conflict and Practice in the History of Japanese Nativism*
246. Yongping Wu, *A Political Explanation of Economic Growth: State Survival, Bureaucratic Politics, and Private Enterprises in the Making of Taiwan's Economy, 1950–1985*
247. Kyu Hyun Kim, *The Age of Visions and Arguments: Parliamentarianism and the National Public Sphere in Early Meiji Japan*
248. Zvi Ben-Dor Benite, *The Dao of Muhammad: A Cultural History of Muslims in Late Imperial China*
249. David Der-wei Wang and Shang Wei, eds., *Dynastic Crisis and Cultural Innovation: From the Late Ming to the Late Qing and Beyond*

Harvard East Asian Monographs

250. Wilt L. Idema, Wai-yee Li, and Ellen Widmer, eds., *Trauma and Transcendence in Early Qing Literature*
251. Barbara Molony and Kathleen Uno, eds., *Gendering Modern Japanese History*
252. Hiroshi Aoyagi, *Islands of Eight Million Smiles: Idol Performance and Symbolic Production in Contemporary Japan*
253. Wai-yee Li, *The Readability of the Past in Early Chinese Historiography*
254. William C. Kirby, Robert S. Ross, and Gong Li, eds., *Normalization of U.S.-China Relations: An International History*
255. Ellen Gardner Nakamura, *Practical Pursuits: Takano Chōei, Takahashi Keisaku, and Western Medicine in Nineteenth-Century Japan*
256. Jonathan W. Best, *A History of the Early Korean Kingdom of Paekche, together with an annotated translation of* The Paekche Annals *of the* Samguk sagi
257. Liang Pan, *The United Nations in Japan's Foreign and Security Policymaking, 1945–1992: National Security, Party Politics, and International Status*
258. Richard Belsky, *Localities at the Center: Native Place, Space, and Power in Late Imperial Beijing*
259. Zwia Lipkin, *"Useless to the State": "Social Problems" and Social Engineering in Nationalist Nanjing, 1927–1937*
260. William O. Gardner, *Advertising Tower: Japanese Modernism and Modernity in the 1920s*
261. Stephen Owen, *The Making of Early Chinese Classical Poetry*
262. Martin J. Powers, *Pattern and Person: Ornament, Society, and Self in Classical China*
263. Anna M. Shields, *Crafting a Collection: The Cultural Contexts and Poetic Practice of the* Huajian ji 花間集 *(Collection from Among the Flowers)*
264. Stephen Owen, *The Late Tang: Chinese Poetry of the Mid-Ninth Century (827–860)*
265. Sara L. Friedman, *Intimate Politics: Marriage, the Market, and State Power in Southeastern China*
266. Patricia Buckley Ebrey and Maggie Bickford, *Emperor Huizong and Late Northern Song China: The Politics of Culture and the Culture of Politics*
267. Sophie Volpp, *Worldly Stage: Theatricality in Seventeenth-Century China*
268. Ellen Widmer, *The Beauty and the Book: Women and Fiction in Nineteenth-Century China*
269. Steven B. Miles, *The Sea of Learning: Mobility and Identity in Nineteenth-Century Guangzhou*
270. Lin Man-houng, *China Upside Down: Currency, Society, and Ideologies, 1808–1856*
271. Ronald Egan, *The Problem of Beauty: Aesthetic Thought and Pursuits in Northern Song Dynasty China*
272. Mark Halperin, *Out of the Cloister: Literati Perspectives on Buddhism in Sung China, 960–1279*
273. Helen Dunstan, *State or Merchant? Political Economy and Political Process in 1740s China*
274. Sabina Knight, *The Heart of Time: Moral Agency in Twentieth-Century Chinese Fiction*
275. Timothy J. Van Compernolle, *The Uses of Memory: The Critique of Modernity in the Fiction of Higuchi Ichiyō*

Harvard East Asian Monographs

276. Paul Rouzer, *A New Practical Primer of Literary Chinese*
277. Jonathan Zwicker, *Practices of the Sentimental Imagination: Melodrama, the Novel, and the Social Imaginary in Nineteenth-Century Japan*
278. Franziska Seraphim, *War Memory and Social Politics in Japan, 1945–2005*
279. Adam L. Kern, *Manga from the Floating World: Comicbook Culture and the* Kibyōshi *of Edo Japan*
280. Cynthia J. Brokaw, *Commerce in Culture: The Sibao Book Trade in the Qing and Republican Periods*
281. Eugene Y. Park, *Between Dreams and Reality: The Military Examination in Late Chosŏn Korea, 1600–1894*
282. Nam-lin Hur, *Death and Social Order in Tokugawa Japan: Buddhism, Anti-Christianity, and the* Danka *System*
283. Patricia M. Thornton, *Disciplining the State: Virtue, Violence, and State-Making in Modern China*
284. Vincent Goossaert, *The Taoists of Peking, 1800–1949: A Social History of Urban Clerics*
285. Peter Nickerson, *Taoism, Bureaucracy, and Popular Religion in Early Medieval China*
286. Charo B. D'Etcheverry, *Love After* The Tale of Genji: *Rewriting the World of the Shining Prince*
287. Michael G. Chang, *A Court on Horseback: Imperial Touring & the Construction of Qing Rule, 1680–1785*
288. Carol Richmond Tsang, *War and Faith:* Ikkō Ikki *in Late Muromachi Japan*
289. Hilde De Weerdt, *Competition over Content: Negotiating Standards for the Civil Service Examinations in Imperial China (1127–1279)*
290. Eve Zimmerman, *Out of the Alleyway: Nakagami Kenji and the Poetics of Outcaste Fiction*
291. Robert Culp, *Articulating Citizenship: Civic Education and Student Politics in Southeastern China, 1912–1940*
292. Richard J. Smethurst, *From Foot Soldier to Finance Minister: Takahashi Korekiyo, Japan's Keynes*
293. John E. Herman, *Amid the Clouds and Mist: China's Colonization of Guizhou, 1200–1700*
294. Tomoko Shiroyama, *China During the Great Depression: Market, State, and the World Economy, 1929–1937*
295. Kirk W. Larsen, *Tradition, Treaties and Trade: Qing Imperialism and Chosŏn Korea, 1850–1910*
296. Gregory Golley, *When Our Eyes No Longer See: Realism, Science, and Ecology in Japanese Literary Modernism*
297. Barbara Ambros, *Emplacing a Pilgrimage: The Ōyama Cult and Regional Religion in Early Modern Japan*
298. Rebecca Suter, *The Japanization of Modernity: Murakami Haruki between Japan and the United States*
299. Yuma Totani, *The Tokyo War Crimes Trial: The Pursuit of Justice in the Wake of World War II*

Harvard East Asian Monographs

300. Linda Isako Angst, *In a Dark Time: Memory, Community, and Gendered Nationalism in Postwar Okinawa*
301. David M. Robinson, ed., *Culture, Courtiers, and Competition: The Ming Court (1368–1644)*
302. Calvin Chen, *Some Assembly Required: Work, Community, and Politics in China's Rural Enterprises*
303. Sem Vermeersch, *The Power of the Buddhas: The Politics of Buddhism During the Koryŏ Dynasty (918–1392)*
304. Tina Lu, *Accidental Incest, Filial Cannibalism, and Other Peculiar Encounters in Late Imperial Chinese Literature*
305. Chang Woei Ong, *Men of Letters Within the Passes: Guanzhong Literati in Chinese History, 907–1911*
306. Wendy Swartz, *Reading Tao Yuanming: Shifting Paradigms of Historical Reception (427–1900)*
307. Peter K. Bol, *Neo-Confucianism in History*
308. Carlos Rojas, *The Naked Gaze: Reflections on Chinese Modernity*
309. Kelly H. Chong, *Deliverance and Submission: Evangelical Women and the Negotiation of Patriarchy in South Korea*
310. Rachel DiNitto, *Uchida Hyakken: A Critique of Modernity and Militarism in Prewar Japan*
311. Jeffrey Snyder-Reinke, *Dry Spells: State Rainmaking and Local Governance in Late Imperial China*
312. Jay Dautcher, *Down a Narrow Road: Identity and Masculinity in a Uyghur Community in Xinjiang China*
313. Xun Liu, *Daoist Modern: Innovation, Lay Practice, and the Community of Inner Alchemy in Republican Shanghai*
314. Jacob Eyferth, *Eating Rice from Bamboo Roots: The Social History of a Community of Handicraft Papermakers in Rural Sichuan, 1920–2000*
315. David Johnson, *Spectacle and Sacrifice: The Ritual Foundations of Village Life in North China*
316. James Robson, *Power of Place: The Religious Landscape of the Southern Sacred Peak (Nanyue 南嶽) in Medieval China*
317. Lori Watt, *When Empire Comes Home: Repatriation and Reintegration in Postwar Japan*
318. James Dorsey, *Critical Aesthetics: Kobayashi Hideo, Modernity, and Wartime Japan*
319. Christopher Bolton, *Sublime Voices: The Fictional Science and Scientific Fiction of Abe Kōbō*
320. Si-yen Fei, *Negotiating Urban Space: Urbanization and Late Ming Nanjing*
321. Christopher Gerteis, *Gender Struggles: Wage-Earning Women and Male-Dominated Unions in Postwar Japan*
322. Rebecca Nedostup, *Superstitious Regimes: Religion and the Politics of Chinese Modernity*
323. Lucien Bianco, *Wretched Rebels: Rural Disturbances on the Eve of the Chinese Revolution*

LaVergne, TN USA
20 January 2010
170659LV00001B/3/P